The Things That Keep Us Up at Night

Reel Biohorror

Biohorror, Biothriller Movies,
the Law and the Science of It

Victoria Sutton, MPA, J.D., Ph.D.

Vargas Publishing
Lubbock, Texas 79410

VARGAS PUBLISHING

This book is typeset in Bookman Old Style. The paper used in this book meets the specifications for 60# white 444ppi.
Cover design by Summer Sutton

In black and white
ISBN-10: 0991420713 (paperback)
ISBN-13: 9780991420711 (paperback)
Printed and Manufactured in the United States of America
First printing, 2014
Second printing, 2018
Typeset in the U.S.A.

Published and distributed in North America by
Vargas Publishing
P.O. Box 6801
Lubbock, TX 79461
http://www.vargaspublishing.com

Dedication

To all my ancestors
who did not die of the
plague, smallpox and other scourges
and passed along their resistant genes
to my family and me

and to

Dennis E. Hackin

Preface

The continually evolving influenzas and the newly emerging infectious diseases which can be carried around the world in twenty-four hours or less are the stuff that pandemics are made of. They are also the stuff that bioweapons are made of, and combine that with an evil hand and you have the makings of true biohorror. Whether the biohorror comes from Mother Nature or the despicable terrorist, these are the things that can keep us up at night.

When the second aircraft hit the second tower of the World Trade Center, it was a horrific realization that it was not an accident. The American way of life, of trust and of security had just become a thing of lost innocence.

As most Americans probably remember where they were on September 11, 2001, I remember standing in front of my own television watching the replay of the second hit, having left my morning meeting to come home to meet my husband-to-be in the wake of the horrifying news. We stood together transfixed to the bitter scene. We had both left the White House at the end of the George H.W. Bush administration in 1992, just over a decade ago, but we were aware enough of the possibility. Allan had written about the possibility of a terrorist attack using aircraft on U.S. buildings in a paper years ago, which some remembered, with this exact method --- aircraft flying into tall buildings. However, the horror of knowing that ordinary civilian citizen-passengers, pilots and attendants and the occupants of the buildings they targeted had died horrifying deaths in this attack against America brought a new level of understanding of the depth of depravity capable of our yet to be known enemies.

Allan and I had also been in the White House during the collapse of the Soviet Union. From the perspective of the White House Science Office, the threat of nuclear bomb research, resources, stockpiles and talent had to be immediately contained before dispersing to all ends of the earth to plant the seeds of the potential destruction of humankind. But we had also been witness to the revelation of the surprising existence of the largest biological weapons program ever developed in the world's written history. Without our knowing, the USSR had built the largest enterprise of military biological weapons in human history. Pathogens were being researched, produced and stockpiled on a massive scale. The program was so advanced that the first defectors were met with disbelief as to their credibility. It turns out that they were largely right.

I took this concern about the risk of a potential bioterrorism attack to my next challenge after leaving the White House. My move further down Pennsylvania Avenue from the White

House to George Washington University led to my next job, which was as Executive Director of the Ronald Reagan Institute for Emergency Medicine in 1993. It was here, that I helped to develop "Disaster Medicine" as one of the five research initiatives for the Institute led by Dr. Joe Barbera. I organized the first meeting of the newly appointed Institute advisory board (which included Eric Holder, now U.S. Attorney General) and together with Frank Young from the Public Health Service, staged a bioterrorism scenario exercise set in Washington, D.C. which at the time was rather shocking and novel.

I began writing about the federalism challenge of taking biodefense to the level of national security out of the backwater of underfunded, neglected state public health agencies. It was a time when I searched the internet for the words "biological weapons" and got a total of three hits from the entire internet which itself was only a few years old. You might say that I could have adapted this song, "I Was Country When Country Wasn't Cool"[1] to the study of bioterrorism and law.

I left Washington, D.C. in 1999 to take a faculty position at Texas Tech University School of Law, an up and coming law school that was ahead of its time in looking for interdisciplinary scholars and teachers.

After the 9/11 attacks, I quickly dashed off an editorial about the risk of biological terrorism that might follow on the ground at the site of the aircraft attacks and placed in the local newspaper, *The Lubbock Avalanche-Journal*, on September 23, 2001 my editorial was published and outlined what might happen if there was a biological attack and how the governments had little in the way of a plan to respond.

Just nine days later, the first victim of the anthrax attacks, Robert Stevens, was diagnosed by an alert infectious disease physician in Florida. Stevens eventually died a few days later. Four other victims followed with fatal infections with various other exposures to the mail.

The anthrax attacks of fall 2001 ended my blissfully lonesome research and analysis in the area of bioterrorism and law and the field of study and practice has continued to advance.

In January 2003, another incident at my home institution, Texas Tech University, brought sudden global notoriety to a scientist who claimed his plague was stolen from his laboratory. This resulted in a two year trial and highly charged political conflicts between law enforcement and the scientific community. The ultimate sentence for this scientist was largely based on his illegal export of plague to a prohibited country and he was sentenced to two years in prison. The profile of the anthrax attacker was a scientist with access and skill to work with anthrax which led to a focus on increasing laboratory biosafety and biosecurity laws and regulations which has become one of the largest areas of regulatory and statutory change in the entire area of biodefense.

The increasing notoriety of bioterrorism and emerging infectious diseases did not go unnoticed by Hollywood. Before the anthrax attacks the occasional movie would focus on the Black Death of 1348 like*The Seventh Seal* (1957) or a horror film that examined an extraterrestrial plague, like *Andromeda Strain* (1971). It seemed to be either the distant past or the far future, but no near or present danger, until 1965 when *The Satan Bug* which ushered in a new fear --- the creation of biological weapons. In 1975 an international treaty, the Biological and Toxins Weapons Convention, was signed by the world's super powers and others, and all nations agreed to dismantle their bioweapons programs. Perhaps the movie brought the problem to the attention of Americans? The box office hit of 1995, *Outbreak* (1995), starring Dustin Hoffman,

---

[1] A song written by Kye Fleming and Dennis Morgan, sung by Barbara Mandrell that rose to number one on the country music charts in 1981.

revisited this issue in a conspiracy theory plot where a government coverup of a bioweapons program went badly wrong with a virus infecting a California civilian community.

In 2002, I began teaching the first course in law and bioterrorism at Texas Tech University School of Law. I used movies in the biohorror and biothriller subgenre for assignments to study hypothetical scenarios that would require legal analysis. After a decade of using this exercise with law students, I decided to share the fruits of these often intriguing, entertaining and horrifying, aspects of what these movies depict and what it might mean in the context of the rule of law.

These analyses will hopefully enrich your experiences with these movies and perhaps help to answer some of the troubling aspects of human nature that make great theater and also provide some answers to some hard questions about our constitutional protection of civil liberties in times of national or global emergencies with diseases or threat of bioweapons.

This book is organized so that you can first explore the dimensions and characteristics of the distinct subgenre of biohorror, biothriller and consider biodrama, biofantasy or bioromance movie possibilities. But at any point use it can be used as a reference to look specifically at any of the 48 movies identified in this subgenre from 1922 to the present.

You may want to have some popcorn and watch one or all of them. If you develop a propensity for using hand sanitizer, or telling perfect strangers to cover their mouths when they cough, do not worry – that's to be expected. After all, these are the things that keep us up at night.

Table of Contents

Chapter 1

What is the Biohorror and Biothriller Subgenre?

The biohorror and biothriller subgenre – and I will refer to it as biohorror for convenience --- is an exploration, examination and analysis of what was previously a latent plot form beginning with *Nosferatu* (1922), now exploding in the post 9/11 fear of bioterrorism and the SARS and Bird Flu emerging infectious diseases of the new millennium. Questions that linger long after the movie is over that fans ask will be discussed – could these things happen? Are they constitutional in America? Is it just Hollywood or is it reality?

The movies in this book depict infectious diseases that are bioweapons or mother nature's weapons where they lead to terror brought on by people, governments, enemies or nature. Quarantine, pandemic, laboratory creations and accidents, all provide plot-ready horror and action for this subgenre. Further indications that you are in this subgenre is the film title: Quarantine; Pandemic; Contagion; Outbreak; Contaminated; Waterborne; Carriers. All of these have served as titles, some more than once.

These movies might be called the "petri dish movies" since they all involve a biological organism, usually a bacterium or virus. Similarly, the "spaghetti westerns" referred to the Italian filming location of a subgenre of westerns and the name came to identify a period of western filmmaking. These names call to mind some kind of unifying, if insignificant, characteristic but in an appreciative way.

To meet my criteria for the biohorror subgenre, the plot, plot devices, the conflict and resolution of the conflict must have an interesting biological organism and syndrome (set of symptoms) as well as have legal and possibly constitutional issues arise in the course of dealing with the bio horror. These could range from legal issues of liability, medical malpractice, wrongful death and anti-hoarding statutes to name a few. Constitutional issues that are natural ones are infringements on the freedom of movement, right of privacy and Fifth Amendment and Tenth Amendment due process. The list is practically unlimited.

Plots often use government conspiracy, criminal schemes for economic gain, terrorism schemes for political coercion, or an ominous appearance of a disease with unknown or natural origins. Almost all plots create a conflict that entail the threat of an epidemic (a local, and contained outbreak) or a pandemic (a worldwide spread of an infection) which must be stopped and cured. The resolution might be seen in several ways. One way is the government conspiracy is exposed and the reluctant officials reveal the knowledge necessary to end the horror in just the nick of time. Another way is for the characters to find, develop or discover a cure. Yet another device is that the epidemic dies out on its own, leaving the ominous prospect for a re-emergence in the future --- or a sequel. Creative resolutions are always a welcome possibility. The plots' overall characterization range from the unbelieveable zombie plot to the magical reality where the impossible becomes an integral part of the scenario to hard realism.

This subgenre of horror is growing, from the beginnings in 1922 with the silent film, *Nosferatu* (1922) engaging Count Orlak (like Dracula) in a plague outbreak on a ship to the present day realism of *Contagion* (2011), depicting a reality-based virus that caused a pandemic. The trend is also seen in a shift from nuclear and radiological horror to biological horror in the choice to change the triggering episode of the origin of Spiderman's powers. Spiderman in comic book, *Amazing Fantasy* #15 (August, 1962) gained his super powers when he was bitten by a radioactive spider (despite the description, "insect") while visiting a science exhibit. In 2012, fifty years later, in *The Amazing Spider-Man* (2012), the movie, Spiderman is bitten by a genetically engineered spider and has to stop a genetically-mutated lizardman, Dr. Connors, from infecting the city's population with his mutation serum.

Over this span of time, the development of this subgenre can be described in three periods triggered by developments in science, biotechnology and terrorism. The first period might be marked from 1922 until 1965, when diseases were mainly naturally occurring plagues. *The Satan Bug* (1965) was the first movie to depict a government military laboratory manufacturing a biological weapon, signaling the end of this earlier age of innocence. The biotechnology revolution had its beginnings and genetic engineering was becoming a part of the societal lexicon in the early 1970s. *Andromeda Strain* (1971) captured this fear of the unpredictable virus and became a classic which was paid homage in future movies, such as its Directive 7-12, which does not exist and is a made up protocol about military destruction of a civilian city, but has taken on a life of its own and used as a plot device in *Venomous* ( ) and . The second period continued until the 9/11 attacks on America followed by the Anthrax Attacks which killed five people, but affected hundreds more, and jolted the entire nation with fear (and terror) about the possibilities of biological weapons. This began the third period, the post 9/11 period, and the increase in movies is notable. The number of movies in this subgenre doubled in the next five year increment following 9/11 (2001-2005) and then doubled again in the next five-year increment (2006-2010) If this rate is indicative, then we can expect to see about thirty of these movies in the biohorror subgenre in the 2011-2015 period, as shown in the graph.

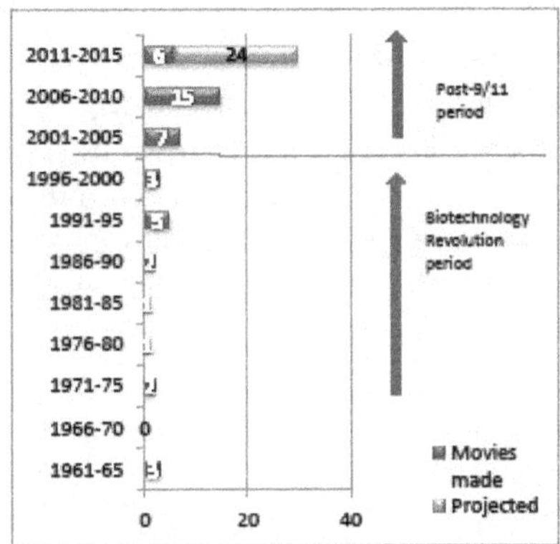

BioHorror movies in five-year time increments in two periods

It is also likely that more of these movies will be independent movies. In March 2012, a Motion Picture Association of America report showed that from 2002 to 2011, there was a 74 percent increase in the number of independent films – companies other than members of the M.P.A.A. ---469 in 2011 compared to 270 in 2002. That increase was occurring while a decrease in films from the member companies like Fox, Disney, Sony, Warner, Paramount and Universal fell by 31 percent --- 141 in 2011 compared to 205 in 2002.[2]

The events that inspired the three periods of the biohorror, biothriller subgenre

The silent film, *Nosferatu* (1922), used plague as the disease agent, an ancient scourge which caused the deaths of ¼ of the world's population in 1341. Thus, plagues were not new, but the new science of the "germ theory" had just taken hold at the beginning of the 20th Century. Slowly antibiotics were developed as a result of World War I experiences for World War II, replacing sulfa drugs, ushering in a new age of antibiotic success over bacterial infections, like the plague. A great epidemic had just hit China in 1921 killing about 8500 people, so the fear was clearly on the minds of Europeans who had suffered through the Black Plague and many outbreaks which followed in the succeeding centuries. The classic in literature, Albert Camus's *The Plague* revealed aspects of human nature when faced with the horror of untimely disease and death. While it was written in 1947, it did not inspire a movie until *La Peste* (1992) was made by France, but it told the story in Argentina, not the original book location, Algeria. The Black Plague or Black Death lost some of its terror with antibiotics, but viruses were still horrifying in reality. The polio epidemics in the 1940s were reminders for contemporary society that we had not yet conquered viruses. In 1970, the World Health Organization announced that smallpox (a virus) had been eradicted from the earth – every last case of it. The world breathed a collective sigh of relief only to be disturbed by the proposition presented by the *Andromeda Strain* (1971), showing that just eradicating a virus from earth may not leave us safe. The movie depicted the arrival of a virus from alien sources and was a box office hit and a cult classic.

---

[2] M.P.A.A., *Theatrical Market Statistics 2011* (March 2012), at http://www.mpaa.org/Resources/5bec4ac9-a95e-443b-987b-bff6fb5455a9.pdf.

Great movies depicting Mother Nature attacks, like *Hud* (1963) which showed the devastating results of animal diseases and economic terror were much more fitting for the period. Nonetheless, bioterrorism was a lurking fear during the Cold War inspiring the classic movie, *The Satan Bug* (1965) playing on a distrust in government engaged in a top secret government laboratory developing a bioweapon. This movie showed just before President Nixon announced he was ending the entire bioweapons program in the United States in 1969. Could *The Satan Bug* (1965) have affected public opinion against the use of bioweapons? It is hard to know what the collective consciousness of American society might have been with regard to bioweapons with certainty, but the popular movie may have made an impression on an already Cold War sensitive population. After the offensive bioweapons program of the United States ended, the Biological Weapons and Toxins Convention was open for signature in 1972 for all nations to also agree to end any bioweapons program they might have. The treaty went into force in 1975, closing a period of state-sponsored bioweaponeering, or so we thought.

The 1970s ushered in a period of what has been called "the biotechnology revolution" where genetic engineering had become a reality finally utilizing the 1950s discovery of the structure of DNA. The period from 1976 to 1991 was one of reduced anxiety about contagious diseases and even some thought the medical profession of infectious diseases would soon be a medical specialty of the past. But when the Soviet Union collapsed in December 1991, the world was horrified to learn that the U.S.S.R. had the largest bioweapons development program ever created, called Biopreparat, ignoring their obligations under the bioweapons treaty ban they signed with the United States and others in 1972. More than 2,000 laboratories throughout the vast empire were employed by both civilian and military bioweaponeering scientists developing chimeras which were combinations of all the worst traits of every bug, imaginable. The U.S.S.R. involvement in bioweapons inspired some of the books in the Ludlum *Covert-One* series (*The Cassandra Compact, The Moscow Vector, the Arctic Event and the Ares Decision*) but none of these were adapted for movies. *Bats: Human Harvest* (2008), an independent movie depicting the use of bioweapons in the Chechnyan rebels and Russia conflict was not widely seen. Otherwise, little in the way of a surge in the bio horror subgenre was based on this revelation of the U.S.S.R. bioweapons program.

But bioweapons movies and government conspiracy plots began to emerge. The movie *Pandora's Clock* (1996) takes place on a flight from Germany to New York where the doomsday virus, a bioweapon developed by terrorists, has infected one of the passengers. The first of the U.S. government conspiracy and police-state plot with biological weapons followed the next year and was a major success at the box office ---the movie *Outbreak* (1995).

The Post 9/11 period and the Anthrax Attacks in fall of 2001 triggered not only $4 billion in federal spending to defend against future bioterrorism attacks, but a revival of the biohorror subgenre in films. A film depicting a conspiracy to assassinate the President of the United States with a terrorist designed bioweapon is the plot in *Contagion* (2002). Then a terrorist plot to poison the water supply with a deadly agent was depicted in *Waterborne* (2005) with an eye more toward the social impacts on different ethnic groups in society. The government conspiracy plot continued in *The Hades Factor* (2006), a Robert Ludlum story in the *Covert One* series, which was a complex thriller leading to the eventual conclusion that the viral outbreak was due to a U.S. government conspiracy that utilized a viral weapon during the Gulf War.

The Mother Nature terrorist plot may have been inspired by the real life events of the 2003 SARS outbreak that began in China and spread rapidly around the world. Fears of bird flu which was an emerging infectious disease tracked by the World Health Organization and the U.S. Centers for Diseases Control and Prevention inspired the television movie, *Fatal Contact: Bird Flu in America* (2006). The movie reflected the fear around bird flu by making it a deadly and horrific death within hours or days of contracting it. The depiction was so frightening the CDC had a cooperative postscript to the movie to assure people that the movie was not an accurate depiction of the course of the disease and sent viewers off to the website to learn about the real bird flu. This was followed the next year by *Pandemic* (2007), an intense three-hour, mini-series, which also used the bird flu for its creatively evolved virus, but with more realism. The ensuing pandemic led to a police-state plot with greater and greater restraints on personal liberties, and some high level officials failing their moral challenges. This trend in Mother Nature terrorist plots was continued in *Carriers* (2009), a movie about a group of teenagers running from a nationwide epidemic. *Contagion* (2011), followed the trend in realism to depict horror in a viral pandemic that was so realistic that the script ended with a depiction of how the virus in the movie evolved and infected humans, plausibly explaining how the pandemic could actually happen, in the closing scenes of the movie. The *Black Death* (2010), a British-made movie and Season of the Witch (2011) a U.S. movie, depicted the plague of 1341 in a Mother-Nature-as-terrorist plot, during a period of ignorance about disease treatment and its causes. These movies depicted another kind of realism by recalling the most devastating "real" single pandemic event in the world's history as we know it ---a reminder that the pandemic horror apocalyptic narrative actually happened.

The investment of billions of dollars in the United States in building new biological safety laboratories and more for the highest level of safety – BSL-4 – was also mirrored in the United Kingdom and other western nations. The possibility of accidental releases became a reality with the escape of foot and mouth disease from the United Kingdom, which is now considered to have presumptively come from the United Kingdom agro-biodefense laboratory, Porton Downs. The result was a nationwide epidemic which led to the widespread slaughter of cattle in the UK in 2001, costing the U.S. equivalent of around $6 billion. Accidental infections in laboratories like the tularemia infection of a researcher who unknowingly worked with the live strain in the Boston University laboratory in 2005 led to the initiation of new safety precautions but frightened the community. In 2007, a brucellosis infection of one of the researchers at Texas A&M University led to the cancellation of their research registration for almost a year. So it is not surprising that a group of films depicted laboratory escapes of deadly viruses. In *28 Days Later* (2003), the movie began with the escape of the "rage" virus from a government research laboratory after animal rights activists who had broken into the laboratory ignored warnings from the laboratory technicians who told them not to free these monkeys. This triggered a apocalyptic epidemic in Great Britain. This was followed by *28 Weeks Later* (2007), the sequel that was based on the same laboratory release of a virus, where the government tries to repopulate Great Britain with Rage-free citizens.

These plots tend to raise questions that are about laws or constitutional rights and provide scenarios for provocative discussions about the possibilities of these disasters or public health emergencies. These ideas will be explored in the context of these movies which will undoubtedly provide some sleepless nights, that can only be cured by watching another reel biohorror.

Chapter 2

The Psychology of Fear and the Rule of Law

The psychology of fear is one of the most basic emotions of humans, and for good reason. It was developed as a matter of survival --- life or death. A movie which evokes those feelings of fear and horror goes to the most ancient and original of our survival skills. We can have adrenaline rushes, tears, screams and even lingering fears long after the movie is over as a result of our reaction of fear.

Horror is a fear that is real and immediate caused by sensorial input that triggers extreme fear. Where in the brain do we find this activity?

Neuropsychologists have physically located the fear center of our brain which is in the amygdala, one of the most ancient areas of the brain. That is, this part of the brain is also found in reptiles, birds as well as mammals, when reaction to a fear by running, crawling or flying away was essential to survival. In many ways, it was the most important emotion to survival. In fact, the word emotion is from the latin words "to move" which is the response to an emotion and a response to the basic emotion of fear --- move quickly and save your life.

Using the most primordial fear response – running away—and make that impossible is a plot device certain to evoke immediate horror. The quarantine or isolation order that prevents the victim from running away from the contagion or running away from confinement like *Outbreak* (1995) in the quarantine of the entire city with a scene where civilians are ordered to stop from escaping the city quarantine boundaries in their pickup truck, only to be shot to enforce the quarantine. The blocking of this basic fear response to flee is depicted in many scenes made for confinement: the commercial aircraft in flight was used to prevent fleeing in *Flight of the Living Dead* (2007), *Pandora's Clock* (1996) and *Quarantine 2: Terminal* (2011). On a ship in *Nosferatu* (1922). Being locked in a biological laboratory with the bioagents was used to prevent fleeing in *Contaminated Man* (2001) and *Warning Sign* (1985) and to some degree in *World War Z* (2013). Being confined with others with the disease and unable to flee in *Carriers* (2009); *Pandemic* (2007); and all of the aircraft-in-flight movies described above are used to evoke that most basic flight response followed by the entrapment panic. Night paralysis plays on that deep fear, by making the sufferer unable to move or run when confronted with an intruder or threat in their dream-like state. Those deepest, most ancient of fears to flee are the stuff that great and memorable horror is made of.

Fear is tempered by risk perception to some degree and helps humans make sense of the world. Risk perception is how likely a risk is to cause harm in our view, and we act sometimes rationally and sometimes irrationally. For example, a mother rushing into a burning building to save her child is irrational for her own safety, but a rational response to saving her child. Humans also use risk perception to help explain fears and consequences. If someone dies of lung cancer, what is the first question that is usually asked? Did he or she smoke cigarettes? Looking for a risk that the unfortunate victim of cancer may have knowingly assumed herself, helps explain the risk and lowers the fear that it will happen to the person making the inquiry. If someone is hit by lightening, which has been established as a one in a million chance, we are still anxious to know how it happened? Was he standing under a tree in a lightning storm? Did he fail to get out of the swimming pool when warned? Did he assume some other risk so that we know that it would not have happened to us because we would not have taken such a risk? These are all mechanisms to reduce our fears about our own mortality. A plot that does not allow an explanation that puts us at ease will be a successful biohorror/biothriller story. In *Hud* (1963), Homer Bannon illegally buys Mexican cattle which harbor the deadly foot-and-mouth disease which leads to the destruction of everything Homer holds dear – his favor cattle, his ranch and finally his life. We are made to feel compassion for Homer, but we still know that he brought it on himself with an intentionally illegal action. This makes us less frightened because Homer just made the bad choice. We would never do that.

Horror and fear of contracting a contagious disease speaks directly to fear about our own mortality. The inability to avoid the risk escalates the fear, which can come from being a targeted victim or an innocent victim. These scenarios make it nearly impossible for the viewer to lessen the fear by attributing the victims of contagion with assuming a risk. It could be considered to be an "act of God" when someone contracts a fatal illness without assuming any of the risk. However, if the victim took a stroll through the smallpox hospital and contracted smallpox, the viewer could lessen the fear of his own mortality by the fact that the victim assumed the risk of contracting smallpox by voluntarily walking through the smallpox hospital. Now change the scene where the victim is handcuffed and walked involuntarily through the smallpox hospital and intentionally exposed to oozing pox sores on a human leg by forcing his hand to rub across the ooze, well then, you have increased the fear and the horror for the viewer, who cannot use assumption of risk to lessen their own fears and perception of the risk.

There are also principles that help explain our perception of risk. It has been demonstrated in risk studies that there are factors which make humans over-estimate and under-estimate risk. For example, if a person is a volunteer with doctors-without-borders and sees patients with plague, routinely, then a movie about plague will not be as horrifying because they are familiar with the risk. So *familiarity* with the threat is a factor in how fearful a movie might be. Another known factor to influence our perception of risk is the catastrophic degree of the risk. For example, a disease with a 90% mortality rate, like the Ebola virus, is likely to cause an over-estimate of the risk. A disease that is highly contagious, like an influenza, which kills only 10% of its victims, may lead to under-estimating the risk because it is not as catastrophic as a 90% mortality rate. Combine that with the fact that Ebola is an exotic disease found in the heart of Africa, and influenza is a familiar disease among us each winter, you also add the *familiarity* factor, which increases the over-estimate of the risk of Ebola. It is no coincidence that "ebola" has become a colloquial term for a horrific sickness of any kind. It evokes a certain edge of fear that over-estimates the sickness in an intentional way to give effect to the statement. Someone might tell their friend, "I think I have some kind of ebola," meaning, I feel really sick, and ebola joins the list of colloquial references unique to our place and time.

Thus, biohorror movies have a ready-made plot for increasing fear and perception of the risk based on the unfamiliarity of deadly and novel disease agents and the catastrophic nature of their consequences. This all adds up to a movie that evokes the most ancient and serious of our emotions --- fear and fear about our own mortality.

The movies are made more horrific by carrying the results of the disease and devastation to its apocalyptic possibilities and even the unlikely, but plausible. The more the plot connects it with a reality they have created on the screen, the more we are horrified. So taking us in an apocalyptic direction, leads us along a path of familiar risks into an unknown world, essentially taking us far out of our comfort zone. Fear. Horror.

One important theory of this method, is based on the principle of the rule of law. We are comfortable and feel less horror when we have the rule of law in order. That is, criminals will be punished for crimes in a legal system that recognizes due process and predictable ways of punishing those who are found guilty. The rule of law, also assures us of an orderly life in such things as banking, grocery shopping and a 9-1-1 number to call when we have an emergency. Take just one of those orderly systems away, and we are taken far out of our comfort zone. Take them all away, and we are suddenly horrified in an unknown, lawless and unfamiliar way of life – the post-apocalyptic plot.

Another source of horror is that of the tension between individual autonomy and power that restraints or influences that autonomy using government powers, diseases that change the human will (zombies) or fantastical constructs that achieve the same end.

The United States enjoys the most liberal human rights protections in the world through the Bill of Rights with the U.S. Constitution. One on which we rely to a great extent is due process, which guarantees that we won't be held to a law about which we have no notice. (Ignorance of the law is still not a defense.) But a law which has been established through the legislative process and through the Executive Branch regulatory process is considered to be one that has given the regulated community notice that they could have some input into the making of the law and some final notice when the law becomes effective. That is the due process that ensures the rule of law not the rule of man is governing us. Take that away, and you have anarchy or dictatorship or a police-state with street justice. All of this takes us out of our comfort zone into an unpredictable environment where the horrors can predictably unfold. The consequences of an epidemic or pandemic where governments react with force (send in the military) or overly constraining individual freedom (quarantine, blockades, isolation in your home) create a tension with an individual's sense of free will. However, unique to the biohorror subgenre, these government forces are presumptively for the greater good or the public well-being and security. All of these actions are to prevent further spread of the disease by limiting individual freedom to move about freely. Then the individual has to cope with the tension between getting food and medicine for the family when the government issues a curfew not to be out of their homes. Several layers of tension in this context of plausibility leads us to --- yes, horror and panic.

Finally, the other plot device for creating horror is the corrupt government or individual in the government that feeds the conspiracy theory suspicions that make the viewer think it is plausible therefore much more horrific.

Outbreak (1995) depicted corrupt government officials who held on to a secret bioweapon from its bioweapon producing past despite the U.S. government's ratification of the Biological Weapons Convention to end all bioweapons production and storage. The motivation for the government officials was not greed or money, but rather an ill-conceived patriotism that an effective bioweapon was a good thing to have and it was a logical action in their minds. It was a case of the bureaucrat knowing better than the government about what is good for national security.

The Satan Bug (1965) depicted a corrupt government developing the ultimate bioweapon, the "Satan bug" in a government laboratory. Interestingly, this was before the U.S. signed and ratified the Biological Weapons Convention (1975) and so an active biological weapons program was part of the U.S. research agenda to create an effective bioweapon at the time *The Satan Bug* (1965) was made. So this corrupt government was really ethically, not legally, acting in a disastrous manner. . *Pandemic* (2007) was the result of a government conspiracy, illegally creating a bioweapon the "Riptide virus", long after the Biological Weapons Convention agreement to ban such activities.

From its early beginnings with pure government corruption, plot devices moved to the government conspiracy with private sector interests taken to a greedy extreme. Much of this was driven by public disdain of corporate greed beginning with the environmental movement in the 1970s and again in the 1990s with the Enron scandal and most recently with the contaminated steroid knowingly distributed by the pharmaceutical-like company, causing hundreds of painful infections and some deaths.

The threat of the military-industrial complex is also food for the conspiracy theorists, but also a threat that has concerned political scientists in the integrity of government and in preserving democracy. Decisions should not be made by industry, but by government by the people and for the people. Movements toward industry collusion and corrupt alliances with government upset that balance and moves power away from the people to individual corporations. Horrifying!

The Constant Gardner (2006) based on the novel by John le Carré, depicts the pharmaceutical company as the greedy villain at the expense of lives in Africa in collusion with the corrupt Kenyan officials. A subtle mass blackmail scheme forced patients who badly needed a tuberculosis drug to forego informed consent and accept injections of a drug, "Dypraxa" in what was ostensibly a clinical drug trial in exchange for the drug they needed to stay alive. The plot leads the characters to investigate the corrupt officials and what is Dypraxa. This horror is much more subtle that any of the other movies on this list, but horrific nonetheless, in part because it is so realistic it leaves the viewer with the idea that this is not only plausible but could easily be happening right now. Could it happen outside of Africa? Could pharmaceutical companies be corrupt, greedy and engaged in clinical trials that kill people, then covering it up? Wait, didn't I just read that in the newspaper? You see where the horror comes from in this clever but subtle biothriller.

The Hades Factor (2006) was another corrupt government plot with a private sector greed component driving the plot action.

Flight of the Living Dead (2007) depicts a government-industry corruption plot device where the industry decides to take its inventions elsewhere to a higher bidder. This virus is designed to reanimate the soldier on the battlefield, taking it out of the typical creation of a bioweapon activity for offensive purposes, but makes it a defensive creation. A defensive purpose makes it more plausible as an activity and not in direct violation of the Biological Weapons Convention like the creations in *Pandemic* (2007), *The Hades Factor* (2006) and *Outbreak* (1995).

So the government power out of balance plot, the government corruption and the government-military-industrial complex corruption plot all have one thing in common that can temper our horror. That is, we have some control over government. Not much, but some, by definition. It will either collapse of its own self-destruction, or the corrupt officials will be convicted and sentenced, or they will be voted out of office. However, there is one force over which we have scant little control and that one may be the most horrific of them all --- Mother Nature.

The Mother Nature villain or plot device has followed the public and medical fears very closely. In the period of epidemics of typhoid fever and polio for the first half of the Twentieth Century, Mother Nature was indeed scary and uncontrollable. There were no reliable antibiotics and vaccines were still in the development stage for safety and reliability, first regulated by the Vaccine Act of 1901. The horrors of the Black Plague in 1341 in Europe which killed one-fourth of the humans on the planet, is not something easily forgettable, even over the next millennia! Then, in the last third of the Twentieth Century, the professionals declared infectious diseases were no longer a threat to humankind, and the days of the infectious disease physician were over. What was left after polio was under control with a vaccine? Smallpox was completely eradicated from the earth, becoming the first disease conquered by man in 1971, and childhood vaccines now ensured the infant mortality rate would drop dramatically. So, too, the movie plots followed this trend.

Mother Nature caused the plague outbreak on the ship with *Nosferatu* (1922) the silent movie based on the book Dracula. The consequences of the plague with no cure were horrifying.

The movie, *Hud* (1963), a western movie about a headstrong and arrogant son of a cattle rancher is played out in the context of a foot-and-mouth outbreak which requires complete destruction of the herd leading to economic devastation. This takes the family out of their comfort zone of wealth and status to one of shunning and economic devastation. These early biohorror movies depict the unpredictable Mother Nature source of terror, which is then followed by a period when Mother Nature no longer seemed threatening. The infectious disease era was dead – or so we thought.

Then the revival of the Mother Nature as terrorist plot returned and ushered in a trend in realism in biohorror. The year 2003 and the SARS pandemic, set the stage for horror plots. Triggered by the emergence of a newly evolved virus from the Guangdong Province of China that was highly contagious and spread around the globe in a matter of days, it was weeks before we could determine whether this was a new virus, a new bioweapon or an old virus ---realism and suspense.

The first of these movies was a made for television movie, *Fatal Contact: Bird Flu in America* (2006) and it was important that it was for television. The threat of bird flu was current and the audience was promisingly large because of the high level of public awareness of this new influenza strain that was emerging. Clearly the U.S. Centers for Diseases Control and Prevention (CDC) was also highly concerned about the public's viewing of this movie. The U.S. CDC was so concerned that they collaborated with the movie producer and the network to include a statement at the end of the movie that viewers could go to the CDC website to learn the true nature of bird flu, and that the extreme reactions and immediate incubation periods leading to illness and death were far from realistic for bird flu. The concern that the public would panic from watching such a depiction of bird flu in the movie was real, in part because of the realism that the movie brought to the unfolding of a pandemic, bird flu, and the consequences and actions of the government in the U.S.

The talking points from CDC and other state public health agencies began with this statement or similar one:

The ABC movie, Fatal Contact, Bird Flu in America is a movie, and not a documentary. It is a work designed to entertain and not a factual accounting of a real event.[3]

Whether CDC's website and other state responses were a success in quelling the panic, or people were just not panicked, it is hard to say. But the reaction to the movie was not mass panic.

The chapters that follow will explore other aspects of this subgenre that make it unique. Whether a criminal copycat could blame his crime on the writers and producers in Hollywood? How these movies use the heroes and heroines, the plots, the disease agents, the villains and the endings to bring out the most in our fears, perceptions of risk and horrors --- the things that keep us up at night.

---

[3] Florida Department of Health, Discussion Points for Fatal Contact: Bird Flu in America at http://www.doh.state.fl.us/rw.../ABC_Movie_Points_for_Discussion.doc. Annex 1 of this book contains the CDC provided talking points for state public health authorities in response to the movie.

Chapter 3

The-Movie-Made-Me-Do-It Defense
Can fictional biothrillers or biohorror movies inspire criminals?

Now of course, that's just fiction,
but that's a damn good idea.

--- Frederick Thomas, Quoted from his indictment for attempt to use biological weapons of mass destruction, 2012

The transcripts of wired conversations between four men conspiring to attack United States Department of Justice attorneys revealed inspiration found in fiction. Frederick Thomas was speaking to co-conspirators, Dan Roberts, Ray Adams and Samuel Crump and his statement was quoted in their indictment for attempted bioterrorism. The book was a biothriller he had read online, a fictional plot to kill federal U.S. Department of Justice attorneys.

The federal crime of conspiracy requires that two or more people take significant steps toward the commission of a crime, and in this case, the crime was attempted use of biological weapons. He had taken significant steps by planning, exchanging information and making contact with a supplier for ricin and made arrangements to buy some.

Two well-publicized cases involving crimes that were very clearly inspired by movies will continue to be a horrific memory for American society. The assassination attempt on President Reagan by John Hinckley in 1981 was the finish of Hinckley's threats to impress the real-life, Jody Foster, who played a character in the movie *Taxi Driver* (1976) with a similar plot. More recently, James Holmes, with orange hair and beard, told police he was "the Joker" from the movie *Dark Knight Rises* (2012) after being arrested.[4] He had entered

[4] Judith Crosson And Carly Reynolds In Aurora, Colo. AND Christina Boyle, Joe Kemp And Rich Schapiro In New York , *'Dark Knight Rises' screening shooting in suburban Denver leaves 12 dead, 58 injured: police,* New York Daily News, July

the theater at the midnight showing of the movie in Aurora, Colorado, July 20, 2012, and opened fire shooting 71 people, leaving 12 dead.

The Seige (1998), starring Denzel Washington and Annette Benning, depicted the terrorizing of New York City by Islamic extremists who used bombs and car bombs to hit federal buildings. In retrospect on 9/11, the targeting of New York City and buildings in New York City where the FBI offices were located paralleled the movie's depiction of a car bomb driving into the FBI building in New York City. The independent terrorist cells that were activated for each plot also closely paralleled the terrorist cell structure and process of the 9/11 terrorists who attacked the World Trade Center and the Pentagon. The terrorists were embedded in sleeper cells in the United States in 1998, living as Americans, and must have also been aware of the widely reported protest against the movie by American Muslims who saw the movie as anti-Muslim propaganda.

How much does the Constitution protect this First Amendment right to free speech and free expression in art, movies and music? The threshold for restricting free speech is very high and only several exceptional circumstances will allow any burden of this express, individual right. One such exception is the "fighting words" doctrine which restricts the right to shout "fire" in a crowded theater, without cause, or to speak words that can incite a riot or violence. If an artist writes a plot or idea that people act out in imitation of the song or movie, does that make the filmmaker or songwriter potentially liable for gross negligence or even malice in publishing or producing the art? The artist or author has the right of free expression and even the acting out of the words to perpetrate a crime if inspired by the expression is not something for which they can be held liable, at least no case has presented thus far that would find that result.

In 1995, two teenagers, Sarah Edmondson , 19, and Benjamin Darras, 18, set off on a drive to a concert after watching the movie *Natural Born Killers*, a movie about a couple who kill countless people and the media made them famous by all the publicity they received. The couple killed George Savage in route to the concert by shooting him in the head twice. Savage had been a friend of John Grisham, best selling crime and thriller author, and Grisham began to speak out about Hollywood's lack of responsibility in what they produce. The next victim of the Edmondson-Darras duo was a convenience store clerk, Patsy Ann Byers, who survived but was left a quadripeligic. Grisham then advised her on her litigation strategy. Byers originally sued Edmondson and Darras for her injuries, but then added Warner Brothers and Oliver Stone, producers of the movie, *Natural Born Killers*. Grisham stated publicly that filmmakers should be held accountable for movies that they make and crimes that they incite as a result of these movies. Grisham allegedly advised Byers to use a product liability theory of recovery, stating that the filmmakers "knew, or should have known that the film would cause and inspire people [...] to commit crimes such as the shooting of Patsy Ann Byers." Grisham also authored an article in the Oxford American, entitled, "Unnatural Killers", April 1996, writing:

> "The last hope of imposing some sense on Hollywood will come through another great American tradition, the lawsuit. A case can be made that there exists a direct causal link between *Natural Born Killers* and the death

---

21, 2011, at : http://www.nydailynews.com/news/national/dark-knight-rises-screening-shooting-leaves-20-injured-deaths-feared-reports-article-1.1118289#ixzz2QMCol2G3 .

of Bill Savage. It will take only one large verdict against the likes of Oliver Stone, and then the party will be over."[5]

The Louisiana courts thought that the movie was protected by the First Amendment and dismissed the case, but Byers immediately appealed it and the court found that she had enough evidence to proceed to trial on the issues of whether the filmmakers were liable for their product's defects in 1998. The case was eventually dismissed by another judge on the basis that there was no evidence that either Warner Brothers or Oliver Stone had an intent to incite violence. That essentially ended the case in 2001, illustrating the high hurdle that a victim will have to try to make a filmmaker liable for their movies, even if there is an established connection between the influence of the movie and the crime. In fact, there are more than a dozen crimes with evidence that they were influenced by the movie, *Natural Born Killers*, including the Columbine High School massacre and the Heath High School massacre in Paducah, Kentucky.

John Bruce Thompson, attorney and activist against video games that incite violence, represented the parents of the victims of the 1997 high school shooting in Paducah. He sued for $33 million, Time Warner, Polygram Film, Palm Pictures, Island Pictures, New Line Cinema, Atari, Nintendo and Sony Computer Entertainment, specifically mentioning the movie, *Natural Born Killers.* Thompson argued that the murder was influenced by the movie and the games, but the suit was dismissed in 2001. This defense of the-movie-made-me-do-it failed to survive in Kentucky courts.

One of the most highly publicized controversies over this issue of copycat crimes involving the arts came with a song entitled, "Cop Killers" by the music group, Body Count, sung by its lead vocalist, Ice-T, released in 1992. The song is a reaction to police violence and the singer's retaliation by killing police officers. Indeed, it has been alleged to have inspired the Los Angeles riots that broke out after the acquittal of the Rodney King police officers tried in that police brutality case. Rodney King and the beating which was captured on video tape was mentioned in the song, "Cop Killer." Clearly it was seen as provocative, because the Combined Law Enforcement Association of Texas (CLEAT) and the Dallas Police officers began a campaign to force Warner Brothers to withdraw the record. Some police officers even went as far as to announce that they would not respond to music stores selling the album with the song. In one case, a young man who shot an officer on a traffic stop from his car, had been listening to the song, "Cop Killer" immediately before the stop.

While it is clear at this point that exceeding the boundaries of free speech and free expression with the content of movie has not yet been demonstrated and filmmakers and film companies have never been held liable for any of the acts or crimes that they may have had a causal connection. The theory of the fighting words doctrine then survives, and that is that the power of the human will should bc able to overcome any words, acting or depictions of illegal acts.

The movie-made-me-do-it defense

However, this does not answer the other question, and that is, could the influence of a movie or a song be used in defense of a murder or a crime.

In 1992, Ronald Ray Howard, a nineteen-year-old teenager in a stolen car on probation was stopped by a police officer for a broken headlight. Howard shot the police

[5] "Unnatural Killers," Oxford American (April 1996).

officer in the neck from his driver's window while he had been listening to the song "Soulja's Story," sung by rapper, Tupac Shakur. The lyrics are about a young black male shooting a police officer who stops him in a traffic stop. This case is not about suing the artist, because the First Amendment is very broad and protective of free speech, even this kind of speech, which some may even say is a kind of political speech with a viewpoint about police brutality. But this case is about whether the influence of lyrics can be used as a *defense* in a murder case. The jury heard the defense say that the violent lyrics were in part responsible for the acts of the defendant, Ronald Ray Howard, causing him to act the way he did formulating a "diminished capacity" defense. The jury was not persuaded and gave him the death penalty.

So the conclusion must be that filmmakers and writers will continue to exercise their freedom of speech and freedom of expression, so why not monitor the writings and films that are being made as lessons for better preparation should a terrorist try the ideas in the movie or the book?

Did you see *Three Days of the Condor* (1975)? Robert Redford's job was reading novels for the Central Intelligence Agency. If someone can imagine a plot against the national security of the United States, then someone else might imagine something like it, or be a copycat. At least that was the logic for creating the unit to review fiction in the movie. In *Three Days of the Condor* (1973), Robert Redford had just submitted a report outlining some elements of a novel which contained potential plots that could be used against the United States. The very day he was expecting a response to his report, he returned to his office from getting lunch to find all of his office mates murdered. When he contacts the CIA headquarters about the incident they send him to meet some agents, which turns out to be a trap which he narrowly escapes.

In real life, the Open Source officers of the CIA have the job of scanning everything that is publicly available and with the explosion of information on the internet since 1993, the availability of e-books and the exchange of books and fiction has increased dramatically. Books and movies would be in the open source category.

Using libraries to track people who may be planning ordinary criminal plots to terrorism through the books and videos they check out from the library has become such a reliable investigatory tool, that after 9/11, the FBI implemented the library and bookstore surveillance program from the powers delegated to it in through §215 of the USA PATRIOT Act of 2001. This also includes electronic retrievals of books and materials from service providers. Now, it was not just probable cause that would send investigators to ask for library records, it was a broad surveillance program that could theoretically see anyone's library records, without probable cause. This was highly controversial and led to public outrage and the usual quiet librarian was vocal. This is not the first time that libraries were used for national security purposes. In the 1980s in the height of the Cold War, the FBI often requested records from academic libraries in search of potential spies who were attempting access to research information and data through the specialized resources of the academic library.

The movie *Seven* (1995) was a thriller involving the investigation of a serial killer who was modeling each murder on the seven deadly sins which led investigators to inquire at libraries who had checked out books on this subject. This provided the missing clue and they used the address to find the suspect. If it can be imagined, perhaps it can happen.

Now with that background, how has bioterrorism been affected by the movies, or have movies been affected by bioterrorism, including that wielded by Mother Nature with naturally emerging infectious diseases like Bird Flu? In Chapter One, the chronology of biohorror movies is told within its historical context and if you review that chapter again, you will observe how many of the more recent movies have followed particular biological events. The projection of the increase in movies in the coming years, based on the rate of increasing numbers of biohorror films, indicates a growing interest and fascination with this new sub-genre. It seems that influence will continue to flow both in influencing and inspiring as well as being potential templates for copycats.

Fiction can also trigger the suspicion of investigators. In the investigation of the Anthrax attacks of fall 2001, Steven Hatfield, a scientist at USAMRIID, the U.S. Army's research laboratory for biodefense, was a "person of interest" in the investigation, sparking controversy over the first time the moniker, "person of interest" had been used. Circumstantial evidence swirled around the target of their investigation, but nothing ever really pointed to Hatfield as a perpetrator and so he was never officially called a "suspect". One of the things that unfortunately triggered the investigators' suspicions was a novel-in-progress that Hatfield had on his computer hard drive which had been seized in one of many searches of his apartment. His draft novel depicted an anthrax attack on American civilians. Hatfield was ultimately cleared of all suspicion and won a judgment of $5million dollars against the FBI for their actions, which cost Hatfield his academic career at one institution and his personal life was also cited in his complaint as a basis for his losses due to the actions of the FBI.

If this is an indication that we should avoid keeping works-in-progress novels on our computer iclouds or hard drives, then it is a sad day for the First Amendment. Grisham's pleas to Hollywood to use moral judgment in their choices of which films to produce has so far fallen on deaf ears and the legal theories he developed were also unconvincing for the courts. Through all of these events of copycats, one thing remains firm and that is our high protection of the First Amendment with no additional exception carved out for the movie that inspires violence. Other exceptions such as obscenity and 'low value" speech can limit movies, but that is already done through the rating system.

The last lines of *Burn After Reading* (2008) at the end of a duplicitous and convoluted dark comedy of misunderstandings in motives and misdirected investigations by the CIA, say it best:

CIA Superior
What did we learn, Palmer?

Palmer
I don't know, sir.

CIA Superior
I don't fucking know, either.

Palmer
I guess we learned not to do it again.
Yes, sir.

CIA Superior
I'm fucked if I know what we did.

Palmer
Yes, sir, it's hard to say.

---*Burn After Reading* (2008)

Chapter 4

The Heroes

Are the heroes scientists? Professionals? Do they tend to be men rather than women or *vice versa*? Are the characters involved romantically with each other? Is the hero expected to do the impossible or the ethical? Is the hero dealing with a realistic threat or a zombie? What is the motivation for the hero? And of course, what are the obstacles the hero faces?

Overwhelmingly, the heroes are scientists or medical researchers. The screenwriters rarely make a government bureaucrat a hero, and more often when they appear they are most likely being villains (anti-protagonists).

Beginning with the *Andromeda Strain* (1971) when the screenwriter proposed to the Director that the novel's male lead character Dr. Leavitt should be a female, many of the hero-scientists have been women. Dr. Nora Hart in *Black Plague* (1992); Dr. Blumenthal in *Formula for Death* (1995); Dr. Landis in *Contagion* (2002); Dr. Levitt in *Global Effect* (2002) who raced to find the cure for the world. *Fatal Contact* (2005), *Pandemic* (2007) and *Contagion* (2011) featured brave, female health professionals who had to break with protocol to get the job done, find the cure, save the patient and save the world.

But even in the male-dominated world of 1950, *Panic in the Street* (1950) depicts women who make the difference in tracing the initial case of the plague. The first one is the wife of a sea captain who knows the infected illegal immigrant he helped to bring into New Orleans. She forces her husband to tell the public health service for fear that he may have the plague and can get treatment, despite his reluctance. The second woman is the nurse who contrary to the wishes of the dominating physician, leaves his presence to contact the public health authorities about the infected patient that the physician has refused to hospitalize. While a third woman falls victim to the plague because of her own dishonesty when she coerces her husband into lying to investigators about their knowledge of the plague-carrying customer who came to their restaurant. A mixed-bag, but with only one exception the women in this 1950 movie are the strong, heroines of their scenes. The main protagonist, however, is the handsome young male physician of the public health service who wants to save New Orleans with a homemaker wife waiting at home for his return, blissfully ignorant of the dangers that lurk where her husband works.

Knowing that almost every biohorror/biothriller had a female heroine who was the physician, public health authority or epidemiologist, I expected that formula to continue. As

I sat in the theater watching *World War Z* (2013), I was stunned when the epidemiologist who was referred to as their "last best hope" was a young man. This was the first male, lone hero in a biohorror/biothriller since Dr. Doctor Bernard Rieux in *La Peste* (1992) and Dr. William R. Whitman in *Contaminated Man* (2000) both characters played by William Hurt!

But it was only minutes until the young epidemiologist either slipped on his gun and accidentally shot himself, or intentionally shot himself upon his first encounter with the zombies of the post-apocalyptic world in which their aircraft had landed. Note to screenwriters: Don't bother writing a male into the script as the epidemiologist or doctor who saves the world --- he probably won't last long, or if you do, be sure to cast William Hurt for the part.

These movies are often driven by the romance as well as the biological threat. *Outbreak* (1995), based on the true life couple who worked at USAMRIID were depicted as still in love, though going through a divorce as they worked to save the world. Even without understanding Japanese, one can observe from the trailer for *Pandemic* (Japan, 2009), that the disease coming between the young physicians is creating tension, despair and grief.

Many of these films have a backstory of a love affair destroyed by the disease which is the focus of the film. *Contaminated Man* (2002) the hero brings home an infection that kills his wife and family, shaping his view of the world; in all of the Matheson inspired movies, The *Last Man on Earth* (1962); *Omega Man* (1971); *I Am Legend* (2007); *World War Z* (2013) the hero's beloved wife had been killed by the deadly disease, also shaping his view of the world. In each of these films, the hero finds a new love interest which ultimately affects decisions that he makes.

Contagion (2011) creates a character whose wife spreads a deadly virus to his children but also to a lover she has stopped by to see on her way home from a business trip. The protagonist struggles with learning the undeniable truth from the epidemiological evidence that his wife was unfaithful to him, making his recovery from the pandemic more complex.

Another group of movies have plots driven by the protagonist trying to save the life of their wife or loved one. Usually, they have had to choose between saving the world or turning their attention to save their loved one.

Contagious (1997) features an outbreak of cholera which is killing people slowly and Dr. Cole (Lindsey Wagner) learns that her husband on a camping trip with her children has suddenly fallen ill with what is probably cholera. Dr. Cole is depicted as a hard working, dedicated professional who does not spend a lot of time with her family, and when her husband becomes sick her character arc takes a turn for the personal and for a time she abandons her fight to save the public in order to save her husband.

Flight of the Living Dead (2007) follows a plot based on a man's effort to save his scientist wife who had become infected with a top secret re-animation virus for the military.

Motivation for the protagonist can be driven by the professional oath to save humanity if they are a physician or a public health official. Motivation for the research scientist has often been how to contain the laboratory accident that threatens to end the world. All three of Richard Matheson-inpsired films end with the protagonist dying in his effort to save the world. The protagonist in *World War Z* (2013), inspired in part by the Matheson book, "I Am Legend", deviates here and survives after saving the world based on his theory of how to create a vaccine.

Perhaps we have the making of a sub-sub-genre, the "bio-romance"?

Chapter 5

The Villains, The Motivations

Terrorists are ready made villains. Are they professionals? Scientists? Males or females? Are the villains involved in romantic relationships or have love interests? What is the motivation of the villain? Is it criminal? Magical? Or is it the motivation of a zombie (the undefined, undead)?

The classic villain, the Devil or Death, is featured in *The Seventh Seal* (1957) (Sweden), a classic tale set in the aftermath of the Crusades and a knight returning from seeing the devastation of the plague, but the real villain is Death who is a character. The unforgettable opening scene of the film is an encounter with Death where the knight challenges Death to a chess game to save his life --- if he wins. The symbolism of the character Death and the Black Plague present its inescapable conclusion, that no one can beat Death.

The government conspiracy and military villains

The government conspiracy plot involving bioweapons and the choice of greed or hubris over the rule of law and/or human life is a central plot device in twelve of the forty-eight movies. The first is *The Satan Bug* (1965) with a government laboratory coverup; *Warning Sign* (1985) was another government laboratory coverup; *Quarantine* (1989) was a government that no longer recognized the rule of law; *Outbreak* (1985) was a military coverup of a bioweapon; *Pandora's Clock* (1996) was a government coverup of the spread of their weapon and they were willing to destroy a flight which had become contaminated in order to keep their secret; *Contaminated Man* (2000) was a government coverup of a bioweapon which affected their own scientist; *Venomous* (2001) was a bioweapons program out of control which led to a coverup to destroy the entire town; *Day of the Dead: Contagium* (2004) is a government trying to quietly stop a rogue scientist who wants to find a cure for a bioweapon he created; *The Hades Factor* (2006) is a government conspiracy in the Ludlum style; *The Constant Gardner* (2006) is a government conspiracy and coverup of the use of human subjects in a failing drug test in Kenya; and *Pandemic* (2009) is a military coverup of a bioweapon that has escaped in a small town. Finally, *Patient Zero* (2012) two scientists in a secret government laboratory uncover a government cover-up. This plot device is used over a broad time frame, from 1965 to 2012.

Greed as the motivation

Greed and corporate greed is a motivation of the villains in six of the forty-eight movies. Greed is a central plot device of *The Satan Bug* (1965) where an "inside job" results in a theft of the killer virus in order to blackmail the government to pay a large ransom for it. In *Killer Buzz* (2001), an opportunistic young man decides the killer bees could be sold if he could get them back to America. In *Global Effect* (2002), an activist group has a plan to start a pandemic from which they think they will profit. *The Constant Gardner* (2006) while identified with the government conspiracy plot, it was intertwined with a greedy pharmaceutical company in collaboration with the governments of both Great Britain and Kenya. In *Flight of the Living Dead* (2007), the contractors who have developed a defensive biological agent to reanimate soldiers to keep fighting, have taken it on a flight to Europe where they hope to sell it to the highest bidder, feeling they were not getting enough money from the U.S. government. In this Bollywood movie, *Azaan* (2011) (India), the villain is stealing a bioweapon in order to sell it for a handsome price.

The Despicable Boyfriend Villain

Two movies feature a villain who is a despicable "boyfriend" who puts greed above any concern for his "girlfriend". An interesting device to make the audience have a more intense dislike for the villain.

Global Effect (2002) features a bioterrorist with a girlfriend who he convinces to let him infect her and sends her into the streets to infect the city, with a promise he will get the cure and meet her before it is too late. Predictably, his villainy is made more clear when he reveals he never intended to save her, and there was now an opening for a new girlfriend. She eventually learns that she has been tricked when her boyfriend does not show up at their meeting place with the cure.

The blogger in *Contagion* (2011) was engaged in a scheme to sell a bogus remedy in the midst of a pandemic, and leads all of his followers to their deaths by relying on his "cure". He defrauds even his pregnant friend, promising to deliver the cure to her. He makes claims that he has been cured by this treatment that he sells to his followers. Eventually he is arrested by the FBI and forced to take a blood test to see if he has the antibodies to back up his claim that he was cured by his treatment. His fraud is revealed.

The bioweapons are not the villains

Terrorism created by animals engineered to be weapons should not make us dislike the animals. The bats in *Bats: A Human Harvest* (2008) and the snakes in *Venomous* (2001) are the instruments of bioterror but it is the mastermind behind each of those – like the wicked witch of Oz, not her monkeys --- who is the true villain.

The problem of attribution and identifying a villain

In a real bioterrorism attack, it is sometimes difficult to distinguish between a natural outbreak and an intentional attack. It is also sometimes very difficult to identify the perpetrator of the bioterrorism attack in part because it may look a lot like a natural outbreak, or because the perpetrator does not leave a note explaining that they have just attacked with a bacteria or virus. The work of the investigators who will likely be public health epidemiologists, disease detectives and crime detectives, is to determine the cause. They will attempt to accurately attribute the attack to the individual or group that is responsible for it. First identifying the biological agent is the essential first step and may help to narrow the list of possible perpetrators. Then once the biological agent is identified, it will be characterized as to its infectivity, fragility and ubiquity. This may also reveal whether it is an engineered biological agent or a naturally emerging infectious disease. Finally, with identification and characterization there is the hope that attribution can be determined.

Some movies play on the difficult of attribution and tell the story without identifying "who did it." Not knowing who did it, can leave the audience dissatisfied (The Greeks who developed the whole three Act structure that answers the questions in Act 3 knew this millennia ago.) *Waterborne* (2005) ends with a newscast saying it was possibly terrorists and no clues in the movie convince us in any way. In fact, *Waterborne* (2005) fails to give us any explanation at all as to what it might have been to cause these deaths, which is a hard sell in 2005 in this period of realism.

Mother Nature, a Villain?

The movies which have a disease emerging from Mother Nature and no bioterrorist, no government bioweapon coverup and no greedy corporate plot open the door for other villains where fear, pressure, self-interest, and loyalty are characteristics that will be challenged in the characters. It also provides an opportunity for a character arc.

Chapter 6

The Settings

The setting for the film is critical to the plot of a biohorror or biothriller movie and can be the source of much of the horror and suspense.

Transportation modes are a prime setting opportunity for spreading the fear and the disease. The use of an aircraft setting utilizes the fear of being trapped with the threat of biological agents. The aircraft and air terminal setting when used to create tension and fear is particularly popular and is the primary setting for the beginning and ending of *12 Monkeys* (1995); and for the much of the movie in *Pandora's Clock* (1996), *Quarantine* (1989); *Killer Buzz* (2001); *Flight of the Living Dead* (2007); and *Quarantine 2: Terminal* (2011).

The aircraft setting plays a role, but not a dominant one in several movies including: *Black Death* (1992) where a teenage girl returning from vacation with her parents brings the plague with her on the flight, infecting those around her. In *Global Effect* (2002) one scene shows the virus spreading beyond South Africa on a flight with an infected flight attendant. *Pandemic* (2007) involves the quarantine of a flight and *Contagion* (2011) involves the rapid spread of the virus due to air travel.

Nosferatu (1992) and *Panic in the Street* (1950) use the passenger ship as the mode of transportation that brings the plague.

The filming location is also revealing of the feel and sense of the story that the director wants to express. A number of biohorror movies are set and/or filmed in places like New Mexico [*Andromeda Strain* (1971); *Pandemic* (2009); *Carriers* (2009)] and Texas [*Hud* (1963); *Andromeda Strain* (1971)] – isolated, desert-like scenes that depict isolation and perhaps reminiscent of the frontier for free-wheeling lawlessness.

Washington, D.C. is also the location for federal government action and conspiracy. *Outbreak* (1995); *Contagion* (2002); *The Hades Factor* (2006) are examples.

California and the Los Angeles area is a frequent location. *The Satan Bug* (1965) in Palm Springs, CA; *Waterborne* (2005) set in Los Angeles; *The Omega Man* (1971) in Los Angeles; and *Warning Sign* (1985) in La Crescenta, CA. *Quarantine* (2008) and *Quarantine 2* (2011) were both set in Los Angeles.

The setting for *Global Effect* (2002) was Uganda and South Africa. The setting suggested that there was a connection with a known biological weapons program in the 1980s, known as "Project Coast." Largely a program with biological weapons aimed at the population of black South Africans. The movie was produced by a British producer, with most of the focus on the aggressive actions of the United States and the influence of the anthrax attacks. Interestingly, none of the widely known biological weapons program of South Africa was used or mentioned.

The Constant Gardner (2005) was filmed in Kenya and Canada, and took place in Kenya and the United Kingdom. This presented the opportunity for corruption and human rights abuses in the poverty-stricken and disease-burdened population.

Other international locations include *Nosferatu* (1922) was filmed in Germany and the Baltic Sea; Sweden was the location for *The Seventh Seal* (1957)]; *Epidemic* (1987) was filmed in Denmark; *The Gerber Syndrome* (2011) was filmed in Italy; *Azaan* (2011) was filmed in India. *Pandemic* (2009) was a movie set in Tokyo and filmed in Japan. (There was another *Pandemic* (2009) set in Los Angeles.)

Just as diseases recognize no jurisdictional boundaries, biohorror and biothriller movies can find a story anywhere.

Chapter 7

The Plague

Mother Abigail Freemantle

Once in every generation, the plague shall fall among them.
That's what it says in the Book. Seems like maybe you went a little too far this time.
--- *The Stand (1994)*

One of the criteria for selecting a movie for this compendium of biohorror movies as a new subgenre is that there must be a biological agent and it should have a name. Beyond the name, such things as its infectivity, lethality and symptoms could be integral to the plot. A contagious disease would call for a quarantine perhaps; whereas a non-contagious agent like anthrax, which can only be transmitted by coming in contact with anthrax spores, not the people infected with them, would not. A non-contagious agent would lessen the fear to some degree, so almost all of these biological agents (except the one in Waterborne, a biological agent used to contaminate the water supply) are contagious, with all the ingredients for fear. The biological agent might be a virus, bacteria, toxin or an engineered organism but it must be developed in the plot to qualify for this subgenre. The effects of the biological organism can range from the realistic to the magical reality to the futuristic science fiction to the zombie effect in horror and fantasy.

The origin of the biological organism can also be an important part of the plot. The origin may provide the back-story, or it may be the plot itself. The first three movies on the biohorror movie list use plague as their biological agent to create the plot. *Panic in the Street* (1950) uses a naturally occurring plague brought into the U.S. by an illegal immigrant from perhaps Armenia, while *Nosferatu* (1922) uses a plague associated with vampirism. *The Seventh Seal* (1957) uses the realism of the Black Plague and the end of the Crusades in the post-1350 world.

This map shows the movement of the plague across Europe which resulted in the death of one-third of the world's population.

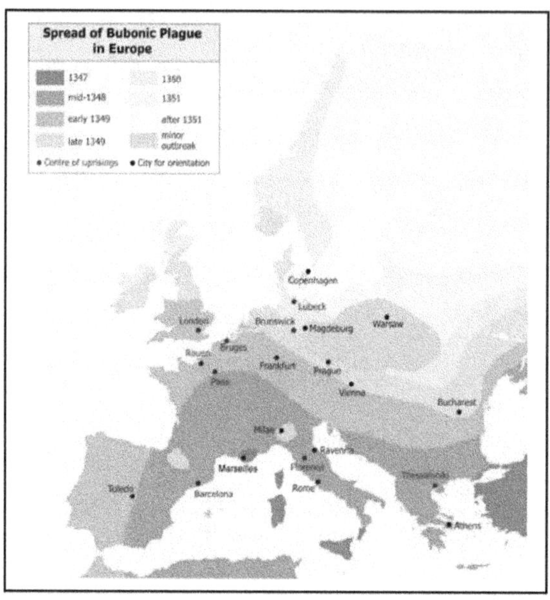

Biological agents can be naturally emerging or intentionally engineered. They can be used as intentional weapons, as in *Contagion* (2002) with a terrorist attack on the President; they can be naturally emerging from Mother Nature, as in *Black Death* (1992), *Contagion* (2011), *Pandemic* (2009), *Carriers* (2009) and *The Stand* (1994) with diseases that naturally emerge from nature and wreak havoc on the human species. A third way to launch the biological agent can be from accidentally releasing it from laboratories. The premise for *28 Days Later* (2003) and *28 Weeks Later* (2007) is the release of a deadly virus, Rage, by a group of animal-rights activists breaking into a government laboratory to free the Chimpanzees, which are infected with the virus. In *Global Effect* (2002) a "new kind of terrorist" makes a sophisticated theft of a rare virus and its cure from an unsecured laboratory in Uganda with an objective of bringing about a "new world order".

The resolution of the biological agent's effect is almost always tied in with the ending of the movie. Whether it is destroyed forever, or it is only controlled for the moment, with an ominous indication that it will return, perhaps in a sequel (*Quarantine and Quarantine 2*; and *28 Days Later and 28 Weeks Later*) the biological agent must be dealt with in the resolution.

The plague, a bacterial disease, has taken on the meaning of just about any disease and has become a colloquialism for describing a much broader range of illnesses than the bubonic plague, for which is gets its name. The bubonic plague, Black Plague or Black Death got its name in the medieval period, for the blackened pockets of blood under the skin in the groin and underarm area from the action of the plague bacteria in the lymph system. The deadly, painful and relatively rapid course of the disease with its contagious feature has forever set the standard for a disease that is a threat to the existence of mankind, even more so than smallpox, the deadly killer that has claimed more human lives in history than any other disease.

But let's look at the reason that we think of plague as a much more threatening disease. In 1348, the beginning of what became a devastating pandemic throughout most of

Europe was triggered when Tartar warriors from the East brought the disease to Europe and the Black Sea port of Kaffa in present day Ukraine. The Tartars were weakened to such a degree by the plague as the battle for Kaffa wore on for weeks, they eventually had to retreat --- but not before catapulting dead bodies of plague victims over the walls into Kaffa as one final gesture of attack.

The plague did spread, but not as they thought at the time from this attack strategy, which has come to signify the first bioterrorism attack in human history. But the strategy probably wasn't needed. Plague is not transmitted between humans unless there is a direct contact with body fluids or coughing and inhaling the droplets containing plague from pneumonically infected plague victims. This is usually the last stage of the disease. The way that the Genovesians probably contracted plague was from the rats that were brought along on the ships with the Tartars. Rats that ran into the walled city to find food were likely carrying plague-infected fleas that were the real transmitter of the plague, not the dead bodies. From this modest beginning in Kaffa, between 1341 and 1357, 25 million people died from plague, comprising about one-fourth of the European population. This disease made the single largest contribution to decimating the human species of any disease in such a short period of time, resulting in a shift in civil order and societal structure, leading to the abandonment of the fiefdom system of land ownership and the opening up of land tenure and more freely tradable property and a resultant shift in wealth. The deaths of such a significant number which were not selected by the plague bacteria based on their wealth or social position, resulted in land and riches being transferred to strangers where the entire families who would normally inherit were all dead. It was a post-apocalyptic world in the most real sense.

So it is no surprise that the most frequently used biological agent used in this group of 29 movies in the biohorror-biothriller subgenre is the plague. The first biohorror movie to establish this subgenre utilizes the plague as the deadly disease that would create drama and conflict in *Nosferatu* (1922). While primarily a vampire movie modeled after Bram Stoker's *Dracula,* the plague creates a central plot feature in the third act, where a ship brings a deadly plague to port in 19th Century Europe.

The Seventh Seal (1957) tells the tale of a knight returning from the Crusades and experiencing the death and destruction from the Black Death which swept across Europe.

The movie *Quarantine* (1989) used the plague or something called the plague as the infectious agent. In the book and movie, *The Plague* (1992) used the plague. *The Stand* (1994), Stephen King used plague as the deadly disease that threatened the disruption of civilization, with many of the elements of the dynamic of the Black Death, with the "chosen" who survived suggesting something of a religious explanation, which was replete throughout the period surrounding the Black Death.

Black Death (2010) and *Season of the Witch* (2011) both revisit the historical black plague setting for their story.

Chapter 8

Cinematic Biological Agents as a Plot Device

These movies each have a biological or biological toxin agent as a plot device. It can be a naturally occurring disease, an engineered bioweapon or animals engineered to be weapons. These range from the accurate description of real human diseases to those found only in science fiction or fantasy. It can be contagious or there can be one source as the infection. Or the transition from non-contagious to contagious may serve as a plot device to increase the tension, signaled with the dialogue, "It has become airborne!".

The origin of the biological agent is often important in determining who or what is the villain. In this group of 48 movies, 22 are naturally occurring, 17 are engineered biological weapons, the remaining 9 have unknown origins. The chart on the following page is a summary of the cinematic names used for each of biological agents used in the movies.

Table of Biological Agents in the Movie Plots

Nosferatu	1922	Plague
Panic in the Street	1950	Plague
The Seventh Seal	1957	Plague
Hud	1963	Foot & Mouth Disease
The Last Man on Earth	1964	Naturally emerging infectious disease
The Satan Bug	1965	Satan bug-engineered bioweapon
The Omega Man	1971	Plague
Andromeda Strain	1971	Andromeda Strain
Virus	1980	MM88 bioweapon reproduces at -10C
Warning Sign	1985	bacillus luminescence
Epidemic	1987	DIN, references to plague

Quarantine	1989	Plague
La Peste (The Plague)	1992	Plague
Black Death	1992	Plague
Outbreak	1995	"Motaba" engineered bioweapon
Pandora's Clock	1996	Doomsday Virus
Contagious	1997	Cholera
Contagion	2001	Level Four Ebola Virus
Contaminated Man	2001	"trinoxin-3" chemical toxin
Venomous	2001	engineered snakes
Killer Buzz	2001	engineered bees as ethnic weapons
Contagion	2002	engineered ebola-like virus
Global Effect	2002	Particularly virulent ebola virus
28 Days Later	2002	Rage
Day of the Dead:Contagion	2004	Military bioweapon blob
Waterborne	2005	"biological agent" terrorist attack on LA
The Hades Factor	2006	"Simitar"engineered virus in Afghanistan
The Constant Gardener	2006	dypraxa for tuberculosis
Fatal Contact: Bird Flu	2006	Bird Flu
Bacterium	2006	Unnamed bacteria sometimes called "blob"
I Am Legend	2007	genetically-engineered / measles virus
28 Weeks Later	2007	Rage
Pandemic	2007	Bird flu
Bats: A Human Harvest	2007	Bats are engineered to become weapons
Flight of the Living Dead	2007	engineered bioweapon
Quarantine	2008	rabies or rabies-like virus
Pandemic	2009	zoonotic virus
Pandemic (Japan)	2009	Blame
Carriers	2009	virus that creates a pandemic
Black Death	2010	Plague
Contagion	2011	like Nipah virus
Quarantine2	2011	rabies-like virus
Season of the Witch	2011	plague
The Gerber Syndrome	2011	The Gerber Syndrome Virus
Patient Zero	2011	H4IV2 smallpox & viremic encephalitis
Azaan	2011	Ebola variant, bioweapon
World War Z	2012	A virus

Chapter 9

The Innocent

"Tragedy is, therefore, an imitation of a noble and complete action [...] which through compassion and fear produces purification of the passions."
---Aristotle, Poetics 1451(b)

The Greek tragedy required a cathartic reaction to the fear produced by the plot, and so can be said about the horror genre. The subgenre of biohorror, too, requires that same thought of fear and an emotional reaction to it to better understand the uncertainty of life.

But there is an aspect of the Greek tragedy which the biohorror subgenre challenges --- that is the need to have a character flaw that drives the bad fortune that comes to the character.[6] This is not enough for the biohorror, biothriller subgenre. An essential if not vital element of the biohorror subgenre is the harm, death even horrifying death comes to the innocent who are struck by the randomness of disease or biologically engineered bioweapons through no fault of their own. Thus, the horror.

The "innocent" represent the tragic consequences of the biological agent to those who have neither put themselves in a position of accepting the risk, do not have character flaws driving the disaster nor seem to be rationally deserving of the infection. They are suffering at the hand of God in a seemingly senseless tragedy that must be resolved by the hero in the conflict with the villain. The dying lie in wait of a hero to miraculously get well, to have a hero find a cure, vaccine or antidote, or to wait for reanimation and live life as a zombie in the meantime. None of these are satisfying outcomes, but are troubling and horrifying. From Chapter 2 and the studies of perception of risk and how humans try to make sense of tragedies to people we know that searching for a reason gives us some sense of control over whether this can happen to us or our family. That is, he has lung cancer because he smoked, therefore I have some control over getting lung cancer and can avoid the risk. That provides some rational way of coping with the sadness and "bad luck" of the victim of lung cancer. But if they have one of those rare forms of lung cancer that occur due to genetics or occupational exposure, then we have a rationale, but not one that held a knowing choice for the victim, yet there is some rationale for the small comfort it provides.

---

[6] Aristotle. Poetics 1453(a), Aristotle in 23 Volumes, Vol. 23, translated by W.H. Fyfe. Cambridge, MA, Harvard University Press; London, William Heinemann Ltd. 1932. *The hero must not deserve his misfortune, but he must cause it by making a fatal mistake, an error of judgement, which may well involve some imperfection of character but not such as to make us regard him as "morally responsible" for the disasters although they are nevertheless the consequences of the flaw in him, and his wrong decision at a crisis is the inevitable outcome of his character.*

Just and "act of God" tends to be the scariest rationale of all, because there is no control over one's fate --- but can lead to massive religious Christian conversions.[7]

The innocent can be the tragic mass execution of the cattle in *Hud (1963).* One of the most tragic scenes in all of the biohorror movies is the scene where panicked cattle are driven into a pit and executed with a blaze of rifle fire from over head. The mistakes of Homer in bringing Mexican cattle infected with FMD into his herd caused his own economic devastation and personal tragedy, but the cattle were also set up in the scene to drive an emotional sadness for their destruction in a manner that was visibly horrifying for the herd.

The innocent in *The Satan Bug* (1965) were seen strewn across a freeway in Florida, when the thief who stole the botulinum toxin used it over a city in Florida. Innocent people were shown dying horrifying deaths.

The more recent innocent depictions in the biohorror subgenre have used the same tragic deaths of innocent people, but before we can experience very much emotional feelings about their loss, they transform into zombies and become the transformed villain perhaps worse than the biological agent or the engineer of it.

The innocent in all of the movies which feature quarantines are those who are unfairly quarantined --- *Warning Sign* (1985); *Quarantine* (1989); *La Peste* (1992); *Outbreak* (1995); *Pandora's Clock* (1996); *Contagious* (1997); *Contagion* (2001); *Contagion* (2002); *Fatal Contact: Bird Flu in America* (2006); *Pandemic* (2007); *Quarantine* (2009); *Carriers* (2009); *Quarantine2* (2011). All of these movies were made in the post-due process explosion which began in the 1960s when the judiciary increased the threshold on the government to justify deprivations of life, liberty and property as interpreted in the U.S. Constitution. Only one movie avoided the opportunity to exploit quarantine, choosing instead "social distancing" a trendy new epidemiological protocol for avoiding contact without depriving individual freedom, and that was the recent *Contagion* (2011).

The innocent in *Global Effect* (2002) are the 40 million people who are the target of the bioterrorist, Nile Spencer. The doctor, Dr. Levitt, who has the cure, is being held hostage by Nile while they watch the numbers of people pouring into Emergency Rooms on a television screen. Dr. Levitt says, "What have you done? Those are innocent people. They have done nothing to you."

In *The Constant Gardner* (2005), the innocent are the focus of the plot and drive the emotion throughout the movie. The poverty-stricken and starving population of Kenya who are already suffering from AIDS and MDR-TB are further used as human subjects in human drug trials by a United Kingdom pharmaceutical company. Through greed, the excessive number of deaths of the poor Kenyans are covered up in the work in order to get the drug to market faster.

---

[7]Rodney Stark, *The Rise of Christianity: How the Obscure, Marginal Jesus Movement Became the Dominant Religious Force in the Western World in a Few Centuries* (1997). During the late Roman period there were a number of devastating plagues: the Antonine Plague (165-180 AD), the Plague of Cyprian (251-270 AD), and the Plague of Justinian (541–542 AD). These are periods of some of the greatest increases in members of the Christian faith.

Chapter 10

Quarantine:
The Governments, Restraints on Liberty

Angela Vidal

[after witnessing Bernard being killed by a CDC Sniper when trying to escape from quarantine]

Scott... They're not gonna let us out of here alive, are they?

Scott Percival

No... I don't think so.

----Quarantine (2009)

Outbreak (1995) is the first movie to receive widespread distribution and to feature the tension of whether to use lethal force to stop an individual who breaks quarantine. The scene where the civilians are blown into a fireball by a military helicopter was a dramatic answer to that question for this plot, but for the due process sensibilities of Americans, this was a dramatic and frightening use of military lethal force.

A second quarantine question was exploited by the plot in *Outbreak* (1995) and that is whether the government can quarantine an entire city? What is not clear in the movie is that quarantine authority is with the state government unless there is an issue involving interstate issues. In this movie, because there was a national security interest, the federal government and federal quarantine authority was part of the scenario. The federal quarantine authority has no more authority to quarantine a town than does state authority. Constitutional due process is widely believed to require individual hearings for each person quarantined. However, some states have adopted statutes to allow for area quarantines such as a building or a geographic area. California was notably the state which was involved in a landmark case striking down an area quarantine around Chinatown in 1900 and the plague epidemic of San Francisco, *Jew Ho v. Williamson,*103 F. 10 (C.C.N.D. Cal. 1900). The court found the delineation of Chinatown was not based on the location of the plague, thus it was unconstitutionally violating equal protection.

Quarantine (2009) as might be expected, involves a quarantine. The quarantine of an apartment building raises the area quarantine question as well as the use of lethal force against those who would break the quarantine. When emergency personnel respond to a call to rescue an ill woman, they never come out again. The CDC has ordered a quarantine of the building. Again, this is set in California and state law would typically be the quarantine that would apply. CDC might be invited to assist California, but the agency would not be the lead on this incident. California would issue the quarantine with the advice of CDC despite its lethal and unusual nature. Since there is no indication it is a bioweapon or a national security event, jurisdiction is still with the state. However, in this movie, the Centers for Diseases Control and Prevention (CDC) which have ordered a quarantine of the building. States have the power to quarantine individuals when there is a threat to public health and safety. Those quarantine orders from the local governments or judicial branches of the state can be enforced with the state's police power. CDC is a federal agency and does not have police power in the states except for a few specifically listed diseases, and must be acting in cooperation with the State to address state public health problems. But when states need public health advice and expertise they may call upon CDC to assist them. This appears to be the reasonable explanation for CDC's involvement with a state quarantine. CDC would also be involved at the borders of states and international borders, but even then, CDC invokes the help of the local state public health departments because without them, they lack police power in the states to enforce quarantines.

The involvement of the military to enforce the quarantine could only be possible with an order from the President of the United States and only to assist local law enforcement personnel. This is one of the exceptions to the Posse Comitatus Act which allows some military involvement with civilians but not in direct law enforcement, unless the state government is unable to function requiring federal government intervention. The best example of this, is the need for the federal government to assist Louisiana in the disaster of Hurricane Katrina in 2005. However, the federalism relationship requires the states to make the first request and seek the assistance of the federal government. Due to political differences between the President and the Governor in this case, the Governor delayed the request to the federal government for three days, extending the time of the chaos.

California presumptively made a decision that this virus was highly dangerous and was a threat to public health and possibly likely to spread beyond its borders. This could result in the kind of complete quarantine of the apartment building, but it would then have to be followed with a due process hearing for those individuals inside who have been restrained and their liberty limited. This should be done in a reasonable amount of time, and in this case, it might be until it was determined that the public health threat had ended.

Then there is the matter of enforcement of the quarantine. Can you ever use deadly force to enforce a quarantine? Scenes from Outbreak and the pickup truck breaking quarantine to escape with the family was obliterated by the U.S. military charged with enforcing the quarantine . Military training to use lethal force to carry out orders, does not fit well with civilian law enforcement and for that good reason, the U.S. strictly prohibits the use of the military in civilian law enforcement, except in the event of a complete breakdown in order and a lack of an operating government. This law, *posse comitatus*, was enacted at the end of the U.S. Civil War as a response to the abuses and harsh results of the use of the military to enforce reconstruction laws in the South.

Back to our apartment quarantine in *Quarantine* (2008), the enforcement of the quarantine results in a sniper positioned on the roof of the apartment building taking aim and shooting an escaping tenant. Even in this extreme scenario, is the use of lethal force ever constitutionally permissible? The example of the kind of instructions for the use of force against civilians during a Yellow Fever outbreak in New Orleans in the early 1900s, was that public health officials should refrain from "brute force" in forcing the public health orders.[8] Even in this extremely dangerous disease, if there was any other option to stop the escaping individual from threating the public health and safety, it would be essential to use only that limit of force. Perhaps a stun gun, or a tranquilizer gun would have been a less lethal alternative. But lethal force will almost never be constitutionally acceptable in the enforcement of a quarantine.

In 2008 when this movie was made, the International Health Regulations (IHR) had been effective since 2007. These regulations bind everyone who is a member of the World Health Organization (WHO) and they require immediate reporting of a Public Health Emergency of International Concern (PHEIC). To determine whether this event in the apartment building is a PHEIC, one has to consult the regulation and follow through each of the questions to make a determination: Is it a listed disease? Is it a disease that is a threat to the International community? The *Decision Instrument for Assessment and Notification* of the IHR would lead the analysis through questions about whether the disease would have a serious public health impact, and whether it has occurred in a highly populated area. The virus appeared in an apartment building in downtown Los Angeles, in a highly populated area. Finally, the criteria that it is both "Unusual" and "unexpected" would have to be answered in the affirmative since this virus appears to behave like rabies virus and seems to have infectivity at a high level. These answers lead to the conclusion that this is a PHEIC which obligates the representative of the United States to notify the World Health Organization. Also, the virus was unexpected because it appeared in an apartment building in the middle of Los Angeles, far away from any place it might occur naturally.

This movie has a lot of value in its depiction of taking the constitutional limitation on restraint of liberty under the U.S. Constitution to its limit and certainly raised the legal question as to whether lethal force may be used against civilians to enforce a civil quarantine order. While it lacks an authentic representation of public policy and constitutional limitations, it posits the possible abuse of those laws when fear of a rabies-like infection is bearing down on the decision makers. But because the movie does not recognize and respond to the conflict, it falls short of some of the value we could take from the effect on human values and behavior.

Pandemic (2009) featured a quarantine over the entire New Mexico small town. Eventually the movie reveals that the small town is being used as an experiment for a biological weapon by the military and they have to be quarantined to avoid the virus escaping into other towns. The quarantine features military blockades, citizen confrontations and cutting off "wired and wireless communications." There were no hearings just a loudspeaker adding, "Thank you for your cooperation."

Two of the most unusual quarantines were in *Black Death* (1992) and *Global Effect* (2002). In *Black Death* (1992), Dr. Hart quarantined the entire Penn Station (the passenger

---

[8] Alfred J. Sciarrino, *The Grapes of Wrath & The Speckled Monster (Epidemics, Biological Terrorism and the Early Legal History of Two Major Defenses—Quarantine and Vaccination)*, 7 MICH. ST. UNIV. J. MED. & L. 117, 167 (2003).

train station) in New York City just because her one contact boarded a train there and was already gone. In *Global Effect* (2002), the National Security Council of the United States quarantined the borders of South Africa and all the airports, traffic was stopped. This would require the United States to ignore all national sovereignty of other nations, which this movie dramatized to a large degree, but the idea is highly unrealistic.

Hud (1963) effectively shows the consequences of a foot-and-mouth disease outbreak on a cattle ranch, and the imagery of hammering a quarantine sign to the fencepost makes the point of government ordered restraint where there is a threat to public health or safety, and ultimately can also order destruction of such property.

ANNEX 2

DECISION INSTRUMENT FOR THE ASSESSMENT AND NOTIFICATION OF EVENTS THAT MAY CONSTITUTE A PUBLIC HEALTH EMERGENCY OF INTERNATIONAL CONCERN

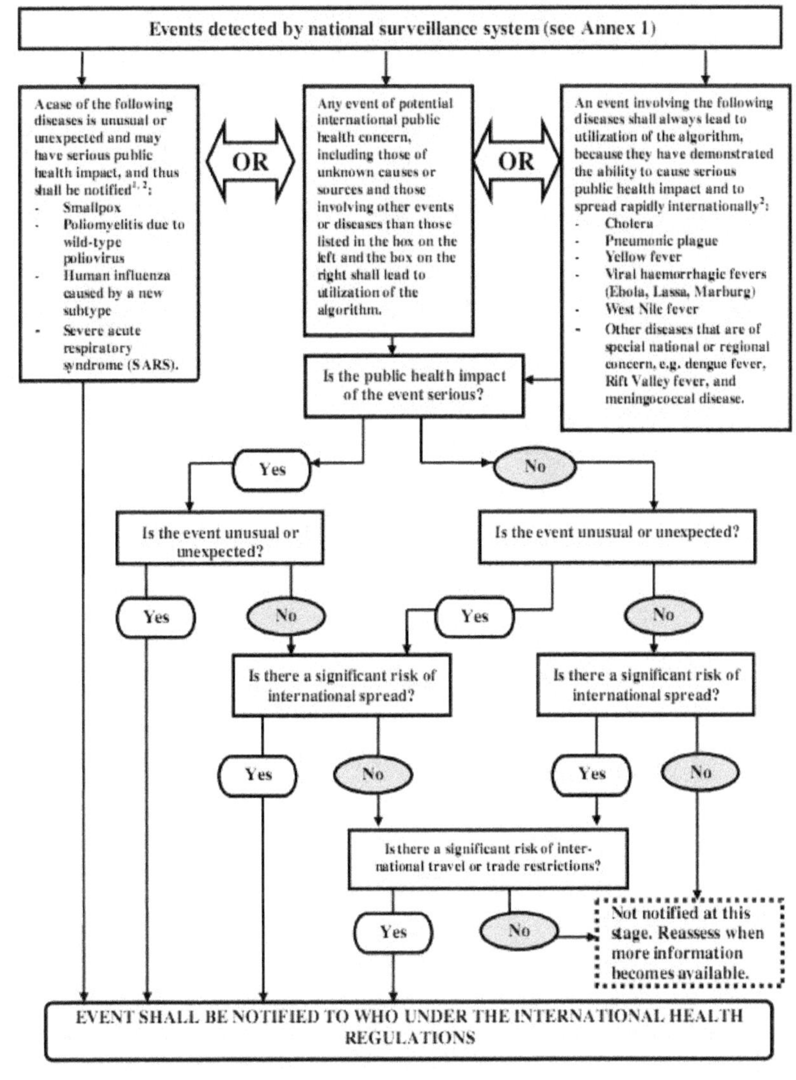

[1] As per WHO case definitions.
[2] The disease list shall be used only for the purposes of these Regulations.

Chapter 11

The Endings

The resolution of the biohorror movie requires some disposition of the biological agent or disease, either to have it die out in a pandemic cycle, find a cure or leave an unsettling apocalyptical ending. This can also indicate a sequel if the movie ends with the ominous suggestion that the disease could return. Movies in this subgenre tend to have endings that fall into one of these categories: apocalyptic ending; hopeful ending; happy ending; tragic ending and ominous prediction ending.

Epidemics and movies. The course of an epidemic runs much like the course of a movie. There is an inciting incident and then an increasing tension to a climax when the most disastrous consequences of the epidemic are felt, and then there is a slow positive relaxing that the epidemic is ending and then a resolution. The ending that is post-apocalyptic is a natural outcome of a devastating epidemic worthy of a biohorror or biothriller movie. It is also a dark ending, but typically some hope, some hero, comes through to start society anew. Movies that are based on the Black Plague of 1348 are based on the realistic post-apocalyptic world after one-third of the world's population was killed. This led to a reorganizing of society, land ownership, wages for workers who were in demand, and other shifts that would change our world forever.

Many movies of the 48 movies had a post-apocalyptic setting or ending. In *Pandora's Clock* (1996), the last line of the movie reveals that the Doomsday virus may have actually been in one of the passengers after believing all were "clean" and released from their quarantine. That suggest the worst is yet to come, leaving the viewers with an unsettling and ominous resolution. That almost 20% of all of the movies are post-apocalyptic is significant, and the reasons are worth examining.

The Post-apocalyptic plot

Movies that start from a post-apocalyptic setting where the world has already been struck by biodisaster are working to come back from the break of extinction.

The three movies that depict the post-apocalyptic world of the post-plague years in 1340s Europe search for blame and search for hope and rebuilding.

The Seventh Seal (1957), shows evil (Satan) winning over good in a dark ending. *Black Death (2010),* follows the people who are changed and become bitter and evil in times of fear of the plague and recovery. It had both a hopeful, yet tragic ending because the protagonist died a hero's death after an epic battle with Satan (I *did* regret seeing the brave knight, Sean Bean, die at the hand of Satan).

In *Season of the Witch (2011)*, the cause of the plague is determined to be Satan and his successfully banishment from the earth averted further plague deaths in an epic battle, ending the Black Death period. Perhaps not coincidentally, the Swedish and German movies portrayed a darker ending, while the United States' movie portrayed the hope of good over evil and a new day. Sweden and German actually experienced the Black Death in their own national histories which must change the perception of these events to their respective audiences.

Modern movies which begin in the post-apocalyptic period include *Carriers (2009); 28 Weeks Later (2007)* both ended not ominously but darkly and with sadness for the world and people lost, with very little hope.

The hopeful ending

The post-apocalyptic plot can also have a hopeful ending, and I would have to move Season of the Witch (2011) in the previous group into this category.

The plot begins somewhere in the post-apocalyptic period or at least a good bit of the movies flashback to the normal period but these movies based on the Richard Matheson book are all in my post-apocalyptic category with a hopeful ending and here is why. *The Last Man on Earth (1964); The Omega Man (1971)* and *I Am Legend 2007* are all based *on* Richard Matheson's novel, I Am Legend (1954), and while they end with the hero's death, the "cure" that he has been developing is used to bring relief from the disease to the world, despite his death.

These movies end on a hopeful note for the survival of humanity: *Virus (1980) (Japan)*, where a vaccine succeeded and survivors were left to repopulate the earth driven by a sense of community; *28 Days Later (2003)*, a few people survive the pandemic and believe they will repopulate. The sequel, *28 Weeks Later (2007)* is the process of repopulating Great Britain has some setbacks but ends with survivors to carry on. In *Carriers (2009)* two people survive the pandemic but they are teens but there is still some small hope as they gaze out to the ocean, where life began.

World War Z (2012) is very much influenced by Richard Matheson's novel and the three movies that preceded it, although not true to the novel. The ending is finding a cure to the worldwide zombie epidemic which gives hope to the survival of humans.

Realism Plots and their Endings

The realism plots tend to drive the horror and thriller tension from events that are based in real diseases or situations that are convincing to the audience that they could happen as soon as they walk out of the theater. These movies tend to have the happy ending or the tragic ending. The ominous ending can be present in either of these categories. Here is where these movies sort out.

The happy ending

Movies in this category are resolved with a happy ending for the protagonist. This could mean ending the disease in a normal epidemic curve where the disease has a peak, a smaller second peak and then slowly ends or finding a cure. These are typically the biothriller rather than the biohorror, but rules are meant to be broken in movies. These endings are pretty flat but give the viewer the satisfaction of a resolution with some certainty.

In Nosferatu (1922) the protagonist and his wife overcome evil, survive the plague and the negative people in their life are eliminated. In *Black Death (1992),* Dr. Hart, the epidemiologist succeeds in stopping the plague with quarantining large areas, and her niece survives. In Pandemic (2007) the city returns to normal after the epidemic.

Panic in the Street (1950) from the film noir period, is dark in that many people die and in the end the hero, a public health officer, was not able to save everyone. He returned home, however, to his 1950s wife who greeted him as if nothing had happened.

La Peste (1992) a movie made in Argentina based on the novel by Albert Camus, The Plague, changed the place of the story from Algeria to Argentina. The outbreak of plague faithfully followed a real epidemic until life returned to normal. The hero survived, but the psychological torment he felt during the plague did not leave him where it found him, yet he survived.

*Contagion (*2011) ended by explaining the basis of a zoonotic disease which evolves from a bat to a pig and jumps to a human, which is the backstory for how a real virus, Nipah, is used as a model for the Nipah-like virus that turned into the pandemic.

Pandemic (2007) the made for television movie, depicted the complete cycle of an outbreak of an unknown virus, similar to the real life plot of the SARS virus of 2003. Life went back to normal and the political conflicts were resolved for a better government. Perhaps this should be in the fairytale category.

Black Death (1992) and *Contagious* (1997) both made for television movies follow a plot where the disease runs its course and life returns to normal. *Fatal Contact: Bird Flu in America* (2006) a made for television movie depicting the bird flu during a bird flu scare, also had the disease run its course and life returned to normal. All three of them featured female heroines with a fan following from their successful television careers [Kate Jackson (Charlie's Angels) , Lindsey Wagner (Super Woman), Joley Richardson (Nip Tuck), respectively].

The tragic ending

The realism category also had its movies that end in tragedy. Tragedy meaning that the protagonist meets a tragic end. These movies were driving by realism but it was the realism that made them all the darker when they ended in tragedy. They could leave an audience feeling that this could happen.

Hud (1963) was the story of an outbreak of foot-and-mouth disease brought in with an illegal purchase of cattle from Mexico. The response requires killing the herd ending the epidemic. However the ending is tragic when the distraught patriarch dies in an accident.

Andromeda Strain (1971) could fall into this category, because with the release of the organism from space into the laboratory, scientists were infected and died, leading to the ultimate destruction of the laboratory and the scientists.

Azaan (2011) protagonist is shot to death in the end after making valiant attempts to overcome the evil forces that stole the bioweapon.

In *Waterborne (2005),* most of the conflicts were left unresolved and relationships were destroyed in the course of this movie. The hero returns home without his friend who has died in the process of struggling to find water to survive.

Pandemic (2007), the Japanese movie, also had a pandemic run its course and everyone returned to normal, but the hero's love interest is killed by the pandemic disease. So many tragic relationships in this movie it almost overshadowed the tragedy of the lead characters.

Quarantine (2008). The presence of infected rats in the apartment left little doubt the rabies-like disease would spread beyond the building, although the ending was tragic with the entire lead cast, dead.

Tragic Endings in Pseudo-Realism

Epidemic (1987) an arty, Danish film, was tragic to the core, with a plot driving by a fictional epidemic that becomes real and the entire cast dies tragically with primeval screams in the end. *The Gerber Syndrome* (2011) an arty, Italian film, convincingly portrays a quiet pandemic that eventually kills characters that are the focus of the plot and in an interesting ending, leave us knowing that the protagonist, the physician who has bravely treated the ill, will die, discovering he has symptoms in the last screen.

These diseases are categorized here as "pseudo-realism" because they are convincingly portrayed without magic or fantasy.

Zombie Diseases

An entire category of zombie diseases have evolved with the biohorror and biothriller subgenre, although not all zombie films are biohorror films. However, the evolution of the zombie in film can be seen from *The Last Man on Earth* (1964) where the zombies speak and recognize their old friends and just want them to join them in their misery, to the zombies of lightening speed and strength in *World War Z* (2013).

The ominous prediction ending

An ending that can be in combination of any of the preceding endings is the ominous prediction that this movie story will continue or repeat itself, maybe with even a worse outcome.

A good example of the ominous ending is *Formula for Death* (1995) which ended with this legend on several screens with ominous music for dramatic effect:

> Ebola is a real virus.
> No one knows when it will reappear . . . as it did in Zaire.
> Scientist think thousands of these viruses wait, hidden in the deep forests throughout the world.
> They are simply the earth's defense systems against the most dangerous of invaders . . .
> Man.

A screaming monkey punctuates the last sentence.

The Satan Bug (1965) is the story of the release of a biological agent that is designed to destroy all life. It is stolen and dropped on the population and in the end there is no guarantee that there will not be more outbreaks of it.

Pandemic (2009) the movie with the veterinarian heroine who uncovers the military plot to use their community as an experiment for a biological weapon, presents an ominous ending when the quarantined town is expected to die out with the test. But a lone dog has wondered out to the road with the infection and is picked up by a boy and his father on their way back home to Los Angeles.

Venomous (2001) ends on a happy resolution with the protagonist developing a vaccine and the Department of Defense announcing they have eradicated all of the snakes. The last frames go deep into their den and the viewers see the snakes are still there.

Pandora's Clock (1996). A passenger goes back to society who may be infected, although they think no one is infected.

Flight of the Living Dead (2007) shows uninfected survivors of the flight after the crash, in a plane filled with infected zombie-passengers. The ending is hopeful until the last frames when you see the zombies re-animate.

The Gerber Syndrome (2011) fell into the ominous prediction category where then last question in dialogue was, "what is wrong with your hand?" which indicates the hero, the doctor, has gotten Gerber Syndrome for which there is no positive outcome.

Quarantine 2: Terminal (2011) The hero is killed in the last few minutes of the movie along with the entire cast except for one child who escapes. An infected cat in the last frame ensures any relief is short lived.

Warning Sign (1985), Patient Zero (2012), Andromeda Strain (1971), Day of the Dead: Contagium (2004), World War Z (2013) are all ended in laboratories where things have gone horribly wrong and the heroes and often the entire cast is killed.

The Laboratory Plots and their Endings

The large number of movies in a laboratory driven plot requires a closer examination of their features. Are they all tragic endings or do any of them end with a hopeful or happy ending?

There are 18 laboratory movies and of those 8 are government laboratories, 6 are rogue laboratories, 3 are private laboratories and one is a World Health Organization laboratory. Without keeping you in suspense, here's the list:

The Last Man on Earth (1964)
The Satan Bug (1965)
Andromeda Strain (1971)
The Omega Man (1971)
Warning Sign (1985)
Formula for Death (1994)
Outbreak (1995)
Contaminated Man (2000)
Global Effect (2002)
28 Days Later (2002)
Day of the Dead: Contagium (2005)
Bacterium (2006)
Flight of the Living Dead (2007)
Bats: A Human Harvest (2007)
I Am Legend (2007)
Quarantine (2008)
Patient Zero (2012)
World War Z (2013)

Laboratory Biosafety and Biosecurity

These movies also show an evolution of biosafety and biosecurity in laboratories from the early government bioweapons laboratory portrayed in The Satan Bug (1965) to the biological safety level 4 (BSL-4) laboratory of Outbreak (1995) a continuum of practices that would be shocking to today's biosafety officer reflect society's understanding of the risks at that time. In fact, some of the plots are driven by laboratory biosafety accidents, some modeled after real laboratory accidents.

Conclusion

The endings of biohorror and biothriller movies are the payback for the tension and fear that we have lived through in the 70 minute to 3-hour movie. It may very well be the endings that are the things that keep us up at night.

Chapter 12

The Movies

The 48 movies which have been analyzed in the preceding chapters are set forth here as individual studies in law and science. Each movie features the poster as part of the cultural and analytical look at its presentation to the public. A ratings system is used to evaluate the public health value and the legal value. The rating appears just below the movie poster for each of the movies.

These movies were selected for the biohorror and biothriller subgenre because they met the criteria: they have a central plot around a biological agent; the resolution of the biological disaster or epidemic is central to the plot to be resolved; and they present interesting public health and legal issues, whether or not these were actually depicted on the screen. The rating system uses each of those two categories: public health and law. Biohazard symbols, 1 to 5, identify how well the movie depicted the biological or public health issues. The scales-of-justice symbols, 1 to 5, rate how accurately and true to reality the movie described the legal issues and made them part of the plot. As you peruse each of the movies, you are welcome to post your comments on the Facebook book page, Reel Biohorror.

Five symbols indicate that the movie was highly accurate, believe and horrifying as a result of its depiction of the possible. Scientifically accurate and medically plausible.

Four symbols indicate that the movie was very accurate but contained some mistakes in the accuracy of infectious disease or science.

Three symbols indicate that the movie was somewhat accurate but contained mistakes that were critical to the plot in the depiction of infectious diseases or science.

Two symbols indicate that the movie had serious flaws in the depiction of science or infectious diseases that detracted from its value.

One symbol indicates that the movie had such serious flaws that it had little value in its depiction of science or public health.

Five legal symbols indicate that the movie probably used a legal consultant and did an almost flawless job of depicting realistic legal scenarios and applied existing laws and regulations to the story.

⚖⚖⚖⚖⚖

Four legal symbols indicate that the movie lacked some component of accuracy in its legal depictions of government action or existing statutes and regulations applied to the story.

⚖⚖⚖⚖

Three legal symbols indicate that the movie had few legal issues and the ones that were presented were not accurate.

⚖⚖⚖

Two legal symbols indicate that either the movie had very few references to obvious legal issues, or they were inaccurately depicted.

⚖⚖

One legal symbol indicates that the movie omitted obvious legal issues and/or inaccurately depicted them.

Nosferatu (1922)

RATING

From the diary of Joham Cavallius able historian of his native city of Bremen:

Nosferatu! That name alone can chill the blood!

Nosferatu! Was it he who brought the plague to Bremen in 1838?

I have long sought the causes of that terrible epidemic . . .

---*Nosferatu* (1922)

Nosferatu (1922) is a silent movie that is a classic in the horror genre, and is now added to the classics in biohorror. It is the first in the line of the biohorror subgenre ---Not because it is a vampire movie, but because it is a plague movie.

The story is based on *Dracula,* but because the producers were unable to obtain the rights to Bram Stoker's *Dracula,* it became *Nosferatu* with character names, Count Orlok and sometimes Count Dracula. The encounter with Count Orlok is triggered by an advertisement in a newspaper in Bremen, Germany from Count Orlok stating that he is looking to buy a house in that city. An opportunistic real estate agent, Reinfeld, sends the young Harkin off to Transylvania to visit Count Orlok to offer him a house that is facing Harkin's own house. Reinfeld's words to encourage Harkin to take the trip reflect the lack of worker's compensation and liability cautions in sending employees to do work which may be harmful. This movie was made in the context of a labor movement in the United States where the U.S. Supreme Court began imposing federal labor laws in place of state law to eliminate employee labor abuses. Reinfeld indicates that the job is likely to cause him harm when he says, "You will have a marvelous journey. And, young as you are, what matter if it costs you some pain --- or even a little blood?"

Near the end of the first act of the movie, a professor is demonstrating new science to the students. First, he shows them a "carnivorous plant" and a video of a Venus Fly-Trap is shown devouring a fly. This, the professor concludes is a vampire of the plant world. Next, he shows what he refers to as a "Polyp" the name for the characteristic of the hydra, microscopic aquatic animals that catch prey in their tendrils and consume them. But the hydra also has a kind of immortality, regenerating tendrils that are lost which may also allude to the immortality of the vampire. Here, the professor shows a video of a microscopic view of a hydra, a polyp, capturing prey and eating it. This, he declares is another type of vampire.

The demonstration of the science of the day, 1922, and the students' impressed reactions to it seem somewhat out of place. But this cutting-edge science demonstration of its day, is cleverly used to convince the viewer that vampires of the human variety may have real scientific plausibility.

There was no science on curing the plague, however. Plague was still an incurable disease and the Black Death still carried a sense of dread centuries after its devastation of Europe. We learned much later in the 21st century that penicillin was effective against plague bacteria, but penicillin itself was not discovered until 1928 by Fleming, a Scottish researcher – six years after the release of *Nosferatu.* Finding a cure for infectious diseases made us feel like conquerors of death, and indeed penicillin was a true miracle drug which would change the percentage of deaths due to infection in the next World War. But even more so, it led many in the medical field to declare the end of the threat of infectious diseases because we had penicillin. Now, decades later, we are faced with having created penicillin-resistant bacteria which shattered our simplistic temporal euphoria that we had conquered infectious diseases forever. *Nosferatu* still provides us with a sense of fear and dread of the most dangerous potential bioweapons --- which still includes plague in its pneumonic form --- among them.

Harkin leaves a distraught wife, Nina, as he travels to Transylvania and says he will be away for possibly several months. On his journey he reads about Count Orlok and vampires but disregards this as not true. However, when his driver refuses to continue his journey to Count Orlok's castle because it is in the land of the phantoms, he has to cross the bridge and pick a ride with a phantom who takes him to Count Orlok's castle.

Here, Harkin has a creepy first encounter with Count Orlok as the castle door mysteriously opens when he approaches the caste. He is met by Count Orlok whose first words are "you are late." Harkin learns very quickly that Count Orlok is after blood. At dinner, Harkin accidentally cuts his finger with a dinner knife, throwing Count Orlok into an uncontrollable attraction and he appears to lick it from Harkin's finger, which causes Harkin to recoil in horror. Nonetheless, Harkin is determined to close the sale, which he does and Count Orlok packs his coffins to go to Bemen, to Harkin's regret. In the meantime, Harkin awakens with two bite marks and starts to feel ill so he uses some sheets to escape out the window of the castle and eventually ends up on a villagers home to recuperate.

Meanwhile, Count Orlok loads himself in a coffin and then has the coffins ferried down the river to a ship which embarks to the Baltic Ocean. The coffins are loaded onto the ship and it embarks with its ill-fated crew.

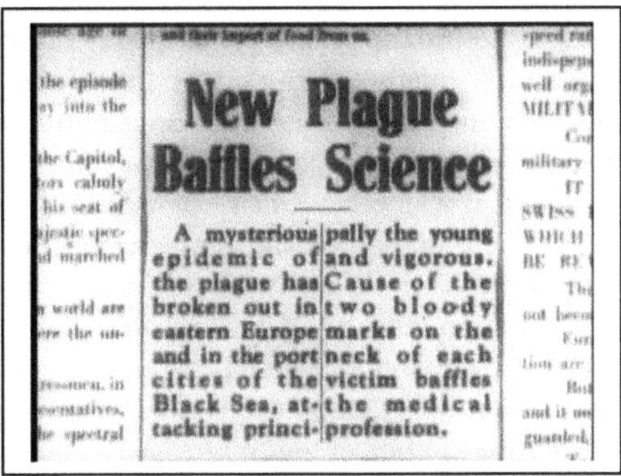

New Plague Baffles Science

A mysterious epidemic of the plague has broken out in eastern Europe and in the port cities of the Black Sea, attacking principally the young and vigorous. Cause of the two bloody marks on the neck of each victim baffles the medical profession.

It is in the last act of the movie that the plague is associated with Count Orlok. A newspaper article documents the strange association with bite marks and the plague, suggesting that plague is caused by the bite of vampires, and the use of rats in the imagery which come from the coffins further associates plague with vampires.

In the course of the ship's journey, a plague ravages the ship and every person on board succumbs to the plague except of course, Count Orlok. "Aboard the *Demeter* first one man was stricken than all," the narration shows us. The narration shows us pages from the Captain's journal and he identifies the plague as the problem killing the crew. It reads, "18 May 1838, Passed Gibraltar – Panic on board – Three men dead already – Mate out of his mind – Rats in the hold – I fear the plague.. . . .. "

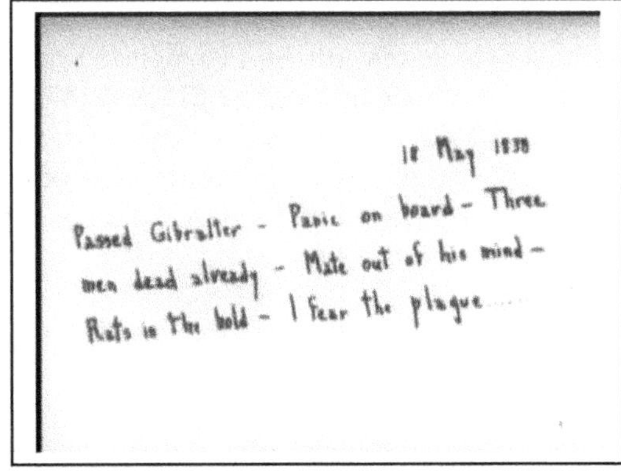

18 May 1838

Passed Gibraltar - Panic on board - Three men dead already - Mate out of his mind - Rats in the hold - I fear the plague....

Before the final moment of death, the First Mate goes below deck and discovers not only rats running from inside the coffins but sees Count Orlok break out of his coffin and stand upright from the box. This is the final straw for the First Mate who panics and runs back to the top deck, falling over the railing. The Ship's Captain seeing this, valiantly ties himself with rope to the Ship's wheel, only to be attacked by Count Orlok, finishing off the crew. Count Orlok continues to navigate the ship to dock in Bremen. Once docked, he disembarks carrying his coffin under his arm to his newly purchased home.

As the ship is approaching Bremen, the real estate agent in Bremen, Reinfeld, appears to be under the influence of Count Orlok. He has gone mad and is confined in an institutional cell and is observed to be capturing flying insects with his hands and popping them into his mouth, suggestive of the demonstration of the Venus Fly-Trap, the "vampire of the vegetable world."

Although the movie is a silent one, the use of language creates a sense of horror: Nosferatu, is a greek word meaning "plague carrier". The use of imagery of rats and the term "Black Death" recall the deaths of one-third of the European population. Max Schrek, who plays Count Orlok, has a surname which translated from German, means "terror."

This is a German film, but it was released in English, and it became a universal classic. It was produced for the silent screen by Henrik Galeen, known for the horror genre in his collaboration as a writer with Wegener on *Golem*, an early classic horror movie. Pre-World War II Germany was the audience for the film, and we can expect that it captured some of the social fears including the plague induced by the evil compulsion of Count Orlok, as well as finding a scapegoat in Count Orlok as the cause of social ills. Who can say what influence this powerful silent movie may have had on its 1922 German audience?

Bremen did have a history of plague outbreaks along with the rest of Europe during the 14th century. However, in 1920-21 a major plague epidemic emerged in Manchuria, China killing 8500 people.[9] Nosferatu as made in Germany in 1922, and this plague epidemic may have brought it to the attention of the producer, Galeen. The previous epidemic in Manchuria of 1910-11 cost 60,000 lives, and was still very much in recent memory when the 1920-21 epidemic occurred.[10]

The use of scapegoats for diseases is a phenomena that has historical roots back to written history. If we knew unwritten history we would likely see shunning behaviors to groups that were ill or who were generally disliked. The "Black Death" plague pandemic in 1341 Europe was attributed to disbelievers, necromancers and witches. The British movie *Black Death* (2010) uses witchcraft as a central plot feature to show the consequences of the scapegoat belief. In 1901 San Francisco, the plague broke out in Chinatown, leading to an illegal quarantine of Chinatown, identifying the Chinese as the cause of the epidemic. This led to the equal protection challenge against the San Francisco Board of Health. The court found that there was no scientific evidence linking the Chinese to the cause of plague and the quarantine was therefore decided based on race, not public health.[11] This, the equal protection of the 14th Amendment of the U.S. Constitution will not tolerate. Citing a case which also found selective enforcement based on race the court said the government cannot

---

[9] Wu Lien Teh, Chun Wing Han, and Robert Pollitzer, *Plague in Mancheria*, J Hyg (Lond). 1923 May; 21(3): 307–358 at http://www.ncbi.nlm.nih.gov/pmc/articles/PMC2167332/ .

[10] Teh, Han and Pollitzer.

[11] *Jew Ho v. Williamson*, 103 F. 10 (1900).

govern based on "an evil eye and an unequal hand." More recently, in 1993, an outbreak of hanta virus in the Navajo Nation and Four Corners area of the southwestern U.S. led news media to report this was a "Navajo disease"[12] which fed into that tendency to find a scapegoat or to blame a group based on race or ethnicity for the social fear. This will probably not be the last example.

A word must be said about the fear that is created about the plague in the silence. Roger Ebert in his review of this movie, found the silence to be the source of its horror, writing:

". . . Nosferatu is more effective for being silent. It is commonplace to say that silent films are more "dreamlike," but what does that mean? In "Nosferatu," it means that the characters are confronted with alarming images and denied the freedom to talk them away. . . . Human speech dissipates the shadows and makes a room seem normal." [13]

In his summary, Rogert Ebert writes, "In a sense, Murnau's film is about all of the things we worry about at 3 in the morning--cancer, war, disease, madness."[14] Yes, the things that keep us up at night.

---

[12] "Death at the Corners," *Discovery* magazine (Dec. 1, 1993) at http://discovermagazine.com/1993/dec/deathatthecorner320 .

[13] Roger Ebert, Great Movie Reviews, *Nosferatu* (1922), Sept. 28, 1997 at http://www.rogerebert.com/reviews/great-movie-nosferatu-1922 .

[14] Ebert (1997)

Panic in the Streets (1950)

RATING

Dr. Reed

And have everyone who had contact with the man leave town? You can't give it to the press. I may be an alarmist and I may be wrong about the entire matter but I have seen this disease work and it if ever gets loose it will spread over the entire country. . .and the result will be more horrible than any of you can imagine, and the key to it lies here within the next 48 hours!

Panic in the Streets (1950) is one of the film noir classics which mark the beginning of this film period. What better subject for film noir than a biohorror? It is the first movie to use a modern-day "plague" as the plot, creating tension between the government and its citizens.

The film opens with a sick man staggering into the room of a poker game with dark lighting and a lighbulb hanging from the ceiling. He wants to leave the poker game, but his poker buddies are not happy that he is leaving while he still has a roll of cash in his pocket. "Got a headache – bad!" the man utters as he leaves the game. He staggers toward his destination, barely missing being hit by a train as he crosses the tracks only to be ambushed by his poker partners led by "Blackie" , played by Jack Palance, whose gang shoots him and takes his roll of cash.

The body of the sick man triggers the public health service to diagnosis his illness, and Dr. Clinton Reed, played by Richard Widmark, is called in to do the job. Dr. Reed leaves his somewhat idyllic home life with his wife and only son for this urgent call to come to the autopsy to make a diagnosis.

In this screenshot, Dr. Clinton Reed, Richard Widmark, is viewing the sputum under a microsope to make the diagnosis of the corpse of the man found shot in the street.

He has not yet made a diagnosis but he starts barking orders to throw the press out of the room. A cadre of photographers who have been flashing photos of the corpse are ordered away from the body and Dr. Reed asks to close the curtains:

Dr. Reed
Can we get this man cremated?

Ben
Well, I suppose. . . .

Dr. Reed
I don't want any "supposing", Ben, I want him cremated right now. Set it up will you?

Ben
Sure.

Dr. Reed
Oh, Cleburn, I want everything that touched him burned or sterilized, do you understand that?

Cleburn
Sure, doc.

Dr. Reed
Paul, get those slides into a sterilizer right away, will you?

Paul
Sure. [pause]
Oh say, they sent over the serum and streptomycin.

Streptomycin had been invented and patented only two years, when this movie was released.[15] World War II was the point where the lack of the ability to control infections was most acute, and while existing sulfa drugs and topical antibiotics tyrothricin, gramicidin and tyrocidin were useful against gram positive infections, there was no drug that could be used for gram negative bacteria, like tuberculosis.

The news of the discovery of streptomycin was before the public because the two inventors were involved in litigation. Albert Shatz, the graduate student working on the invention of streptomycin, and co-inventor on the patent, was asked by Dr. Waksman to sign a patent assignment on May 3, 1946, which he did. The agreement stated that both would receive $1.00 but Waksman did not disclose to his graduate student, Shatz, that he had an agreement with Rutgers Research and Endowment Foundation that would give him 20% of the royalties from Streptomycin if he could get Shatz to sign the assignment. When Shatz learned of this in 1949, he commenced litigation to recover royalties he believed were due to him. The lawsuit was started the year this movie was released, 1950, and settled December 29, 1950 when Shatz was awarded an undisclosed percentage of the $350,000 in royalties already received by Waksman, as well as an acknowledgement that Shatz was entitled to the royalties as a co-inventor. The Rutgers Research and Endowment Foundation had received $2,600,000 in royalties by that time. Dr. Waksman received the Nobel Prize for the invention.[16]

The diagnosis is finally revealed in a meeting with Mayor Murray and the Police Captain Tom Warren, played by Douglas. The diagnosis puts pressue on the detectives to find the murderer within 48 hours. Here is the dialogue that sets up the tension to solve the crime and to find the potential carrier of the disease:

---

[15] Streptomycin was patented by Selman Waksman and Albert Shatz, patent No. 2,443,485, June 15, 1948; and Improvement in Streptomycin and Processes of Preparation. No. 2,449,866 issued Sept. 21, 1948, to S.A. Waksman and A.Schatz.

[16] Albert Shatz, "The True Discovery of Streptomycin," *Actinomycetes*: Vol. IV, Part 2: 27-39: August, 1993 available at http://www.albertschatzphd.com/?cat=articles&subcat=streptomycin&itemnum=001 .

Mayor Murray

No. We've got to work on the supposition that the doc's right. . .

Dr. Reed

If the killer is incubating pneumonic plague you can start spreading it within 48 hours.

Police Captain Warren

48 hours?

Dr. Reed

Yes, we have 48 hours.
Shortly after that, you'll have the makings of an epidemic.

Police Commissioner

If you want to believe the doctor - I am sorry sir, but frankly I honestly don't believe him. . . the only way to handle this is to release it to the press. Get on the radio . . .

Dr. Reed

And have everyone who had contact with the man leave town? You can't give it to the press. I may be an alarmist and I may be wrong about the entire matter but I have seen this disease work and it if ever gets loose it will spread over the entire country. . .and the result will be more horrible than any of you cn imagine, and the key to it lies here within the next 48 hours!

The police are assigned the job of finding the murderer in the next 48 hours. The next time we see the police officers there is a crowd of suspects being questioned at desks scattered throughout an interrogation room. Some of the dialogue would raise the hair on the back of your neck:

Arrestee with crutches

You can't hold me without a lawyer!

Police officer

Why don't you just shut up.

Well, it was pre-Miranda rights in 1950, so this was probably not an unusual response.

Meanwhile, the police officers are being inoculated with streptomycin and Police Captain Warren, is forced to be innoculated on order of the Commission, too. In this screenshot, Dr. Reed has ordered him to roll up his sleeve for the inoculation.

In the meantime, Blackie is trying to figure out why the police are picking up everyone, and he concludes that the man they shot must have brought something into the country. He then extends to the dead man's cousin and says he suspected him all along. They are off on the wrong track creating another subplot of conflict in the criminal underworld.

Dr. Reed has become frustrated with the lack of success of the police investigation and cynicism about the likelihood of finding the murderer. Dr. Reed goes to a dock and offers a $50 reward to the dock workers for anyone who might know the murdered man, and he passes a photo around. He is approached by Barbara Bel Geddes, at his appointed place at Frankie's.

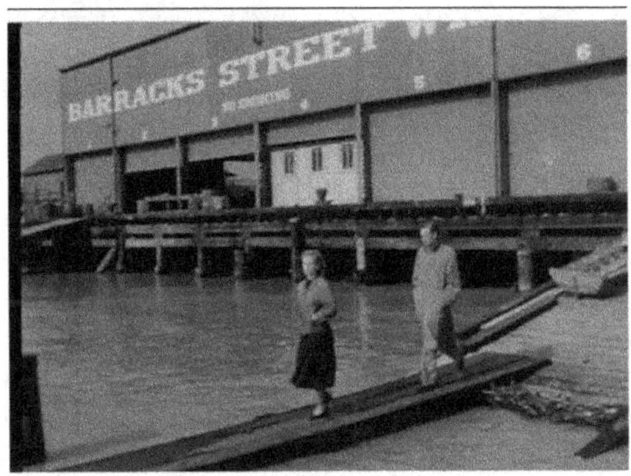

This screenshot is where he is led by her to the informant, with a sea shanty playing in the background. The woman brings Dr. Reed to her alcoholic husband who admits that he picked up the illegal immigrant in the photo from a ship named "Nile Queen."

From there, the investigation picks up Police Captain Warren who accompanies Dr. Reed on a flight to the "Nile Queen" in international waters. When the captain of the ship is confronted about picking up the illegal immigrant he denies it and resists their inquiries, only to suffer the backlash of his crew, now concerned that they may be infected with the plague. The public health officer with Dr. Reed points out to him, "We're in international waters – we have no authority here!" The captain does have authority over his ship in international waters. Despite this warning, Dr. Reed continues to question the crew and the captain warns him, "You are inciting my men to mutiny!" When one of the men comes up from the galley to report one of the cook's men is sick with a fever, the captain relents, and says, "What do you want me to do?" to which Dr. Reed tells him he wants to quarantine his ship.

Dr. Reed also speaks Chinese and handily determines that the illegal immigrant wanted shishkabob, which indicated to the Police Captain that he must like Greek food and so they went ashore to investigate Greek restaurants.

At this point we learn that the Public Health Service doctor, Dr. Reed, smokes cigarettes. Probably works well for the theatrical effect, but it would be abhorrent to see a Public Health Officer smoking today.

Blackie shows up at the Greek restaurant after Dr. Reed and Captain Warren have left, empty handed. In the next screenshot, Blackie asks the little person selling newspapers outside the restaurant who came and went from the house and pays him off as his informant.

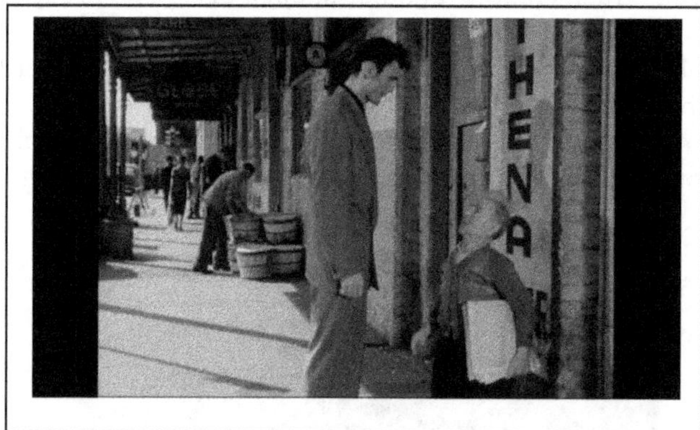

The restaurant owner who lied to the investigators ends up with his wife dead, and Dr. Reed shows up to make the diagnosis and quarantines the entire apartment building. He orders the bedding burned and lies on the death certificate as to the cause of death – pneumonia.

The news reporter finally shows up and demands to know what is going on – first there is the death and city wide sweep of suspects, then the quarantine of an apartment building. The news reporter says to Captain Warren and Dr. Reed, "An idiot could figure it out." Captain Warren quips that this makes him qualified so what does he think? The answer is surprising to a current day audience but in 1950, it was not so absurd. The report replies that he thinks it must be "cholera or smallpox."

The last case of smallpox in the United States was in 1947 in New York, when a businessman from Mexico was visiting New York, was hospitalized and was not diagnosed until two other people in the hospital had contracted the highly contagious disease.[17] It would not have been unusual then, for the report to suspect a case of smallpox.

---

[17] Garrick Utley and Sanjay Gupta, "NY faced last smallpox case," CNN.com/Health online edition, Saturday, December 14, 2002 at http://archives.cnn.com/2002/HEALTH/12/13/smallpox.ny/ .

Incredulously, the Captain have the reporters arrested to keep the news away from the public! Obviously, this is a violation of the First Amendment protection of free speech, and high value speech such as the news about the government's handling of a plague outbreak and coverup is of the highest political value requiring the highest protection. The freedom of the press, another First Amendment protection which prohibits the censorship of publication except for threats to national security and other very specific criminal information is another right that is clearly infringed by arresting the news reporters.

Finally, with only 19 minutes left, Dr. Reed announces that it is time that he notifies Washington!

In the next screenshot, Blackie is still determined to get whatever he thinks the police are after out of the deceased man's cousin, who himself is dying of plague. Blackie is clearly being exposed to pneumonic plague as he threatens the man on his deathbed.

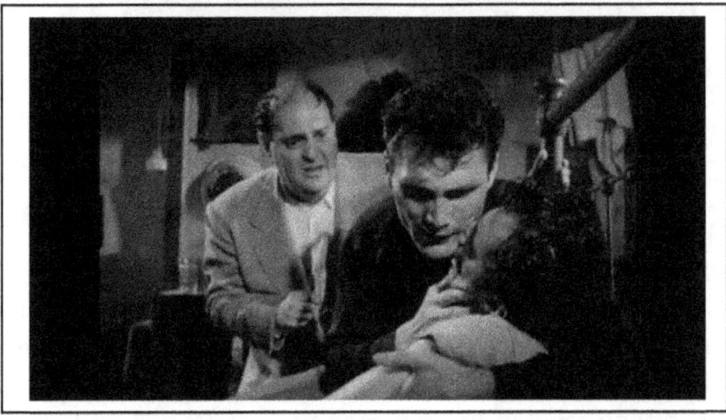

Blackie manages to get a doctor to come see Polti, the dying cousin of the deceased man. The female nurse who comes with him is not as easily bought off as the male physician, and alerts public health authorities as to the man's condition. As Dr. Reed closes in on Blackie, they dump Polti down the steps to kill him so he does not confess to the police.

The chase scene through the New Orleans dock district is fascinating with the 1950s Ford police cars and the pursuit through a coffee warehouse. This screenshot from that scene appears on posters used to promote the movie.

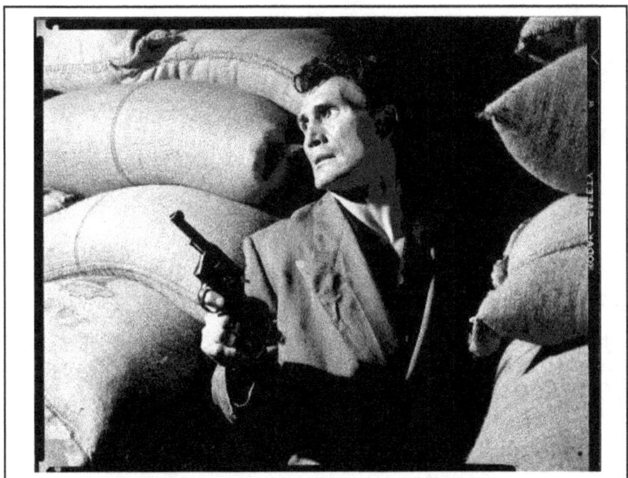

The next screenshot is the final struggle of the now plague infected Blackie as he descends a rope metaphorically and realistically designed with a big disk to stop rats from running aboard the ship. Captain Warren just waits for Blackie to fall into the water and then the "fish him out."

As Dr. Reed returns to his idyllic home after saving the city of New Orleans, his neighbor tells him he should spent more time with his son. A radio broadcast is heard with the public health director announcing that all contacts have been located and there is no need for panic. Then the movie ends as he meets his 1950s wife on the front walkway of their picturesque home as they revel in her pregnancy.

Ah, the idyllic 1950s.

But the truly dark side of this film noir has to be the censorship of the press, the refusal to provide lawyers for arrestees, the false arrest of newspaper reporters for the purpose of censoring their freedom of speech, and it would be hard to miss the fact that not a single black actor appeared in a movie set in New Orleans where the African-American population in 1950 was 30.9%.[18] The suppression of the press and the failure to make public the potential for coming into contact with pneumonic plague may have prevented *Panic in the Streets*, but at what cost?

---

[18] Campbell Gibson and Kay Jung, "Historical Census Statistics On Population Totals By Race, 1790 to 1990, and By Hispanic Origin, 1970 to 1990, For Large Cities And Other Urban Places In The United States," Population Division, Working Paper No. 76, U.S. Census Bureau, Washington, D.C. 20233 (February 2005) available at http://www.census.gov/population/www/documentation/twps0076/twps0076.html .

The Seventh Seal (1957)

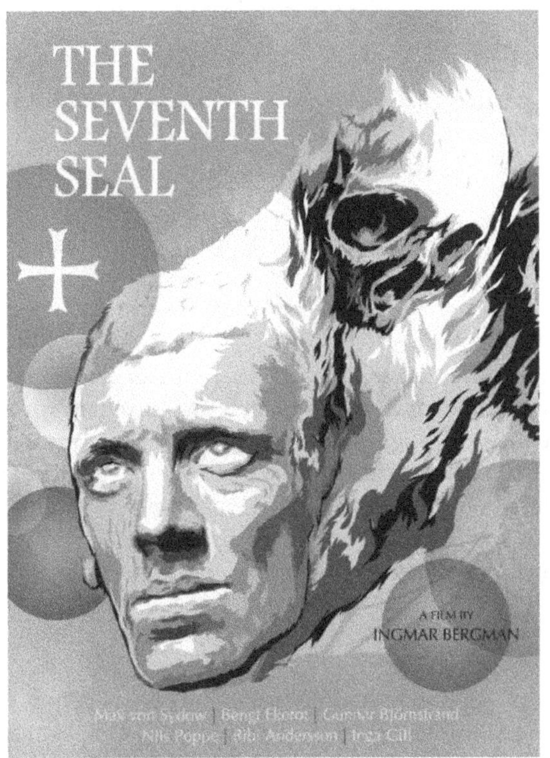

RATING

[the church painter explains why he is painting a mural about death]

Church Painter
Why should one always make people happy? It might be a good idea to scare them once in a while.

Jöns
Then they'll close their eyes and refuse to look.

Church Painter
They'll look. A skull is more interesting than a naked woman.

Jöns
If you do scare them...

Church Painter
Then they think.

Jons
And then?

Church Painter
They'll become more scared. . . .
The Strange thing is that people see the plague as a punishment from God. Supplicants trail through the land and whip themselves into God's favor.

Jons
They beat themselves?

Church Painter
Yes it's an awful sight.

---*The Seventh Seal* (1957)

The Seventh Seal (1957), a Swedish movie, captures the elements of the biohorror subgenre with its connection of death to the plague that ravaged Europe in 1341 and those who saw its effects and survived. Life would never be the same in this true-life post-apocalyptic story told to a mid-1950s audience. And this movie questions belief in God, religion and the meaning of life, brought to its full metaphor in the opening scene when the knight returning from the Crusades is confronted by Death.

The opening legend reads over the sounds and scenes of the ocean washing the rocky shore:

It is the middle of the 14th century,
Antonius block and his squire after long years as crusaders in the holy land have at last returned to their native Sweden a land ravaged by the Black Plague.
[pause]
And when the lamb opened the senventh seal, there was silence in heaven, which lasted about the space of half an hour,
And the seven angels who had the seven trumpets,
Prepared themselves to sound.

The opening legend quotes from the Bible, Revelations 8:1, about the opening of the seventh seal. The four horses of the apocalypse are the first four seals, and then there are two more that are described in Revelations, but it is the seventh that director and writer, Ingmar Bergman leads us to believe we are about to witness.

The knight returning from the Crusades to Sweden is confronted on the beach by Death depicted by a shrouded and hooded white-faced, Bengt Ekerot. He eludes Death for awhile by challenging him to a game of Chess which has been depicted in stories and art about the Devil, to which Death succumbs to the flattery as might be expected by saying, "Why yes, I am a very good chess player." The knight continues to win throughout acts one and two of the movie as Death follows him.

The behaviors that occurred during the Black Death are portrayed in the movie – stealing jewelry from the corpses, drinking excessively in the taverns with no regard for the future, and engaging in talk about the end of the world. One tavern patron said, "This is the end, that's what it is. We all know it, but no one dares to say it."

In real post-plague Europe, not only did the survivors steal jewelry from the corpses but they took their land, their manors, their crops, their houses and their wealth. With no heirs to take these things, why not? This was the real impetus which ended the form of land tenure holdings, and broke up the large fiefdoms that had come to completely block the free transfer of lands and the inability of people to break out of their lower levels of poverty no matter how hard they worked. In a perverse way, the Black Plague opened up a new freedom for pursuing happiness for the majority of people in Europe that had no hope of existing before the Black Death.

The flagellates portended in the scene in the church with the painter and Jon, appear during one of the performances of the traveling entertainers,

The metaphor of the plague as love is a theme throughout. Jons gives advice in the tavern to the sulking husband whose wife had left him for one of the actors, "Love is the blackest of plagues. If you died from it there'd be some joy. But it almost always passes."

At one point, the traveling band of entertainers now accompanied by Jon and Antonius Block meet a traveling band of men who are carrying a witch in a wooden cage to be burned because she brought about the curse of the plague. Antonius Block seeks her insight into Satan. She has been convinced by her accusers that she is at one with the devil and shares that with a disbelieving Antonius who finds himself no closer to his questions about death and Satan. They try to prevent her death from their plans to burn her, but he finds that it is Death himself in charge of the entourage. To ease her pain, Antonius Block gives her something that he says will "ease her pain," a show of compassion but also of exerting some control in an uncontrollable and hopeless context. He may have given her an herb like yarrow. Knights were known to carry dried yarrow (*Achillea millefolium),* an herb that was known to kill pain from wounds on the battlefield.

Further on their journey through the forest, they are confronted by one of their actors who had run away, returning with the plague. He is warned to stay away from them, but begs for water. Jon cautions Jof's wife that it is useless to try to give him water. The actor dies a dramatic death in front of them, staggering, crying for water, falling, getting up again and finally crashing to the ground in his final moment. The agony of a death from plague creates fear and tension that is increasingly growing as the group senses a dreadful future as they continue on their journey.

Death from pneumonic plague was usually swift and judging from the short time the actor was away and his curse by Death, one could conclude this actor died of pneumonic plague. It typically comes with severe chest pains from the lung adema, spitting up blood and profuse sweating. The movie depicted none of the gory aspects of the death rather the emotional appeal for help in an utterly helpful and hopeless situation for the victim of the plague.

The infected plague victims throughout the movie were under no constraints as far as law or quarantine. While isolation of individuals who are sick can be found in Biblical references, the use of a legal quarantine for a set number of days was first used in Dubrovnik, Germany and immediately thereafter in Venice, both triggered by the Black Plague in the late 1340s. The period of forty days is not clear about its origin, but it has been suggested it is based on the forty days that Christ was in the desert in the Bible account, or that it is simply an arbitrary period during which anyone who had contracted the plague, would die.

The biohorror in The Seventh Seal comes from the core response to a confrontation with a complete lack of control over death. Bergman shows that even with some control --- the game of chess which brought the knight some more time on earth, the use of yarrow to ease the pain of burning to death, status, power and money --- none of these could keep death away for long. The metaphor is as true today with the best of modern medicine, as it was in 1348 or in 1957. A true and haunting biohorror.

Hud (1963)

RATING

Hud

[*after illegally shooting some buzzards*]

Well, I've always thought the law was meant to be interpreted in a lenient manner. Sometimes I lean one way and sometimes I lean the other.

---Hud (1963)

Hud (1963) is a drama that is not only a three academy awards winning movie, with seven nominations, but it also makes the List as a biodrama which transmutes into a biohorror. The economic devastation of the family cattle business for the foreseeable future through the purchase of cattle from Mexico carrying foot-and-mouth disease is shown through a slow and painful unfolding in the context of brittle family relations.

Let's begin with importation of cattle. Currently, the United States allows the importation of cattle if it s from a country that is on the USDA list as free of three diseases: foot-and-mouth disease, rinderpest and bovine spongiform encephalopathy (BSE). Mexico is now on the list as free from all three of these diseases. In fact, rinderpest has been eradicated as a disease in the world, but the USDA is still vigilant. An import permit is required and a 60-day quarantine period for cattle is required before they are exported to the United States. Once imported into the United States, another quarantine period is required. A 30-day quarantine period for the cattle is imposed on all countries except Mexico and Canada. In addition to these requirements, a health certificate showing the cattle are free of these three diseases is required. There are additional testing requirements and pesticide sprays for parasites that are also required during these periods.

The FMD outbreak on Homer Bannon's cattle ranch, the family patriarch in *Hud* was not only devastating to the family but could have caused the infection of neighboring cattle, deer, sheep and any other hooved animal. It would have taken the U.S. off the list of FMD-free countries and impacted the entire cattle industry in the United States.

Homer Bannon's cattle ranch is in Texas, and Texas has some additional requirements regulated by the Texas Animal Health Commission (TAHC). In additional to USDA requirements for importing cattle from Mexico, Texas requires that they be branded with an "M" before coming into the state.

The last FMD outbreak in Texas was in 1924. The Texas outbreak infected 148 herds made up of 8,473 cattle, 27 sheep, and 69 swine. The quarantine was ended January 1, 1925.[19] In order to make his point about the significance of FMD, the state official in Hud told Homer that the last outbreak in the United States had caused the destruction of "77,000" head of cattle and "20,000 deer." The numbers indicate he was referring to two outbreaks. The 1915 outbreak in the Chicago stockyards was the biggest in the U.S. and caused the destruction of 77,000 cattle and 9 deer. Then in 1924, California had an outbreak of FMD leading to the destruction of 20,000 deer. Artistic freedom was used to make the point that large numbers of animals are slaughtered to control FMD, probably to prepare Homer for the inevitable destruction of his entire herd that was threatened.

In order to control cattle diseases and protect the economic interests of the state's industry, the 23rd Texas Legislature, in 1893, passed Senate House Bill No. 112, establishing the Livestock Sanitary Commission, now named the Texas Animal Health Commission (TAHC).[20]

The TAHC can order the destruction of cattle.

Homer considered whether a long quarantine would help, rather than killing all of them. Hud and Homer get into a conflict about what will happen to the cattle ranch. Hud tells him to sell all the cattle before they come back. Homer asked "and try and pass bad stuff out on my neighbors?" Hud says, "Why this country is run on epidemics!" He then describes the tax schemes, etc. "You're an unprincipled man, Hud," Homer concludes.

---

[19] *History of Foot and Mouth Disease Outbreaks in North America*, ARS 91-58-1 -- May 1969, *Agricultural Research Service / U.S. Department of Agriculture at* http://members.bellatlantic.net/~vze4hqhe/history/fmdars.htm .

1. [20] *How the TAHC Began*, at http://www.tahc.state.tx.us/agency/History.pdf.

Hud was reflecting a sentiment not uncommon in private business owners regarding privacy and the desire to avoid government intrusion. When he was called back to look at a dead heifer to see what he thought the cause might be, Hud concluded that he just did not know. Homer responded that he would call the state veterinarian to see if he knew what it was. To this, Hud objected vehemently and said, "This is our land. I don't want any government men on it --- anytime, anywhere." Later during the movie, Homer had a similar sentiment when the state official came by to shoot his remaining longhorns which he had personally raised and were his favorites. Homer told them to get off his land and he would take care of it, expressing his own resistance to state imposed authority on his land.

While the constitution protects against seizing property in the 5th Amendment, it also provides for "just compensation" if the government has to take property out of public necessity, to protect the public's health or for eminent domain purposes. The state official came to Homer to report the test results had revealed the cattle were infected with FMD and said, "Your cows are public enemies now."

The quarantine sign mounted on the gate was imagery that forebode the inevitable end of the ranch.

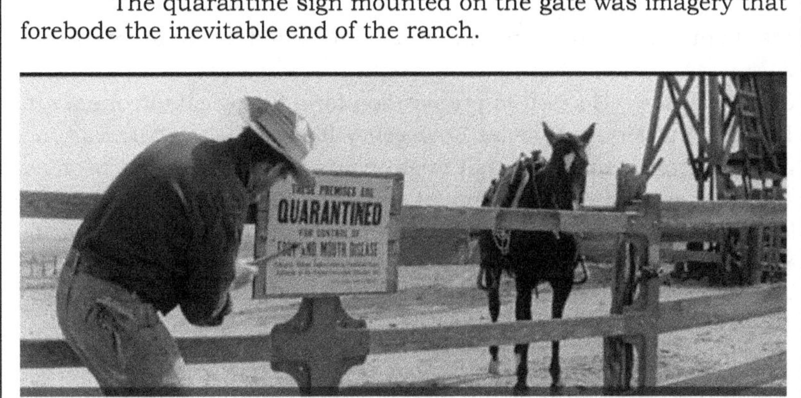

When property becomes a public nuisance and a threat to health and safety, the government can destroy it without compensation which was decided by the U.S. Supreme Court.[21] However, Congress saw the need to compensate farmers and ranchers when their livestock had to be destroyed due to public health and safety and provided for a compensation plan.

The Congress passed legislation to give authority to the USDA to compensate farmers for livestock that has to be destroyed on an order from the federal government at "fair market value."[22] As Hud put it in disgust after Homer talked about his lifetime of selective breeder that would be lost, "The government will pay us 4 bits on the dollar." Compensation for cattle destroyed on order of the federal government is compensable at a rate determined by the federal government.

[21] Lucas v. South Carolina Coast Commission, 505 U.S. 1003 (1992).

[22] 7 USC §8306(d) requires the Secretary (USDA) to pay up to the fair market value for animals, articles, facilities, or means of conveyance destroyed by the Department.

The personal protective equipment (PPE) worn by the state agriculture workers for the spraying of the carcasses after the cattle were put down is very lightweight in comparison to today's PPE.

The treatment of the carcasses with lime is the standard for animals as well as human bodies.

In the aftermath of 9/11 and in preparation for a biological terrorism attack, the USDA created a Foot-and-Mouth Disease Emergency Plan in 2002. FMD was considered to be the most likely agroterrorism agent that might be used. The plan has been continuously updated and coordinated with the Department of Homeland Security and the Federal Emergency Management Agency. The MAC is the coordination team across the federal and state governments in the event of a FMD emergency. This organization chart for coordinating a response to an FMD emergency is show in this chart.

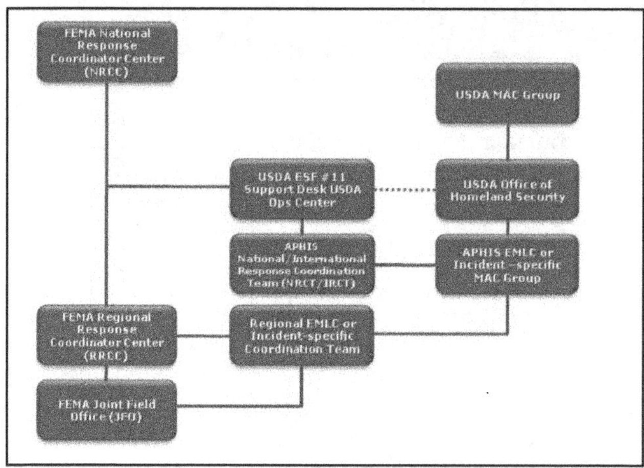

Unlike the state level response in Hud, an incident of FMD would trigger national resources and an investigation, due to both the potential for use as an agroterrorism weapon and because of the economic consequences nationally.

Specifically, the FMD Emergency Guide for a single incident (like that in Hud) is handled like this:

At the start of any FAD outbreak, the State Animal Health Official (SAHO), or designee, and Area Veterinarian in Charge (AVIC), or designee, will initially serve as the co-Incident Commanders for the Unified Command. The AVIC and SAHO may be relieved by an Incident Management Team (IMT) if there is a delegation of authority to the IMT.

Figure B-2 illustrates an overview of a MAC system according to NIMS. The figure shows the transition over the course of an incident. The incident begins with an on-scene single Incident Command (IC); as the incident expands in size or complexity developing into a Unified Command, the incident may require offscene coordination and support, which is when MAC Groups are activated.[23]

This chart shows how an incident would progress overtime.

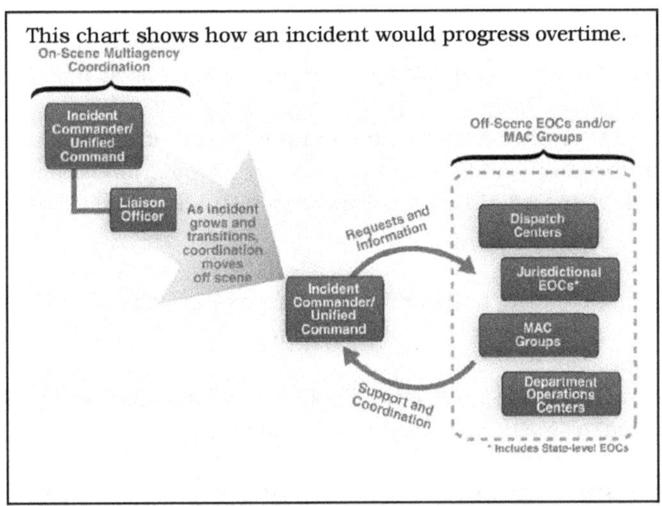

Waiting for the testing of cattle was a major point of tension in the movie. The state official told Homer they were going to infect some cattle and other animals and wait to see if they got the disease. The international animal health organization (with a French acronym, OIE) gives these times for incubation: (Incubation period = 7+/- 4days; OIE= 14 days). Home would have to wait about two weeks for the results. However, the test today is a much more sophisticated antigen blood test to determine not only FMD but which of the strains of FMD are present.

The destruction of the cattle on the ranch in the manner shown on Hud is still one method of mass depopulation and certainly the most dramatic for the big screen and to evoke a powerful emotion. The real life depopulation can also create human health impacts that can be devastating. The USDA in the FMD Emergency plan lists these methods of mass depopulation which are further described in another document called an SOP or Standard Operating Procedure. Here is what the Emergency Guide describes:

This SOP offers FMD-specific information on mass depopulation and euthanasia, including evaluation of various euthanasia methods, such as

[23] *USDA APHIS FMD Response Plan: The Red Book (June 2012).*

· *gunshot,*

· *penetrating captive bolt,*

· *electrocution,*

· *injectable euthanasia, and*

· *carbon dioxide and other gas.*

In an FMD outbreak, euthanasia or mass depopulation should be provided to the affected animals as safely, quickly, efficiently, and humanely as possible. In addition, the emotional and psychological impact on animal owners, caretakers,their families, and other personnel should be minimized.

When the state official came back to shoot Homer's two remaining longhorns, he failed to try to minimize the emotional damage to Homer, which is clearly required in this guidance, above.

Destruction of the cattle is required to stop the spread of FMD. However, because there is now a vaccine for strains of FMD, a determination would be made as to whether vaccinated cattle could be spared. The FMD Emergency Guide describes the process almost exactly as it unfolded in *Hud*:

1. Physical Resources

1.1 Slaughter capacity FMD infected/ high-risk animals should be slaughtered on-farm. Thus farm technology and mustering facilities, intractability of livestock are factors..

1.3 Disposal capacity - If on-farm disposal available, heavy equipment would be required for burial or incinerator facilities for burn. . . .[24]

Among the cull strategies, this one would have answered Homer's concern that all of his life's work in selective breeding was being destroyed. The use of genetic preservation of cattle before slaughter could have saved Homer's selective breeding program if it happened today. The FMD Emergency Manual has this direction:

1.4 Social - economic status of producers/ region - What is the sophistication of the producers in the

[24] USDA APHIS FMD Response Plan – The Red Book, App. B (June 2012).

affected region? What is their social-political influence? Are there genetic preservation considerations against pre-emptive slaughter?[25]

FMD would still devastate a ranch and a country. The experience in the United Kingdom show how the economic costs of an outbreak of Foot-and-mouth disease (FMD) are tremendous. The FMD outbreak in the United Kingdom in 2001 resulted in the destruction of 10 million sheep and cows at a cost of $16 billion dollars (8 billion British pounds) by the time the disease was declared eliminated in October 2001.

In 2003, in a rumor that there might be an FMD case in Arizona, Mexico closed its border to cattle from Nogales, AZ because of possible FMD in cattle for export to Mexico.

So what happened to the Bannon family in Hud? The destruction of his cattle ranch was too much for Homer and he died from falling from his horse. Lonnie, Hud's nephew left his ranch with disgust at his Uncle Hud's behavior and for not caring about anyone. Hud was left with his inheritance of a ranch contaminated with FMD which will have to be cleared to be restocked with cattle. If you were looking for a character arc that made Hud change his irresponsible and uncaring ways, it didn't happen. In the closing scene after Lonnie had left him for good, Hud thought about it for a few minutes then he gave a sneer and a back-handed wave of his hand to Lonnie.

But can Hud get a loan to buy his cattle? The USDA has been given authority to make loans to ranches which have had losses due directly to a quarantine issued by the government, when no banks will be willing to do so.[26] The statute authorizes the USDA Secretary to make and insure loans to *established farmers, ranchers . . . Who are US citizens, where the Secretary finds that the applicants' farming, ranching or aquaculture operations have been substantially affected by a quarantine imposed by the Secretary under the animal quarantine laws.*

But two conditions to make a loan are required and they are if *(1) they have experience and resources necessary to assure a reasonable prospect for successful operation with the assistance of such loan and (2) they are not able to obtain sufficient credit elsewhere.*

Hud's drunkened bar brawling and general avoidance of responsibility days are over, if he hopes to qualify for this federal loan to get the ranch started again.

[25] USDA APHIS FMD Response Plan – The Red Book, App. B (June 2012),

[26] Consolidated Farm and Rural Development Act, 7 USC § 1961.

The Last Man on Earth (1964)

RATING

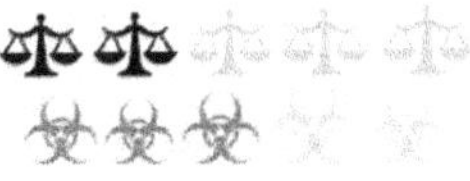

Dr. Robert Morgan

I am sorry Ben, I just cannot accept the idea of universal disease.

---*The Last Man on Earth* (1964)

The Last Man on Earth (1964) is the first film adaptation of Richard Matheson's book, *I Am Legend.* Dr. Robert Morgan, Vincent Price, appears as he awakes to another day and reflects on the three years it has been since the disaster. They live in a suburban single family home with a picket fence.

In the next screenshot, Dr. Neville is picking up the dead bodies on his front lawn and putting them in his trunk.

The next screenshot he is dumping one of the dead bodies from his lawn into a large dump.

During the day he goes about looking for where they hide, in the process killing a lot of the living dead. He knows he must get his windows repaired by sundown because the living dead come out and attack. He uses mirrors on his door because they "hate the sight of their own image." Using a string of garlic is also useful, but he has to keep fresh garlic for the door. He also spends a lot of his day sharpening conical spikes to drive into the hearts of these living dead he calls, "vampires."

He went to a church where he has a marble sepulcher for his departed wife, and laments her passing. He falls asleep on her sepulcher and sleeps past sunset. He awakes with the horrific realization that he has slept past sunset and will have to battle the vampires to get home. The vampires are traditional vampires in the sense that they sleep in the day and come out at night.

Dr. Neville identifies bacilli that are present in every person with the illness but Dr. Mercer, the laboratory director refers to it as the "virus theory." Bacteria and viruses are two very different categories of disease causing agents. Dr. Neville in the laboratory makes a conclusion about the disaster, "There is a germ floating around the world that is highly contagious and it has reached plague proportions."

Dr. Neville finds his wife and daughter sick and as he leooks out his front door, he sees a neighbor screaming as they carry away a dead body from her house. The military in gas masks are loading bodies into a military truck.

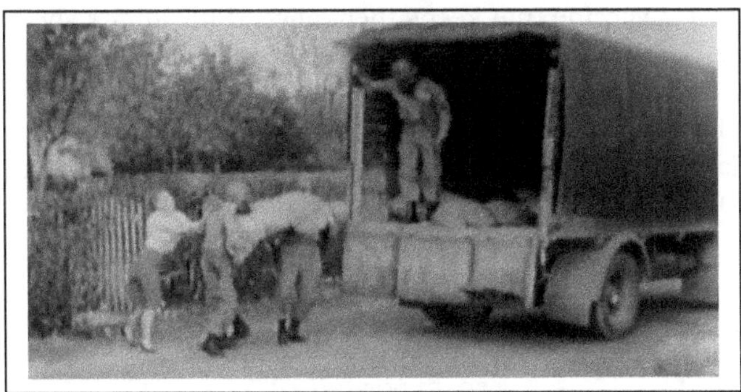

Dr. Neville goes home to find that his daughter has died and has been collected and carried away to the dump and incinerated. He drives to the dump to try to stop them but he is too late. One of the military guards tells him that his daughter is in that dump, too. Dr. Neville returns home and shortly thereafter his wife dies. He promises her that she will not be put in the pit and he buries her himself in a grave that he digs.

This screenshot is the scene at night when Dr. Neville goes to retrieve his daughter's body.

Taking possession of the human remains of family members is regulated by state laws. Permission must be given by the family members, unless is is a matter of public health and safety and then the body can be taken and disposed by public health authorities. This authority would most likely be accomplished through a public health disaster declaration by the Governor or the Secretary of Health and Human Services.

Dr. Neville tries to continue to determine the cause of the disasease and finally says, "oh, what's the use?"

He attributes his survival to The vampire germ entered his system in an attenuated form, and that gave him immunity. He explains this to a woman who appears to be normal but she is infected he comes to find. She explains that she is part of a society of survivors who are infected but have a vaccine that keeps them alive. She admits she has come to his house to make sure he never leaves because the society considers him to be a big threat. They believe he has killed many people.

He discovers she is taking a vaccine, and confronts her about whether she has a cure. The following dialogue resolves some questions about the theory of Ruth's vaccine and why they want to kill Dr. Morgan.

Dr. Robert Morgan

What do you mean? You found the solution

Ruth Collins

That's rright it's exactly as you said it would be.
I take that for it.

Dr. Robert Morgan

What it it?

Ruth Collins

Its fabricated blood plus baccine.
Blood keeps the germ and the

vaccine keeps it isolated and keeps it from multiplying. We have had it for some time now.

Dr. Robert Morgan

We? We?

Ruth Collins

There are quite a number of us.

Dr. Robert Morgan

And I thought you were alone. I was going to cure you! Does that amuse you?

Ruth Collins

To find out if you know anymore than we do. You know far less. We are alive. We are an organized society. We are neither alive nor dead.

Dr. Robert Morgan

And you want me to join?

Ruth Collins

You can't join you are a monster to them. Why do you think I ran? You are a legend in the city, living in the day. Many of the people you killed were still alive!

When she passes out from not getting her vaccine, he performs a transfusion on her to give her his antibodies and make her immune to the disease.

Immunity takes weeks to build in a body, and in this movie she becomes immediately immune and is normal. Dr. Neville tells them that they can save the other people in her society and they will never be alone again.

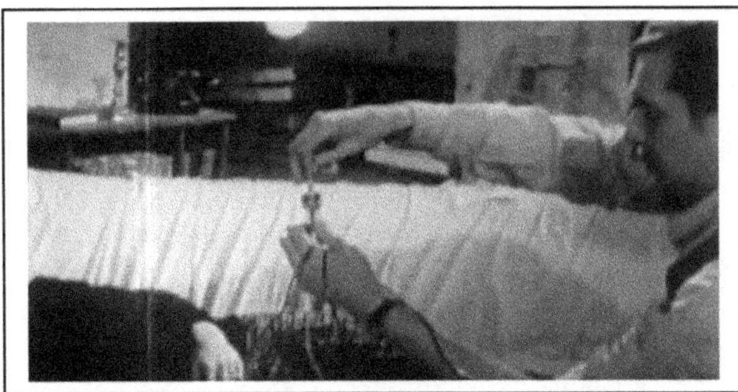

Her society of infected but functional people come to his house and try to kill him, hunting him down with guns and spikes. They chase him into the church where his fie's sepulcher is located and they shoot him.

He dies inside the church when they throw a spear that ends his life. His last words are that "they were afraid of me."

This early biothriller, categorized as a science fiction/horror movie, raised questions about naturally occurring diseases and whether they could spread from Europe to the United States. Dr. Robert Morgan expressed disbelief that this could happen. Commercial airlines had begun the Jet Age from 1956 and an explosion in air travel was beginning making the spread of disease much more possible. The rate in international travel increased 400% from 1970 to 2005 and the ability to spread disease increased along with air travel. This depiction portrayed a time of innocence before AIDs, before SARS and before the need for International Health Regulations that regulate how nations will control and report disease outbreaks of public health events of international concern. But this was not the last movie that would interpret Robert Matheson's novel, *I Am Legend.*

The Satan Bug (1965)

RATING

Dr. Gregory Hoffman
More than forty chemical weapons are being developed at Station 3. I will confine myself to two which we have developed here, at E Lab. The first, botulinus. We have twelve hundred grams in six flasks. If ten grams of it were allowed to contaminate a city, that city is a morgue in four hours. It is an ideal weapon, if you will forgive the phrase, because it only destroys people. It oxides itself, and in effect dies after eight hours.

Lee Barrett
Well, then it's safe to go in there. It's been over eight hours since that vault door was closed. And if all twelve hundred grams of botulinus were spilled, it would still be safe. The closed-air circulation system is still in operation, so it would be oxidized.

Dr. Gregor Hoffman

That is correct, but there is something else in there. It is only three weeks since Dr. Baxter refined it, and only three days since he communicated its existence to anyone.

Gen. Williams

There's something beyond botulinis?

Dr. Gregor Hoffman

Yes, the second weapon. Also a virus, airborne. But self-perpetuating. Indestructible. Once released it will multiply at a power beyond our calculations. It perhaps will never die. To this virus we have given a highly unscientific name, but one which describes it perfectly. "The Satan Bug." If I took the flask which contains it and exposed it to the air, everyone here would be dead in three seconds. California would be a tomb in a few hours. In a week all life, and I mean all life, would cease in the United States. In two months, two months at the most, the trapper from Alaska, the peasant from the Yangtze, the Aborigine from Australia are dead. All dead, because I crushed a flask and exposed a green colored liquid to the air. Nothing, nothing can stop the Satan Bug.

---The Satan Bug (1965)

The Satan Bug (1965) is a sci-fi, thriller which fits in the biohorror, biothriller subgenre with its plot centered on two bioweapons that are stolen from Station 3, a secret government laboratory.

The period of 1965 was at the height of the Cold War with the U.S.S.R., and our biological weapons program was actively pursuing research on building and disseminating bioweapons. This movie captures the fears of what might happen if a megalomaniac stole the most virulent weapon ever created along with the formula for the vaccine. The questions about laboratory security and safety are prominently part of the opening, yet laboratory biosafety and biosecurity did not change until after the events of 9/11 and the Anthrax Attacks.

The beginning of the movie shows someone arriving from out of town, we learn is Mr. Reagan and he enters the laboratory through a ramp that goes underground to an opening with no door. He passes a delivery of crates he is told is equipment on his way into the building. Mr. Reagan talks to a few people who appear to be scientists and one walks into the room wearing a full biosuit. The point of a biosuit is to shield the person from contamination, but if there is any contamination on the suit, it would expose all the people in the room to the biohazard by wearing into an area where people have no protection.

Mr. Reagan talks to Dr. Baxter about his visit to Washington, D.C. setting up the concerns about laboratory security.

Dr. Baxter
Were they worried?

Mr. Reagan
They are always worried about the security of this place.
Tired men make mistakes.
God help us if a mistake is made here.

The end of the day at the laboratory shows a staff of security guards, but the protocol for entering is signing in and leaving is a friendly nod to the security guard. In the frame shot below, the theft of the flasks of bioweapons is removed from the secured safe. Red and green flashing lights with a humming noise signify the "hot" zone for the materials. The man leaving with the metal box is wearing a suit and tie and entering and leaving a highly dangerous hot zone.

At 10 minutes into the 2 hour movie, the laboratory door is closed like a safe. Red and green lights add to the effect.

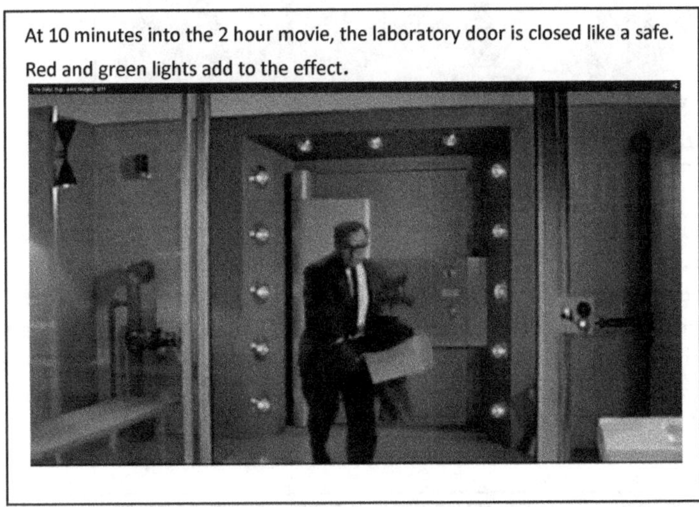

Laboratory biosecurity would have required an entry key pad at the door to note who was entering and exiting, all done with an identification card that is magnetized, a fingerprint reader or a retinal scanner. This helps to avoid using hands that are heavily gloved with two layers of rubber. The records are kept for three years. A security camera would likely be installed to cover the ingress and egress of this special safe storage area. In this highly secured laboratory, there appears to be no camera and no use of a camera.

Laboratory biosecurity refers to the locks and doors and protecting the materials from theft; whereas laboratory biosafety refers to the practices that ensure against accidents with dangerous pathogens that result in harm to the researcher or those nearby.

Laboratory biosafety in 1965 was still in its early stages. Handling deadly pathogens led to laboratory accidents which led to newly developed biosuits and laboratory equipment. New designs of laboratories ensured that ventilation systems were contained and filtered. Waste water that left the building was required to be treated to kill any pathogens that might have been washed off in cleaning and disposal processes.

In the next frameshot, Barrett, the CIA official, uses himself to determine if the area is contaminated. This would be unethical and completely illegal to use a human entering a hot zone to see if the zone was hot and infective. He admitted that he knew that if the space was "hot" he could not come out. Carrying in the hamster was a test that they used to determine if the area was hot. After just a few minutes, they determined the hamster was alive and therefore the room must be safe. Barrett had no training in biosafety nor was he a scientist, but he was the one who dressed in the biosuit and entered the hot zone.

Once inside the laboratory, we can see the range of equipment. The most interesting piece is the wooden box on the right edge of the frame with two holes. The two holes are used to place gloved hands while looking through the glass in the closed box. This device was created as early as the 1940s and used in bioweapons facilities, but a wooden box would not allow disinfection of the surface. A modern gloved box would also be ventilated so that any aerosols could be evacuated from the box so no accidental contamination could take place.

Throughout the movie, the ten flasks that were stolen from the freezer were handled without gloves and carelessly put in pockets, bags and at one point teetering on the seat of a helicopter with the door open.

Two bioweapons are revealed as the stolen material from the laboratory. One is botulinum and the other is the "Satan bug". Botulinum is a toxin produced by a bacteria which is one of the deadliest toxins on earth. The "Satan bug" is a fictional pathogen that we never learn anything about except that it will spread through the air and sea until everyone on earth is infected and dies. Neither of these bioweapons is contagious by spreading from one human to the next, as are many of the top candidates for bioweapons. Botulinum is on the top tier of regulated pathogens and among those considered to be candidates for bioweapons.

The investigators are contacted through telegrams and telephone calls, the rapid communications means of the day. In one call, they learn that the thief plans to use botulinum in Florida and Los Angeles to show his willingness to use these weapons. It is never clear that he wants anything for the weapons; he just wants to be powerful and use them.

In the next frameshot, a video has been taken from the air and sent to the investigators to view the dead bodies that are peeling out of their cars and boats in the wake of the botulinum attack in Florida.

Barrett was shipped video to see the death and carnage from the attack in Key West, Florida with botulinum toxin.

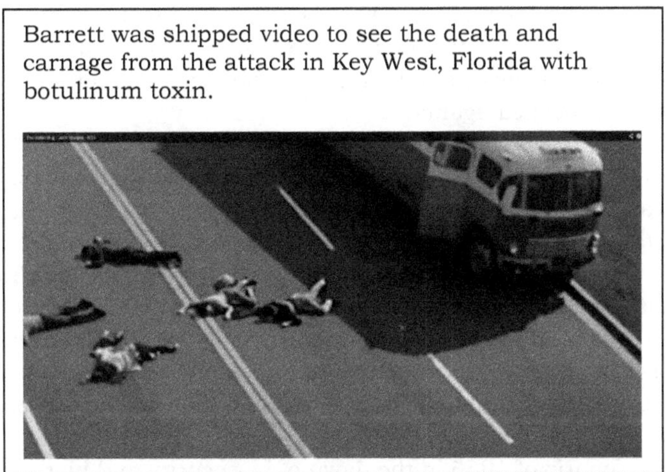

At one point, the question is asked about what Washington is saying about this, and the response is "quiet panic" but no action is ever evident coming from Washington, D.C. throughout the movie.

They also discuss the need to evacuate Los Angeles since this is the next target. One of the investigators says, "We can't evacuate Los Angeles, we don't have time." The helpless reply is, "We'll have to try." Evacuation plans are an important part of any city's emergency response plans, and this would be a plan that could be activated by the emergency services and the Governor should evacuation from Los Angeles be necessary today.

Later in the movie, they learn that an imposter who killed Dr. Baxter, and who looked like him, walked past the security guard and left without being detected. He had gotten into the laboratory through the crates that were delivered to the laboratory. The security guards remarked that their job was to keep things in the laboratory not keep things out.

The timing of *The Satan Bug* (1965) is indicative of the public sentiment against bioweapons and the uncontrollable destruction that they could cause. Unlike other weapons, once released, these weapons cannot be controlled. The only possibility of control is to vaccinate against them, and the thief in *The Satan Bug* (1965) had not only vaccinated himself, but had stolen the formula for the vaccine and killed the inventor.

Barrett the brave CIA operative who fearlessly entered the potential hot zone, also managed to get the flask back from the thief, wealthy megalomaniac, Ainsley. The movie ended with the flask safely back and Barrett remarking that they were back where they started.

The timing of *The Satan Bug (*1965) was just prior to President Nixon ending the bioweapons program in the United States in November 1969. This was the groundwork for the establishment of the Biological Weapons and Toxins Treaty which was signed in 1972 and entered into force in 1975. The U.S.S.R. was a signatory on the same day as the United States but instead of ending their program, they began building it, believing that the United States was also doing the same. It was not until the collapse of the U.S.S.R. in 1990-91 that we learned the extent of their extensive bioweapons research program.

In 2002, Congress passed new legislation to strengthen biosafety and biosecurity in laboratories and hundreds of new facilities were constructed to do research and provide resources for testing. This was amended in 2005 and 2012. The regulations, called the Select Agent Program, requires biosafety measures, training and biosecurity measures of using locks and inventories and background checks of scientists to ensure that accidents as well as intentional theft is protected against.

Would any of these new laws prevent the theft in The *Satan Bug (*1965) ? Not if it was an inside job, as it was in *The Satan Bug (*1965), even with video cameras. The theft of a testube of a bacteria can be easily replaced with another testtube with bacteria from another testtube. That would take care of the inventory part of the regulation. Could someone leave the laboratory without scanning their identification? The answer is, yes, and not something that is secured. It is assume that if you are cleared going in, that you will be cleared leaving. The delivery of wooden crates with equipment which are really Trojan horses with thieves inside, is also very possible. Inventories are checked and verified with the laboratory, but it is possible that an crate could go unnoticed for just enough time for the contents to escape into hiding.

The Satan Bug scenario of 1965 in the dawn of biosecurity and biosafety, predates major biosafety and biosecurity regulations, but it manages to still find weaknesses that exist in human nature that prove to be the most serious vulnerabilities.

Andromeda Strain (1971)

RATING

Senator from Vermont
You're absolutely sure it worked? You'd better be!

Dr. Jeremy Stone
All reports continue to indicate that the experiment was successful, Senator.

Senator from Vermont
Then we can feel confident your so-called "biological crisis" is over?

Dr. Jeremy Stone
As far as Andromeda is concerned, yes. We have the organism at Wildfire, and we continue to study it. We know now beyond a doubt that other forms of life exist in the universe.

Senator from Vermont
Thanks to Scoop?

Dr. Jeremy Stone
Yes.

Dr. Jeremy Stone
[pause]
However, with this new knowledge, there is no guarantee that another so-called "biological crisis" won't occur again.

Senator from Vermont
Hmm. What do we do about that?

Dr. Jeremy Stone
Precisely, Senator. What do we do?

The Andromeda Strain (1971) is based on the book by the same name by Michael Crichton, a master sci-fi, thriller author. *The Andromeda Strain* (1971) offers all of the elements of a biohorror, biothriller or biofantasy movie and makes the List.

The movie begins with a simple recovery of a satellite which has landed in a small town in New Mexico with a population of 68. The duo that goes to recover it reports there are bodies everywhere and then there is a scream and silence. It is clear they are dealing with something to do with the return of the satellite. All of the top brass and scientists are collected in secret and a message goes out that there is an issue at Wildfire, the name of the top secret laboratory that has been developed for the highest biosafety containment of any organism that might be highly pathogenic. The first message about the incident is shown as it is being typed onto a piece of paper in a typewriter.

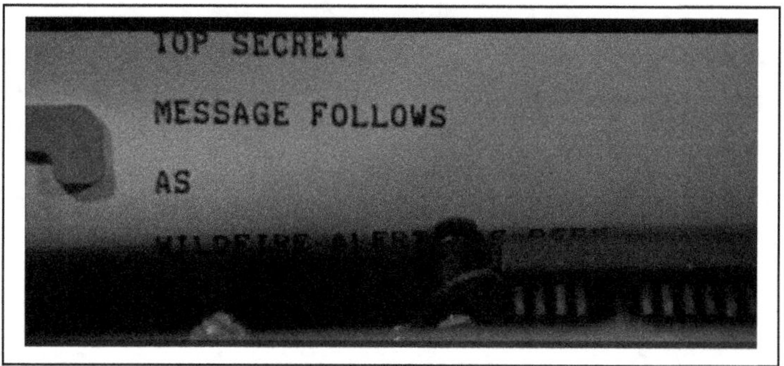

The five level underground laboratory is state of the art and the scientists that have been brought in to do the investigation are given a tour through the facility as they enter. This floor is all red, and its design indicates it has all the makings of a futuristic laboratory – no corners or creases in this deep red level.

The discussion of what to do about the new alien form of life that shows up as having elements common to life on earth, but lacking amino acids and other typical structures, refers to several legal documents.

This movie uses some interesting references to legal documents which make the context more believable and so more horrifying. The investigative team gives some thought of how to eliminate the contamination in Piedmont, NM where all of the residents are dead, and the two survivors – a baby and an old man --- have been rescued for further study. The first document is "Directive 712" which in the context of the dialogue is a protocol for eliminating cities when necessary. There are directives with different acronyms for each Presidency. There is no directive 712, and most of them never issued more than three hundred or so, during their administrations. The next document mentioned is the "Moscow Treaty of 1963" which they cite as a reason they can't drop a nuclear bomb on Piedmont. This treaty is very real, and is also known as the partial nuclear test ban treaty signed with the USSR to mutually agree that no testing of nuclear weapons would be conducted above ground. Interestingly, the investigative team was more concerned about the legal constraints than on the consequences of a nuclear bomb being detonated in NM to obliterate a city.

The movie's theme to combat this threat from outer space is decontamination and the consequences of failing. The laboratory which is set up for such testing including testing for bioweapons was explained by Karen Karen Anson a technician in the laboratory.

NASA isolates returning astronauts as well as the materials they retrieve from the moon, etc. This is because of the precautionary principle. It does not entail a large burden to isolate people and materials for a short time in order to prevent a catastrophe if any dangerous contamination becomes evident. SETI, the organization for the Search for Extraterrestrial Intelligence, was once a part of NASA but after a Congressional rejection of further funding the search from the NASA budget, it became a "spin-off" but still relies heavily on federal money for its existence. The work has extended to a field called "astrobiology" and they produce scientific publications in this field, many on the topic of extremeophiles, forms of life on earth that exist at the extremes of our environment – in extreme heat, cold, acidity, alkalinity, etc. But the organization is also considering how to contain materials that may be retrieved from other planets in order to avoid contamination on earth. This has led them to inquire into systems for biological safety laboratories and the regulations that control biosafety in them. The idea of a Wildfire laboratory may not be that far from reality.

The nuclear explosion safety feature of the Wildfire laboratory, which features an automatic nuclear explosion if any virus is at risk of escaping, would at least comply with the Partial Nuclear Test Ban Treaty or Moscow Treaty of 1963 with the explosion occurring underground. But if any of the workers estates hope to recover for radiation effects or their death, they will have a difficult time overcoming sovereign immunity, the discretionary function exception to mistakes that are made, and the causation element of whether the explosion caused their later cancer. At least two plaintiffs have failed to make their causation cases against the federal government where they were accidentally exposed to a nuclear bomb test and suffered leukemia and died four years later. No causation proven, the court held.[27]

Another legal issue in the movie involved the surprise vaccination of the civilian scientists who had been summoned to the laboratory for the investigation. During a lengthy "body analysis" procedure, a screen with flashing colors was used to distract the subject, while a mechanical arm moved into position to inject an arm with vaccines. After the injection the music and flashing colors on the screen stop and a pre-recorded voice is heard saying, "You have received pneumatic injections of booster immunizations." Noting the past tense of the announcement, there was no warning and no informed consent disclosures about the risks or side effects from the vaccine boosters before they were injected which is a requirement for administering vaccines, but not until the mid-1970s when a federal court found it was medical negligent not to have disclosed risks to a patient who had suffered predictable but not probable side effects from the polio vaccine. Even military troops who may be ordered to take a vaccine are provided with informed consent disclosures although they may be limited in their ability to refuse or be dismissed.

Here is the frameshot of Dr. Hall's surprised look at the mechanical arm in action.

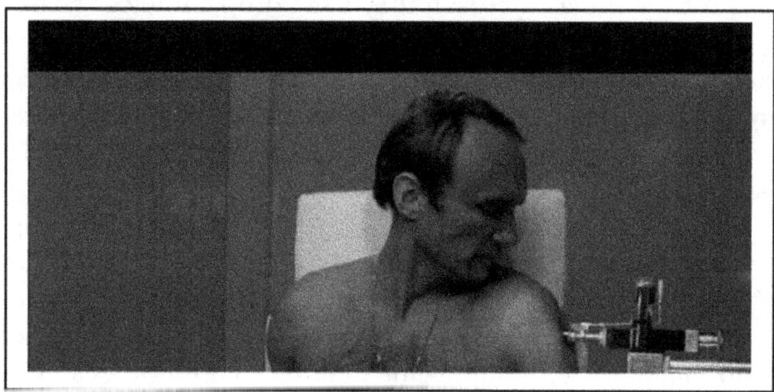

The investigative team is working around the clock to isolate the organism. The process of finding what it is made of with mass spectrometry and then checking its size by exposing a rat at different filter sizes until the organism gets through tells them it is less than two microns in size. The size of a cell, they remark. (A red blood cell is 5 microns in diameter.) And finally they isolate it on some fabric and the magnification on the fabric gives the viewer a good idea of its size.

---

[27] *Roberts v. United States*, 85 F.3d 637 (9th Cir. 1996).

Dr. Ruth Hatchett: *They do look like splatters of paint.*

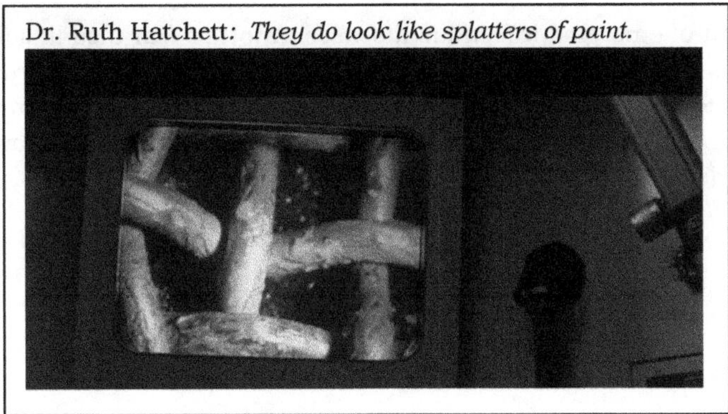

Meanwhile they have had a laboratory malfunction embarrassingly simple, and that is a simple bell that rings when a telegram comes in, has been blocked by a sliver of material. This creates a chain of events that prevents the investigation team from finding out that the mission to bomb the town has been called off, and a jet flying overhead crashed when all its rubber dissolved. (Funny they didn't mention the pilot dissolved, too, leaving his bones in the cockpit!)

The commander on the video monitor responds to their desperate demands to bomb the town: "It's because of rash statements like that that makes the President not trust scientists!"

It is Dr. Mark Hall who finally finds out why the old man and the baby survived Andromeda Strain. Their behaviors have blood that is too acid (baby) and blood that is too alkali (old man who drinks sterno), which was outside the survivable range for Andromeda. Just at the point they had solved the mystery about how to control it, they find it has eaten the seals and a leak has set off the automatic self-destruct safety feature of Wildfire. It is only the heroics of Dr. Mark Hall that eventually allow him to disengage the self-destruct timer and they all survive. Andromeda has floated out to sea in a non lethal form and they have formulated a plan to seed the clouds to obliterate it from the earth.

The movie ends with Senate hearings on the "biological incident". Did we break any laws with the mission to collect a bioweapon from space with our satellite. No, but we were well on the way to violating international law. And yes, the laboratory directors were violating the President's orders, which is at best insubordination and could result in dismissal. But the movie made the President complicit in the activities at Wildfire, so the movie did not reflect the legal reality of the time, given that President Nixon had already announced the end of the bioweapons program in the United States in November 1969. Perhaps it is the movie, *Andromeda Strain* that further gives momentum to our change in heart about bioweapons in the United States? The Biological Weapons and Toxins Convention was signed by the United States in 1972 and took effect for all signatory countries in 1975.

Biological weapons laboratories would seem a thing of the past, when the treaty was signed, but after the anthrax attacks in 2001 the infusion of 18 billion dollars into research and development of countermeasures for biological weapons established hundreds of new laboratories including five at the highest containment level.

The fear in the 21st Century now shifted to laboratory accidents or thefts, but biological laboratories are essential to understanding the threat of not only intentional uses of biological agents, but of emerging infectious diseases. Another fear also lingered, and that is fear that bioweapons were still being kept long after they were ordered destroyed by President Nixon. This fear resurfaced more than two decades after *Andromeda Strain* in the 1995 movie, *Outbreak*, and the question of bombing a city also resurfaced. How much difference a couple of decades can make? You will see.

The Omega Man (1971)

RATING

Newscaster

[V.O. television video images of people dying in the streets]

Martial law is now nationwide. . .
Our fellow countrymen are dying. The very foundations of civilization are beginning to crumble under that dread assault of that long feared horror, germ warfare.

---*The Omega Man* (1971)

The Omega Man (1971) is a post-apocalyptic action, sci-fi, thriller about germ warfare which makes the List for the biohorror, biothriller subgenre. The attack against the United States with plague bacilli carrying bombs was met with the order, "Abort firing! Interception will fragment bacilli carrying missles!"

The Omega Man is Charlton Heston, a military scientist who searched for a vaccine that would counteract the plague attack. After failing to find a cure and the collapse of civilization in the U.S., he finds himself possibly the last man on earth. He is living alone in a row house being constantly attacked by the packs of people who lived through the plague and look as if they have chronic sores and bleeding gums set against a pale chalky face. The movie was inspired by the book, *I Am Legend* by Richard Matheson. The book also inspired *Last Man on Earth* (1964) and as you will see in the coming pages, *I Am Legend* (2007) which also makes the biohorror, biothriller subgenre List.

Newscaster announcing marital law is now nationwide.

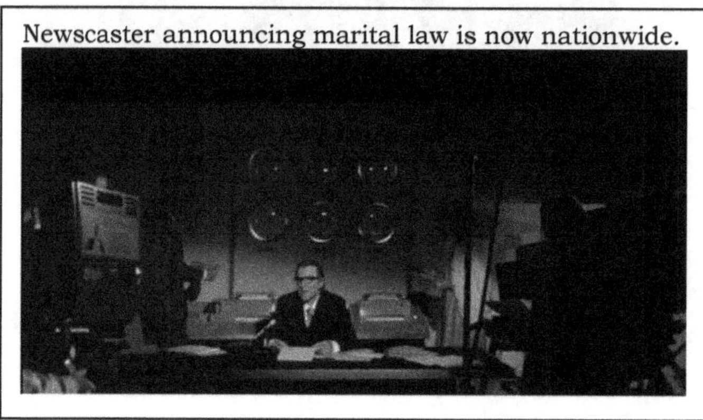

The movie was released in 1971 and was set just a few years ahead which we learn from a calendar hanging in an old building, turned to March 1975. Since he has been living like this for two years, it must be around 1977. The possibility of germ warfare was a reality because the United States as well as the U.S.S.R. were engaged in full scale bioweapons research and development programs. Movies like *The Satan Bug* (1965) followed by *The Omega Man* (1971) showed the risks of the dangerous possibilities from the research and development programs themselves, as well as the consequences of carrying the bioweapons to their full purpose in an attack by the U.S.S.R. against the United States in the movie.

Interestingly, the movie foretold what would later be a major shock to the West, and that was the extensiveness of the U.S.S.R. biological weapons program, Biopreparat. Defector Ken Alibek, the second to disclose the existence of the program, wrote extensively about the developments that had taken place in the U.S.S.R. program over the two decades that the U.S. had stopped their bioweapons program. Biopreparat was staffed by thousands of scientists and located in 2,000 laboratories across the U.S.S.R. Advances in engineering bioweapons were helped by reading the scientific literature in the U.S. as well as their own efforts, in one of the best kept military secrets in history. The collapse of the U.S.S.R. and the investigation by the United Nations groups confirmed the defectors' disclosures. Arsenals of bombs capable of carrying bacteria and anthrax spores were in the 10,000s and vats holding 1,000s of gallons of bacteria slurry were constantly being refreshed to ensure a ready supply of enough biological weapons to fill the missles at a moment's notice.

The year that this movie was released, an incident in the U.S.S.R. raised suspicions of a possible bioweapons program. The deaths of hundreds of people in and around the city of Sverdlovsk, Russia died of anthrax. Pneumonic anthrax is rare, because it requires inhaling spores, yet the Russians reports were that the deaths were caused by anthrax contaminated mean bought on the black market. Extensive investigations and groups visiting the U.S.S.R. could never confirm that this was the result of an anthrax bioweapons mistake. In 1991, however, it was disclosed that the deaths were caused by an air filter being left off the building in a routine maintenance operation that released the spores into the air and they traveled downwind killing everything in its path.

Meanwhile, the movie depicted plague deaths to cause death in a few minutes. While exaggerated, the U.S.S.R. had developed chimeras or combination pathogens that had high infectious rates and high mortality rates. The newscaster in the first 18 minutes of the movie declares that "martial law is now nationwide." But what does it take to have martial law? Many believe this is a natural consequence of bringing order after a disaster, but that is not the case, as most state governments are capable of responding to and recovering from disasters with federal assistance, without martial law.

The United States tried martial law at the end of the U.S. Civil War, placing military troops in the South to ensure that reconstruction was taking place and the new social order was in effect. The experience was such a negative one with severe consequences for the civilian population that Congress declared that the U.S. would never again use martial law in domestic law enforcement unless certain conditions existed, including not using martial law unless the Governor of the state where martial control might be imposed requests it, which would mean the state had no law enforcement infrastructure left. This law called, *posse comitatus,*[28] is still law and consulted when any use of military human resources or military resources are contemplated for use in response to a hurricane or tornado disaster.

A post-apocalyptic context doesn't have even martial law, but reverts to tribal power and control, much like we see in countries that have such weak government structures that it is really tribal governance that controls the lives of its citizenry. The rule of law becomes the rule of man and abuses of power become the law.

This tribal form of law and rule by man was depicted in the scene where Col. Robert Neville, the Omega Man, is strapped to a table is in what was once a courtroom, with the leader, Mathias, sitting as the chief judge with his two henchman on either side. The large audience acts as a jury. The trial is conducted with a large book opened in front of Mathias, but with no apparent connection to what he is saying. The judgment against Col. Neville is based on a broad philosophy of cleansing the world of those who had not paid the price and suffered with the disease, bearing the marks, and who represents the past age of science and medicine. All of this philosophy came from an epiphany Mathias had as he was wandering around after having the plague, and he managed to collect hundreds of followers.

---

[28] 18 U.S.C. § 1385 (2013)

The Judge

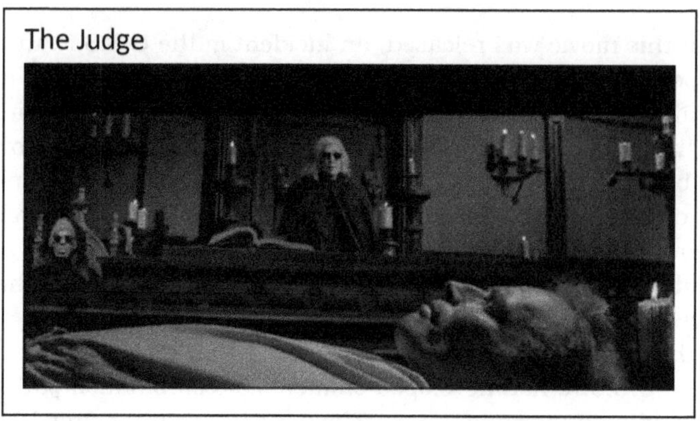

The judgment was made by asking the jury predictable questions generally about whether Col. Neville is among those they needed to wipe off the earth. This led to a "questioning" in the small room. There is no recognition of a right to an attorney from the Sixth Amendment of the Constitution, and no opportunity for a defense from the defendant, Col. Neville.

The Jury

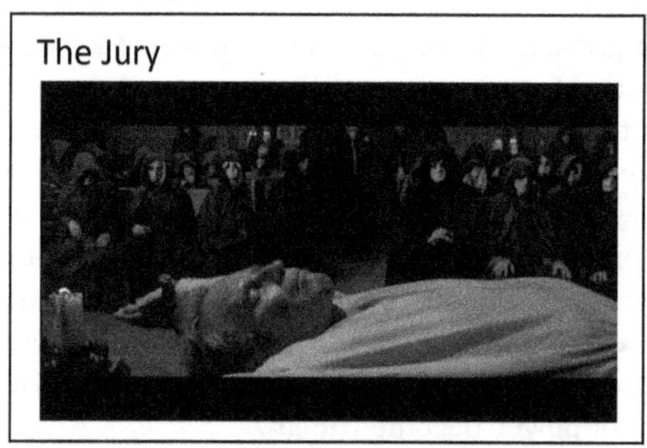

After an unknown rescuer switched on the lights in the stadium where they were located, blinding the mass of miscreates who could not see in the light, Col. Neville was able to escape with the help of his rescuers. This is a discovery for Col. Neville to find that there are at least a couple more people on earth who had not succumbed to the plague attack.

At one point, Col. Neville describes how he tried to find a cure by capturing one of Mathias' people and experimenting on him. This frameshot shows how he had to omit the "informed consent" requirement to fully inform human subjects of the consequences and possible side effects of experimental drugs and vaccines allowing them to make an informed decision as to whether they would agree to the experiment.

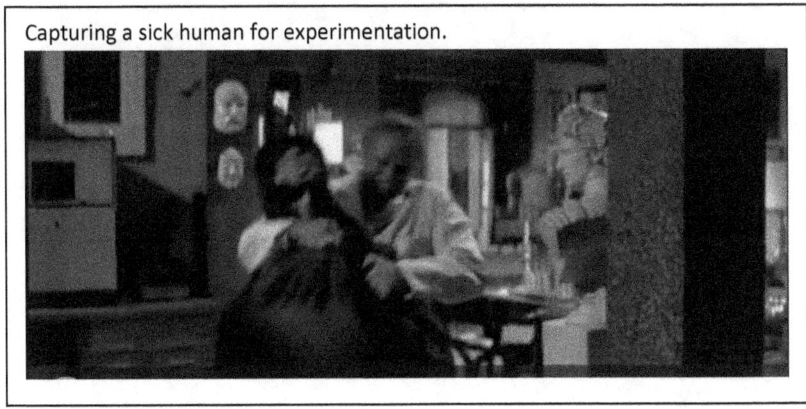
Capturing a sick human for experimentation.

Here, Col. Neville did not follow the Nuremberg Code of rights for human subjects, created to ensure that humans were never forcibly used for experimentation. In a post-apocalyptic trial should the rule of law be re-established, it is unlikely that anyone would have the political will to pursue Col Neville for a crimes against humanity trial given his good intentions.

Col. Neville's experiments continue with treating a sick patient who is in the "second stage" of the plague. Col. Neville uses his own blood to infuse him with his antibodies.

The young man he cures of the plague tries to persuade Col. Neville to treat the plague zombies with the blood serum to see if they can recover. Unfortunately, this starts a chain of events which pulls everyone into the wave of "the family" and all of Col. Neville's efforts to resist them fail when he his killed with ancient technology as Mathias throws a spear from the balcony of his own home at Col. Neville as he stands in the water fountain. He lives just long enough to give his bottle of serum to the young medical student who is taken the children away from the city to start again, "like the Garden of Eden."

They are going to need a Constitution and a Bill of Rights as soon as they get organized enough to begin trading with each other.

Virus (1980) Japan

RATING

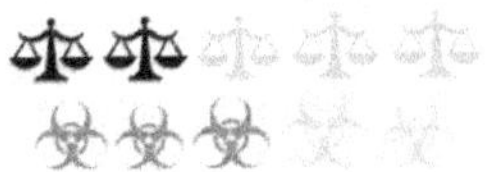

[Upon surveying the skeletal remains of the Japanese people from the virus via telescope from the safety of their submarine.]

Sargent
The Japanese appear to have licked their smog problem.

Captain
That will be quite enough, Sargent.

---*Virus* (1980) Japan

Virus (1980) with a second title, *Day of Resurrection*, is based on a science fiction novel by Sakyo Komatsu. The film is a long 2 hours and 50 minutes in the English version, although long scenes are in Japanese without subtitles.

The plot is based on the release of a stolen biological weapon, MM88, when the helicopter carrying it crashes into a mountain. The virus container shatters, causing the virus to be released. Predictably, it eventually kills most of the world's population. This movie is noted for being the most expensive film made in Japan to this time in 1980.

The MM88 was stolen by underground criminals but their helicopter crashed in the snowy mountains. The camera zoomed in on the broken vial of the doomsday virus, MM88 that broke on the snow.

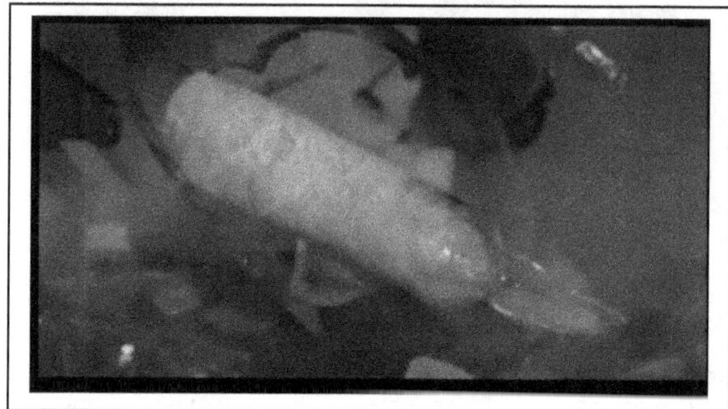

Meanwhile, back in the military, the military scientist has a confrontation with the scientist they have asked to work on the vaccine for MM88. They told him that it was necessary to develop a vaccine because it had been stolen. However, it argues that he believes they are keeping it as a weapon, but Col. Rankin shows him the newspaper and says they need it because the Soviets have installed the same defense system and bioweapons are all we have.

Dr. Myer, Scientist

There's not a vaccine in the world that can stop it. Not likely to be one either. . .I'm scared to death of this thing.
It's not just a vaccine you want to develop from this little monster of ours, is it?

Col Rankin

I don't know what you are talking about.

Dr. Myer, Scientist

I know how the system works!
Develop a part of the weapon here, another part over there --- the trigger someplace else again and nobody knows what the hell they are working on until it is all put together!

Col. Rankin then discovered a fax on his fax machine that disclosed his scientist was about to leak this information to the Senate Defense Oversight Committee. So the Colonel ordered a "routine medical examination" that afternoon for the scientist. The screenshot below shows the scene at the medical examination where the scientist is being taken away as he is shouting that he is not crazy.

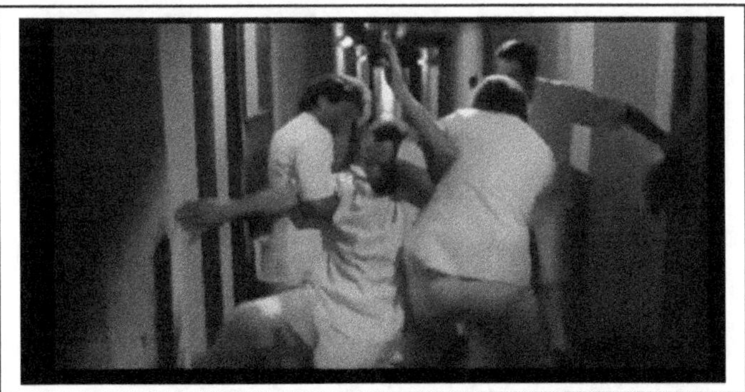

Meanwhile, the virus which escaped in the snowy mountains is affecting populations in Japan. The Japanese are panicked and a scene where mothers are holding their babies trying to get medical treatment at a hospital shows the widespread panic only thirty minutes into the movie.

The panic spreads around the world and the cabin and President are watching the television coverage. This is a scene in Japan. HHS might have been in a better position to develop a vaccine had they not had their budget slashed from Congress. Another member is astonished that what they are giving the public is not a public. The dialogue in the Oval Office proceeded as follows:

Pres Richardson

What vaccine?
Alright, how long will it take to manufacture this vaccine in quantity?

DHHS Secretary

Mr P we have not even been able to isolate the cause. The virus—if it is a virus ---it's like the common cold. It is everywhere, it is nowhere.

U.S. Senator, Robert Vaughn

I would like to say at this point, Mr. Presidenet that HHS might have been in a better position to develop the crash program if its budget hadn't been slashed against the specific wishes of Congress.

Pres Richardson

Damn it Senator I don't have to hear that from you.

Cabinet member

What do you mean? There is no vaccine? Then what is it we are giving the police and fire department personnel? The essential services, the military alert crew Its just that we don't have enough for the general populace - that's right? Isn't that right?

Secretary

We have a vaccine of sorts. We put together a soup of every flu vaccine we know. Its effect leaves something to be desired. In fact, it is more of a placebo.

President Richardson

You gave me a goddamn placebo?!

The cabin members and the Joint Chief of Staff comes into the room and announces that all evidence points to only one enemy. Then the red phone rings form the Kremlin. The message to the President was that the Soviet "Chief of State" died this morning, dashing their suspicions of the Soviets as the perpetrators of a bioweapons attack. It is being called the "Italian Flu."

Then it is revealed that "Operation Phoenix" is a paper study about bioweapons attacks. It was a top secret biological weapon system study and it was claimed to be a theoretical study, but then in the Oval office, the truth is revealed. Col. Rankin is called in because it was his project, but he claims it was a failure and never worked. The scientist who had been put into the mental institution, Dr. Myer, was found by the Senator and took him out. Col. Rankin was fired on the spot. The President asks the scientist whether the virus is actually MM88. The scientist replies, "Im sure of it, sir." The scientist urges the President to involve all the scientists around the world, but the President refuses and wants to keep it top secret. Another call interrupts their meeting and he learns that his wife is infected.

The next scenes are focused on the Japanese couple. The wife, a nurse is in Japan fighting the epidemic while her husband was serving in a submarine. Very few people are left.

The President is lamenting that they may be seeing their last sunset. The Senator mumbles, the quote, "Those that cannot remember the past are condemned to repeat it—those of us who can." This is a clear reference to the arms race of the Cold War, still unway in 1980. The President wanted his name in the history books for something "meaningful – something lasting." The President has a heartfelt conversation with the Senator.

President

What could I have done to make the slightest damned bit of difference?

Senator

Maybe it will snow?
. . .might give us a little more time.

President

How?

Senator

"Myers said that the virus remains dormant in cold temperatures.

President

Well it's not going to snow, Senator.

Everyone is coughing, the Senator is coughing and about to die. He recommends that the President and his staff fly to Palmer Station in Antarctica where they can survive. "The government must continue," were the Senator's last words.

Admiral Conway at Palmer Station responds to the President and he reports that the illness is in Antarctica. The President dies of a heart attack at this desk.

The General demands that the President activate the "ARF" system which is the missle defense system of the United States, in this movie, aimed directly at only the Soviet Union. Right before he dies, the President says, "You are a fool, General. There is no one left."

One hour into the movie, the President is dead.

Wild laughter follows the activation of the ARF system by the General.

Meanwhile, up at the Palmer Station, the survivors from all nations represented by nations with stations in Antarctica have convened their own cabin led by the Admiral. Chaos breaks out.

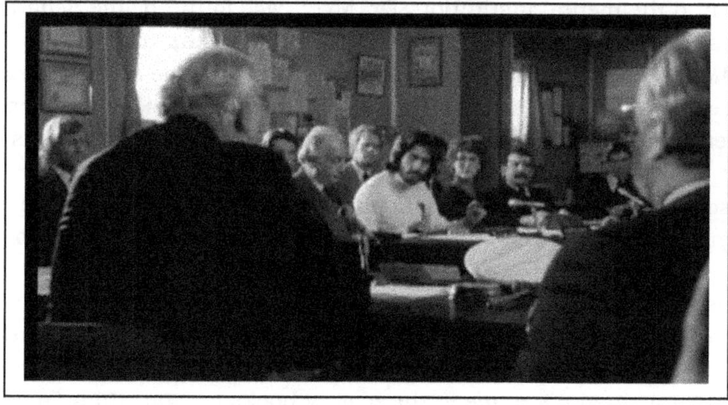

An American breaks up the chaos when he walks in with a gun and gives it to them to use on each other.

The problems of forming a new society are before the new "council." For the first order of business they congratulate the arrival of a new baby and offer to be the godparents for the baby. The next issue is that a woman comes before the council and complains that they have to stop the rapes. Without a better solution, she declares that they are the most important natural resources and they will have to accommodate more than one man. She urges everyone to "suppress their instincts....but can we?" she asks.

Then they receive a distress signal from the submarine and they disclose they have personnel sick with Italian Flu. They are refused permission to land by the Federation of the Supreme Council, Chair, American Admiral. The Soviet physician joins the conversation and tells the submarine they cannot land due to the fear of infection. The British submarine intervenes in the communication, Capt. McCloud, who is the defense submarine commander. He volunteers to blow up the submarine if it attempts to land. They attempt to land and the British submarine blows up the Soviet submarine. Capt. McCloud certifies that they have no Italian Flu on board, and they are invited to join the Federation of the Supreme Council in Antarctica.

The movie offers geat cinematography of Antarctica, the missle attack and submarines. But the most touching and bone-chilling longshot is the view of the last community on earth.

But the most telling statement was at the Christmas party of the inhabitants which the British Admiral remarks that he doesn't know if it was a mistake to allow him to bring that vial of virus here. Dr. Latour is working on the vaccine.

As the Christmas party unfolds, the viewers observe that the old traditional "secret Santa" game where a present would come from a surprise giver. Except in this game, it involved opening up an envelope to see which woman the man receives to impregnant as they try to repopulate the world.

The next scene is concern over some work done by one of the geologists who believe there is an earthquake that is a month away from happening on the east coast of the United States. The activation of the "ARS" which was triggered by the General right before everyone died. The British Admiral confirmed they had heard the signal setting the system since they cooperate. The Soviet General also confessed that they had constructed a defense system to strike Palmer Station if the U.S. set off the ARS which would strike the Soviet Union.

"How long will our past haunt us?" was asked by the Chair of the Council.

They determine that someone must go to Washington and disarm the ARS. They use a playing card drawing system in the General's hat to determine who must go. I assumed the cowboy with a Texas accent, Major Carter, would pick the "lucky" card, but instead, he dumped the cards out of the hat and just volunteered. The Japanese scientist volunteered to go with him, and not surprisingly, the American rejected his offer.

Dr. Latour offers the vaccine that he has created by introducing radiation to human cells making a vaccine against the Italian Flu. He instructed them not to inject themselves until right before they leave the submarine in Washington, D.C. And if they have symptoms and it doesn't work, they should report what happens to them --- as long as they can. At the two hour mark in the movie, the submarine sets off from Antarctica to Washington, D.C..

Upon reaching the shores of the United States they inject themselves with the vaccine. Since vaccines work by making the body produce antibodies to the virus, it is unclear why the scientist who developed the vaccine would have wanted them to wait until they arrived in Washingotn, D.C. to inject themselves. The pair doned SCUBA gear and left the submarine. They ran toward the Oval office. It was refreshing not to have the obligatory infected zombies consistently used in movies in the last decade. They made it to the White House without seeing another human being and that may be more terrorizing than any number of zombies at a deeper level of fear. The earthquake begins to hit as they are looking through the White House. Colonel Carter is smashed by a heavy shelf, and the Japanese scientist is forced to leave him there. He makes it to the room with the ARS and amazingly the map and all the lights are still working. He tries to disable the ARS system as it is activated but he watches the missles disengage from their silos on the screens. Major Carter frees himself and struggles to the room, still in shock. The Japanese scientist tells him it is too late.

Then the missles are seen striking the Soviet Union and shortly thereafter the mushroom clouds arise over Washington, D.C. Then we see the implosion of the Palmer Station and the Federation.

Somehow the Japanese scientist survives and is depicted as the last man on earth in this dramatic scene. He wanders toward the north.

Then we see the survivors of the Palmer Station are alive four years later. The scientist who developed the vaccine credits their survival to the vaccine (although it is not clear that they have encountered anyone with the virus). The women are tired and one of the children has died. They are immoralized. But Olivia Hussey walks outside and sees that her love, the Japanese scientist has returned, having walked all the way to Antarctica from Washington, D.C.

The theme song with lyrics, "It's not to late to start over," plays as the credits role over the bleak landscape of ice and blue in Antarctica.

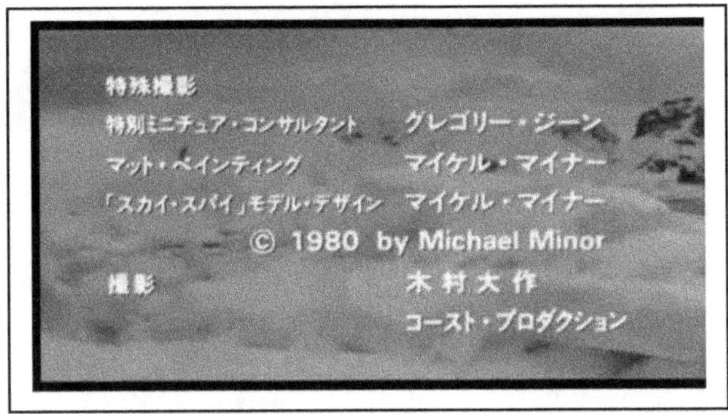

This entire plot would have been unnecessary if the transporters of the virus in the opening scenes had used approved packaging for an infectious disease. This kind of packaging requires triple packing the vial, first in one box and then that box is placed in a second. The vials would be secured in another container before being placed in the first box and padding would be wrapped around that container as well. This packaging is designed to withstand a nine meter drop.

The shipment of infectious substances is regulated by non-governmental organizations, ICAO (International Civil Aviation Organization) and IATA (International Air Transport Association), who develop consensus regulations for the requirements to ship these materials safely. ICAO governs the international transport of dangerous goods or hazardous materials by air, and with IATA they have developed the document, IATA *Dangerous Goods Regulations* which combines additional industry standards with shipping requirements.

The criminals who stole the virus would not be concerned about violated the law, but they should be concerned about safe shipping. The section that applies to shipping containers and labeling requirements is Division 6.2 and reads as follows. The biological material in this case would be a "Category A" material.

Division 6.2 Infectious Substance:
A material known or reasonably expected to contain a pathogen, such as bacteria, viruses, rickettsiae, parasites, fungi or prions, that can cause disease in humans or animals.
Category A An infectious substance transported in a form capable of causing permanent disability or life-threatening or fatal disease in otherwise healthy humans or animals when exposure occurs.
Category B An infectious substance not in a form capable of causing permanent disability or life- threatening or fatal disease in otherwise healthy humans or animals when exposure occurs.

The requirement to package the material in triple containment is shown in this diagram.

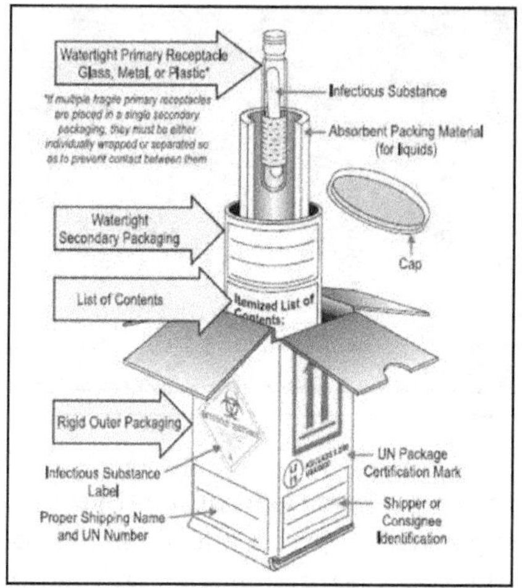

But the theme for the movie was clearly the threat of our national security policy of MAD – mutually assured destruction. With missles poised to be launched if one of the two super powers launched first, was the best deterrent during the Cold War.

One incident which has become public was the near miss nuclear war that almost occurred. It was on September 26, 1983 when the Soviet early warning system reported that the United States had launched an attack of American Minuteman ICBMs. The officer in charge at the time, Stanislav Yevgrafovich Petrov, an officer of the Soviet Air Defense Force, made a decision not to retaliate and launch Soviet missles first investigating to see if this was a malfunction. He had only minutes to decide. He was correct and were it not for his thoughtful decisionmaking process, a nuclear war could have been launched. This was three years after the release of Virus (1980) – a vision that should make anyone hesitate in triggering the MAD strategy.

Warning Sign (1985)

RATING

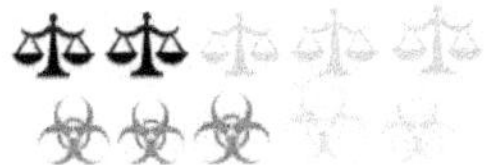

Sheriff
Wait a minute, I'm the civil authority in this county.

Mike Connelly
I know. This is government property.

---*Warning Sign* (1985)

Warning Sign (1985) is set in a biological research laboratory, a private company called Biotek, which is really involved in the development of bioweapons against agriculture. The plot is built around the accidental release of one of their bioweapons inside the laboratory. This movie fit squarely in the biohorror, biothriller subgenre and is quite a bit of an update in technology for biocontainment from the 1971 *Andromeda Strain,* the previous movie in this chronological tour.

This movie could be used as a demonstration film of bad practices in biosafety. The viewers are presented with one common sense violation of biocontainment after the other. Where are their training records?

While working inside the highest biocontainment level, evident by their full biosuits and air lines, they lift their face shields because the photographer can't see their faces. The leader assures everyone that it is safe and he holds up a vial for the camera. At least he is still wearing his safety gloves.

While going through the shower with his biosuit on, which is the normal protocol for leaving a biological safety laboratory (BSL) room, he takes his contacts out in the shower and puts them on his contaminated gloves and reinserts them into his eyes. One would have to wonder how he ever became a microbiologist!

After the photo, the closeup on the vial which is crushed by one of the scientist's boots

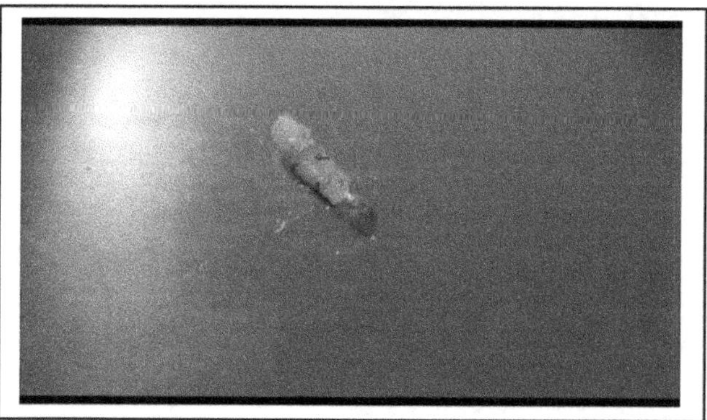

When the alarm goes off that there has been a contamination incident, the security guard who is the wife of the Sheriff, activates Protocol One, which is a lockdown of the facility. The lockdown appears to be ribbons of incident tape that falls from a doorway as you see in this frameshot.

When the sheriff took off to find the scientist who had left the company, Dr. Dan Fairchild, to help out with the disaster back at the lab, he discovered that they were not just growing genetically engineered plants, they were creating bioweapons.

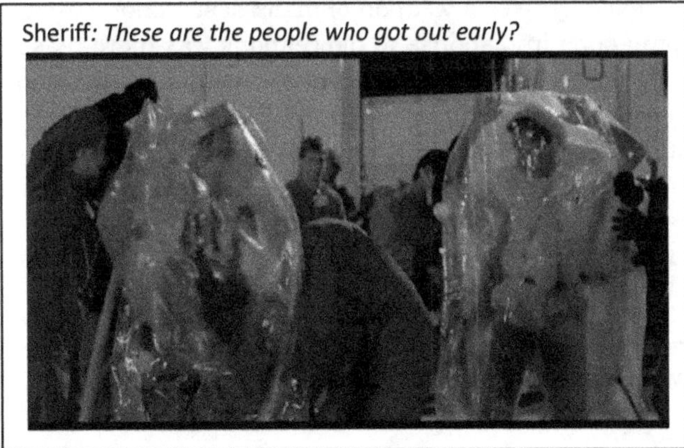

Sheriff: *These are the people who got out early?*

Major Connolly cautioned his investigators, "The bug is virulent. 80% mortality rate." The decontamination team of eight people go into the laboratory and discovery nightmarish zombie-like survivors who hack them all to death with an ax. The BioTek spokesperson reports that they have news that there are a few low level human infections.

At one point this dialogue reveals the BioTek position on the work being done there:

Dr. Fairchild
[speaking to the Sheriff]
Why are you limping?

Sheriff
[embarrassed]
Polio. I had polio.

Dr. Fairchild
I knew you had a thing about germs.

Sheriff
No I don't! I don't think we have any business fighting wars with them.

Major Connolly
It's called deterrence-in-kind.
What do you want us to do?
Start a nuclear holocaust if the Soviets infect us?
We need the proper reply.

When the United States announced the end of the bioweapons program in 1969 and signed the Biological Weapons and Toxins Treaty of 1972, effective in 1975, the end of our "in-kind" response with bioweapons came to an end, based on two ethical aspects of war. There is an ethics of war, and the first principle in this context is that you cannot use a weapon that will kill civilians in a disproportionate way with the military objective. Because bioweapons are indiscriminate and uncontrollable once released you can never assure that this will not happen, so bioweapons are by definition, ethically prohibited. The in-kind response is also by definition prohibited if we are attacked with bioweapons. And yes, Major Connolly, we would response with nuclear weapons because of our MAD policy – mutually assured destruction --- if one party uses a weapon of mass destruction. Major Connolly seemed to believe that bioweapons in response to bioweapons was more reasonable than a nuclear bomb response, but it is not at all clear that this would reduce human suffering. Actually, when President Nixon was asked by William Safire who was drafting his renunciation speech whether they should retain some biological weapons for deterrent effect, President Nixon replied, "We'll never use the germs, so what good is biological warfare as a deterrent? If somebody uses germs on us, we'll nuke 'em."[29]

Later, Dr. Dan Fairchild returns to help his friend the sheriff who has saved him from more than one drunk driving ticket. Here, in this frameshot, he shows the Sheriff the

---

[29] William Safire, "On Language: Weapons of Mass Destruction," The New York Times Magazine, April 19, 1998, p. 2, quoted in David Hoffman, The Dead Hand, fn 45, p. 124 (2009).

front page reporting what he calls "the lies that are being told" by the company. The headlines read, "Yeast mishap quarantines 85."

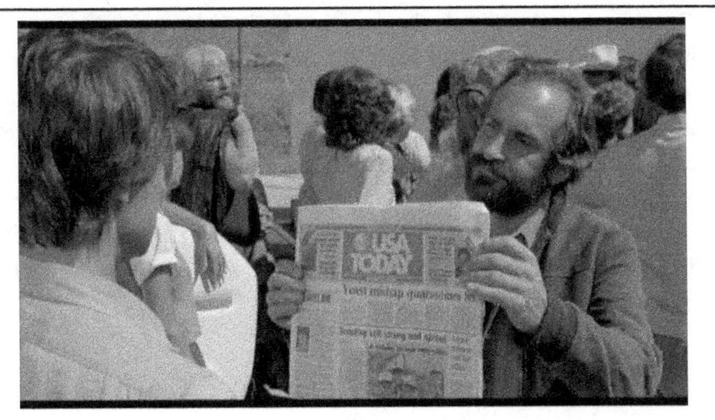

But it is not yeast. The bioweapon called *bacillus luminescence* is conveniently visible on its victims under a light that shows its luminescence. After realizing that the company intended to let the disease runs its course and just let people die inside, the Sheriff and Dr. Fairchild decide to break in. The Sheriff has to overcome his fear of germs to enter the laboratory which he does when he realizes they are being pursued.

Once inside the Sheriff finds his wife, the security guard, but they also encounter the many scientists inside who have succumbed to *baccillus luminescence* and are now zombies in a rage, the purpose of the bioweapon. Dr. Fairchild's biosuit is ripped and he is exposed to the disease which causes a major rush to find the anti-toxin. He experiments with a cocktail of drugs that fortunately work on him. The Sheriff who is horrified of germs also becomes infected but is also saved by the anti-toxin.

Many scientists and workers were killed inside the laboratory, once all the damage is assessed. Because BioTek is a private company doing business as a contractor for the military, they are probably strictly liable for the injuries, deaths and damage because they are working with what the law would define as "ultra-hazardous" materials. This would make any accident they had, predictable in the law. The law suits against the company for negligence and wrongful death would likely put the company into bankruptcy. The fact that they may have been working as a government contractor is almost always not a defense to liability, even if they were following the government formula.

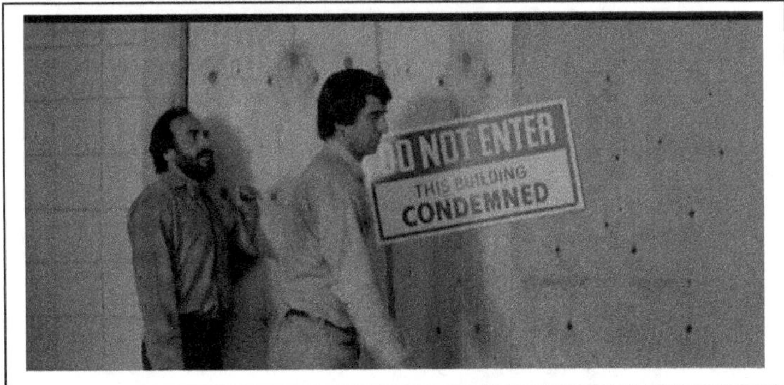

This movie is another in a line of laboratory accident scenarios which are built on the fear of what might be the residuals of the bioweapons program of the United States. Interestingly, at the time of the release of the movie in 1985, we were merely suspicious that the U.S.S.R. was engaged in a bioweapons program, and they had signed the Biological Weapons and Toxins Convention the same day as the United States. Major Connolly's statement that the Soviets might poison us with bioweapons was very unpredictable in 1985. While the Soviets had a group of anthrax deaths, they explained it away and only a handful of people remained skeptical. It was not until 1991 when the U.S.S.R. came to an end, that we discovered the extensive bioweapons program in the U.S.S.R..

Major Connolly was certainly right to be concerned about the Soviets in 1985, but his in-kind-deterrence was prohibited in the Geneva Protocol of 1925, when it prohibited nations from responding to biological attacks in-kind. Certainly, President Nixon would have retaliated with "nuc's".

Epidemic (1987)

RATING

THEME SONG
(play with roll credits)

The end is near, the plague is here.
We all fall down - EPIDEMIC.
We all fall down -EPIDEMIC.

---*Epidemic* (1987)

Epidemic (1987) is a very arty film that is a story within a story. A group of writers who are writing about an epidemic in Europe begin to confuse their fictional story with reality. In an interview by Mark Kermode of Lars von Trier, director and co-writer of *Epidemic (1987),* he says, "Lars seldom leaves Denmark due to a bizarre assortment of phobias and anxieties."[30] Who better to write a biohorror movie?

There are only 21 scenes in this movie of 106 minutes, where maybe 60 scenes would be normal for a movie of this length. The camera techniques described in the press kit employee "pan and tilt" with "other parallel camera movements" giving it an unedited but free flowing feel, twenty years before we saw *Paranormal Activity (2007)* using similar home video techniques.

1. Day One
2. Rewriting
3. The Red Death
4. Library Research
5. Doctors and King Rats
6. Day Two
7. Story Line
8. The Wine Expert
9. Helicopter ride
10. Day Three: Germany
11. Toothpaste
12. Udo Tells a Story
13. The Priest
14. Day Four: The Hospital
15. Autopay
16. Bodies in Water
17. Day Five: The Girls From Atlantic City
18. Twelve Pages?
19. It's Pathetic at Best
20. Mesmerized, Part 1
21. Mesmerized, Part 2

The entire movie takes place over five days, and the subject of the movie is triggered by a disastrous loss of their screenplay, "The Cop and the Whore," a work of 215 pages, as he describes to presumably his producer on the telephone. When they realize they can't recover their file on their floppy disk, a plastic thin sheet of magnetized material that was used for a memory storage device in the 1980s, they face trying to recreate it.

In the second scene, Lars, the actor playing Lars the screenwriter, says "I would like it if we wrote something more dynamic" to which his co-writer Niels, the actor playing Niels the screenwriter, types the words "Epidemic" onto the paper in his typewriter.

---

[30] Lars von Trier interviewed by Mark Kermode on The Culture Show http://youtu.be/Mav_WGpOLdU (date unknown).

In the scene four, the writers are doing research and the librarian is lecturing on the atmosphere around the 1348 great Black Plague. He tells of the Priest Visconti who ordered the families with plague, bricked into their homes to starve and die. In this way, the librarian says, Milan avoided the plague. They find the death certificate of Dr. Mesmer, the physician who created the concept of "mesmerism".

In the scene five, called "Doctors and King Rats," begins the story about Dr. Mesmer who wants permission to go into the "infected areas" but his Chair of the "Crisis Commission" does not want to grant him his request. His colleagues tell him about the symptoms and the infection source from the air and from the water. The letter to the Chair tells him that the government has decided to withdraw from managing the epidemic and has asked the Chair of the Crisis Commission to form a "provisional government". Dr. Aim is given this power in the letter from the Prime Minister. All the doctors proceed to name their friends to the cabinet of this new provisional government.

Every government should have a Continuity of Government (COG) plan which would include the setting up of a provisional government. The delegation of the work of setting up a provisional government to the Crisis Commission suggests that the doctors as the ruling plutocracy or technocracy will be the provisional government, themselves.

He refers to the King Rat theory, that of rats who have their tails entangled and they eventually starved to death. The King Rat theory is an omen of a plague to come, and this is supported by the discover of the five rats tied together from the past. A few days ago, the Chair relates that a King Rat tangle of seven rats was discovered ---an omen of an epidemic.

In scene seven, "Story line" they draw the timeline on the wall as well as places.

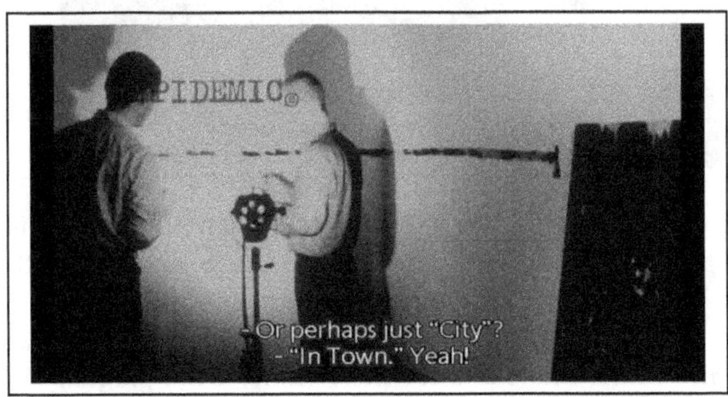

They explain it is a bacteria that is approaching with strains of the Wagner overture, *Tannhauser.* That the disease will move beyond the city because the infection will be carried in the doctor's bag.

Scene eight, "The Wine Expert" is a strange deviation from the development of the story as they sit around drinking wine and discussing its bouquet with their guest, the wine expert. Their wine expert recommends white wines, Puligny-Montrachet or a Meursault Santenots. So the conversation turns to a plague that attacked grapevines in France a few hundred years ago.

The next scene, scene nine, "Helicopter Ride", the doctor appears to be floating with a medical flag on a rope with his doctor's bag, but he is hanging from a rope from the helicopter. He approaches a house with the cross symbol indicating someone has the plague inside.

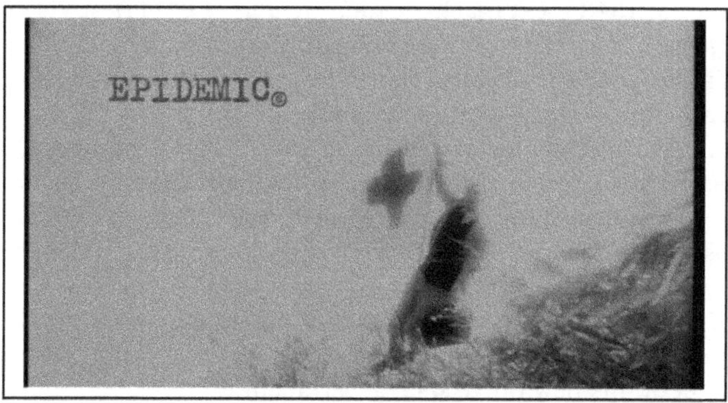

The next scene, "Day Three: Germany" is a trip to Germany for the writers, with a penchant for typing in the car—both driver and passenger.

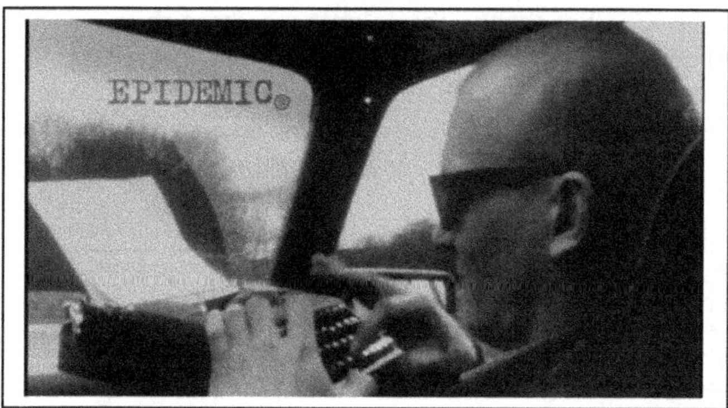

They talk about their character, Dr. Mesmer who is on his way to disease-ravaged Europe. They plan out their story of the epidemic and want to structure a theologian so that they can "poke fun at religion, and the educational system as well." This is a bit of humor they hope to use in this tragedy. Niels, Lars co-author, wants to make Dr. Mesmer's wife the victim of being buried alive in the haste to bury the victims of the plague. The next scene shows her trapped in a coffin buried underground, trying to get out.

Despite the name "Epidemic" the writers have the plague spread globally in just a few hours, which would meet the definition of a "pandemic." Epidemic is more regionalized and contained. They name the disease "DIN."

Then in the scene entitled, "Toothpaste," they play out their earlier discussion of stripes coming out of a boil that never mixed their colors. They found some "Signal" toothpaste which they identify is the kind of toothpaste that would typify the boil. They dissect the toothpaste tube and find its "secret" as they say.

In scene thirteen, "The Priest," he talks to the physician about his abbreviated education during the epidemic when education is shortened due to their shortened lives. He studied for two days to become a priest. He has to invent rituals, which he does when they find a piece of wreckage in the water. The Priest is truck with the plague and the physician gives him an injection which presumably saves him.

In scene fourteen, "The Hospital," Lars goes to find his co-author who had a surgery he had "completely forgotten about." Lars goes to see the pathologist in the hospital to discuss their story and to see an autopsy.

Scene fifteen is predictably, "Autopsy." They discuss the growing number of cases with their strange symptoms in the lymph nodes. "We don't usually do autopsies wearing masks and gloves," the pathologist says because this is something unknown. (They have no eye protection unless they are wearing regular glasses, risking a splash in the eye which would cause an infection.)

Scene sixteen, is the most bizarre with people standing in water while the Priest prays then screams. He seems to be praying for the infected areas of the city.

Scene seventeen, "Day Five: The Girls from Atlantic City," seems disconnected from the story and is more about the process of writing. Niels, the actor, pretended to be sixteen and solicited young girls in Atlantic City so that he could learn about the city for writing about it. He was modeling this plan after Kafka who got his information from his uncle, who lived in America.

Scene eighteen, "Twelve pages," where he presents his producer with twelve pages, generates a question that this is all you have done for one and half years? They have invested a lot of money in the project and he explains that the board which runs the film industry in Denmark, requires a script of at least 150 pages, the producer tells Lars.

Scene nineteen, entitled "Its Pathetic at Best," is the remark the producer makes as Lars gives him the ending of the film. The ending is the doctor realizes that he is the carrier of the disease when everyone around him dies and he gives thanks to God for the life that once was. He continues, "I am worried."

Scenes twenty and twenty-one, "Mesmerized, Parts 1 and 2", finish the movie. The producer tries to salvage what he has to work with and compares it to Camus's story about a writer who wrote the same line about a horse coming down the boulevard for years.

The scenes are dark and shadowy as the other guests arrive for their dinner. The dinner guest is a hypnotist with his patient, and he proceeds to hyptotize her to the delight of the other guests. He asks her to enter the film, Epidemic. She says the people look terrible and they are screaming. She is distressed as she continues to describe the scenes in the movie much like the movie has already described.

The girl who is hypnotized grows more hysterical, screaming and will not listen to her hypnotist to come out of the film. Instead, she deteriorates, eventually manifesting signs of the disease which become huge boils on her neck as seen in the next screenshot.

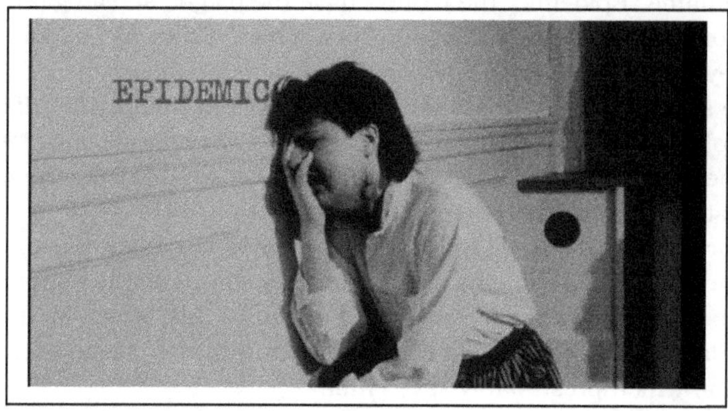

Everyone at the dinner party is affected, and several seem to succumb to the disease. Lars is left in a catatonic star sitting on the floor as the film ends.

With the rolling credits, the closing music lyrics are, "The end is near, the plague is here." The repeating chorus is taken from the legend of the nursery rhyme that is said to have been passed down from the days of the Black Plague, "We all fall down – Epidemic. We all fall down --- Epidemic."

The artistic blending of the fictional epidemic with the manifestation of the disease in the writers and everyone around them may express one of the persistent problems that in reality are problematic in treating a widespread epidemic. The phenomena is known as the "worried well." With excessive talk and fear about an epidemic, people may imagine any symptom to be indicative of the beginning of the dreadful disease, whatever it might be. This leads to overcrowding in emergency rooms and exposing people to sickness by going to emergency rooms when it is unnecessary to take the risk. In this movie, the worried well ultimately generated the symptoms, but in reality the worried well, do not manifest any symptoms at all related to the epidemic disease.

While the world that was created for their film was one of fantasy, the ideas of the worried well, death all around, suffering of children and dying neighbors, marks on houses identifying the sick, the formation of a provisional government, all are elements of a film in the biohorror subgenre.

Quarantine (1989)

RATING

Senator Ford
[on a television screen]

Declare war on bacteria!

---*Quarantine* (1989)

Quarantine (1989), not to be confused with *Quarantine* (2009) or *Quarantine 2* (2011), depicts an America in the year 2000 where a massive quarantine is implemented by the Congress in response to a devastating epidemic. People live in fear of being determined to be "infected" from their routine tests and put into quarantine. The plot of the fear of quarantine drives the action and the characters throughout this movie. For this reason, *Quarantine* (2009) makes the biohorror, biothriller List.

It is unclear what the symptoms of the disease might be because it does not really matter. It is not clear what started the epidemic because that no longer matters. No signs of the disease are needed to quarantine an individual, only that they are determined to be "high risk" by the Quarantine Commission or that their "test" shows they are "infected." While the Commission is made up of several members, it is Senator Ford who presides over the "hearings". The hearing procedure is so fast that the defendants never slow down on the literal conveyor belt that brings them across the room in front of Senator Ford's podium. Each of the individuals are standing on a conveyor belt which passes in front of the podium and Senator Ford makes a judgment: "high risk", "quarantine." Those are the only rulings he makes.

This frameshot is the hearing procedure in front o f the Quarantine Commission and Senator Ford, played by Jerry Wasserman, is standing at the podium giving his judgments.

In one trial, Sen. Ford has ordered the arrest of "Dr. Jim" who has been running illegal clinics for the infected, which is against the quarantine law according to Senator Ford. Dr. Jim's daughter has already tried to assassinate Senator Ford, but astonishingly with all their advanced identification and tracking equipment they do not know that the girl they identified as the would-be-assassin is the daughter of Dr. Jim. In the middle of the trial, Spencer, a bright, young computer software engineer who is programming software to replace the police force, has been forced to cooperate at gun point by Dr. Jim's daughter, but he also seems to be sympathetic with her. Spencer interrupts the trial and asks Senator Ford to delay the hearing because he has something very interesting. Senator Ford, seeing Spencer as his computer programming wonder boy, agrees to do as Spencer asks over the objection of the police chief, Captain Beck. A conflict between Spencer and Captain Beck is escalated and Beck wants to find a way to eliminate Spencer.

In this frameshot, individuals are arrested and taken from their homes to presumptively have a hearing as to whether they will be quarantined or as a result of their tests being positive. The defendants are not allowed to present any evidence, but simply stand on the conveyor belt as they glide past the podium where Senator Ford makes a judgment.

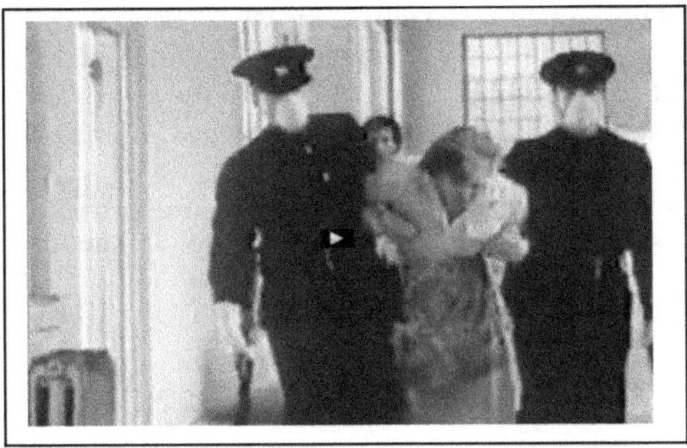

The U.S. Constitution, 5th and 14th Amendments quarantees due process for any deprivation of property or liberty and the highest standard of due process is required for deprivation of liberty. The U.S. Constitution 6th Amendment quarantees the right of counsel,, but only for criminal cases, not civil detentions, so in the case of quarantine, the 6th Amendment does not guarantee counsel, even though it is a deprivation of liberty. However, some states through their state constitutions have provided for the right to counsel even in a civil hearing in addition to criminal proceedings.

In this movie, there is no attorney because this is a Congressional hearing and the procedure does not comply with judicial procedural due process, because the Congress typically does not deprive individuals of liberty on civil matters. However, if individuals are subpoenaed to appear before the Quarantine Commission, then if they failed to show, this would be a contempt of Congress criminal matter if the committee certified it as such. The U.S. Attorney for the District of Columbia must then order the empanelment of a grand jury to determine whether to move forward and indict the individual in a criminal proceeding of Contempt of Congress. Only then, after the Grand Jury, would a defendant have the right to an attorney in this criminal matter. This would seem to be a much better alternative to the conveyor belt justice, but apparently this system may have very well been done away with in this new order, as well as normal procedural due process.

Spencer is also having an affair with Senator Ford's wife complicating his conflict with Captain Beck who attempts to catch them in the act, only to end up with a dead Senator's wife. Spencer and Dr. Jim's daughter escape into the night. The society is filled with a subclass of "refugees" escaping from the quarantine which exists around open campfires and wrecked automobiles.

Spencer is still needed by Senator Ford to build the ultimate computer that will replace the police force, so when he returns with Dr. Jim's daughter, they have a brief tense meeting, but then the Senator allows Spencer to go to work on his computer. From there, we see unfold Spencer's sinister plan to program in data that it is Senator Ford's test that is positive as infected. Within minutes the police force appear to escort him away as he shouts in protest. Senator Ford is placed on the conveyor belt before an empty Senate chamber as he babbles about cleanliness and happiness.

But Senator Ford's removal as Chair just means he is replaced by Senator Campbell as the Chair who announces that it is day 1,846 of the quarantine, and the viewers realize that the quarantine is likely to never end in this new society.

The U.S. Constitution contemplated situations where deprivations of freedom with no certainty to their term might occur, and for that, the writ of *habeus corpus* was created. Meaning in latin, literally to "have the body" brought before the court to adjudge whether they should be held. If this provision were available, those quarantined by the Senate would at have another avenue to gain their freedom.

Quarantine (2009) showed the consequences of a quarantine without any basis in science (as one individual shouted out from the conveyor belt), without any constraints on the deprivation of liberty, without procedural due process, without the right to counsel and without a right to appeal or even have the rare remedy of a writ of *habeus corpus*.

The Plague (La Peste) (1992)

RATING

Jean Tarrou
[being wheeled into ambulance] Cottard, what was it we were supposed to learn?

Cottard
That it will always come back.

----*La Peste (The Plague)* (1992)

La Peste (1992) is a movie set in Argentina and based on Albert Camus's classic book, *The Plague* (1947). It was written and directed by Luis Puenzo who changed the original book's location from Oran, Algeria to a fictitious "Oran in the south of South America." The story follows the course of a plague epidemic through the perspective of the doctor, Dr. Rieux, played by William Hurt, who struggles with his own dedication to his profession that challenges his beliefs about life and what he cannot control. This movie is an artful interpretation of the original classic book, in the existential tradition of dark and deliberate depictions of unfortunate turn of events. This film makes the List of the subgenre biohorror, biothriller, biodrama.

The movie opens with the early period of the plague. Rats are everywhere. A radio host interviews someone about rats being found in the Department of Public Health and laughs. A woman is caught on an elevator with a rat, and a sick rat, at that. Within the first ten minutes of the movie the city enters a citywide quarantine.

Public Health official

The Provincial government has been transferred to another city. The Governor is getting out this evening.
Oran is to be sealed off at midnight

Doctor Bernard Rieux

Has that been announced yet?

Public Health Official

Not yet. They need a few hours to station the troops.

The news crew which Dr. Rieux met at the airport when he put his wife on the flight to the capital for medical tests, are isolated in the city and so they decide to report on the plague. Martine Rambert, reporter from Paris stands at the end of the bridge that is blockaded in the quarantine to give her report. (This version of the movie is in English but she is giving her report in French so there are English subtitles.)

Martine actually tries to get out of the city to return to Paris, but each try fails. She is attracted to Dr. Rieux who professes to be there for nothing else than to help victims of the plague.

Dr. Rieux visits the quarantine center to find out why a mother of a dead daughter who died of the plague in her home is still in quarantine at the center. The mother has been held there long after her quarantine period has ended – one and a half months, Dr. Reiux tells the

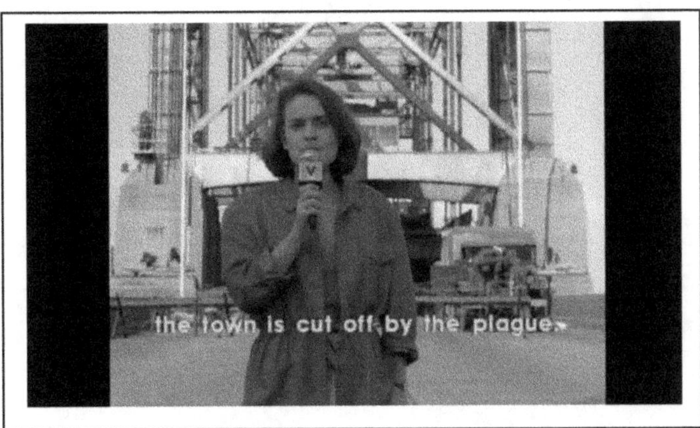

Director. The Director of the quarantine center asks if Dr. Rieux is challenging their decision and points out that he is the one who recommended isolation in the following dialogue:

Center director
You were the first to
support isolation.

Dr. Rieux
In their homes, not
in a concentration camp!

Center director
You're very naïve Reiux.
No one voluntarily
shuts himself away.

It is evident that the system of quarantining individuals has led to quarantining entire families presumptively based on their exposure inside the same residence as the plague victim. But after an established quarantine period which for plague due process would require they be released unless further public health need is indicated. The APHA manual on communicable diseases recommends a 7 day isolation period for someone in a household who has been exposed to a plague victim.[31] Placing all of the people together in the stadium ensured their exposure to others with the plague, putting individuals at risk.

[31] James Chin, ed., American Public Health Assoication, Control of Communicable Diseases Manual, 385 (2000).

The plague eventually causes the death of a little boy who his wife and mother had taught to sing. This, in addition to the news of the death of his wife the previous day, sends Dr. Reiux into a tormented rage.

A conversation between the Priest and Reiux contrasts two ways of dealing with the plague epidemic. Reiux 's way is fighting and as he says, the Priest's way is acceptance, which Reiux cannot do. The next scene is a confessional by the Priest as Reiux sits in the pews of the cathedral.

Priest

(in confession)

I accepted belief in everything
because my faith did not
allow me to deny anything.

Please forgive me.
I am simply a man. My faith
allowed me to forget anything
but not any longer.
I have made the only
decision a man can make.

The viewpoints in this movie are from the medical and religious and to a minor degree the government public health authorities who administer the quarantine and cause it to be enforced in the city or Oran. The dialogue between the priest and the physician juxtapose the acceptance of the plague against the fighting against the plague philosophies that each of them hold. This is in the context of what seems to be an out of control disease and an out of control governmental authority that has exceeded its authority out of either neglect, incompetence or incapacity to handle the massive numbers of people being quarantined, cremated and buried ---perhaps all three.

In 2009, Argentina experienced an epidemic of H1N1 in the outbreak that was first reported in Mexico. In 2009, the International Health Regulations were in effect and required any country with a disease that represented a Public Health Emergency of International Concern should be reported to the World Health Organization within 24 hours of making a determination. The World Health Organization declared a pandemic shortly thereafter, meaning it had spread globally based on a determination made by an expert panel at the WHO.

Argentina implemented a public health emergency and took steps to quarantine people who were sick, including providing a "sanatorium" for those who needed it. Schools were closed by the government and universities were urged to do the same. The government stopped short of ordering no public gatherings of people, and fortunately the epidemic began to subside and did not continue on the predicted trajectory of infections and deaths.

In *La Peste* (1947) the entire city was quarantined. No one was allowed to leave the city but people were allowed to come into the city, as Dr. Rieux's mother said when she appeared in Rieux's home to take care of him while his wife was away being treated. Could such a quarantine be used in Argentina? In the United States?

In the United States, each state government has quarantine power, confirmed by the U.S. Supreme Court in a case in the early 1800s. States also have to recognize the U.S. Constitutional due process and liberty interests of individuals and must balance that in any quarantine which burdens those freedoms. That means a quarantine would necessarily involve notice to an individual of the individual circumstances and reasons that they are being held, and for how long, and when they can appeal the decision at a later time. This does not fit as well in an area quarantine, because it is nearly impossible to have an individual hearing for each individual.

An area quarantine would have to have the same circumstances for every individual to make such a blanket determination affecting everyone based on their presence in a geographical area. But if it is determined that every person in that area should be isolated for the public health of the people outside the region then it may stand up to Constitutional scrutiny. Some states provide for a mass quarantine of a building or area for example for a very short time until a determination can be made about the public health's safety. But it is up to each state's determination on how they want to structure their quarantine and isolation laws.

In Argentina, similar quarantine measures would exist, as they have been a part of the international sanitary conferences since 1914 wherein countries in the Pan American Health Organization agreed to provide isolation and quarantine and notice of the existence of plague. But individual rights and due process may not be as carefully protected in the administration of constraints.

The end of the movie includes a quote from the book, in the dark grays that pervaded throughout the movie as the consequences became darker.

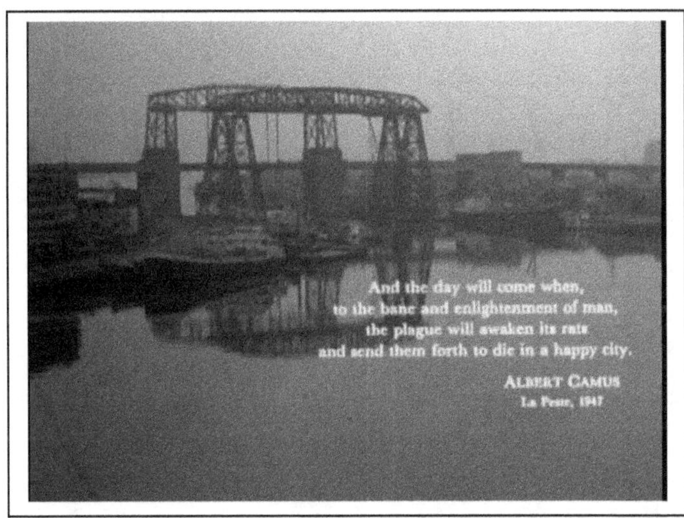

The return of the plague is probably as certain as the ending predicts, because plague does stay in mammals like cats and dogs and rats as reservoirs. In places like Oran, Algeria, the plague has emerged in several different centuries causing epidemics that ran their course much like the movie. But at some point, it may evolve to become more infectious or present a more difficult case to treat with antibiotics.

When the next plague occurs, the use of antibiotics is our frontline weapon. The APHA Manual recommends streptomycin as the drug of choice for the plague.[32] It is particularly effective if administered within 8-18 hours of the onset of the plague. Should we need a patented drug, the federal government has a statutory authority to obtain a license for the production of the drug or to set a price for it, although the U.S. has been reluctant to demand patent rights because of our political interest in the protection of patents and payment for intellectual property. Even during the anthrax attacks and the swell in need for Cephaloclor, which at the time was patented and required a license to make, the U.S. did not use its compulsory license authority, but instead negotiated with the pharmaceutical company on the price. Alternatives, gentamicin and tetracycline which are no longer patented could also be used for plague treatment, avoiding the patent issue.

The quarantine scenes of *La Peste* (1992) juxtaposed against later quarantine movies in the realism style like *Pandemic* (2007) and *Contagion* (2011) show how much the expansion of legal due process has changed our ideas about quarantine.

As Jean Tarrou is quoted as saying to Cottard in the opening of this discussion as he is being wheeled into an ambulance, "Cottard, what was it we were supposed to learn?" To which Cottard replied, "That it will always come back."

Indeed, what have we learned about the plague in the last seven hundred years? It seems it will remain the same answer for the foreseeable future, "It will always come back." We could also add, laws may change and science may change but human nature stays the same.

---

[32] James Chin, ed., American Public Health Association, Control of Communicable Diseases Manual, 385 (2000).

Black Death (1992)

RATING

Jake
What it is?

Dr. Nora Hart
It's the plague, Jake.
The Plague.

---*Black Death* (1992)

Black Death (1992) is a made-for-television movie, starring Kate Jackson, and depicts an outbreak of plague in New York City. Based on the book, *The Black Death (1978)* by Gwyneth Cravens and John S. Marr, this is the first movie in this subgenre to use realism both from the medical as well as the legal perspectives, to depict horrifying consequences. This movie is a biothriller and makes the List.

Diagnosis came with the first patient, the teenage girl who had returned from a family vacation to New York City. The test was a simple gram negative staining which showed the bacilli under the microscope. This screenshot shows the slide with the glass pipette used much like a straw to add reagent to the sample. The laboratory practice was frightening, because even under ordinary conditions, the technician should wear latex gloves. This laboratory technician was handling the slides with no gloves and no eye and face protection. Fortunately, this was not a setup for an accidental infection of the laboratory technician.

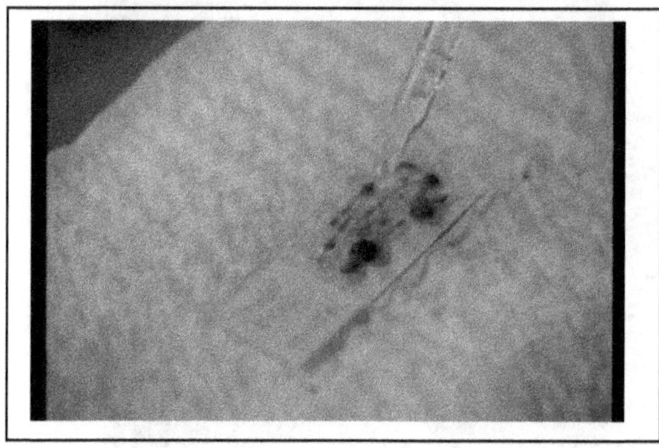

The next scene, the team dutifully packages up the samples to send to CDC for confirmation that they have identified the organism correctly, as yersinia pestis, or the common name, plague. Legally, federal law requires states to report the presence of certain diseases that are considered to "affect interstate commerce" which is the authority by which Congress can make such laws. Otherwise, all public health matters are within the scope of power belonging to the states, under state sovereignty.

The next screenshot is a very accurate and correct process of packaging the infectious substances for shipping to CDC. Airlines have their own regulations developed under the trade association IATA, which publishes the restrictions for shipments on each airline. There is no uniformity between airlines, so packaging, labeling and confirmation that the substance is allowed to be shipped on the particular airline is important. Because of this complicated set of rules, shipment companies often handle packages that must be shipped by air. The shipping regulations for infections substances were made federal law in 1996, with the Antiterrorism and Death Penalty Act for select agents, which is the designation given to a list of infectious agents that are more closely regulated by CDC. Later in 2006, the U.S. Department of Transportation assumed responsibility for shiptments of select agents and the law was re-codified under the U.S. Department of Transportation law. Specific procedures including completing an EA-101 form for every shipment, which requires notification to CDC both before shipment and after receipt of the package.

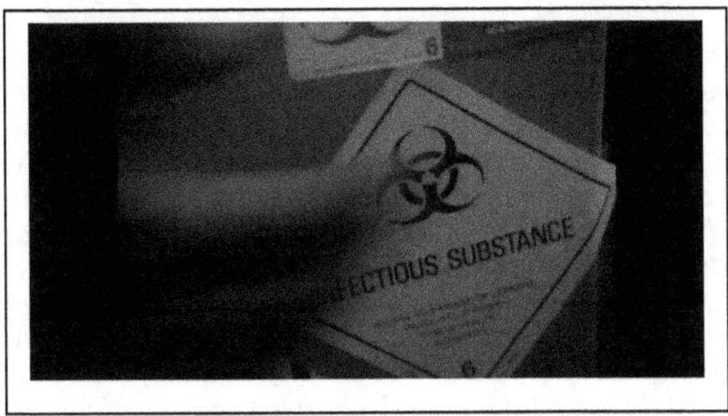

The first meeting with city government regarding powers is on "Day 4" when the medical team, led by Dr. Nora Hart, Kate Jackson, meet with the Mayor and his staff. Dr. Hart explains that plague has appeared and it will require them to take emergency measures. Dr. Hart says, "I need my detention powers increased." This would suggest the New York law had not been kept current, like most state quarantine and isolation orders in 1992.

The Mayor is very concerned about the national convention that is coming to New York City and refuses to make any of this public. In the meeting, the Mayor asks his assistant to consult the emergency preparedness plan for the city. His assistant reads from the plan, "Epidemics are beyond the scope of the Task Force for Emergency Preparedness." To this, the Mayor responds, "we'll just wing it."

Dr. Nora Hart has a colleague with whom she confides and discusses her thoughts, Dr. Jake Prescott, played by Jeffrey Nordling. He is a new doctor from Indiana which is a point of humor for the medical team who are saavy about the ways of New York City.

On Day 4, the two doctors discuss the possibility of the teenage girl's travel on an airline and whether she might have infected other passengers. To that, Dr. Prescott discusses the massive amounts of air that are exchanged on airline flights and says, "Catching a disease on a plane would be like catching a disease on a beach with a 5 naught wind blowing." Dr. Prescott did not have the benefit of the SARS outbreak in 2003, which was geographically widely disseminated mainly due to the infections on the flight from Hong Kong.

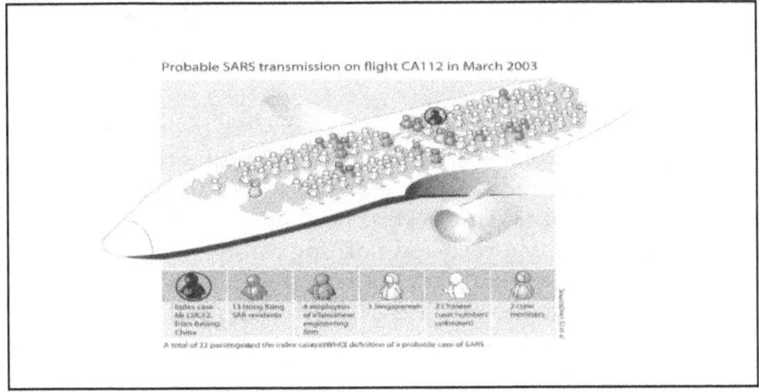

The graphic shows the circled index patient and the location of the passengers sitting on the flight who were infected with SARS on this single flight. Had Dr. Prescott had the benefit of knowing what happened 11 years later, he would not have been as confident that infections of pneumonic plague would have occurred on this flight boarded by the teenage girl.

Also by Day 4, Dr. Vincent Califano, played by Jerry Orbach, announces to the medical team that he is going to recommend a "declaration of imminent peril" to Mayor Carmichael. A Declaration of Imminent Peril is the NYC ordinance for how to declare a public health emergency, codified at 22 NYC Code § 563, and reads in its entirety as follows:

> *In the presence of great and imminent peril to the public health, the board of health, having first taken and filed among its records what it regards as sufficient proof to authorize a declaration of such peril, shall take such measures, and order the department to do such acts beyond those duly provided for the preservation of the public health, including the power to take possession of and occupy as a hospital any building or buildings in the city, as the board, in good faith may declare the public safety and health to demand, and the mayor shall in writing approve. No expenditure shall be incurred in the exercise of such extraordinary power, however, unless provision is made therefor in the budget or unless such expenditures are financed pursuant to sections one hundred seven or section 29.00 of the local finance law. Such peril shall exist when and for such period of time as the board of health and mayor declare.*

The penalties at 22 NYC § 562 are simply trial by a judiciary with a penalty at the level of a misdeamenor, which means a most, less than a year in confinement, but probably nothing more than a fine.

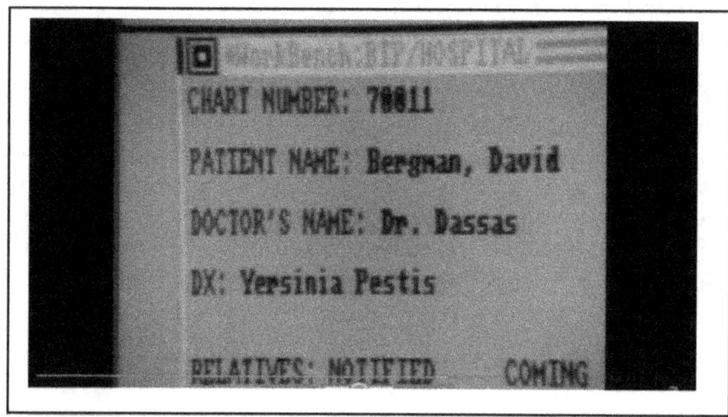

The screenshot of the record of his friend shows *yersinia pestis* and they have kept it a big secret. In 1992, the digital recordkeeping was new, and interestingly, the diagnosis of plague is clear in the record, although they have consistently lied to every patient and family about the illness and the cause of death. This record was found by this patient's roommate who is also a newspaper reporter. Having received nothing but silence from the doctors even after issuing quarantines of apartment buildings, the reporter does his investigation by impersonating a doctor and finding the record. He calls from his cell phone to have his assistant look up the diagnosis in a medical dictionary. Once he learns it is plague, he panics and runs through the hospital screaming that it is the plague. Then, for the first time, the news leaks to the press.

The withholding of this information from the public is not something that would be possible in the post-internet world. The internet became public one year after this television movie was made. Misrepresenting the illness to the public and to individual patients could have led to many undiagnosed cases and failure for people to recognize the symptoms.

The medical team goes out in the Pest Control van for the City of New York to collect rats, and it is at this time they are overwhelmed by a mob which overturns the van. The doctor ends up in the hospital to recouperate but no serious injuries are added to the drama. Interestingly, they pointed out accurately, that the majority of rats in NYC are not the kinds of rats that typically carry plague, but they continued to trap rats to test them.

One of the final contacts that they needed to locate was a Congressman, but because he was staying for the weekend with another Congressman's wife, he was unlocatable. They followed his trail to Penn Station and then on a train from New York City to Washington, D.C. and as a result Dr. Hart ordered a quarantine of the entire Penn Station and also the diversion of the train. This would have been far beyond the recommended public health action, being far too broad to warrant the risk, cost and burden put on all the other passengers. Simply waiting until the train arrived at the next stop and locating the Congressman would have been a much better balance of risk and burden on society.

The end of the movie is simply that the plague begins to go away, just like the normal curve of an epidemic. The medical team stands in the hospital room where one of the doctors is recouperating in bed from his injuries in the rolled van. Dr. Hart cites the statistics from the epidemic, "22 dead, 46 dead from riots and panic." They discuss that the Governor is considering an investigation of the Mayor for the way he handled the epidemic, and the Deputy Mayor Kapro resigned .

In the course of the investigation, it will likely come to light that Dr. Nora Hart, Kate Jackson, will have to face her medical licensing board about her action in lying to her patients and lying to the public about the truth about the epidemic.

Formula for Death/Virus (1995)

RATING

LEGEND ON THE OPENING SCREEN

The virus is man's ultimate predator.

---Robin Cook, M.D.

---*Formula for Death* (1994)

Formula for Death (1995) begins with a hemorrhagic fever in Zaire and carries it to American hospitals. But all of the cases are presenting at HMOs, the health care system that corporate boards feel may be destroying quality hospitals. Could someone be motivated to devise an elaborate bioterrorism attack across America, aimed at discrediting the ability of HMOs to provide quality healthcare? The urgency to find the perpetrators of the spread of *ebola* in America before more people die puts our intrepid rookie researcher in constant danger. A biothriller based on a book by Robin Cook, physician and novelist, this movie makes the List.

This movie is based on the Robin Cook novel, *Outbreak* (Putnam, 1987), which would have made an excellent name, but the same year another movie was being released with that name. *Outbreak* (1995) became a widely recognized movie, while *Formula for Death* also known as Virus (1995) was a television movie which was largely unnoticed. The movies were very different, but especially different in the choice of villain. *Outbreak* (1995) has the government and Department of Defense as the heart of the conspiracy; while *Formula for Death* (1995) has hospital corporate board of directors as the villain. Who does the viewing public love to hate the most? Corporate greed? Government corruption? Both provocative choices.

Dr. Marissa Blumenthal, Nicolette Sheridan, is the CDC researcher who is the rookie assigned to investigate the strange disease outbreak in Los Angeles. She is better than they expected and she finds it looks like *ebola.* Her confidantes are a male colleague and her love interest, Dr. Harbuck, played by William Devane, who is a powerful doctor in Atlanta's medical society.

Dr. Leland, a physician on the hospital Board, with a deep southern accent, complains about HMOs and immigrants who are getting free care, and how they are putting good hospitals out of business. He begins this rant on his first meeting with Dr. Blumenthal at a cocktail party, but then gives a feigned apology. This is an ominous warning for what unfolds, when a dubious plot to discredit HMOs takes Dr. Blumenthal on a criminal and medical investigation of who is behind it all.

It seems that all of the corpses of the victims of *ebola* have a strange mark that appears on every body. No police ever investigate the incident because they are never alerted by medical examiners in this movie, which tends to make it less believable. The only person who notice the unique wound is the rogue investigator, Dr. Blumenthal.

In this frameshot, they show the electrophoresis test that identifies the common DNA among the strains from the victims and compares it to the ebola strain found in Zaire. This is the state of the art test in 1995 for comparing strains which involves placing the genetic material on a gel covered surfact and an electrical current will cause the DNA to move up the gel. If they are the same, then they will move up the gel leaving the same marks for each test. She points out that the same strain could not possibly be naturally occurring because it would have evolved from the Zaire strain. The only conclusion is that someone is using the Zaire strain intentionally. Her colleague does not want to believe her and says she is "crazy."

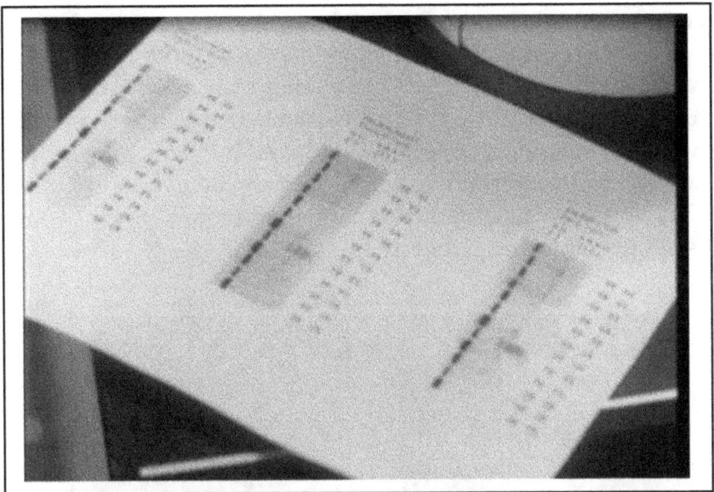

She is taken off the case and reassigned. But she continues to track down the source. Her meddling gets her set up as the thief who stole a vial of *ebola* from what the researchers call a "Max" lab which is the equivalent of a BSL-4 since they have air pumped into their biosuits and wear full protective gear.

Dr. Blumenthal is attacked in a motel room with an injection gun which the viewer can now conclude is the device that is used to make the unusual mark on the previous victims.

She manages to disable her attacker and take his gun and inject him, in the process. She carries the gun to her love interest, Dr. Harbuck, and asks him to keep it as evidence. Dr. Harbuck appears on donor lists and corporate boards with the same group of friends, but appears to be unaware of any wrongdoing. He encourages her to go to the police on a number of occasions which she always rejects and says she must keep looking.

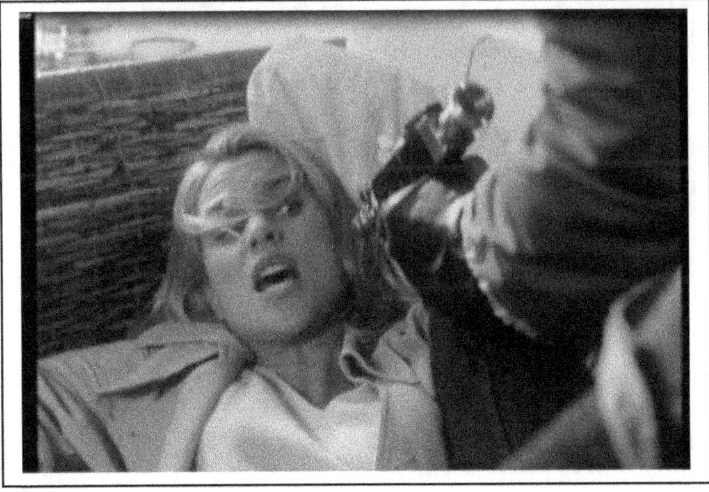

Victims are showing up all over the U.S. – in Los Angeles, then St. Louis then Atlanta. It is not clear who is being tasked with all of these *ebola* injection assaults, but our imagination must be suspended on that one.

A word about the security in the "Max" lab. In this frameshot, she is seen entering her code after she has swiped the identification card she took from her colleague's coat, after hers had been confiscated by her supervisor. Note, that she has to touch the pad with her ungloved fingers, because afterall, it would be impossible to touch the keypad numbers with bulky gloves that would be required for this level of biosafety. Touching also spreads bacteria and viruses. While this keypad was used in many labs, because of this risk with kind of keypad, many labs are using methods that do not require physical contact, for example a retinal scan reader for researchers.

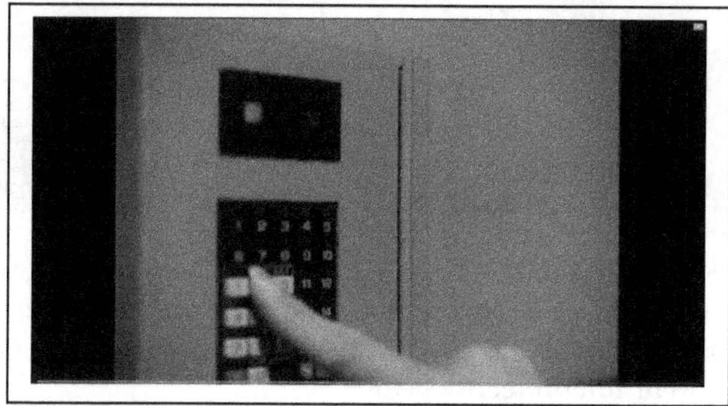

The interior of the "Max" lab is a hazy blue and makes a nice visual, but the dark conditions in the laboratory would make it very unsafe.

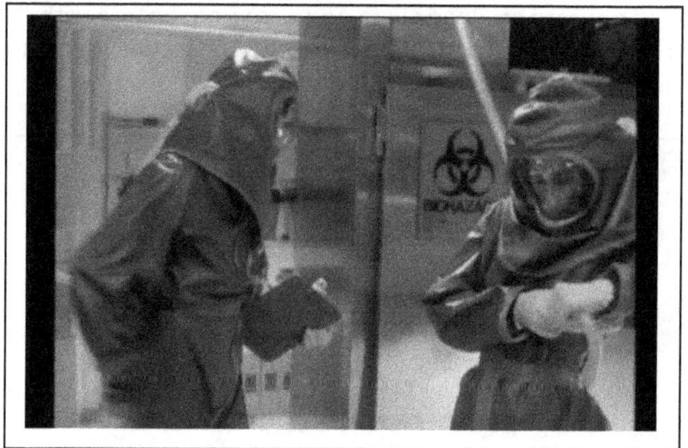

Dr. Blumenthal does use the law on a couple of occasions and impresses her male colleague with her knowledge. She first finds out the connection between all of the hospital Board members and donations to a member of Congress who we later learn is complicit in the scheme. Her colleague asks her how she found out, and she explained her inquiry to the Federal Election Commission (FEC) and that they sent her the list of donors, which he found to be incredulous. The list of donors is part of the transparency the federal election law hopes to achieve. By around the year 2000, the FEC reports were posted on the internet, and easily searchable.

On another occasion, Dr. Blumenthal tells her colleague she discovered the members of the Board of Directors of a corporation who own a "Max" lab; and he again, is incredulous that she discovered this information. The state corporation commission keeps this information for the public in order to identify the owners and officers for several purposes including serving legal documents on the appropriate responsible official and for many other uses.

The final stages of the movie draw our attention to the throngs of protestors at CDC who demand that this plague be stopped. If the perpetrators of this bioterrorism scheme succeeded in discrediting HMOs it is not evident from this protest.

The movie begins with the words of wisdom from the author, Robin Cook, a medical doctor-novelist, noted at the beginning of this analysis. The movie ends with unattributed words that appear as the legend on several frames at the end of the movie with this warning:

> Ebola is real virus.
>
> No one knows when it will reappear . . . as it did in Zaire.
>
> Scientists think thousands of these viruses wait, hidden in the deep forests throughout the world.
>
> They are simply the earth's defense systems against the most dangerous of invaders . . .
>
> Man.

A screaming monkey ends the movie, which may be what the viewer feels like doing when left with all the loose ends in this story.

Outbreak (1995)

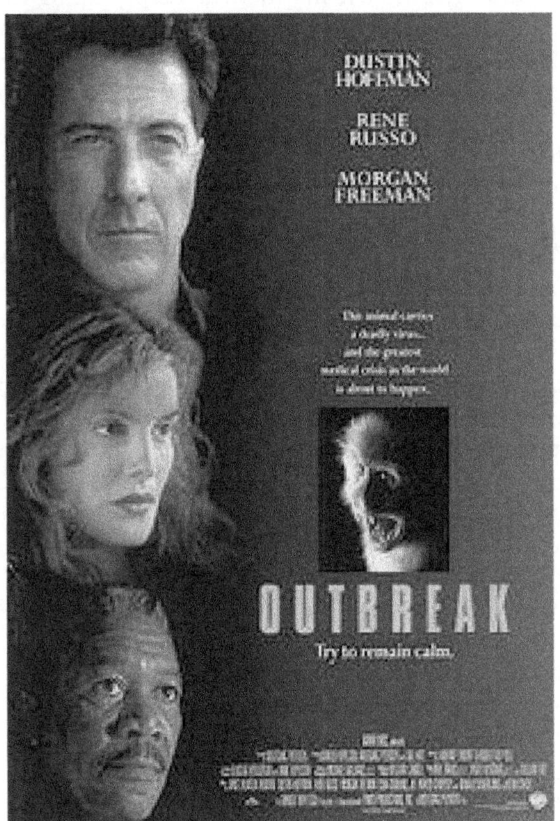

RATING

LEGEND ON SCREEN -- OPENING

The single biggest threat to man's continue dominance on the planet is the virus.

---Joshua Lederberg, Nobel Laureate

Outbreak (1995) is a landmark movie in the chronology of the biohorror, biothriller, biodrama subgenre for the List, in part because it was written and produced in the pre-9-11 period, six years before the anthrax attacks in America. Also, casting Dustin Hoffman, Morgan Freeman and Donald Sutherland, A-list actors brought immediate notoriety to the film. The plot turns on the deadly disease that is ravaging a small California town and the government's actions to both contain and conceal its origin and effects, making it a classic in this subgenre.

The story reveals a government conspiracy to keep its most valuable biological weapon developed in 1967 during the pre-Biological Weapons Treaty era. The opening flashback to a village in Africa shows the origin of the deadly virus, called Motaba for the Motaba River Valley in Zaire, Africa. In 1967, the United States as well as other developed countries were engaged in biological weapons programs and it was not until 1972 when the United States signed the Biological Weapons Convention that countries followed and decommissioned their bioweapons development operations and turned them into defensive operations. In 1995, the treaty was already in effect for twenty years, and biological weapons would have been long ago destroyed according to the terms of the Treaty.

The disease that emerged from the village in the Motaba River Valley in Zaire, Africa is shown in scenes of almost 100% mortality during the visit of Maj. Gen. Donald McClintock, played by Donald Sutherland. He is on the scene presumptively to collect a virus that could be useful in the United States's biological weapons arsenal. The scene is very similar to video footage of the remains of an outbreak of ebola when it first emerged in the area of Yombaku in northern Zaire in 1976. What they found was 17 of the 20 healthcare workers had died of the disease and all of the people who were infected. In this 1967 flashback, the U.S. Army destroys the village by bombing it so that nothing is left of the virus or anyone to transmit it. But their sinister purpose we learn is to keep it as a bioweapon.

The practice of collecting new viruses for the purpose of weaponizing them is not a creation of Hollywood. The U.S.S.R. typically sent scientists to investigate new outbreaks. For example, the Marburg virus, a viral hemorrhagic fever, was secretly obtained from corpses in Germany in 1967 from an outbreak, there.[33]

The U.S. biological weapons program with its major laboratory at the U.S. Army facility at Ft. Detrick, called USAMRIID (United States Army Medical Institute of Infectious Disease) is where the two scientists work, our protagonists, Dustin Hoffman, playing Col. Sam Daniels and Rene Russo, playing Robby Keough, his wife from whom he is recently divorced.

---

[33] See Ken Alibek, *Biohazard* (1999).

The opening of the movie takes the viewer through the increasingly secure areas of the laboratory. The laboratory levels designated Biological Safety Laboratories 2, 3 and 4 --- 4, being the highest level --- lead to the biosuits connected to air supplies where infectious agents which have no cure are handled.

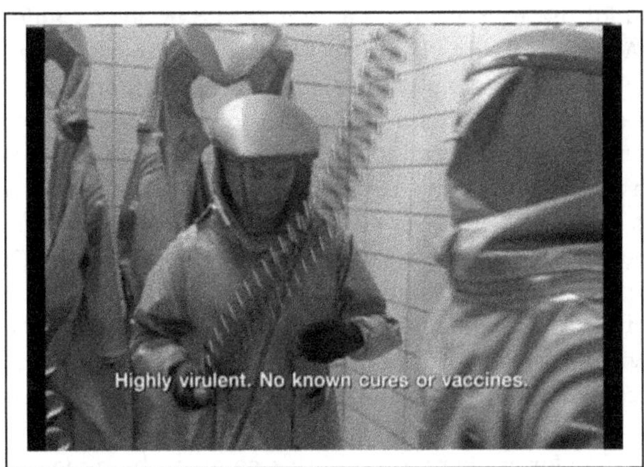

Now, the Motaba River Valley has another outbreak of a virus, thirty years later. Col. Daniels and Dr. Russo are sent with a team to investigate and rookie, Major Salt, played by Cuba Gooding, Jr. The reality of investigating a new and lethal virus is made real by the warnings about panicking with a contained biosuit when he sees the rotting corpses that they expect to find in the village. When they arrive, despite Major Salt's resolve to not panic, he does, removing his face protection and oxygen supply. Fortunately, the local healthcare worker announces that the virus is not airborne and is infecting people through the water. They learn the virus has a 48-hour incubation period and a near 100% fatality rate.

When Col. Daniels returns and alerts Maj. Gen. McClintock that a warning should be announced, he is rebuffed, telling him that the virus kills too quickly to be a threat to spreading. It is a reasonably good epidemiological reason, but it becomes increasingly clear that Maj. Gen. McClintock is protecting the knowledge about the virus and has his own agenda.

The virus is on its way to the United States, through its host, a capuchin monkey, which has been captured for use in a medical laboratory in San Jose, California. An employee at the Biotest Animal Holding Facility in San Jose, Jimbo Scott, an opportunistic fellow, steals the monkey to sell to a pet store in Cedar Creek, California.

Jimbo Scott has done this before and sells the monkey to the pet store owner. The pet store owner releases the monkey but after a bite, he soon succumbs to the disease dying in his pet store. When a technician, Henry Seward, is testing the pet store owner's blood to attempt to determine his cause of death, the test tube breaks in the centrifuge as it is spinning, splattering blood in the face, eyes and mouth of the technician. This is a very realistic and unfortunate way that technicians can become infected. One of the first laboratory infections occurred this way at Yale University in 1994, where a technician working with the exotic viruses collection, was splattered by a test tube containing Sabia virus that broke during centrifuging, splattering him with blood. Sabia virus causes an infection for which there is no cure. The case became important for implementing new protocols for laboratory safety for workers to avoid this common breakage risk that could prove to be deadly. This movie is just a year after the incident and after these protocols were instituted and the technician in the movie would have had training to avoid such an accident. Nevertheless, carelessness and failure to follow protocols can still lead to laboratory accidents even with the best training. The technician in the movie was concerned about HIV, unaware of the source of the blood he was testing. He attended a movie with his girlfriend and began coughing in the theater, leading to the conclusion that the virus had now evolved to become airborne when the theater patrons begin lining up at the emergency room in Cedar Creek, California. With the growing numbers presenting with similar symptoms, the physician contacts the Centers for Prevention and Diseases Control (CDC) for help. In 1995, this would have been an acceptable protocol, except that the state health department should always be notified first, before the federal agency, due to the federalism relationship with the states and the federal government. Once invited to assist, CDC can trigger other federal agencies' involvement in the state incident. However, if it is a suspected bioterrorism event, the FBI can be immediately contacted by anyone.

Meanwhile, Jimbo Scott was already becoming sick on the flight to Boston to see his girlfriend. When he arrives he collapses and dies soon thereafter, but he has already exposed people on the flight who disperse to Boston and other areas. Interestingly, it is only Cedar Creek that becomes the focus of eradication.

The discovery that people are infected in the town of Cedar Creek leads Maj. Gen. McClintock to propose the same cure he had used effectively in Zaire thirty years ago—fire bomb the entire city before anyone can escape and infect other people in the United States. They will also be able to save their biological weapon, and will not have to use the vaccine that they have created and held in secret.

Col. Daniels and his ex-wife, Dr. Russo are looking for the index case or "patient zero" the term for the first person to exhibit symptoms of the disease. The term "patient zero" was first used in relation to the first HIV patient The patient zero may also carry the disease without dying leading to its spread, but also harboring potentially antibodies which prevent the original patient zero from dying. Maj. Gen. McClintock is doing everything he can to prevent Col. Daniels from finding the host and the cure, including sending a fighter jet to shoot down his helicopter as he is piloted by Major Salt on a chase between Cedar Creek and USAMRIID in Ft. Deterick, Maryland. Col. Col. McClintock intends to initiate "Operation Clean Sweep" with the approval of the President in order to destroy the entire city of Cedar Creek, California and everyone in it.

It is during a high level executive meeting where the options for stopping the epidemic which threatens to spread to the rest of the United States, that *Posse Comitatus* is mentioned as an objection to using the military to control civilians in Cedar Creek.

Quarantine of the city is a questionable legal order, because due process requires that each individual have a hearing at least at some point as to the evidence of why they are being held. There is no appeal process for being held in the quarantine, which is also a violation of due process. But because the city is put under martial law even after the discussion of *posse comitatus*, due process is subjugated to military command. The writ of habeus corpus would be suspended, also an unconstitutional action, unless the entire national security of the national was at stake, and that is the argument that is being made to justify the quarantine. Maj. Gen. McClintock makes the comparison of saving 2600 people or saving 260 million people to justify the quarantine and Operation Clean Sweep, which will eradicate the town.

Individual rights protected against unrestrained government is one of the most important principles of the Constitution, and *Outbreak* (1995) makes this a theme.

Can lethal force be used to enforce the quarantine? Lethal force is a military objective, but civilian police officers have an objective of protecting the lives of citizens, including the ones they arrest. Using the military which are trained to use lethal force presents an immediate conflict when they are presented with orders to prevent civilians from leaving a militarized zone that is quarantined. Orders to prevent their escape, without specifically eliminating lethal force, would require the officers to follow orders, using lethal force to achieve the military objective of maintaining the integrity of the quarantine. When two families in their pickup trucks decide to try to break out of Cedar Creek, the visuals of the military response was particularly striking and these remain some of the more memorable moments in the movie.

This frameshot is the beginning of a car chase leaving the city. The blockaded road guarded by armed military on a sunny day in California contrast the peaceful lives of Americans in a small California town with the transformation this outbreak has caused.

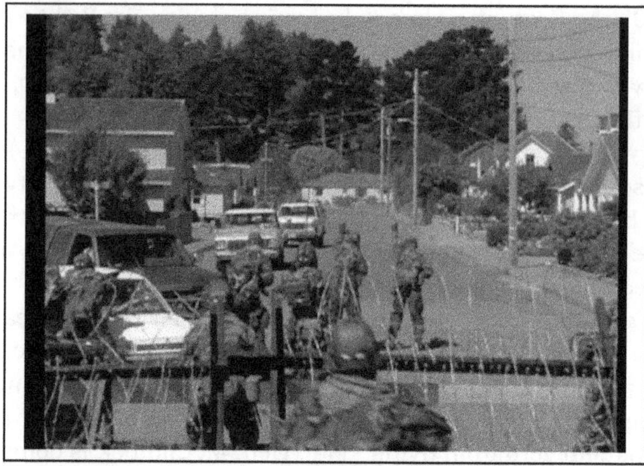

The next frameshot is the use of helicopters in addition to the military vehicles which have given chase, escalating the conflict with a show of force.

The consequences of using lethal force to enforce the quarantine are vividly and dramatically played out where the helicopter opens fire on the family pickup truck and it bursts in to flames as the horrified looks on their faces observe.

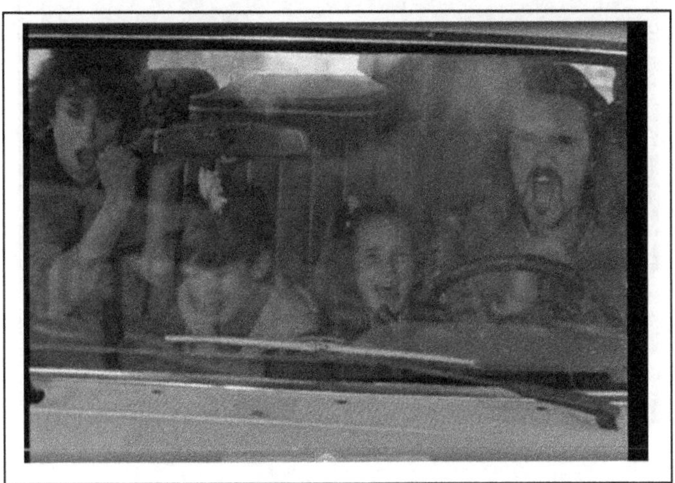

The family in the second pickup truck are arrested at gunpoint by military officers wearing biological safety masks, making it all the more incongruent with our legal statute which makes civilian law enforcement contact off limits for the military.

Immediately after the civilians were killed breaking quarantine, the newscaster simply continues to report on the quarantine of the city without any outrage about the deaths of an American family at the hands of military orders to stop their exit from the city.

The military loudspeaker issues a message from the middle of the street in Cedar Creek on a sunny day, "If you are feeling sick in any way, you should hang a piece of white cloth on your door. Soldiers will take you to a testing facility and you will know the results in less than an hour." The people of Cedar Creek are largely compliant and wait dutifully to be taken away by the military to the testing center. Most of them know they will not return. One emotional scene is a mother leaving her family and children who cannot hug her and say goodbye. *Posse comitatus* allows local governments to utilize the equipment and expertise of the military but no contact directly with civilians. This might be one of the few moments in the military occupation of Cedar Creek that is legally compliant with the federal statute and the Constitution.

The CDC Director, Dr. Reynolds remarks to Renee Russo about the cost of sending out an alert to health care workers (pre-internet communications), "Both you and I know that the chances of this virus showing up in this country are virtually nil." The next scene is Jimbo letting the monkey go into the forest in the United States, contradicting the CDC Director's prediction.

Wildlife smuggling into the United States is a crime that is all too common, and the possibility of infections coming with them is high, especially primates like monkeys. Even monkeys brought into the U.S. for experimental purposes have had hidden infections. A colony of monkeys brought to Reston, Virginia for experimentation in 1989 harbored an unknown monkey strain of ebola. (Fortunately, it was a strain that was only infectious for monkeys, not humans, but the whole colony had to be destroyed.) In this movie, the thief, Jimbo, who stole the monkey, became infected as well as the pet store owner who was scratched, all from illegal behavior. The lab tech who was centrifuging the blood from the pet store owner was not at BSL-3 or 4 levels which might have been indicated by the symptoms of the patient who died. Without proper biosafety precautions, the exploding centrifuge was lethal. A real-life incident happened in the same way at Yale University with a deadly virus that proved lethal to that lab technician, as well.

At what appears to be a National Security Council meeting, one of the members gives a speech about the unconstitutionality of firebombing a city in the U.S., "This is the Constitution and I have read it cover to cover and I don't find anything about vaporizing 2600 American citizens, but it does say several times that no person shall be deprived of life, liberty without due process." He then goes on to demand the unwavering support of everyone with the President and not to go to *The Washington Post* claiming to be the one dissenting voice. Otherwise, it appears they are approving Operation Clean Sweep despite the unconstitutionality of it.

The two military leaders, who are complicit in covering up their plan to retain "Motaba" as a bioweapon, discuss their options regarding the elimination of Cedar Creek, California:

Maj. Gen. McClintock

We are at war…
Everybody is at war.
I have a presidential green
light on Operation Clean Sweep
and I am going forward.

Gen. Billy Ford

Donny, these people are Americans.

Maj.Gen. McClintock

2600 dead or dying Americans.
If that bug gets out of there
260 million Americans will be dead or dying.
Those people are casualties of war, Billy
I would give them all a medal if
I could but they are casualties of war.

Using a military ethical code of conduct, an operation is ethical if the loss of civilian casualties is outweighed by the importance of the military objective. Based on this principle, Gen. Maj. McClintock is justified in his decision.

Back at the laboratory, another colleague is working long hours without sleep. In a moment of perhaps slow reactions, his biosuit is ripped open in the BSL-4 laboratory, when the air tubing is caught on an open drawer, and we see the dramatic closeup of the gaping hole in the biosuit.

Lisa Hensley, microbiologist, USAMRIID, was interviewed about this incident in the movie.[34] She explains that an infection is unlikely to result from such an incident for three reasons: (1) these suits are reinforced and she has never had one rip, so it is unlikely to happen in the first place; (2) the positive air pressure inside the suit would keep air rushing out of the hole, and nothing going in; and (3) the air is circulated in the room continuously so if there is an accident, the air is likely not to be contaminated. In the movie, Casey Schuler, played by Kevin Spacey, keeps the tear a secret, but becomes ill and collapses in the BSL-4 laboratory a short time later.

Biosuit integrity is very important, and several points throughout the movie: there was a tear in Col. Daniels suit when he was concerned about his divorce and not paying attention to checking for safety; Robby Keough, played by Renee Russo pricks her finger through two layers of rubber glove; Major Salt removes his biosuit in a panic when he is in the field; and Casey Schuler has the accidental rip from the air tube catching on a drawer. Part of the protocol for dressing up in the biosuit is to inspect it for tears or other issues that might create a risk. The movie made biosafety an integral part of the plot.

Major Salt, played by Cuba Gooding, Jr. and Col. Daniels, played by Dustin Hoffman become superhuman for the last part of what was otherwise a movie based on realism. Major Salt gives us superhuman, marksmanship to shoot the monkey, superhuman helicopter piloting, and superhuman scientific development of antigens to cure Motaba, under fire.

In the meantime, Operation Clean Sweep is underway and Maj. Ford musters the will to order the pilots not to rearm after they intentionally missed hitting the city of Cedar Creek with their bomb. They were persuaded by the radio messages coming from the voice of Col. Daniels who is being helicoptered by Maj. Salt. Maj. Gen. McClintock orders them back to the base to rearm, but Maj. Billy Ford orders Donny's arrest for the crime of "withholding

[34] http://hosted.ap.org/specials/interactives/wdc/biosuit/index.html?SITE=VASTR .

information from the President." Billy will be tried in a military court of justice for this military crime.

Finally, one obvious change in the regulations effective in 2012,[35] is the personal assurances requirements. These regulations require other colleagues or self-reporting of anything that might disturb your concentration when working in high level containment. This would include going through a divorce or other conflict. In the movie, both Robby and Col Daniels would have been completely removed from high level containment given their overt expressions of being preoccupied with personal conflict.

Outbreak (1995) has some striking visuals and for that reason many of these frames are included. It makes the review from John Simon in National Review[36] particularly distasteful, with his comment about all disaster movies as disasters, but then fingers "Outbreak, which could have been a good disaster film, is an artistic catastrophe." Wrong, John. Almost two decades later, *Outbreak* (1995) remains a landmark – and an artistically remarkable --movie in the biohorror, biothriller subgenre.

---

[35] Select Agent Regulations, 42 C.F.R. §73 (2012).

[36] John Simon, *National Review* (April 17, 1995).

Twelve Monkeys (1995)

RATING

Airport security personnel
Excuse me sir, would you mind letting me have a look at the contents of your bag?

Passenger, Dr. Peters
Me?
[Security opens the bag,looks at the cylinders, takes them out, holds them up to examine them.]

Passenger, Dr. Peters
Biological samples. [pause] I have the papers right here.

Airport security personnel
Well, I'm going to have to ask you to open this up, sir."

12 Monkeys (1995) is a story of a plague that has killed 5 billion people (and we just passed the 7 billionth person born on the earth). But by 2035 only 1 percent of the population has survived and they are living underground.

This opening text describes the pandemic in 1997 and the consequences. But the quote is delivered by a man diagnosed with paranoid schizophrenia, James Cole, played by Bruce Willis, a man from the future who has been sent back to 1990 to discover clues about the virus so it can be prevented.

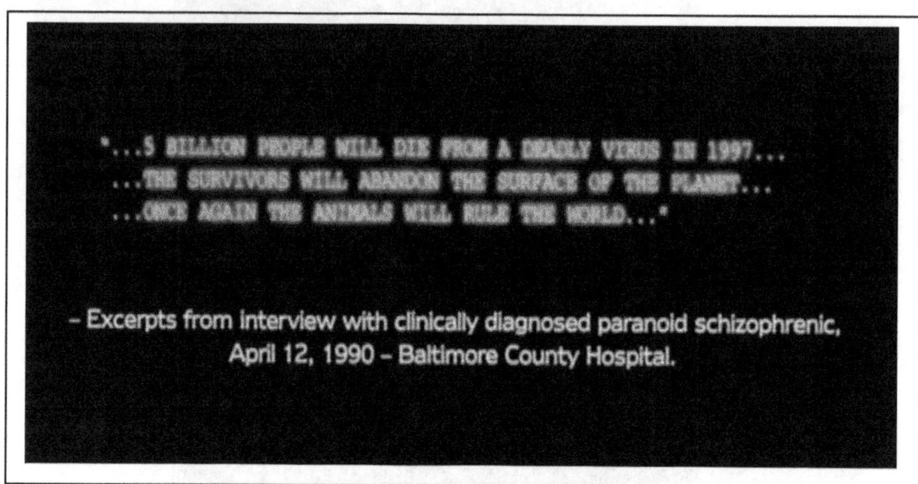

While the credits are still rolling in the opening, Bruce Willis, James Cole, has been "volunteered" from his imprisonment for some wrongdoing, to go on an assignment. As we learn from his roommate, he might get a reprieve, but Bruce Willis counters, that no one ever comes back from their assignments. His cellmate does not want to believe it. This shows some optimism is still left in this post-apocalyptic world.

And that is not all that is left. Bruce Willis is instructed to go find information about the pandemic that destroyed much of the world, and he finds a cockroach in the snow, always reputed in popular culture to be one of the living organisms most likely to survive a nuclear attack. The truth is that this is a Madagascar Roach and would not be found in a United States city. You may recall in the closing scenes of *Carriers* (2009), one of the last humans sees some surviving cockroaches, also Madagascar Roaches.

They are said to make good pets. (There are special rules for handling animals, including Madagascar roaches, for movies.)

He plucks it from the snowy ledge and pops it into a jar.

Before Bruce Willis is sent to the surface for his mission, he has a form of a hearing before what seems to be scientists acting as a parole board. The parole board is a panel of about six scientists who ask what his offenses are. The baliff responds that he is serving 25 years for violating orders to comply with the rules. They ask him, "You wont hurt us will, you?" He responds, "no sir." Then he is scooped up in a chair that is going to propel him into the year 1996, the past.

Once on the surface, he is arrested after assaulting police officers, beaten and given heavy sedatives. The community services psychiatrist, Dr. Kathryn Railly, visits with him and in his sedated state he appears to be schizophrenic. He was sent to the year 1996 on the surface of the earth to find out more about the virus, but there was an apparent mistake, sending him back to the year 1990. (Terry Gilliam, the director, must be well acquainted with time travel coming from the British tradition of *Dr. Who*, the time traveling time lord who always had trouble getting to the targeted time period, leading to his decades of adventures in the wrong time periods.) Dr. Railly, the psychiatrist believes he thinks he is living in the future and thus commits him to the psychiatric ward. Bruce Willis is introduced to Brad Pitt, another inmate in the psychiatric ward who is heavily sedated but behaves in a way that suggests he is also schizophrenic---has a fear of germs, distorted sense of reality, etc.

Here in the psychiatric ward, he appears before the board and tells them "this is a psychiatric hospital and I am not crazy." Here he tries to explain that his scientists have sent him to the wrong time period and that he needs to make a phone call to let them know. When they finally grant his wish he finds the phone call goes to a woman who knows nothing. He tells them the number doesn't work yet because he is in the wrong time zone. They are not convinced but the psychiatrist continues to think she has seen him before.

He tries to escape after Brad Pitt gives him the key to the door, making a connection between monKEY and key, in his schizophrenic exchange. This screen shot shows him fully sedated and fully restrained. He mysteriously disappears from his restraints when he is recalled to the future.

Note the long shot in the next frame, showing his seemingly helpless capture.

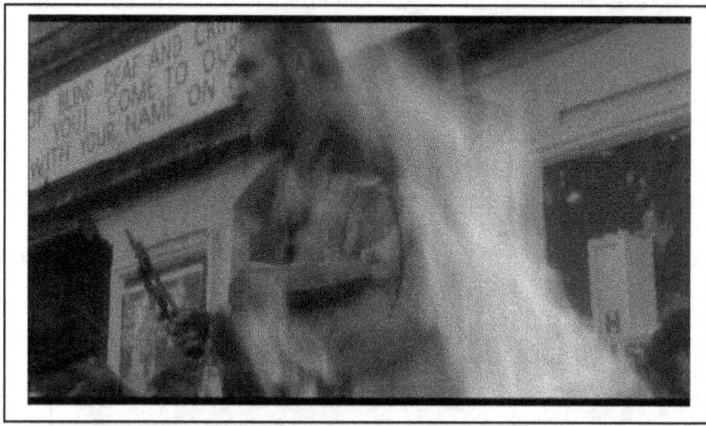

James Cole kidnaps Dr. Railly in 1996 when he is sent to the correct time period on the second try. She begins to become sympathetic with his objective, but probably more impressed by his passion for his mission at this point. She agrees to go with him into the seamy areas of Philadelphia and look for the cults, the Army of the 12 Monkeys. They end up finding a great underground rotunda and eventually find their way to the lab of the Army of the 12 Monkeys, which Bruce Willis has told the psychiatrist he needed to find.

James questions the young kids in the laboratory and finds that they are led by a crazy activist virologist behind their work.

After taking a stolen car, he finds the virologist giving a speech in a deep southern accent at a formal black tie party. He discovers that the son of the famous virologist is Jeffrey Goines, Brad Pitt, who he had met in the psychiatry hospital in 1990. Jeffrey told James that he had given him the idea of making a virus that would wipe out the human race. Bruce Willis, James Cole, now bears the burden that he inspired the mad man who developed the virus that killed 5 billion people, when he was babbling in his sedated state.

Railly and James Cole are being pursued by law enforcement believing she has been abducted by this escaped insane asylum patient. James Cole eventually convinces his psychiatrist, Dr. Railly, that he knows the future when he knows the outcome of a news story that is being followed by the nation about a little boy who fell down a well. James knows that the little boy was actually hiding which the news eventually reveals, to the psychiatrist's astonishment. She begins to believe his prediction about the Army of the Twelve Monkeys and the virus that they will unleash in just a few weeks and will wipe out 5 billion people.

The television news continued to cover James Cole as a missing person from an insane asylum, dangerous and on the run.

Dr. Railly called the virologist and questioned whether his son had access to his dangerous viruses. The virologist directed his staff to increase security – "beef it up."

Dr. Railly, on her own, begins to try to find the Army of the Twelve Monkeys. The perspective changes to the kids inside the building, allowing the viewers to see the virologist's son, Jeffrey, inside with the Army of the 12 Monkeys.

In desperation, Dr. Railly paints a large sign on the building warning people that they have a lethal virus with a can of red spray paint.

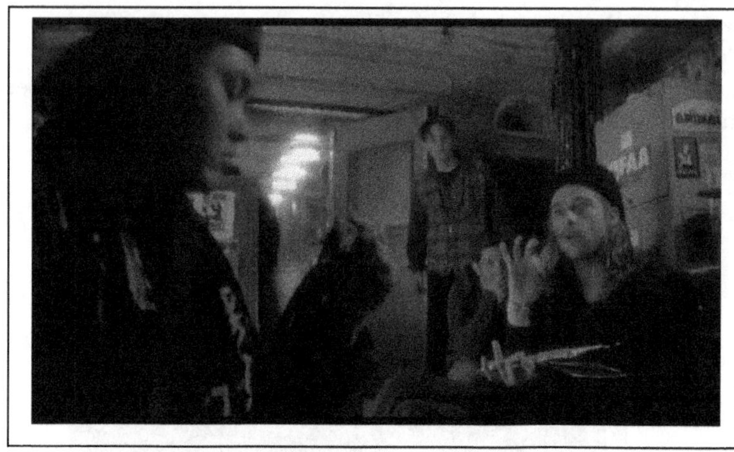

The psychiatrist spray painted the wall outside that explained the future. James Cole looked at it and said, "I have seen that before."

Meanwhile, Jeffrey, insane as ever, kidnaps his father with his followers, the Army of the 12 Monkeys. He explains he no longer has the code to the virus and they tell him that's not what they want. What they actually wanted was to free all of the laboratory animals. So they release all the zoo animals onto the streets of Philadelphia.

Once Dr. Railly and James realize the Army of the 12 onkeys are just a bunch of harmless kids who want to free animals, they decide to go to the ocean, which James says he has never seen. Before they go, they see a movie where they apply their wigs and mustache disguises to escape to the airport, knowing they are being hunted.

They go to the airport, purchase their tickets with cash, no identification required. (This scene certainly takes today's audience back to the past to see how easy it was to buy a ticket for a flight.) But as she is waiting to meet James, she spots someone who was at her booksigning at the beginning of the movie and realizes he is part of a cult and it must be him, Dr. Peters.

In the meantime, James calls the phone number to the future and tells them he isn't coming back and that he has done his job – forget the Army of the Twelve Monkeys – they are just a bunch of kids, he tells them. Then someone from the future appears in the airport and they tell him that they have been instructed to shoot the psychiatrist, Dr. Railly, if he doesn't come back.

Dr. Railly then spots James in the airport and runs to tell him about the man she spotted who she believes has the virus. As they push toward the gate, the perspective changes to Dr. Peters going through security. As he is putting the suitcase through the security scanner on the belt, the security personnel see the cylinders and testtubes through their scanner and he is stopped to examine his bag. (Nice job, in pre-9/11 airport security.)

The airport security personnel takes out the clear containers and examines them. The passenger explains they are biological samples.

Airport security personnel
Excuse me sir, would you mind letting me
have a look at the contents of your bag?

Passenger, Dr. Peters
Me?

[Security personnel opens the bag and
looks at the cylinders, takes
them out, holds them up to examine them.]

Passenger, Dr. Peters
Biological samples. [pause]
I have the papers right here.

Airport security personnel
Well, I'm going to have to ask
you to open this up, sir."

Passenger, Dr. Peters
Open it?

Airport security personnel
[nods his head in the affirmative]

Passenger, Dr. Peters
Yes, of course.

The rest of the exchange involves Dr. Peters taking off the stopper from the testtube and allowing the airport security personnel to sniff it. The airport security personnel remarks that you can't see it or smell it. Dr. Peters tells him he assures him that it is there.

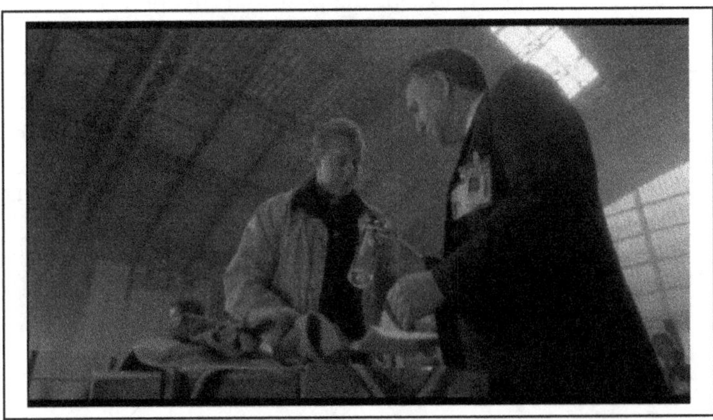

James Cole and Dr. Railly are battling the crowds to reach Dr. Peters with the suitcase, but they are slowed to a stop at security. James bolts through the airport x-ray machine and has a gun that he is trying to use to shoot the passenger but people keep darting between them. Two officers shoot James in the back and he goes down. Dr. Railly tries to save him, but it is clear he is dying. She looks around the room looking for the little boy that is James and makes eye contact with him for a magnetic moment. The movie ends with a closeup on the boy's eyes.

This was a 2 hour and 10 minute movie, developing the story through time travel, flashbacks and interspersed bouts of insanity on the part of the hero, making it a movie that required close attention or else you might find you were lost in the unreality of James's struggle to keep realty distinct from unreality.

The theme of the movie would have to be "you can't change the past," until you see that seated beside the cult leader on the plane after he has successfully boarded with his suitcase of vials, is the woman from the parole board of the future. She introduces herself to the man and the last line of dialogue is simply, "I'm in insurance." We have to assume that her line of insurance is to make sure 5 billion people don't die as a result of Dr. Peters's biological weapon.

The perception of the rule of law takes an interesting character arc with the psychiatrist. She is a psychiatrist, researcher, lecturer and book author with very structured rules and beliefs. She tells her colleague that she is beginning to lose the faith as she talks about what psychiatry can provide for answers. As she begins to believe James, she witnesses first his murder of a couple of men in self defense and is horrified, but then joins in the act of self defense. In fact, we know she has truly arc'd when she demands that James rob the man that just tried to assault her --- "rob him?" He asks with astonishment. "Yes! We need the cash!" Dr. Railly responds. The rule of law becomes diminishingly less of a guiding principle as the tension to follow the rule of survival becomes increasingly urgent, for Dr. Railly. James Cole had long ago abandoned the belief in the rule of law as protection and stability.

It bears mentioning that in a small credit in the opening of the movie it reads, "inspired by the film 'La Jetée' written by Chris Marker." Chris Marker was also giving screenwriter credit along with two other writers, Peoples and Peoples.

The movie, *La Jetée* (1962), is a French film made entirely with still, black and white photos but the story line is very similar except the post-apocalyptic world was caused by a nuclear accident. *12 Monkeys* (1995) uses a biological pandemic, consistent with the trend from the first *Spider Man* caused by an irradiated spider bite to the *Spider Man* of the new millennia, given his powers instead by a genetically engineered spider. Biological pandemics and disasters have taken the place of our previous worst horror – nuclear war.

Pandora's Clock (1996)

RATING

Iceland Ground Crew
[speaking to the pilot]
I am under orders to absolutely prevent any human being from leaving that aircraft --- that's a deadly force authorized order. Do I make myself clear?

---***Pandora's Clock*** (1996)

Pandora's Clock (1996) takes place on a commercial flight to Germany from New York. However, when a man dies and other people become infected, it becomes clear that no government wants to flight to land. The urgency to find a jurisdiction to land before everyone is infected on the flight places this movie squarely in the subgenre of biohorror, biothriller movies.

A virus from a laboratory, the Hauptman Laboratories in Erlangen, Germany that was engineered by the Soviets was accidentally released, infecting a researcher when a petri dish broke.

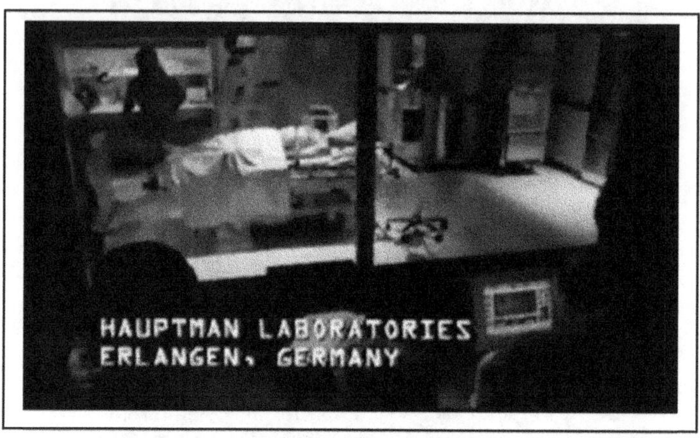

An Ambassador-at-large is on the flight with his assistant and they help interpret the political decisions that are being made in Washington and in other countries as the plane is denied landing in every country they approach.

The infection begins when an American professor is in an isolated wilderness area taking photographs and an escaped man tries to take his car. A helicopter traps the man in a net, and the American professor drives away.

The American professor boards his flight for JFK, but is becoming feverish. The flight leaves late from Frankfurt, Germany and before they are as far west as the UK, the American Professor appears to have a heartattack . This incident triggers the pilot to try to land in the United Kingdom, but right before they are to land they put them in a holding pattern and refuse to let them land. The pilot is annoyed, and told he must fly back to Germany because they have a nasty influenza requiring the plane to be quarantined in Germany. The dialogue between the pilot and the air traffic control in the UK explains:

Air Traffic Control -UK
The British Ministry of Health has been informed by the German Ministry of Health that one of your passengers has been exposed to a particularly nasty strain of influenza.

Pilot
Flu? We've got plenty of aspirin.

Air Traffic Control - UK

I have no other information, but because of
that exposure you must return to Frankfurt
ofr processing and quarantine.
Your company has been informed that you cannot
land in the U.K.

Since 1992, the federal government has been negotiating for an international bilateral and multilateral agreements in the "Open Skies" partnership. The objective of these Air Transportation Agreements (ATA) is for governments not to interfere with routing decisions made by commercial airlines. These allows stops for connections and refueling or just flying over the sovereign territory of a country. These agreements are between two partners (bilateral) or agreements between more than two partners (multilateral).

In this movie, the effort to find a country for the flight to land was the major conflict points in the plot. The aircraft was denied landing in the United Kingdom at Heathrow, then they were rejected when they returned to Frankfurt, Germany when they had a change of mind. Then the aircraft tried to land at a U.S. Air Force base in the UK but they were thwarted at the last minute by UK officials. Then the pilot tried to land in the Netherlands, saying that they would never turn down a flight in distress, but again, the Netherlands were persuaded to turn away the flight.

The CIA and the White House become the predominate agencies in the lead on the situation, and they have given orders not to allow anyone to leave the plane when they are finally given permission to land at a U.S. Air Force base in Iceland. The Iceland ground crew leader communicates with the pilot and says, "I am under orders to absolutely prevent any human being from leaving that aircraft – that's a deadly force authorized order Do I make myself clear?" The use of deadly force is warranted if it is an immediate threat to public safety or national security, and that determination was made when this order was given.

Aboard the flight is the Ambassador-at-large who is a target of Al Aqbar, noted as the worst terrorist group in the world and a threat to the U.S. In order to make them more of a priority, a CIA operative begins a rogue operation to use a pilot to attack the commercial flight while it is in the air, and then blame it on Al Aqbar. The CIA rogue agent then tries to stop Dr. Ronnie Sanders, the CIA medical doctor who is advising on the Doomsday virus infection believed to be on board.

While on the ground in Iceland, they remove the now dead body of the American professor and they also have to shoot a woman trying to escape from the plane.

A dramatic moment when a civilian passenger is shot on the tarmack in Iceland.

Some of the passengers become agitated, and shove the stewardess. The pilot says, "you just committed a felony" which is a true statement concerning federal law which prohibits assaulting airline personnel.

In the White House, the President's aid is briefing him on the situation The President says, "If we have to sacrifice 150 people to save 260 million American lives, we will, John, but we do not make it our first choice." The President lives to regret his signature on an order to blow up the flight with a low yield nuclear bomb which specifies if they all die of the virus, but the order appears much more strident.

Can the President order the destruction of a civilian aircraft? In 1996, the answer would be that yes, but it is unprecedented. However, during the morning of September 11, 2001, the President of the United States was asked to give Rules of Engagement for shooting down commercial aircraft that might be seen in the air after FAA had ordered all aircraft to land. At 10:25am, the 9/11 Commission Report finds that an order was given by Vice President Richard Cheney to shoot down commercial aircraft. The protocol requires that it is the President who gives orders to "engage" and those are to be given directly to the Secretary of Defense. Given the disarray that morning and the President's absence from the White House on a visit in Florida, confusion as to the President's involvement in this order has remained unclear.[37]

Turning now, back to Flight 66 in *Pandora's Clock*, the commercial aircraft is now being escorted by four F-16 fighter aircraft but they are not sure if it is to protect them or to ensure they never land.

They are given permission to go to Mauritania in the Sahara Desert at an abandoned air strip to land but in route they are attacked by the terrorist flight.

CIA medical doctor, Dr. Ronnie Sanders manages to reach them via satellite phone using the Iridium satellite, and tells them about the double agent plot to have them shot out of the sky and blame the Al Aqbar terrorist organization. The pilot is skeptical about whether she is really from the CIA or a terrorist herself, but he soon discovers he is under attack and one of the engines is blown off of the jet. They manage to recover and he changes his plan and heads for Las Palmas, Canary Islands. There, they refuel, and the terrorist pilot sees them and continues to pursue them, but the terrorist plane goes down in flames in a runway game of "chicken".

The pilot then plans to go to Barbados or the Virgin Islands, concluding that if he gets close to the U.S. and Miami the news crews will be watching so closely that the U.S. will not allow them to be blown up or bombed.

Plans change again, and they land in the Ascension Islands, in the Atlantic Ocean and people are allowed to deplane because the quarantine period has passed and no one is ill.

The end of the movie is a meeting at their beach house with the pilot who has married the Ambassador's assistant and a visit from Dr. Sanders. Just after Dr. Sanders arrives at the beach house for a visit, the phone rings and they are told that one of the crew members was hospitalized with a fever and flu-like symptoms and died in 48 hours. Someone says these are the symptoms of the Doomsday Virus, and the movie ends.

This is a made-for-television movie that runs 176 minutes.

---

[37] The 9/11 Commission Report (July 22, 2004) pp. 36-37.

Contagious (1997)

RATING

Dr. Hannah Cole
It's cholera. Ever seen vibrio?

First Medical Examiner
No. Nasty Looking aren't they?

---*Contagious* (1997)

*Contagious (*1997) takes cholera and makes it a biohorror scenario. Starting with the drug mule who arrives from Bogota, Columbia bringing the disease to the spread through city after city, the real-life rapid spread of cholera needs no sensationalization to make if horrific.

Lindsay Wagner plays Dr. Cole, the intrepid epidemiologist who works for "Pacific Health Services" a fictitious government public health agency, who is the first to diagnosis the disease. Dr. Cole comments, "The problem with cholera is that it just kills *so* fast."

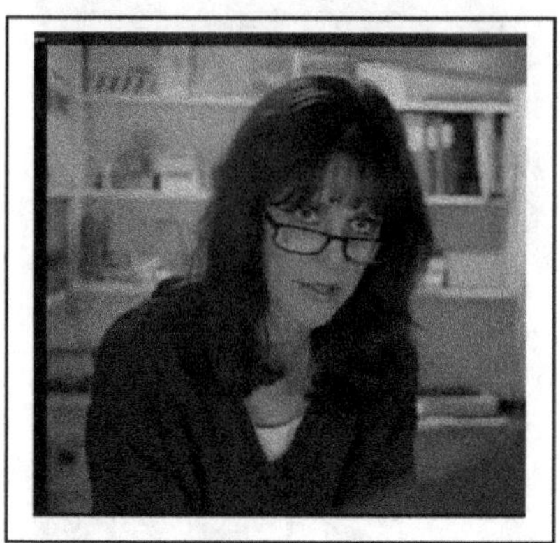

A bigger problem seems to be Dr. Cole's credentials for having patient contact and performing autopsies. It is revealed that she worked for CDC and she introduces herself as an "epidemiologist", but not a physician. To have patient contact for treatment purposes she would have to be trained as a medical doctor, nurse or physician's assistant, yet she treats patients and is participating in several lifesaving procedures in the emergency department. In these two screenshots, she is involved in an autopsy in the morgue and making a determination as to cause of death. Typically, a medical examiner would be certified by the American Board of Pathology, having done a post-medical school residency in pathology. An epidemiologist would have an advanced degree in the field of epidemiology which is the tracing of diseases through the population using interviewing and mapping techniques.

The police are not very interested in the case, but assign detective "Lou" to the case, who is a rebellious woman

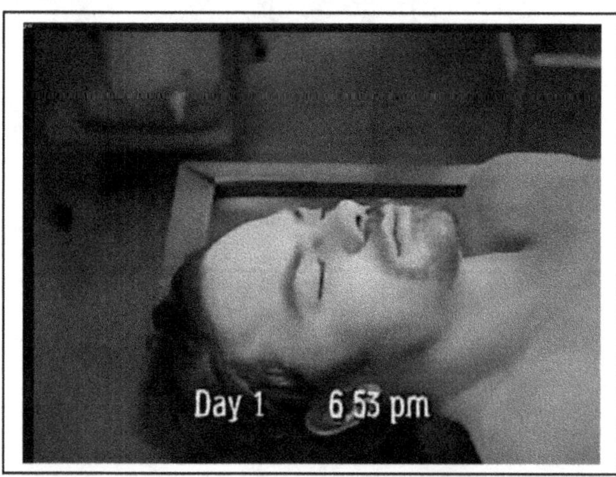

among a department of male detectives. She is happy to take on this challenge. Lou befriends Dr. Cole and vows to help her solve the crime to get at the source of the cholera.

The Emergency Room is overflowing with sick patients and one man confronts Dr. Cole about his unhappiness with the treatment his wife is receiving. When he threatens to leave with his wife, Dr. Cole and her colleague have this exchange with him:

Doctor
Sir, your wife has a
contagious disease. Until .

Husband
I am not listening to
some loser public health doctor.

Dr. Cole
Yes, you are.

Husband
Excuse me?

Dr. Cole
I am an epidemiologist with the
Pacific Health Service and
I am telling you . . .

Husband
I can walk right
out of here, too.

Dr. Cole
Oh no you can't. If you don't
cooperate I have the power
to detain you for public safety.
Shall I call security?

Husband
No. But you are looking
at one hell of a lawsuit!

The epidemiologist could ask the Board of Health to issue an order to quarantine the woman, but without that order, security really has no power to detain them except for a period long enough to obtain the emergency order. It is possible that in California, the local Board of Health could issue such an order very quickly and detain an infectious person who is immediately dangerous to the public. As far as the lawsuit that the husband threatens, it is highly unlikely that a court would second guess the judgment of the agency in its area of expertise unless his wife was held beyond a time when she was no longer a threat to public health and safety. Courts typically defer to the expertise of agencies on matters that require specialized knowledge such as public health determinations.[38]

At the end of Act 2, Dr. Cole is confronted by a reporter who asks,

Reporter
How many are dead? [pause]
You have an epidemic!

Dr. Cole
No, we have an outbreak.

The Pacific Health Services has known for two days at this point that they have a cholera outbreak, yet they are attempting to keep it from the press in order to avoid panicking the population, according to Dr. Cole.

In 1997, the use of the internet, and instant electronic communication was not available, or the news would have leaked within hours. In 2007, ten years later, the year the International Health Regulations were effective, the occurrence of a case of cholera in the United States would have triggered a report to the federal Centers for Diseases Control and Prevention (CDC) and a report from the Department of Health and Human Services to the World Health Organization that a Public Health Emergency of International Concern (PHEIC) had occurred. This would be required within 24 hours of making an official determination at the DHHS level that this outbreak met the requirements of a PHEIC, which includes risk of international transmission. Given this case came from Bogota, Columbia, this would indicate there is already international risk.

With Act 3 left, Dr. Cole's husband who has taken his own biological children on a hiking trip begins to get ill. The search in the state park to find her husband and his rescue and treatment complete the cycle of the five day outbreak of cholera. Also during Act 3, Detective Lou tracks down the cocaine bosses and during the sting arrest, she is shot in the arm but shoots two of the suspects as they try to escape. Since they shot at her first, she had an easy case of self-defense to protect her police record. A flight attendant is also taken ill and is evacuated by biosuited Taiwanese at the Tapei airport, with no real connection to the rest of the story, except that he was a flight attendant on the ill-fated flight from Bogata, Columbia with the contagious drug mule. At that point, the epidemiologists had already made the connection with flight 117 and had tracked the passengers and alerted them that they might be infected.

The tracking of the passengers from the flight posed a legal problem which was a confrontation between Dr. Cole and her public health agency supervisor. Dr. Cole follows her supervisor to his American-flagged office (although she was part of the Pacific Health Service, a fictitious public health agency in California, not a federal office) and inquires about the airline's passenger list:

Supervisor
That's what they said - no.

---

[38] The *Chevron* doctrine is named after a case which set forth a procedure for courts to defer to government agency decisions that are highly technical with specialized knowledge unless they are just contrary to written law or are not reasonable interpretations of the law.

Dr. Cole

How can they do that, do
they understand what is going on?

Supervisor

Absolutely. Hanna, if the airlines
served contaminated seafood they
are open to all kinds of litigation
not to mention bad publicity.

Dr. Cole

That's ridiculous. I need that
passenger list now.
Can we force them to give it to us?

Supervisor

Their CEO is looking at this.
It's going to take a little time.

Dr. Cole

We don't have time! There were
as many as 60 passengers
on that flight who were exposed.

Interestingly, the airlines in 1997 kept only paper manifests of flights and any search would take days to find the information. Even if they found the manifest, the airlines did not keep contact information.

In 2006, the FAA proposed regulations that would require the airlines to keep contact information and manifest data for up to three years, and to collect a long list of personal contact information including the destination and contact information at their destination. This was an unprecedented proposed regulation that infringed on privacy interests to such an extent, it was questionable whether this might exceed constitutional protections. It did exceed privacy protections in Germany, and this was only a concern because airline reservation data was routed through the international reservation system called "Amadeus" which is based in Germany. The fact that the private information would pass through and be stored in Germany meant that it was a violation of their own privacy laws and they objected to being a part of this new regulatory requirement. The regulation failed in 2006 and it was several years before the FAA sought to ask for any private information, again.

Dr. Cole also asked the key question – can we force the airlines to give us the passenger list? Airlines are required to disclose the passenger manifest to the CDC for "contact tracing" purposes and CDC can send an administrative order to the airlines requesting the data. Airlines today would likely see the wisdom in making an attempt to notify sick passengers to seek treatment rather than being seen as withholding information that would have saved the lives of its customers. This would be a much better position for the airlines in the event of litigation.

In one of the most important scenes in the movie, and one which was anticipated from the first few moments of the outbreak, a patient with cholera presents in the

Emergency Department with a positive cocaine test. When he is presented with this information by Dr. Cole, he simply refuses to answer any questions and demands a lawyer:

Patient
[to the nurse]
I want a lawyer.

Nurse
That's one thing we don't have on tap here, thank God.

Clearly, having a lawyer to respond to these questions was not wanted by the medical staff. (It is also somewhat clear, that the film producer also did not want lawyers around to give technical advice on this movie.)

This may be the most difficult legal question in this movie, and that is whether you can require a person to give incriminating evidence to a public health official for purposes of responding to a public health emergency. An analysis might flow from the urgency of the situation. If the information was needed to respond to an emergency public health event, then it would be warranted for the individual to disclose the source of his cocaine, for example. However, this would be contrary to the protection of the Fifth Amendment which prevents the individual from making statements that are incriminating. The statement made to the public health official could be revealed by a subpoena to the public health official or a deposition. Even a confidential statement to a physician is subject to discovery in a court of law. The only person to whom such a statement could be made that would not be discoverable would be to an attorney representing the individual. So the hospital might have been wise to find a criminal lawyer appointee for this patient as soon as possible. The criminal lawyer would likely have sought to make a deal with the state prosecutor to avoid liability for his client in exchange for the information to help the public health agency, and then his Fifth Amendment protection would be preserved and the public health agency would have their vital information. The law enforcement officials would likely want to seek the information given to the public health officials, but without an order to force them to disclose it to law enforcement officials, they would not be obligated to disclose.

The issue of simultaneous interviews of individuals who had both public health information and criminal information has occurred in one state investigation. The case involved a rape in a mental institution. The victims of the rape had contracted a sexually-transmitted disease. Public health officials needed to know with whom these individuals had sexual contact in order to stop the spread of infection. Criminal investigators needed to know who had raped the victims. Each victim had what could only be two psychologically painful interviews. Later efforts have been made to design interviews that could be done only once, and shared with both law enforcement and public health officials without disclosing private health information or criminal information inappropriately.[39]

The legal questions and the realism of the cholera outbreak are interesting and challenging for 1997, many of which are still problems decades later.

---

[39] Victoria Sutton, " Dual Purpose Bioterrorism Investigations in Law Enforcement and Public Health Protection: How to Make Them Work Consistent with the Rule of Law," *6 Houston Journal of Health Law 165-185 (2005).* Practitioner's guide to criminal and public health investigations in a potential bioterrorism event. http://www.law.uh.edu/hjhlp/Issues/Vol%206.1/Sutton.pdf

Contaminated Man (2000)

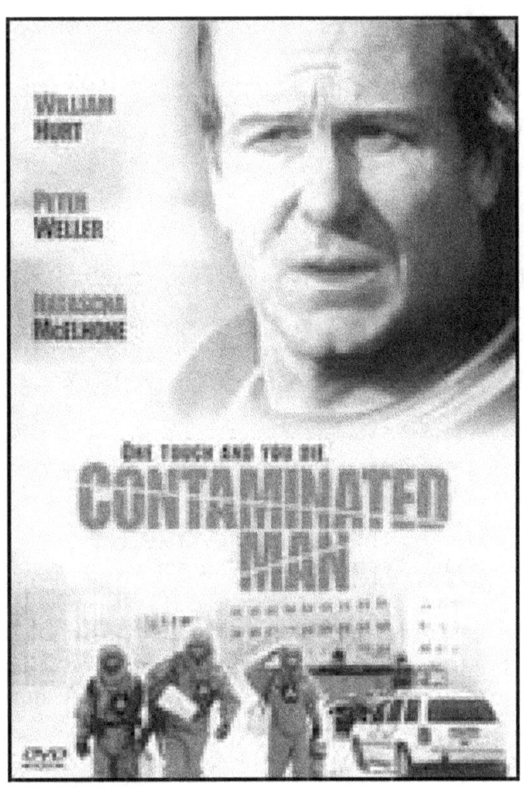

RATING

David Whitman

Whatever happened they are a one man walking plague.

---*The Contaminated Man* (2000)

Contaminated Man (2000) is a pre-9/11 movie about a toxin so powerful that it causes a fatal heart attack preceded by neurological and other physiological reactions within one to two minutes ending in a painful death with foam from the mouth and a swollen tongue protruding from the mouth. This deadly agent called Trinoxin-3 is a weapon designed as a "surgical strike tool – the first strategic chemical weapon," so says Holly, the CIA operative on site.

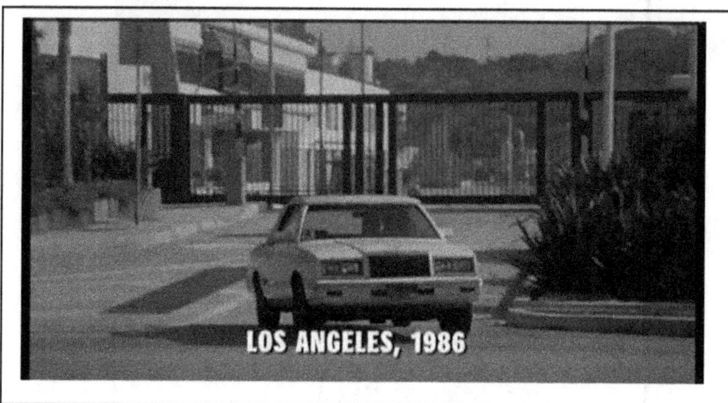

The movie opens with David Whitman driving home in a casual conversation with his wife on his car phone.

William Hirt plays David Whitman, the environmental expert from the United Nations, the international organization of the nations of the world. He is called away from his lake cleanup duties to attend to a laboratory accident. Holly Anderson, played by Natascha McElhone, is the CIA field officer who appears on the scene and meets David who does not welcome her intrusion as he sees it. An NSA (National Security Agency) operative makes his fumbled appearance by hiding in the back seat of Holly's car, which does not go unnoticed by Holly. She circles around her car and confronts him with a gun to his head, then she recognizes him when he turns around. NSA is an unwelcome appearance, as he tells her that they are there to protect this vital "surgical strike tool" as Holly later describes this encounter to David. Holly has been enlisted by NSA to help them.

NSA seems a rather strange choice as a government entity with interests in the toxin, since there expertise is in communications and internet traffic. Most NSA folk do not operate by hiding in the back seats of cars. A Department of Defense laboratory like DTRA or DARPA would have been more likely the agency interested in the recovery of an uncontained toxin weapon.

The trinoxin-3 we learn was developed as a weapon, and this is expressly forbidden by the Biological and Toxins Weapons Convention, to which the United States is a party, effective 1975, as well as the nations involved in this drama – Germany, Hungary, the United Kingdom.

The laboratory accident is caused by a disgruntled employee, Joseph Muller, who has been laid off, putting pressure on his ability to pay alimony, a condition of his visitation of his eight-year old son. By 2000, most state courts were clear about not making alimony payment a condition for visitation by the non-custodial parent. However, this was the key element of the story that drove the laid off employee to try to talk to his boss. Not getting any satisfaction from his brief encounter with the boss, he follows them into the most secure area of the laboratory and then begins turning over cabinets, crashing glass testtubes and dishes and equipment. The toxin

escapes into the air, killing some of the people, but the disgruntled employee just picks himself up, dusts himself off and scurries away into what is the Balaton Region of Hungary according to the opening legend.

The scene which introduces Joseph is his early morning trip to work and he is entering through a security gate to which he no longer has access. His colleague opens the door for him and he passes through, his colleague believing from their conversation that Joseph is also not one of the employees laid off. Laboratory biosecurity protocols in general specifically prohibit using an access card for another employee but this movie shows how easily this can happen. Safeguards for entry now include retina scanners, fingerprint pads and/or passcards, but most of these are designed to allow someone with legitimate access to allow anyone accompanying him or her to enter at the same time. Once inside, Joseph becomes more desperate to talk to the managers who then put him off, leading him to begin vandalizing the glass-walled laboratory which he enters by following closely behind the managers. Again, laboratory biosecurity would have required all of them to have on biosuits and to go through several rooms before entering this level of security. At one point, the toxin is described as needing handling at "Level 5". While this is a meaningless numbering reference, there are four biological safety levels for handling toxins and biological agents on the select agent list, a regulated list for dangerous pathogens. This would seem to indicate the highest level of containment for the "Trinoxin-3" toxin.

The biosuits are an accurate depiction with yellow suits for the United States and white suits for Europe. During this period, these were the colors of biosuits purchased. However, the use of the biosuits in the movie showed the wearers walking out of the building during the investigation and hosing down on the building steps, but before they were hosed down, they stopped and chatted with Holly who has no biosuit on at the time. This would have unnecessarily exposed Holly to whatever might have been clinging to the biosuits during their investigation of the destroyed laboratory.

Joseph Muller, played by Peter Weller is the "contaminated man" and he carries a toy airplane with him throughout the chase scenes, at one point dropping it off the roof when a police officer chases him. The police officer is immediately affected and falls off the balcony but Joseph continues on his way to find his son, retrieving the model airplane on the way. He infects a number of people on his journey – a police officer, a hotel clerk, a gaming casino customer and finally, Holly.

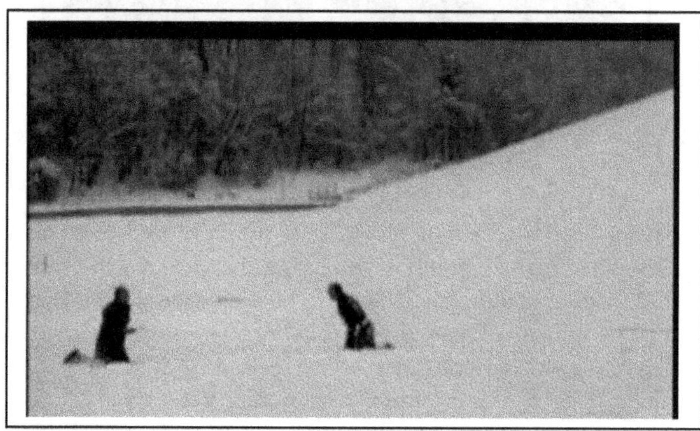

Yes, Holly, in a brave move in the last scene to save Joseph Muller from a sniper is splattered with his blood as the sniper successfully plants a bullet in Joseph's neck and presumptively the juglar vein judging from the spewing blood that reached Holly's face. David and Holly recognize this, and he quickly recovers from his the sniper bullet that had gone into his back. He uses the antidote he has handy which had been prepared to help Joseph Muller before the snipers took him out.

This biohorror drama illustrates the failures of the United States to adequately control its toxin-based weapons but more importantly the extent to which ethical behavior is forfeited in favor of protecting the weapon resource. The bad guys are the NSA and to a lesser extent the compromised CIA operative, Holly. The affected innocent are those nice people who were touched by the contaminated man, Joseph, and died a terrible death in a minute or two. The heros were Holly and particularly David, an idealistic scientist who learns in the course of the movie that his own wife and child's death had been due to the NSA making him a human experiment without his knowledge.

In 2000 when Contaminated Man was released, the federal government had a history of admitted experimenting on human subjects without their knowledge. The Clinton Administration had just settled with members of the military who had been intentionally exposed to radiation in experiments. In 1996, the United States paid $4.8 million to the victims and their estates for this wrongdoing.[40] The use of human subjects without informed consent in 2000 was illegal and violated the "common rule" for informing human subjects of the risks before engaging in any experimentation. The rule has roots in the Nuremberg Code, developed from the hearings at the Nuremberg trial which tried Nazis from World War II who had engaged in human experimentation and torture.

Contaminated Man is an interesting scenario of the consequences of the release of a toxin that is not contagious, but is spread only by one index case, even though the 1-2 minute time to death was unrealistic. Even the polonium-210 poisoning of Alexander Litvinenko, the Russian journalist in 2006 took three weeks to reach death after contamination.

---

[40] http://www.nytimes.com/1996/11/20/us/us-to-settle-for-4.8-million-in-suits-on-radiation-testing.html?pagewanted=all&src=pm

Venomous (2001)

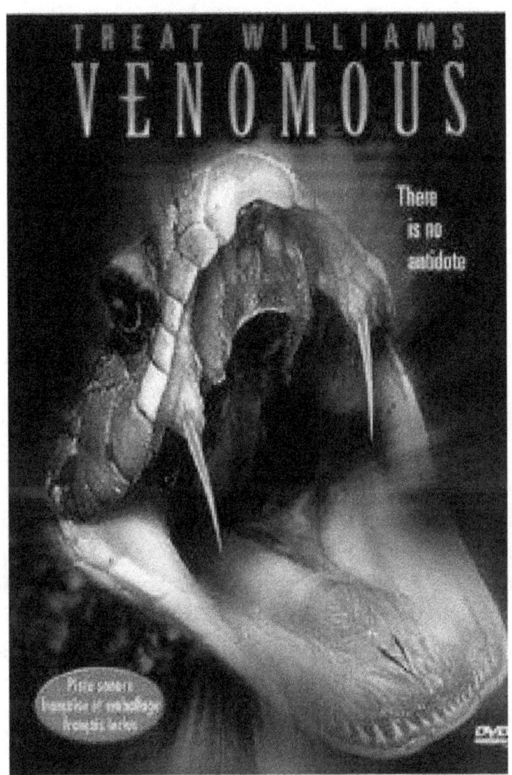

RATING

General Arthur Mancheck
I want an immediate and total blackout of all non-military communication.
[walks into Sheriff's office]
Are you in charge here?

Sheriff
Yes, I am and I would advise you to keep that in mind.

Gen Arthur Mancheck
Santa Mira Springs is under immediate quarantine for purposes of controlling a lethal infection.

Sheriff
By whose authority?

Gen Arthur Mancheck
General Arthur Mancheck, U.S. Army. I'll expect your full cooperation to help control the citizenry. No one is to enter or leave the area without further notice. Sheriff?

----*Venomous* (2001)

Venomous (2001) should not be dismissed because of its choice of snakes as the delivery device for a virus. After all, fangs make a convenient method of injection and the snakes just do what snakes do naturally. A race for an antidote, a government coverup and a citywide quarantine --- this movie has all the elements of the subgenre of biohorror and biothriller and makes the List. But this movie is most important because it marks the first movie to adapt elements from movies in the same subgenre, a strong indicator that biohorror and biothriller movies have earned the distinction of a singular subgenre.

The opening legend reads "November 1990". Early in the movie the audience is introduced to the snakes after terrorists gain entry into a government laboratory and see the development of snakes as weapons. The jihadi terrorists use a suitcase filled with C-4 explosives to demolish the building thinking they are protecting "their people", but the snakes escape into the surrounding desert.

This frameshot is the manner in which these aggressive new genetically engineered snakes emerge from the ground. The earthquake activity suggests that either it is bringing the snakes out, or the snakes are causing the tremors by their massive numbers. However, throughout the movie, the snakes are not depicted in any manner beyond their normal horrifying natural behavior. Those who live in the desert will tell you it is not unheard of for a rattlesnake to enter a house, and this is part of the horror experienced with these rattlesnakes.

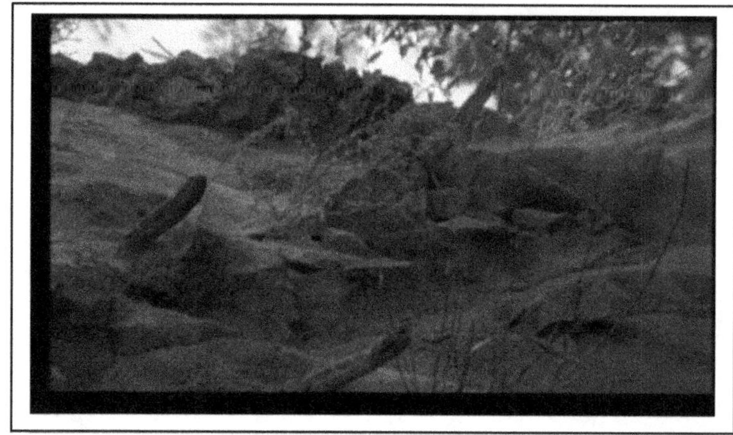

The first indication that this movie is paying homage to other movies in its subgenre is the leading characters. There are two scientists who are in the middle of a divorce and find they have to work together to save the world from a lethal virus. If that sounds familiar, then you probably watched *Outbreak* (1995). Dr. Sam Daniels and Dr. Robby Keogh from *Outbreak* (1995) find counterparts in Dr. David Henning and Dr. Christine Edmonton Henning. Newly separated, Dr. Edmonton, has just moved away to start a new job with the Department of Defense Virology Research Center. Dr. Henning plays the small town emergency room physician. The analogies do not stop with the characters, but extend to their conflicts and plot turning points.

The opening dialogue in this review, is the point where General Arthur Manchek assumes control of the city of Santa Mira Springs, California. Here is the frameshot of the Sheriff as he relinquishes control to the General with nothing more than his verbal order.

The quarantine lacks the grand imagery of that of *Outbreak* (1995), but many of the same angles depict news reporters standing at the barbed wire as they discuss the quarantine. This is the low budget version of a town quarantine compared to the Outbreak (1995) citywide quarantine with the border staffed with dozens of military officers, tanks and long fencelines.

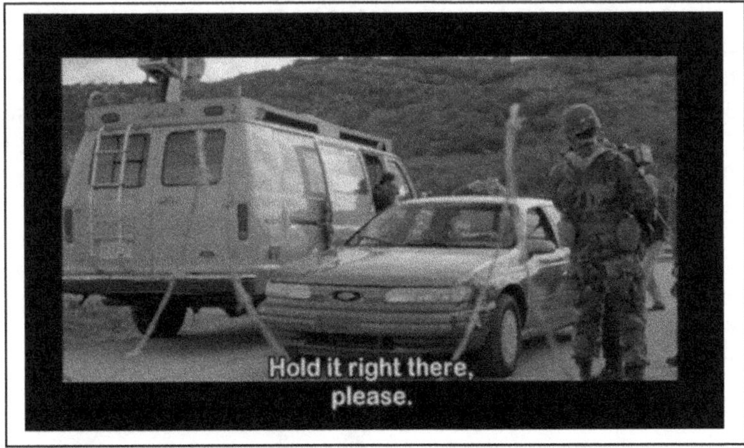

If "Directive 7-12" has a familiar ring, then you watched Andromeda Strain. It is an order given by the President to fire bomb a site, village or city where a biological disease threatens to destroy society. In *Andromeda Strain* (1971), Directive 7-12 was being activated to firebomb Wildfire, the government laboratory, but after receiving a report from Manchek, he postpones the firebombing for 48 hours and quarantines Piedmont and a hundred miles around it.

Major Manchek from the *Andromeda Strain* (1971) also finds a namesake in *Venomous* (2001) with the General Arthur Manchek, as well as Major Sparks from *Andromeda Strain* (1971)finds his counterpart with Commanding General Sparks in *Venomous (*2001).

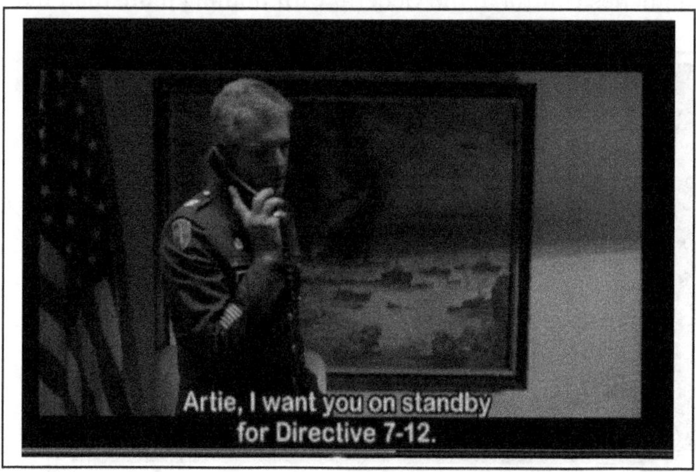

In *Andromeda Strain (1971),* the government did not obtain the support of the President's Science Advisor, although Ed David was the science advisor, who thought he was ignored by President Nixon who promptly abolished the position after his re-election in 1972.

But here in *Venomous* (2001), the President's Science Advisor in the time period of the movie, 1990, was D. Allan Bromley, and I was a member of the staff. My conclusion is that there is no such document as a Directive 7-12, but it has taken on a life of its own as a plot device in the biohorror subgenre.

The military quarantine, omits the entire discussion of *Posse comitatus* and whether the President is the authority needed to order the quarantine. Commanding General Sparks from the Pentagon is not ordering the quarantine – it is the lower ranking General Arthur Manchek who announces the quarantine is on his order. That is so far outside the constitutional jurisprudential legal framework of *Posse Comitatus* one would have to begin with the question of where is the media and the ACLU when you need them?

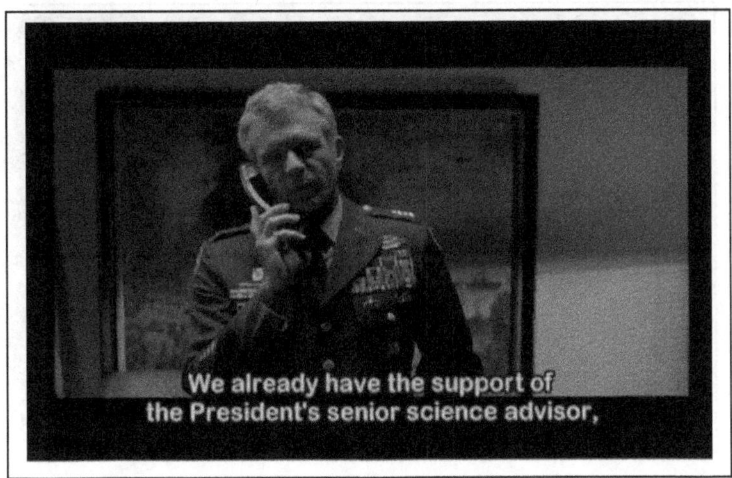

The next frameshot is a blast directed from a helicopter to the civilian car, fleeing from the quarantine.

Two cars attempt to break quarantine. The first is tracked and shot by a helicopter, reminiscent of the famous scene in *Outbreak* (1995), but in *Venomous* (2001), the driver modifies this scene when he gets out of his burning car, goes to his trunk and pulls out his shoulder-fired anti-aircraft missle launcher and takes down the helicopter! However, a second helicopter quickly retaliates with deadly force, the Commanding General finding that the military was simply acting in self-defense.

Meanwhile, Dr. Henning is out looking for a rattlesnake to use for its antibodies to create a vaccine to save the town. Just like *Outbreak* (1995), Dr. Edmonton develops an infection and it is up to Dr. Henning to develop the antibodies and make the vaccine. In Outbreak, Dr. Robby Keogh stabs a needle through her glove; and in Venomous, Dr. Edmonston falls in the laboratory and a broken testtube shard pokes through her glove. virology institute is shocking, unless you conclude that it is the fault of the military for not bringing in appropriate gear for the investigation of this epidemic.

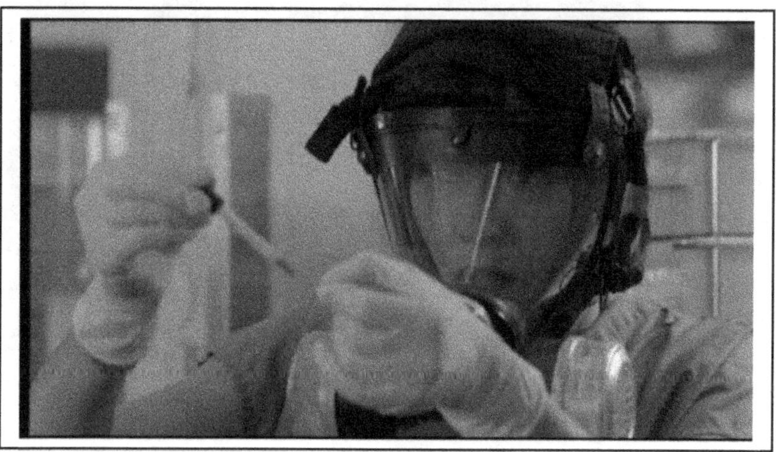

The critical difference here for quality is that in Outbreak, Dr. Keogh had single layer rubber gloves on to give an injection to her colleague who had fallen ill, and had the accident without her full body protective equipment, level four biosuit. In *Venomous* (2001), Dr. Henning is working on a virus that should be held in BSL-4 containment, but instead, she is wearing a short-sleeved scrub and simple, one layer rubber gloves! The respirator she is using is a simple filter which will not stop viruses as effectively as a full PAPR device that has pumps oxygen from an outside source into the suit. The lack of biosafety for a scientist at the nation's top military virology research center.

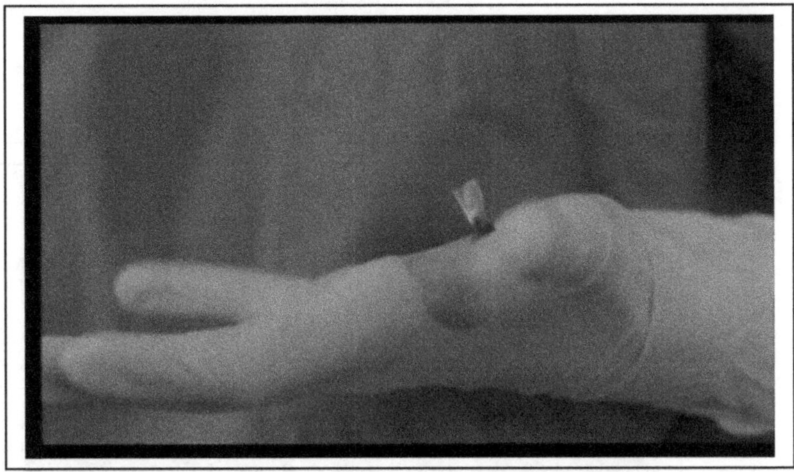

The analogies continue when aircraft are summoned to carry out "Directive 7-12" with a bomb. The aircraft leave Vanderberg Air Force Base in northern California, the same Base from which the fighter jets were deployed in *Outbreak* (1995). Except in Venomous (2001) they use a Stealth bomber which looks amazing, but since the media are reporting on every movement, it is hardly a stealth operation.

In a moment between the Generals, reminiscent of *Outbreak* (1995) where Gen. McClintock is arrested by General Billy Ford for "withholding information from the President," it appears there will be another arrest. However, instead, there are no other military troops around when Gen. Manchek confronts Maj. Gen. Sparks and says, "Tom, all due respect, they have the vaccine. It's not too late to save those people." Almost exactly the same sentiment as expressed in the moment between the Generals in Outbreak. But it is here that the scripts diverge. Gen. Manchek makes no arrest and instead, Maj. Gen. Sparks simply shoots him! A rather disappointing outcome in the battle of good verses evil.

Maj Gen. Sparks has had a conversation from the Pentagon with who must be the Chief of Staff to the President, about using Directive 7-12, and much like *Pandora's Clock* (1996) where the President is coerced into signing an order to eradicate American civilians, the Chief of Staff is passing along false information that everyone in town is dead from the epidemic:

Chief of Staff
[on phone with Gen. Sparks]
I'll meet with the President immediately. In the meantime I want a door-to-door search. Check all the outlying areas within the quarantine. The President will need 100% assurance that there are absolutely no survivors before he will even consider something like this.

Gen. Sparks

It's being done as we speak. Your country thanks you, sir.
[Hangs up the phone, and sneers.]

So far, *Venomous* (2001) has paid homage to *Andromeda Strain* (1971), *Outbreak* (1995), *Pandora's Clock* (1996). But there is one more --- the first of the modern classics in this subgenre, *The Satan Bug* (1965). Here is a monologue from Gen. Sparks:

Dr. Edmonton

[speaking to Gen. Sparks after he shot Gen. Manchek]
You created this bug didn't you?

Gen. Sparks

We call it the Satan bug. Not entirely original, I am afraid. But the biblical connotations proved irresistible, given the bug's carrier.
A genetically engineered breed of supersnake for more aggressive and cunning than its mundane cousins to be deployed against Saddam's troops during Desert Storm.
Unfortunately, a messy security breach some years ago caused the program to be suspended. Though not before a number of the prototype specimens escaped into the wild, and began to breed.

When Gen. Sparks goes off in his helicopter to supervise the operation, they are attacked by snakes that have boarded the helicopter and in his panic, Gen. Sparks shoots the control panel of the helicopter sending them to a firey finish.

Meanwhile, Dr. Edmonston has gotten to the media at the fenceline and told the world that there are still people in the town and to call off the bombing. Just in the nick of time, the Chief of Staff sees the broadcast and the stealth pilot is told to abort his mission and return. Dr. Henning has done his part and gone into town and shot a flare at the Stealth apparently delaying him for the split second he needed to hear the order to abort his mission.

The resolution is what you would expect – they still have to eradicate the snakes. The Department of Defense is seen on the desert killing the snakes in their den. "A spokesman for the Department of Defense Virology Research Center confirmed that all of the snakes infected with the virus have been accounted for."

Anytime an announcement like this is made by the government, be afraid, be very afraid. The final scene is deep in the snake pit and the audience sees that a few rattlesnakes survive.

Killer Buzz (2001)
Also known as **Flying Virus**

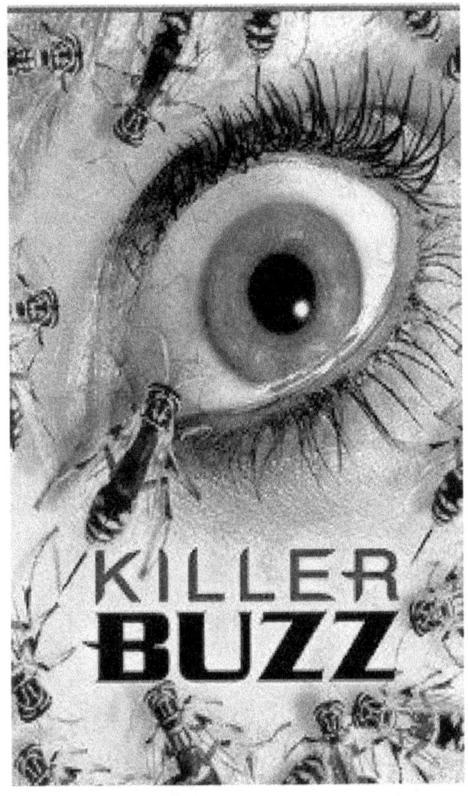

RATING

Worker

```
These babies really are the perfect killers.
These bioengineered beauties cleared six towns.
No wonder they call them demons from the sky.
```

---*Killer Buzz* (2001)

Killer Buzz (2001) opens with a political setup that the United States has failed to sign the Kyoto Protocol leading to global unrest, the treaty that would bind nations to limits on the rates of increase of carbon dioxide to slow global change. This led to an agreement to build a road into the villages in Brazil, the setting of this movie.

The petroleum companies that are being given access have indigenous tribes attack them, so they begin a project to develop a killer bee species that will attack the tribes and allow the drilling to continue. A Caucasian physician, a Vietnam Medi-vac doctor and helicopter pilot, becomes their "savior" and joins the tribes and finds a cure for the bee venom.

The two leading characters are newly separated couple. You may be reminded of the similarly situated couples in *Outbreak*(1995) and *Venomous* (2001) which ultimately are thrown back together because of their work and old differences begin to seem trivial or they are resolved in the throes of a deadly virus. The wife, Anne Bauer is a reporter who has gone off to report on the roadbuilding in Brazil. Her husband, Martin Bauer, has come to Brazil to convince her to return to New York and stay together. The personal conflict is about selfishness and whether to have children and appears insurmountable.

Anne's reporting takes her to the village of indigenous people in the rainforest. Here, at a pivotal moment, the bees re unleashed and attack the representative from the U.S. Department of State who is complicit in the grooming of these bees with some unsavory characters.

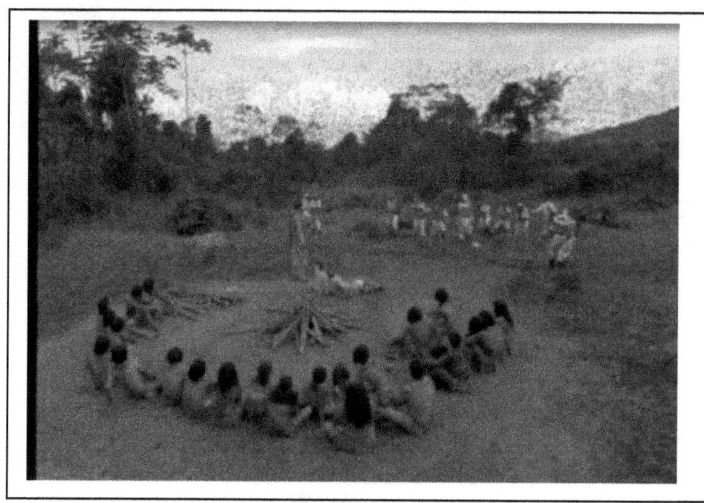

The bees are a superbee engineered with a venom that contains an ebola-like virus. Like *Venomous* (2001), which used the natural fangs of the rattlesnake for injecting a virus, *Killer Buzz* (2001) uses the natural stinger of bee for injecting the virus. Both are ebola-like viruses. The bees are seen as a secret bioweapon that one of the opportunistic news media people with Anne decides to take back to the United States to sell to the highest bidder. Predictably, the bees escape on the flight back to the U.S., and begin attacking the passengers. Martin Bauer, Anne's husband, who is returning to New York, happens to be on the flight and turns out to be a hero by cleverly and bravely letting the bees get sucked out of an open door.

A missle is launched to shoot down the aircraft, and the State Department seems to be behind it. This would be highly unusual for the State Department to be involved in a fast moving and unfolding incident. It would be more likely the CIA or the FBI. However, in this scenario which was triggered by the failure for the U.S. to sign the treaty and the negotiated road building project, which would have been led by the Department of State, it is logical that the Department of State would have the self-interest to keep this a secret. Apparently, they have been made aware of the virus on the way to the U.S.

Shooting down a civilian aircraft can only be done on the order of the President, and at no time does it appear that the President is involved in the decision. The computer nerd, teenage boy, on board finds the encrypted password for the missle that has been launched toward their aircraft and diverts it, just in time, but theshock waves from the blast cause damage to the fuel line, increasing the urgency and tension to land. However, this act of saving the plane eventually does the trick to impress the teenager's love interest on board, a teen girl who has been less than receptive to his earlier advances.

Can bees be boarded on a flight to the U.S. from another country? Anytime an agricultural pest or agricultural organism is imported into the United States, the Department of Agriculture has statutory authority to control it. Bees are used in the honey trade, but they can also be an invasive species that would harm other bees, bring in bee viruses or take over habitat that belongs to indigenous bees. The USDA office that handles these permits is the APHIS, which allows only honey bees and a few other specific species into the U.S. and only from two countries – Canada and New Zealand, at least at the time of this publication.

In this frameshot, Dr. Stephen North who hopes to get rich quick on the bees, checks them as organs for transport, raising no questions from the desk agent.

The smuggling of the bees is done by packing them in a box marked "organs"

Bees may be transported on commercial aircraft even in carryon luggage, as long as the travel is all within the continental United States.

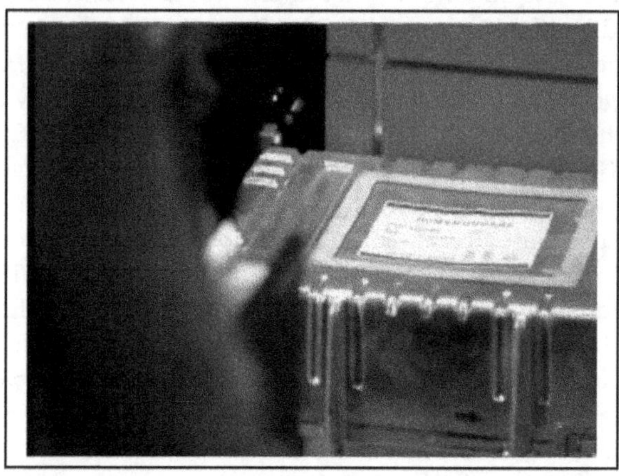

What might happen with bees on a plane? Well we have an example. In May 28, 2011, the Russian newspaper, *Hurryat Daily News*, reported that a man had boarded a flight from Moscow on its way to a city in eastern Russia with a box of bees, stored in the business class section of the aircraft. The container came open and began swarming the cabin. The passengers were said to have been in shock and panic, but there were no reports about stings. The investigation showed that the Assistant Airport Manager had helped the man in taking take them aboard and had assisted him in circumventing security to get to his flight without discovery of the bees.[41]

As the disaster on the flight heightened, the pilots were confused as to why they were not being allowed to land. The first pilot then discovers the reason:

Pilot
I know why they won't let us land.
I just talked to a friend over in
Ecuadorian Air National. Rumor is
we are carrying a type of virus
like ebola or something.

Robert Hauer
[standing in the cockpit]
What?

Pilot
Someone got a call from the
U.S. State Department confirming.

Robert Hauer
U.S. State Department?

[41]"Bees on Russian Plane Panic Passengers," *Hurriyat Daily News*, Aug 18, 2011
http://www.hurriyetdailynews.com/default.aspx?pageid=438&n=bees-on-russian-plane-panic-passengers-2011-08-18 .

Pilot

No one is ever going to
let us land with a virus on board.

In practice, the pilot may be right, that no airport will allow them to land. However, legally, the air traffic controllers would direct the aircraft to an airport with an international quarantine station, of which there are about thirty in the U.S.. Here, they could better assess the health of the passengers.

The transport of ebola is regulated by the U.S. Department of Transportation and the U.S. Centers for Diseases Control and Prevention. International importation of an ebola virus would require a CDC import permit and identification of all the individuals involved in transporting the virus – the sender, the receiver and the contact information from the originator. It is a felony to fail to include the emergency contact information on the shipping container. However, if the virus is undiagnosed, the bees could be brought in as "diagnostic specimens" and avoid all of the strict transport requirements, which many see as a serious gap in regulating viruses that may come into the United States.

There is a bit of suggestion that the writers are asking us to suspend our imagination that a good pesticide would not kill these bees. High altitude, low humidity and a pressurized cabin threatens the lives of the hardiest insects.

A cure? Yes, the "savior" found a cure in the frogs, which make a memorable visual in the next frameshot. A little juice from these frogs and the victims of the beestings begin an instant recovery.

Ann Bauer sees Martin as a hero, now; and the teenage girl sees the teenage boy as a hero, and they all end happily hand-in-hand as they walk away from the successfully landed aircraft and cured victims of the bee ebola strain.

Much like *Venomous* (2001), *Killer Buzz* (2001) involves a deadly ebola-like virus but the focus is on the delivery device – the snakes, the bees. In bioterrorism, the most difficult part of the attack is often the method of dispersion and these movies make a creative and believable dispersion device which is relatively realistic. They join the subgenre List of biohorror and biothrillers.

Global Effect (2002)

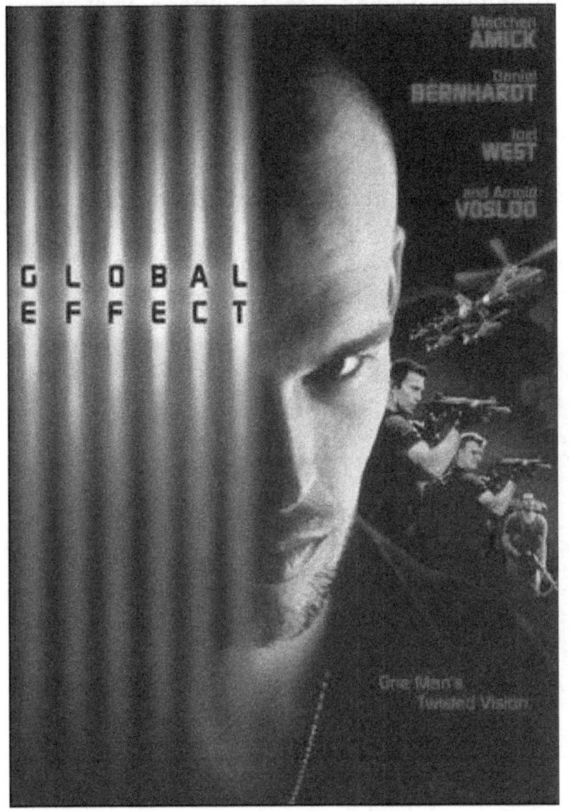

RATING

Conrad Lee
(National Security Advisor)

So you discovered a disease that is quite possibly the most destructive mankind has ever encountered and you stick it in an unprotected facility to fiddle with?

So just exactly what is the timeframe for informing the world leaders on the planet that you have the world's demise in a petri dish?

---*Global Effect* (2002)

Global Effect (2002) is very likely the most *James Bondesque* of the biohorror, biothriller subgenre List of movies. It is the first movie to mention the anthrax attacks in America in the fall of 2001 and use it as a trigger for other acts of bioterrorism. The race to find the researcher with the cure before the United States decides to firebomb infected cities is the plot which makes this an entry on the List.

The virus appears to begin naturally in a village in Uganda. The disease is identified as a particularly virulent form of ebola. The disease has a strange side effect of leaving the victim with ice blue eyes, which seems rather odd considering ebola causes bleeding from the eyes and every orifice. Nonetheless, the victims are easily identified by the cold, blank blue-eyed stare.

The movie begins with a boy about eight years old, who returns to his Ugandan village to find his mother and everyone dead with the virus.

He sees aircraft overhead and starts running away. The aircraft fire bomb the village. The next screenshot is that of two biosuited investigators who announce, "Gentlemen, I am getting a reading here." Apparently they have invented biosensors for the particular disease and a handheld unit. This was science fiction in 2002, but these realtime biosensors they were under early development at the time.

Back at the Environmental and Disease Control Agency (EDCA) laboratory, the investigators are celebrating Dr. Levitt's discovery of the "cure" for the virus in this outbreak. Just as they are getting started, a van of thugs arrive and shoot their way into the laboratory looking for the virus and the cure. It is an inside job and the informant is the one who told them they had found the cure.

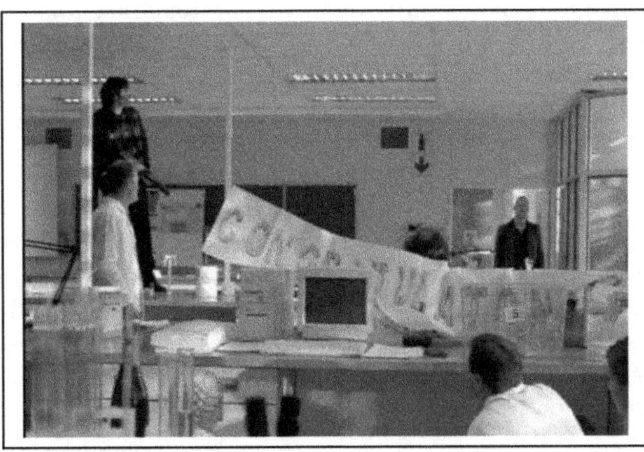

This group of thugs shoots or gives the disease to everyone in the lab except Dr. Levitt who he demands to give him the cure. She gives him some vials from the freezer and he kidnaps her.

Meanwhile back in the Pentagon or the Situation Room of the White House, what looks like the National Security Council is convened. It is not clear except the aerial shot of the Pentagon. However, operations like this would take place in the White House, not the Pentagon.

The briefing is on the laboratory break-in, assault and murders of the staff and theft of the virus. The Director from the Environmental and Disease Control Agency, Dr. Richard Hume walks into the room, and President Meredith Tripp introduces him. He describes the thieves as a new kind of terrorist. Nile Spencer, played by Joel West, who put up a website discussing his plans for a "new world order" after the success of the anthrax attacks. Then he describes the backstory of how the virus came to the laboratory. He said the small boy who escaped had the disease and they harvested the virus from him and gave it to the laboratory in Uganda to find a cure. That is where the thieves stole it and the cure. The National Security Advisor, Conrad Lee remarked:

```
        So you discovered a disease that is
quite possibly the most destructive mankind
has ever encountered and you stick it in an
    unprotected facility to fiddle with?

        So just exactly what is the timeframe
for informing the world leaders on the planet
that you have the world's demise in a petri
                   dish?
```

This is one of the most significant legal questions in the movie, because the storage of viruses is not uniformly regulated from one country to the next. The nations who are signatories to the Biological Weapons Convention agreed to pass domestic laws against using a biological weapon. In the last meeting of the parties, the decision to make laboratory safety an important confidence building measure of the convention was strongly supported. However, there are still many laboratories that are not secure. President Obama made a visit to a biological laboratory in a country in Africa, and remarked about the lack of security at the abandoned facility which still contained vials and samples. The United States can provide support for guarding the laboratories and cleaning them, but not without the sovereign nation asking for assistance. This can be done with an agreement between nations to assist in the clean up. One successful example of this, was the trilateral agreement between the United Kingdom, the United States and Libya to clean up the old weapons of mass destruction remnants. Otherwise, many facilities have low security in resource-poor countries. These are often the very countries where the viruses may originate.

There is a clear conflict between the National Security Advisory, Conrad Lee and Meredith Tripp. The Council then receives intelligence about where the thieves are located and despite the possibility that Dr. Levitt is with them, Conrad Lee orders the bombing. Only the President could authorize such an operation. In this next screenshot, the Council is watching the firebombing on two video screens.

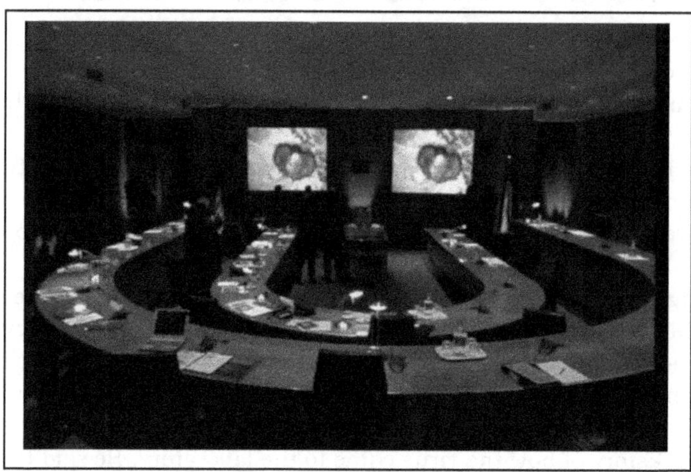

The next intelligence that is handed to Meredith Tripp is a correction, that the warehouse they just bombed is actually a shoe factory in Uganda. Meredith Tripp tells Conrad Lee he will have to do things her way, now.

Meanwhile, Nile Spencer has his kidnapped victim, Dr. Levitt strapped to a chair in a mansion, another very *James Bond-esque* scene. The objective seems to be that they get the cure and what she gave them was not the “cure”.

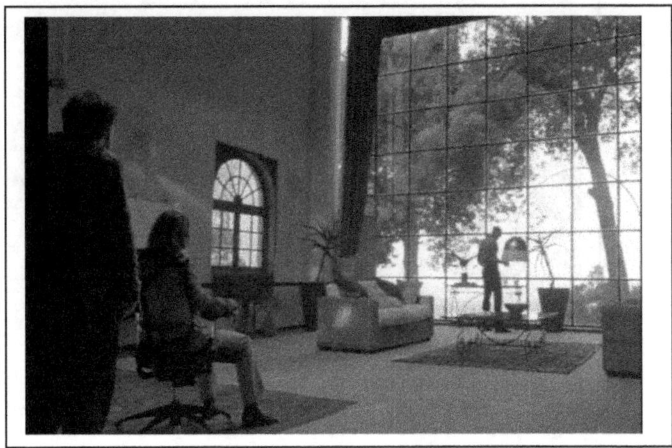

Nile's girlfriend, Sasha, played by Rolanda Marais, is the infection source for their plot. She injects herself with the virus and the cure, but he promises her he will get the cure in time for her. She then wanders through the streets of Capetown, South Africa in order to infect as many people as possible.

The victims then start pouring into the Emergency Rooms in Capetown, as seen in this screenshot.

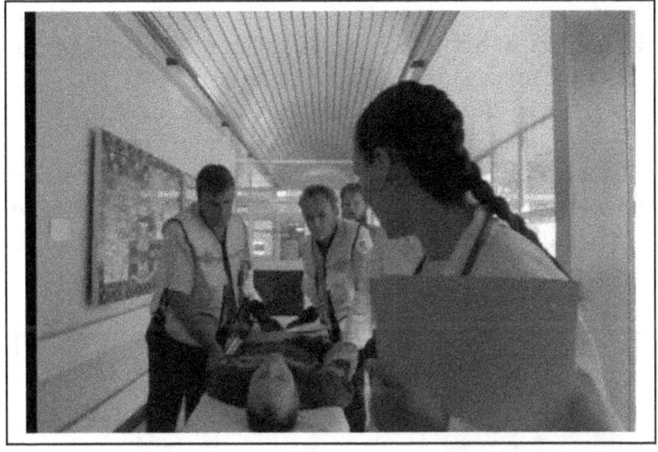

A man who is sick with the virus lumbers into the hospital and rips open his shirt to show he has C-4 packs of explosives strapped to his body and he blows himself up along with the entire Emergency Room. No real explanation for this or tie up of why a suicide bomber came to the Emergency Room bent on destroying himself and the ER.

In this screenshot, the terrorists watch the death count rise in Capetown from this television monitor with Dr.Levitt whose response is, "What have you done? Those are innocent people. They have done nothing to you."

Meanwhile, back in the Situation Room, the National Security Council is also watching the death toll rise and spread from Capetown and Conrad Lee continues to propose bombing including using nuclear bombs. He proposes killing 40 million people of Capetown to prevent the spread, and Meredith objects, but finally relents and just as a Special Forces team extracts Dr. Levitt from the kidnappers, they barely outrun the nuclear bomb that is dropped on Capetown.

Meredith insists that they have contained the virus because they have shut down all the airports and the borders in South Africa, but when it starts to appear outside of South Africa she realizes that those measures have not been effective.

Could she seal the borders? Only with the agreement of the United Nations which would most likely be in collaboration with the World Health Organization. No where in this movie, did the international organizations play a role nor were they consulted. The United States acted alone, with a propensity for bombing entire cities until the virus came to Washington, D.C.. The United States could refuse air traffic from South Africa in 2002 for preventing the disease from entering the United States.

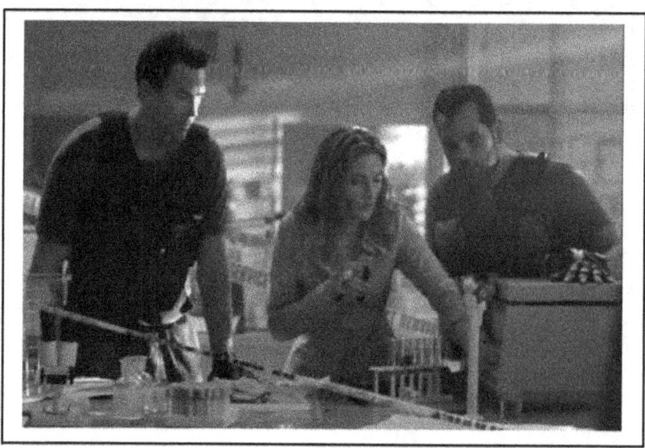

The Special Forces team is convinced by Dr. Levitt that she must return to her laboratory to make more serum for the cure. In the screenshot below, they are working quickly to collect blood from a rat and then make the antibodies for the "cure"--- but not before they save the white rat with the antibodies from a large python in the laboratory cabinet.

No sooner had Dr. Levitt gotten the serum for the cure in a vial, the bioterrorists invade the laboratory again, and this time, they take the cure and infect Dr. Levitt. They also killed the white rat (but fortunately not in view).

The Special Forces team which is now down to Marcus and Dr. Levitt and they find them on an abandoned ship after locating Sasha who now realizes that Nile was leaving her for dead and never planned on curing her. She helps them find him.

Meanwhile on the ship laboratory, Nile is handling the deadly virus without gloves and hands it to his laboratory technician to check to see if it actually kills the virus. The laboratory technician has thin latex gloves, but has no eye or face protection from splashes as he works with the serum.

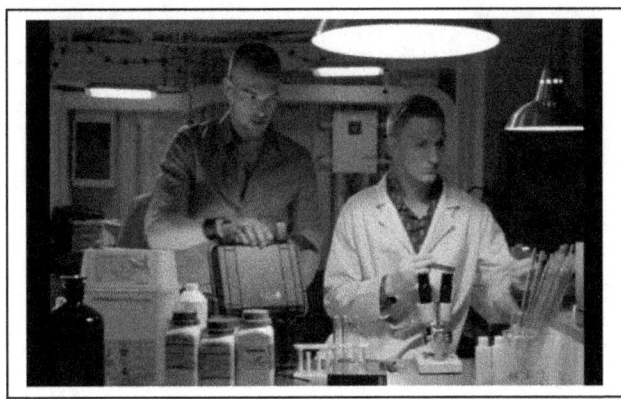

It turns out to be the least of their worries, however, because Dr. Levitt and Marcus soon show up and there is a shootout but not before Dr. Levitt gets the serum back from Nile, although she is shot in the arm while doing it. In a slow-motion toss, she throws the vial to Marcus who is at the door opening fire on Nile.

Nile lives just long enough to experience the dozens of C-4 explosives that have been planted on the ship by Marcus. Marcus and Dr Levitt jump into the ocean and appear to be miles from shore, but without further explanation, they are soon back at work.

In the last exasperating effort for Conrad to bomb something with his underwater nuclear submarine, Marcus uses the code to intercept the bomb and just in the last few seconds, saves the next city.

The voice over announces that the effort to get the cure to the sick is being led by Dr. Levitt.

While the movie was intended to dramatize the spread of the disease, it probably underestimated the rate of spread, not having had the benefit of the SARS outbreak the following year, 2003. Within 48 hours of the index case leaving Hong Kong, the virus had spread around the world.

Contagion (2002)

RATING

Secret Service Agent
We have a biomedical emergency. The Department of Disease Containment says you are the best virologist they have.

Dr. Diana Landis
I'm speaking at the Epidemiology Intelligence Conference in 20 minutes. I can't help you.

Secret Service Agent
There's been an attack on the President.

---*Contagion* (2002)

Contagion (2002) takes the bioterrorist motivation to the President in this biothriller . A deadly virus, a rush to find a cure or the criminal, a race against the ultimate sterilization of the disease and an orphan combine for a biothriller that makes another contribution to the subgenre.

The heroine is a Dr. Landis, Meghan Gallagher, a divorced virologist and physician who we are told is the "best virologist" at the Department of Disease Containment (DDC), a fictional substitute for the real-life federal government Centers for Diseases Control and Prevention (the official name), also referred to as CDC.

The attack comes on President Howard, Bruce Boxleitner, with a hefty syringe-dart to the neck as he is leaving a building, reminiscent of the attack on President Reagan as he was leaving the Washington Hilton Hotel, surrounded by secret service agents heading for the Presidential limousine. This frameshot shows the moment he is struck by the syringe-dart.

The similarity does not end there, and just as Reagan made his famous quip to Nancy after he was shot by the would-be-assassin's bullet, "I forgot to duck," our fictional President also has his quip for the occasion: "I'm the first President in history to be attacked by a game piece."

The President downplays the seriousness of the attack, until the intrepid Dr. Landis takes the President's blood sample and shortly thereafter tells the President he has "ebola."

Dr. Landis bumps into an old friend, Dr. Amos, Andy Lowell, who is brought into the frantic response to the attack. Both are sitting at a table in an open area of the hospital with nothing more than a labcoat and latex gloves when Dr. Landis announces to her colleague she has found that the President has "ebola." No respirator, no self-contained oxygen (PAPR) and no protective clothing. The fact that she is working in space that is open to others and this unsuspecting colleague suddenly realizes he is leaning on the table where the "Level 4 hot agent" is located is a stunningly inaccurate depiction of how this agent would be treated. Audiences are already acquainted with *Outbreak* (1995) which had some of the most accurate biosafety visuals, to date, and this movie ignores all realism and in doing so, has lowered the dramatic tension inexplicably.

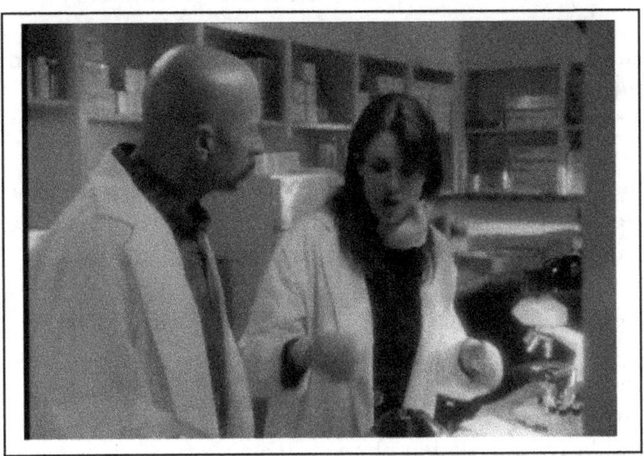

Dr. Landis
We have a Level 4 agent in this hospital.

Dr. Amos
In the hospital?

Dr. Landis
Right there on the table.

Dr. Amos
[recoils in horror]

But after announcing to Dr. Amos that she is looking at "ebola" under the lens of her microscope, she puts her latex gloved-hand on her face and mouth, which would make even a rooker biosafety officer cringe in horror.

In the meantime, Secret Service agent, Maxwell, receives an anonymous call from the terrorist who says the President has received a "Level 4 hot agent."

The calls continue and a bargain is struck for a temporary 'cure" until the President can deposit $100 million in a Swiss bank account. The female partner on the terrorist team, the thought-dead, Dr. Laura Crowley, gets into a status argument on the phone during a discussion about the antiserum. The sparring is over who came from the most impressive medical school. "Harvard, phi beta kappa," Dr. Laura Crowley snaps back and Dr. Landis replies, "Johns Hopkins."

Dr. Landis's biggest challenges come from a young orphan boy who runs around the hospital unescorted although he is there recovering from an appendectomy. It is his probing questions about marriage and children that cause her angst, not even the invasion through the duct system into the quarantined "hot zone" of the hospital. He is simply escorted out like a bad boy, seemingly forgotten that he has been exposed to ebola.

"It's airborne" is the pronouncement by Major Daniels, Dustin Hoffman, in *Outbreak* (1995) which sends the tension soaring. Dr. Landis makes this same pronouncement after taking a look at a dead cat in a storage room under an air vent and utters the memorable and fear-laden phrase, "It's airborne." This evolution of a virus to being "airborne" is a mechanism to perpetuate itself, and all evolution tends to have that objective. Since viruses replicate more times than even bacteria, there are more chances to evolve and change for viruses than any other disease. That is the reason our influenza vaccine may not be effective –by the time we get the vaccine, the virus could have evolved so far from its original form that the vaccine may be less effective.

The hospital has been quarantined and the mother who wants to be with her child, the same character-type as in *Pandora's Clock* (1996) presents an opportunity for an individual to break quarantine, as she did, with lethal consequences in Pandora's Clock (1996). But in this movie, the mother simply collapses in the hospital waiting room, on the floor.

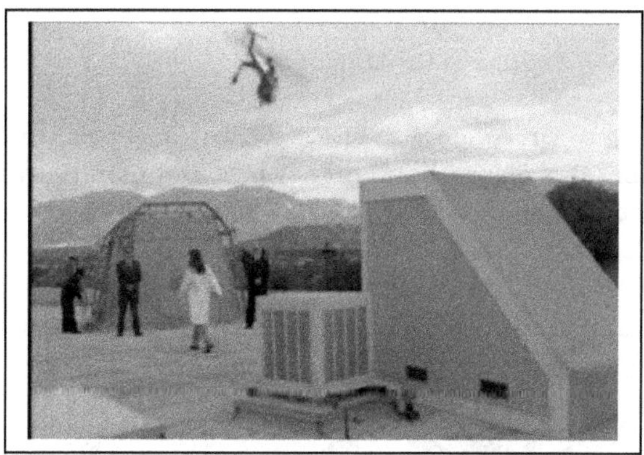

Perhaps we can forgive Dr. Landis for observing no biosecurity training in the first hours, because almost a full day later, the portable containment unit arrives from the DDC by helicopter. There are portable BSL-3 laboratories which operate with positive air pressure inside it's walls, and this appears to be serving some similar purpose. They also arrive with biosuits, and PAPRs, self-contained air supplies, which are suitable for BSL-3 work.

In an inexplicable move, the federal government declares isolation and a curfew. Military troops roam the residential neighborhoods flanking tanks. But then later, the curfew changes to a quarantine and people are made to leave their homes and are loaded into military trucks and taken to presumptively detention centers. One couple tried to make a run for it, but was stopped at gunpoint by two armed and masked militia, seen in this frameshot.

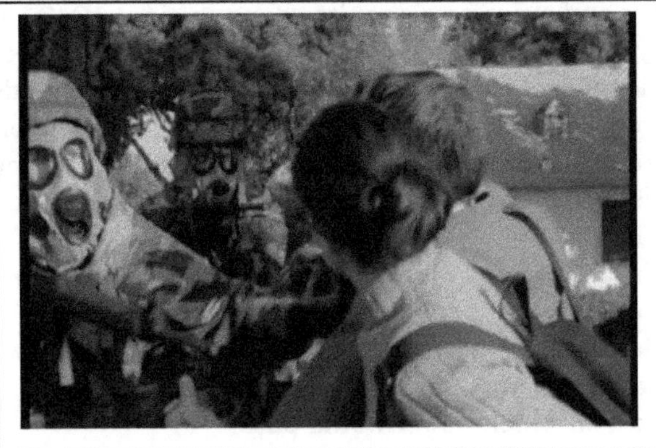

Election Day arrives, and without explanation, there is no quarantine, and the people are out in the streets holding posters supporting the President while he is quarantined with "ebola." In the next frameshot, a voter holds up a t-shirt with a good-spirited slogan about the President and his illness which reads, "I Survived the Plague with the Prez."

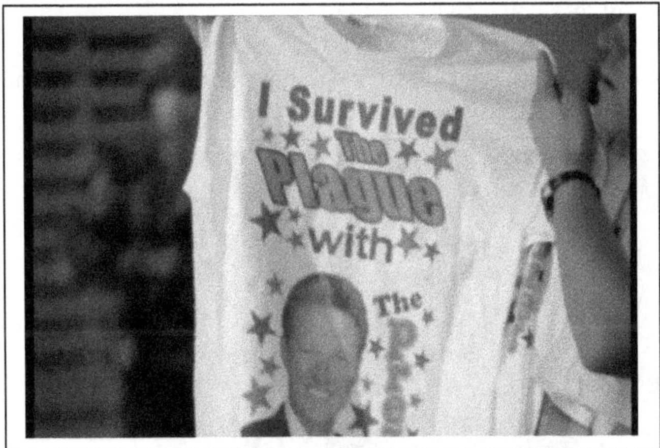

Slowly, we learn the motivation behind Dr. Crowley's bioterrorism with her partner-in-crime, whose accent suggests he may be a former Irish terrorist. When told that the President will not take the antidote she has prepared she remarks, "He deserves to die for what he did to me."

Another conflict is brewing with a presidential hopeful, Gen. Ryker, who wants to seize the moment to be a hero. He storms through the roof of the hospital with his troops ostensibly to take over, since the President might be "incapacitated."

Surprisingly, Gen. Ryker is unacquainted with the Continuity of Government directives which provide for exactly who will take over for the President to keep the government operating. These Continuity of Government orders have been in existence since the National Security Act of 1947 with President Truman. It is the President, who plans for Continuity of Government and every president has done so since 1947. The most recent directives were issued by President George W. Bush which would have been in effect at the time of this movie. President Bush '43 began a second category of directives, the Homeland Security Presidential Directives, and HSPD-20 describes the continuity of government and is classified. The other category of presidential directive is the National Security Presidential Directive and NSPD-51 is the continuity of government directive for national security purposes and it is also classified.

However, there is also the constitutional form of continuity of government where the President is incapacitated, and that is the Vice President, and then the Speaker of the House. The infamous statement by Secretary of State, Al Haig, that he would be in charge after President Reagan was shot, highlighted the problem that even cabinet secretaries were ill informed about the order in which power would pass.

When Gen Ryker, US Army, stormed into President Howard's room, he was greeted with this statement by the President's staff: "I suppose you still know who your commander in chief is, sir?" The looks of a military coup right in the hospital seem inevitable until Dr. Landis interferes and gives both men a lecture about the virus and tells them to put the guns down. They dutifully obey. The, Gen. Ryker has to stay in the quarantine, and the President tells him he will "look forward to a court martial." President Howard probably missed Outbreak (1995) and Venomous (2001) where the commanding officer told his reporting officer that he would not make general. When he needed the disgraced officers they were less than helpful, in fact down right hostile.

In a "Psycho-esque" move, Dr. Crowley, the female terrorist who just introduced herself to Dr. Landis on a hospital elevator, tries to inject her with something lethal in a hypodermic syringe.

Fortunately, this is a fast elevator, and the door opens before she makes the fatal plunge.

Dr. Landis, no fool, discovers that this woman is actually Dr. Laura Crowley and shows the personnel file from DDC to President Howard, who is doing remarkably well with ebola and the temporary "cure" from the terrorists. Although, Dr. Landis and the President identify the female doctor as someone who was in the jungle researching the ebola virus three years ago, and Dr. Landis tells the President she just saw her in the elevator, astonishingly no one looks for her! In fact, she is spotted by multiple people on the team and no one knows who she is. Finally one person --- the orphan boy in the hospital recognizes her as the doctor in Rwanda who gave his parents the "cure" for their sickness and they died.

Meanwhile Dr. Amos tells Dr. Landis that the orphan boy is not sick and he is immune, but then it occurs to them it was his time in Rwanda with his parents that must have exposed him to "ebola" and he has developed antibodies against it.

Dr. Amos
He's got the antibodies.

Dr. Landis
He's got the cure.

Before President Howard learns there is a cure, and knows only that the Americans are about to be infected downwind, he tries to seal the hospital. This involves throwing yellow banners down the side of the building, but little else.

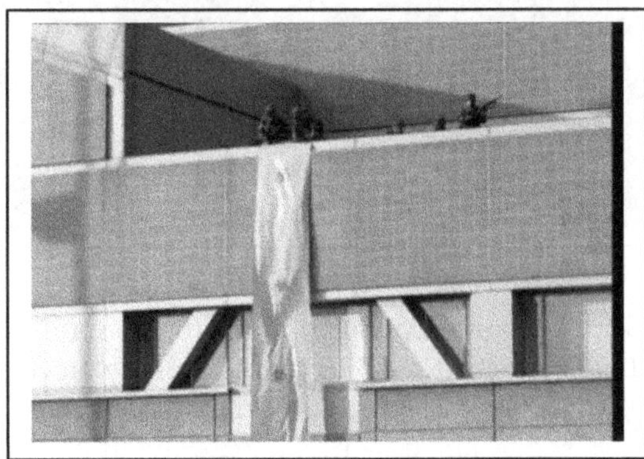

An interesting visual is where the two terrorists who have been operating out of the hospital basement, peer out the window and wonder what they are doing?

The President and the General have a reconciliation faced with their own imminent death-suicides as they contemplate how to sanitize the place and stop the spread of the virus. Instead of bombing a town as in *Andromeda Strain* (1971), *Outbreak* (1995), *Venomous* (2001) they are just selectively bombing the hospital in which they both happen to be quarantined.

The General when asked his approach says he would "order up a 60-ton inversion bomb with a blast radius that would incinerate one square mile. Fry the virus before it spreads." As casually as he might make a fast food order of French fries, the General is sent off post-haste to activate the plan. The next frameshot, below, is the movement of the bomb into place.

Still frantically looking for the orphan boy with the cure to "ebola," Dr. Crowley tries to find him, too, so that Dr. Landis will not find him. The showdown occurs on the roof of the hospital between Dr. Crowley and Dr. Landis and the hostage orphan boy, where Dr. Landis outsmarts Dr. Crowley, distracted by her diatribe about her sad history of being underappreciated and unrecognized for her brilliance as a DDC researcher, which proves to be her flaw as Dr. Landis releases the containment tunnel which, like a giant slinky, pushes Dr. Crowley off the building and presumably to her death. Oh, and the orphan boy saw this coming and jumped out of the way just in the nick of time. Cure, saved.

The victims of "ebola" are saved and a happy exit of the President proves once again, that Dr. Landis is the top virologist at DDC. As the President leaves the building he pauses long enough to invite Dr. Landis and the orphan boy to visit him at his House.

There are a number of loose ends with the law that are naggingly unresolved that look like setups for future conflict, but were instead just left unresolved. For example, right after the hospital announcement came that the building was being quarantined, two young boys ran out the door before the guards could stop them. Dr.Landis inexplicably walks around without her biosuit after she discovers she has "ebola" exposing everyone to her illness. The fact that Dr. Crowley was identified as a suspect, yet no one ever looked for her, is equally mystifying. The FBI which has the lead in the investigation of bioterrorism incidents (another presidential decision directive) is never present or called, without explanation. No one questions the authority or basis for the city-wide curfew and then the quarantine roundup as an unreasonable burden on individual liberty. And maybe the most important question – where was the Vice President?

Contagion (2002) was weak on public health processes, biosafety protocols and the legal and constitutional aspects of their story but because of that, it is an intriguing scenario that challenges our confidence that the real world might just have some of these same weaknesses.

28 Days Later (2002)

RATING

Major Henry West

This is what I've seen in the four weeks since infection. People killing people. Which is much what I saw in the four weeks before infection, and the four weeks before that, and before that, and as far back as I care to remember. People killing people. Which to my mind, puts us in a state of normality right now.

--- *28 Days Later* (2003)

28 Days Later (2003) is a biohorror that revives the zombie concept as the result of an epidemic that is limited to the island of Great Britain. The avoidance of becoming infected is still a very important part of the plot, and 28 Days Later falls squarely into the biohorror and biothriller subgenre.

Exposure -- Infection---Epidemic---Evacuation---Devastation ---the opening legends, floating with the number of the day it occurs, respectively, *On the first day, Day 3, Day 8, Day 15, Day 20,* on the screen with regretful music sets the stage for the movie's tagline, "the days are numbered."

The beginning of the movie and the root of all evil is the laboratory breakin by animal rights activists, who want to free the Chimpanzees. But the monkeys are infected and they attack as they escape, beginning the epidemic in Great Britain. Laboratory biosecurity is once again at the center of the conflict or the triggering event for the disaster. Laboratories would be highly unlikely to use chimpanzees and instead, they would be more likely to use rhesus monkeys. In fact, experimentation on Chimpanzees is regulated differently, in the United States, but this movie is made in Great Britain.

In this screenshot, the animal rights activists are forcing the laboratory technician to release the chimps despite his warning that they are infected.

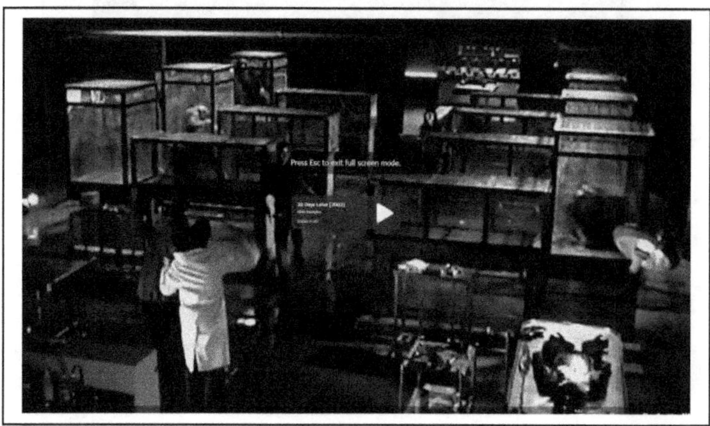

This screenshot is the dramatic reality that faces Jim, the bicycle courier who wakes up in the hospital after 28 days, and is confronted with the aftermath of the virus epidemic.

As Jim wanders through the city he eventually finds other survivors and they describe what has happened to the United Kingdom. Jim questions the state of the government:

```
                    Jim
        How about the government?
          What are they doing?

                    Mark
         There is no government.

                    Jim
           Of course there is a
       government.  There's always
           a government they are
      in a bunker or a plane . . .

                    Mark
          There's no government.
           No police. No army.
         No t.v.  No radio. . . .
```

The process of infection is very quickly demonstrated when "the infected" break into their space and one of them bit Mark. Selena immediately hacks him to death. She explains to Jim that she has 10-20 seconds to kill him before he turns into an "infected" and attacks them.

From here, they continue on and find more survivors, this time, a father and a daughter.

The decision to leave safety is made from this rooftop where they hear on a crank radio from a recorded message to go to a safety point where there is "salvation". Despite the uncertainty, they decide to leave and he feels that his daughter will be safe with them.

After taking a car through the city and getting a flat tire, a swarm of rats signal them that "the infected" are coming and the rats are running from them.

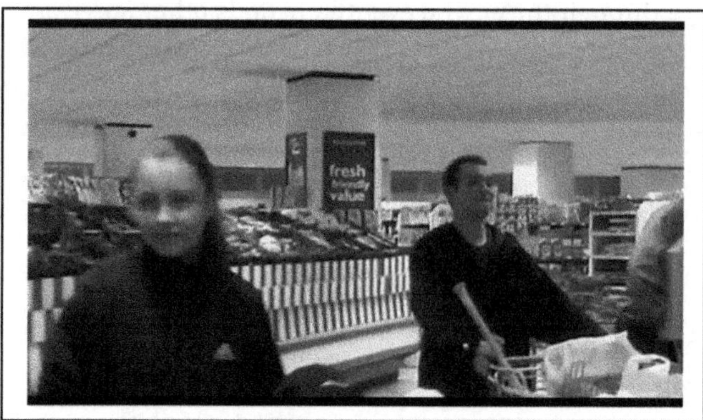

The screenshot above, is a raid on a grocery store. This is in the UK, but in the U.S., pillaging a store in a disaster is a crime, but since there is no government or judicial system, there is no enforcement, so only at some future date could this be a crime that is enforced. Symbolically, the father places his credit card at the check out as he leaves.

With 50 minutes left of the 113 minute movie, they arrive at the army base that is their destination that they have been following since they heard the pre-recorded message on the radio that there was "salvation" here. Predictably, no one was there when they arrived.

The father, Frank, is determined to find something there and he is angry and sits down to think. This is the most poignant of any scene in this movie and I didn't forget it even after ten years. The father walks over to scold a blackbird which is picking at the flesh of an "infected" overhead on the beams of the building and as he walks under the beam, a drop of blood falls into his eye and he has just enough time to tell his daughter he loves her. He then transforms into an "infected" and military snipers shoot him from a distance. Selena, Jim and the daughter are rescued by the military personnel.

They enter a new society that is the rebuilding of the United Kingdom by the military. They are ruled by no particular martial law, but just a survival instinct.

The interesting philosophical discussion at the table began with one of the officers pointing out that man has only existed on the planet for a fraction of a second:

```
                Officer
   If the infection wipes us out,
  then that is a return to normality.
```

The Commanding Officer has to stop a rape attempt of Selena, and there is no punishment only a statement "My apologies" from the Commanding Officer.

Throughout, there is a continual confrontation with murder and hopelessness. There are only nine men in the army base, and there is only one woman on the base.

```
       Commanding Officer
    I set the recording and I
       promised them women.
       Women mean a future.
```

They begin to realize that the island of the United Kingdom has been quarantined from the rest of the world.

The rape scene is a frightening psychological tension between survival and the rape of two women, one the young daughter of Frank. They delayed until there was an emergency call to defend against "the infected." Rape is the crime, but is the interest of survival a crime? This seems to be a point that the movie lays out as a conflict for the viewer.

This screenshot is intended to convey a dark look at these women waiting on the inevitable rape, if the military officers return. Hannah and Selena wait for the return of the military officers, and Hannah talks about the effect the drug is having on her that Selena gave her. But when the rapist have to go and defend the compound and are "infected" the worst nightmare occurs for the women.

In the next screenshot, Jim who was shaken by his first murder of a young boy who was infected has not evolved into a killer willing to plunge his thumbs into the eye sockets of his attackers (not infected).

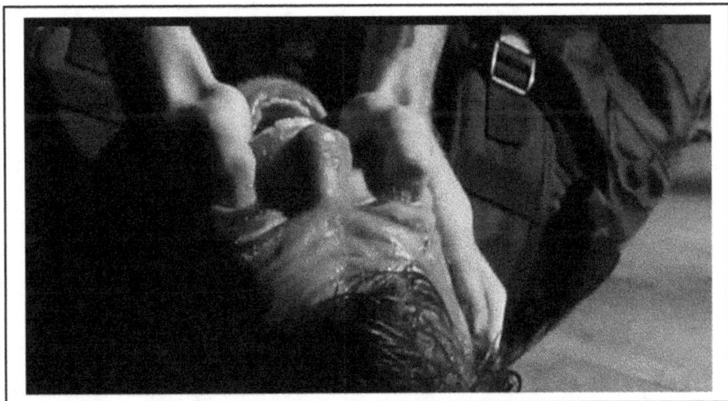

The three of them, Selena, Hannah and Jim escape from the military base as the Commanding Officer is attacked by the enlistee he has chained up after he was infected to see how long it would take for starvation to kill him. The three of them crash through the locked gate and somehow get to a hospital where they recover, dress their wounds and find their way to a country cottage and sew a large banner. The banner is strung out over the meadow for the low-flying figher pilot to see their message which reads, simply “HELLO.”

They end when Hannah says, “I think they saw us this time.”

This movie was much more of a psychological depiction of survival and horror without leaving any comfort zone. The law and health depiction in this movie was lacking except for the extraordinary demonstration of what happens in the absence of the “rule of law.”

This movie is probably most remarkable for its revival of the zombie movie and the plot focus on the undead. Despite its lack of law and health depictions, its central plot focused on the epidemic and how a country might be isolated from the rest of the world and in this case, the United Kingdom provides a perfect scenario of an island that can be isolated from the rest of the world.

Day of the Dead 2: Contagium (2005)

RATING

Jerry (Deluca's son)
That's right you're dead.
On human standards anyway.
I guess you opened the vial.

---*Contagium: Day of the Dead* (2005)

Day of the Dead 2: Contagium (2005) begins with the backstory of a government laboratory in 1968 with a bacteriological weapon that gets out of control turning people into zombies. The opening scene is an exterior shot of the government laboratory, with the legend, *Ravenside Military Installation, Pennsylvania 1968.*

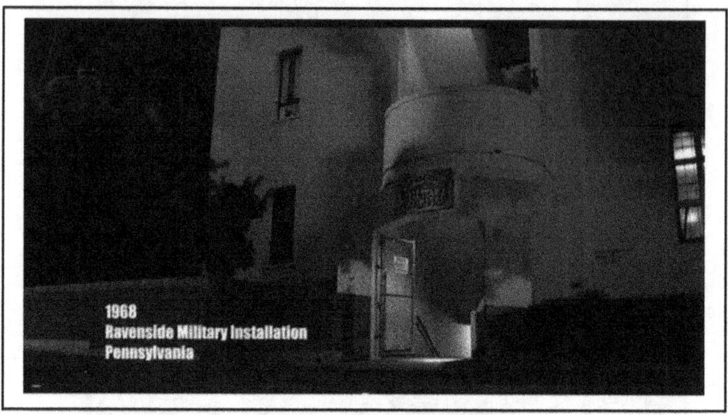

A telegram is sent to alert the government's military that the biological weapon has escaped in the lab, and they respond by storming the laboratory on foot with armed troops, shooting everyone, well or sick. At one point that were given instructions over the radio:

Radio communication
Shoot to kill!
All units shoot to kill!
Aim for the head.

The impression was that the military had been overwhelmed by the zombies that were created by the biological weapon, because all of the troops seemed to disappear in an attack of the zombies. The laboratory was destroyed.

The next scene away from the bloodbath at the laboratory is a group of mentally ill men in the forest wearing uniforms indicating their institutionalization, which is in the present, about 37 years later. In their walk in the forest, one of the mentally-ill patients finds a missing thermos, too rusty to open. One of the men perportedly suffering from supernatural fantasies, predicts bad things will happen if they open the thermos. They point out his delusional condition and he is not taken seriously. He does not argue with this because he wants to be released on schedule, tomorrow, from the institution.

The curiosity about what is in the thermos finally gets the best of them after returning to the institution. One of the patients takes the thermos to the men's bathroom. His friends follow him into the men's room and tell him not to open the thermos. In the scuffle the vial inside the thermos drops on the bathroom floor and in this creative shot, the camera focuses on the vial and the men looking down at it.

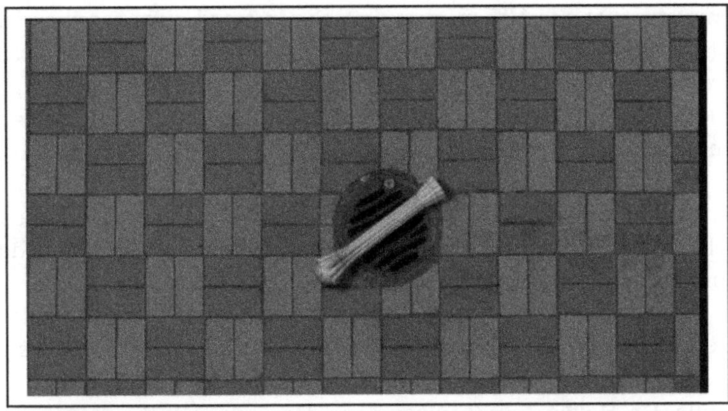

At this point in the movie, the scenario would be one of the most creative "worst-case-scenario" exercises that has ever been devised. The creative of a "worst-case'-scenario" was part of the Environmental Impact Statements for biological laboratories planning. Eventually, it was determined by the regulators that these worse-case-scenarios were providing more information to terrorists that was necessarily helpful for biosecurity, so these worse-case-scenarios were eliminated as a requirement for these environmental impact statements.

The patients at the mental institution seem to make more sense in their philosophy than many of the other characters in the movie which is probably an intentional mechanism for contrasting the insane with the greater insanity of building a bioweapon.

The use of the mentally-ill as victims of the bioweapon, makes the element of the "innocent", an element of the biohorror/biothriller subgenre, a real focus of the plot.

The unfolding symptoms of the disease begin with a cough and their skin begins to peel off even while they are the 'walking well". They think it is like a snake poison because they are shedding their skin like a snake. One of the infected patients had foaming from his mouth, a symptom of a rabies-like virus. Symptoms are largely inconsistent from one person to the other, except that they all eventually have an insatiable urge to eat people, while maintaining cognitive ability to talk about their condition and even to chat with their old friends while convincing them to come over to their side.

At 45 minutes into the 103 minute film, the infected were communicating the same response to a slap when Emma was slapped by a guard for biting him to defend herself from what might have been an attempted rape. This was followed by throwing up their food, then throwing up blood, but they are still walking well. The ability to communicate with each other was a line that just dropped from the script along the way with leading to nothing else in the film.

It is hard to take this movie seriously because it does not take itself seriously. Quips that mark ridiculous moments are almost out of character and provided comic relief but not intentionally. For example, when Donwyn learns from Jerry via the internet video communication that they should not open the thermos because there is a deadly virus that will result in the government killing anyone with it by fire, Donwyn remarks glibly, "And of course, it just gets better and better."

Meanwhile, Dr. Heller, the despised doctor in charge of the mental institution pulls out an old metal locked box and removes a map. In the next screenshot he puts his finger on the place where in 1968 Deluca disappeared and the thermos was located. It is not clear why the thermos was not found and destroyed if they had it pinpointed on a map, but nevertheless, the situation is now that the inmates have the thermos and have opened it.

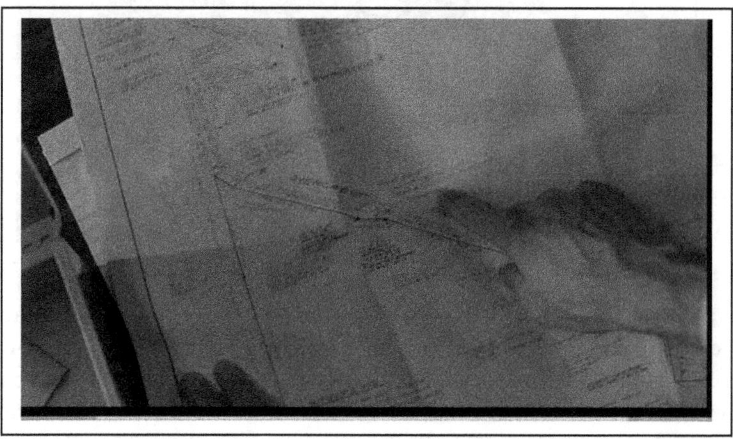

The burning issue for us at this moment when the inmates are turning into zombies who are attacking each other with an insatiable appetite for human flesh and organs, is what legal rights do the institutionalized mentally-ill have?

A subplot involves Emma's pregnancy by her fiance who saw her without supervision by Donwyn, at his encouragement to do so. This created an interruption in the chase scene in the hospital after the infected soon outnumbered the uninfected. Legally, this would have created a criminal investigation resulting in some privacy issues that would have to be infringed. Emma and her finance did not survive to cope with this intrusion on their privacy, however.

People who are institutionalized are still entitled to the right of privacy in health matters and pregnancy matters, too, unless there is a rape involved, and mentally ill persons are not considered capable of consent so any pregnancy is presumptively a rape. When rape is associated with the pregnancy, this involves carefully avoiding intruding on the right of privacy as much as possible in a criminal investigation. A case where both a health investigation into a sexually transmitted disease and a criminal investigation of the pregnancy of a mentally-ill woman was given as an example of such investigatory complications to sharing criminal and health information in testimony before Congress in 2001 on barriers to sharing information in a bioterrorism attack.[42]

Donwyn's friend, Jerry came to the mental institution to see his friend. He looked at the thermos and sat around casually chatting with the infected, telling them about the course of the disease and what they could expect. Much of the backstory is revealed here which connects the opening scenes where a Russian pilot in 1968 crashes his spy plane and is recovered. He tells the hospital personnel that the bioweapon was stolen from the United States and he is just bringing it back. Then he becomes infected and the entire hospital has to be destroyed.

The viewer at last sees the telltale markings on the bottom of the thermos when Jerry identifies the thermos as the one his father took from the Ravenside Military Hospital. (What was the motivation for Jerry's dad to take the thermos is not clear.) One of the lines of dialogue that is consistent with this movie not taking itself seriously, is the line delivered by Jerry, when the infected ask him if they are dead. Jerry replies, "That's right youre dead. On human standards anyway. I guess you opened the vial."

The infected chatting with Jerry eventually succomb to the temptation and are overwhelmed by the scent of Jerry's blood from a headwound. Then they eat him.

In fact, eating bodies by one or more of the almost 150 "infected" actors and actresses named in the credits kept the blood flowing throughout this movie, almost non-stop. The next screenshot had become so commonplace by the time this scene appeared, it was not even surprising to see someone casually munching on fingers at the end of a bloody arm.

[42] Patricia Quinlisk, Testimony before the Committee on Government Reform, Subcommittee on National Security, Veterans Affairs, and International Relations, "Combatting Terrorism: Federal Response to a Biological Weapons Attack," July 23, 2001.)

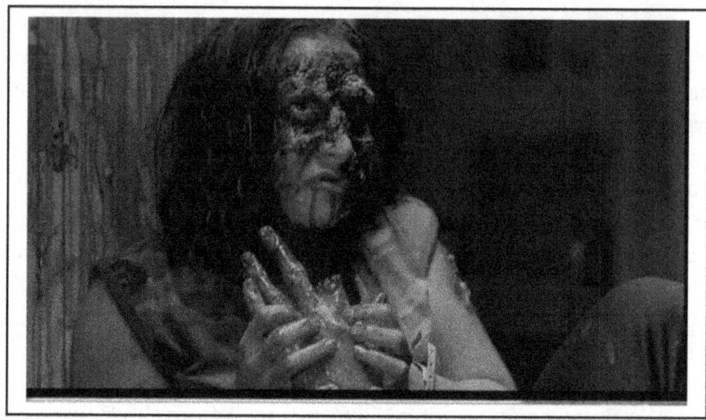

There was never a government response to this outbreak in the Ravenside Mental Institution. There are no named characters that are uninfected at this point, leaving little to care about in this film. Then the infected manage to march orderly out of the mental institution front door on a sunny day into the community. Predictably, they drag people out of their cars in their driveways and eat them.

This is the end of the movie, so we enjoy no particular resolution, and the vaccine is lost inside of the laboratory where anyone who knew about it is dead.

This last scene recalls some unfounded fears of a community who sought to block a home for the mentally-ill from being located in their neighborhood. This case came before the U.S. Supreme Court on an equal protection theory that an ordinance in Clebourne, Texas, which excluded the mentally-ill from their neighborhood. Perhaps using the mentally-ill as a basis for creating horrifying zombies portrayed in this film, adds to the discrimination against the mentally-ill. The U.S. Supreme Court ruled that communities cannot discriminate against the "mentally-retarded" by excluding them by ordinance from their neighborhoods and that they could live without any risk to the community. [43]

This film distinguishes itself, despite not taking itself seriously, as the only film to use smell to identify the bioweapon --- "it smells like ripe fruit." It also distinguishes itself as the last in an era of zombies that were just no longer very scary, and even the dialogue didn't take them seriously. The next movie to revive the zombie as the product of a biological weapon or epidemic was the sequel, *28 Weeks Later,* five years after the original *28 Days Later,* and two years after *Day of the Dead2: Contagium.* Zombies will always be with us, but their character is changing.

This film's tagline, "every day has a beginning" speaks for itself---but certainly not for the movie.

[43] ***City of Cleburne v. Cleburne Living Center, Inc.***, 473 U.S. 432 (1985),

Waterborne (2005)

RATING

TV Reporter

This is the first attack on U.S. soil since 9-11 and the first attack ever using a biological agent.

---*Waterborne* (2005)

Waterborne (2005) is a story of a terrorist attack on the Los Angeles public water system with a biological agent. It is a film that is rich with racial tension that proves to be a weak link in society's web of cohesiveness that may begin to unravel in time of disaster. The news reporter announces that this is the first attack on U.S. soil since 9-11 "and the first attack ever using a biological agent". This is certainly fiction, since the first attack was during the colonial period when Sir Jeffrey Amhearst delivered smallpox-infected blankets to the Indian tribes in the northeast U.S. with the intent of infecting them with smallpox. Then the second biological attack in modern U.S. history against humans was in 1984 in The Dalles, Oregon by the Rashashnee cult who poisoned the local salad bars to sicken people in hopes of changing the outcome of an election the next day.

Zach (Chris Masterson) opens with a first person monologue which is a foundation for his decisionmaking throughout the movie.

The writer Ben Rehti in an interview said that he was always fascinated with water rights, so it is not surprising that he did not shy away from the legal questions in the film. Not only water rights, but equal protection, gender and racial discrimination, hate crimes, hoarding in an emergency, price gouging in an emergency and military interaction with civilians within the context of *posse comitatus.*

The trigger for panic occurs with a televised news story that announces "the biological agent has killed 3 people since this morning." The warning not to drink the water from the public water supply until future notice, sets the events in motion where the panic grows.

The focus shifts to a store run by an American-Sikh family. The mother has decided to increase the cost of water by 300% and limit sales to two bottles per person. Her son challenges this practice as unethical and she rebuffs him.

In California, Cal. Penal Code sec. 396 prohibits price hikes of more than 10% of the price, prior to the emergency, of emergency supplies, for a period of 30 days following a declared disaster, and is punishable with a maximum county jail term of one year or a maximum fine of $10,000, or both. However, if the merchant can demonstrate that a price hike of more than 10% resulted from additional costs imposed by the supplier, then this may be a defense.

Gender issues are raised when a private talks about his experience in Afghanistan and the lack of gender equality where they "drug a woman in the street" and beat her. Further discussion about the U.S. policy of involvement in other foreign affairs between Zach and Bodi his jobless friend, over a chess game leads to a decision to leave Los Angeles and they decide to drive to Zac's father's house.

On Day 2, the news reporter announces that there have been 23 deaths in Los Angeles. The military confront what looks like two men pulling water out of an aqueduct, and have another political discussion. The man trying to take water is told it is a federal offense. He argues he pays his taxes and is innocent, and who is going to bring water to his wife and baby?

Bodi is able to get water for them with his wiley personality. First he trades two grams of marijuana for a bottle of water from someone stuck in traffic on the freeway in the next car. Then he flirts with a convenience store clerk and she gives him a bottle of water. The friends have their first mild conflict over the bottle of water, but the situation has not become so desperate that they still believe they will find water.

The racial/ethnic tension continues with another subplot of a relationship with the American-Sikh family's son Vic (Ajay Naidu) and his Jewish girl friend Lilian (Mageina Tova) from New York. The traditional Sikh mother is very unhappy with her son's interest in a non-Punjabi girl and makes her feel unwelcome when she is around the family, despite her son's feelings.

In the meantime, Zach and Bodi spend the night at Bodi's friend's mobile home, who happens to be a survivalist. Conveniently he has water. He a gas mask that Bodi jokes around by wearing it. His friend poses the problem of fighting over oil in the Middle East as just a prelude to the problems with water and the future fights that will be had in the future. Survivalists and their groups have been listed on domestic terrorists groups because of their extreme views about government but also because they tend to collect arms, ammunition and explosives in addition to food and water. There is no indication that Bodi's friend has crossed the line into illegal activity.

The Safe Drinking Water Act of 1972 was passed to ensure that systems supplying drinking water would strive to meet certain maximum contaminant goals (MCGs). The goal of the SDWA is "to reduce contaminants as closely as feasible to levels where no adverse health effects will occur and which allow an adequate margin of safety. . ." But the threat changed from environmental contaminants to intentional bioterrorism after 9/11 and Amerithrax. The SDWA was amended to include safety and security for drinking water systems which included such things as the installation of security cameras, monitoring systems, locked gates and guards. A "public water system" is defined in the SDWA that it "must have at least 15 service connections or serve at least 25 people per day for 60 days of the year." The security regulations gave the bigger systems a short time to comply, and smaller systems were allowed 2-3 years to comply with the new security requirements.

The use of the Civil War-era law, *posse comitatus,* to gain military control of a civilian jurisdiction was evident when the National Guard was employed in a law enforcement capacity. Federal activation of the National Guard under Title 10 would be less likely than deployment under Title 32, the state level militia controlled by either the Governor, or potentially the President. Further there were actions by the soldiers that would raise some rules of engagement questions when they engaged citizens. For example, when the California National Guard Sergeant Ritter (Jon Gries) and his private drive to Acadia, they confront a man who is robbing a water truck. The private is too aggressive and despite being ordered to stand down, shoots the civilian driving away with the water in this screenshot in the dark and rain.

The ethics of Sargeant Ritter final erode into stealing water himself for his family, despite this being an act prohibited by his military orders. His private confronts his Sargeant about his actions: "Here we are busting people for stealing water and you are doing the same." His Sargeant tries to use his shooting of the civilian to shame him into backing off of his confrontation about stealing the water for his wife. The two men are very conflicted about using lethal force against civilians. Using lethal force against civilians for anything other than self-defense or defense of others is homicide in California, even for National Guard law enforcement.

The American-Sikh family is attacked by customers who use racial slurs and assault them, leading their son, Vic, to demand the police investigate the crime as a hate crime. During this scene, a conflict arises between Vic and his girlfriend, when he becomes angry that she can't understand how he feels to be discriminated against. This further heightens the racial and ethnic tension in the movie. The penalty for a hate crime is heightened beyond the normal sentencing range for an assault not involving race. The Matthew Shepard and James Byrd, Jr. Hate Crimes Prevention Act of 2009 makes it a federal crime for acts of violence that cause physical injury. In 2013, a Sikh man was assaulted by a passenger who he had driven in his taxi, and the man plead guilty to a crime under this Act for a hate crime.[44]

In the meantime, Bodi and Zach leave Bodi's friend's mobile home after an altercation over an old conflict. They do not have water and now they have panicked. They try every convenience store, and they are closed with signs that read "no water" as in this screenshot.

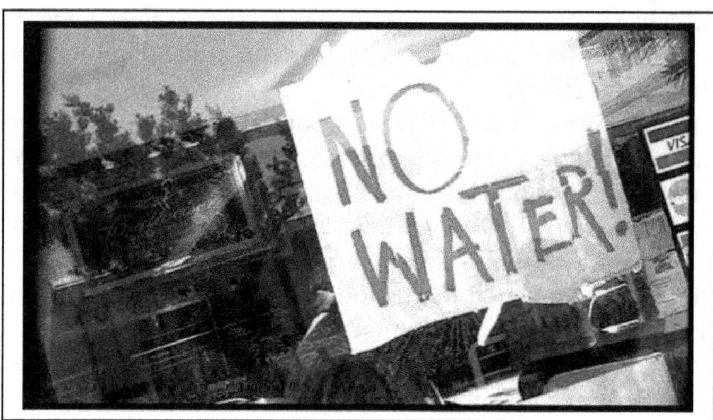

Zach starts to panick and sob, and Bodi repeats his population control conspiracy theory that he believes is underway with the government. Zach becomes angry then apologizes. Bodi passes out for lack of water.

A screenshot of the National Guard delivering water follows the scene where Bodi and Zach panic.

---

[44] *United States v. Larson* (D. Wash) FBI press release at http://www.fbi.gov/seattle/press-releases/2013/washington-state-man-pleads-guilty-to-federal-hate-crime-in-attack-on-sikh-man.

The three subplots merge: Bodi and Zach are dying of thirst when they enter the convenience store owned by the American-Sikh family. Sargeant Ritter's wife and daughter enter the store just at the time Bodi has completely degraded into threatening Vic with a gun for water. When Sargeant Ritter's wife contacts him about the robbery with her cell phone he rushes to the store and shoots Bodi who still has a gun in his hand. This does not end well for Sargeant Ritter who is hoping for an honorable discharge at best. His private re-enlists for military duty overseas. Zach has lost his friend, Bodi. However, Vic's girlfriend is finally accepted by his mother.

The science in the movie was never explained and for good reason. Although a suspect was arrested for the crime at the end of the film, they did not identify a motive. The film also did not describe the biological agent. Modern drinking water treatment involves adding chlorine in addition to filtration, which would make it almost impossible for a significant amount of a biological agent to survive in the water.

This film focused on the racial/ethnic tensions that can become heightened during a panick and it also focused on the role that religion plays in coping with emergencies and disasters. This film presented an array of legal issues that were well developed, but the science was clearly left to the imagination.

The movie ended with Zach returning to his home in Los Angeles with these last lines of dialogue:

Zach

I thought the water would always flow when I turned on the tap. Honestly . . sometimes you need a splash of cold water to the face.

The Constant Gardner (2005)

RATING

Arthur "Ham" Hammond

No, there are no murders in Africa. Only regrettable deaths. And from those deaths we derive the benefits of civilization, benefits we can afford so easily... because those lives were bought so cheaply.

---*The Constant Gardner* (2005)

The Constant Gardner (2005) is perhaps the most unlikely movie in this subgenre because the plot revolves around the pharmaceutical company's drug for treatment of a contagious disease. But the contagious disease, MDR-TB does not create the ticking time bomb of urgency, but rather the deadly results from the use of the drug to treat it. There is a sense of urgency not because of the course of the disease but because the drug is killing the patients. The movie is based on the novel by the same name, by John le Carre.

Why would a pharmaceutical company, the Three Bees Pharmaceuticals, use Africans to test a new drug? The laws for liability in Kenya are based in British law, just as is United States' legal heritage. However, the culture of using liability for equity is almost non-existent in Kenya compared to the United States, known as one of the most litigious countries in the world. Logically, pharmaceutical companies would fare much better economically to perform their human subject research in a country that does not have tort lawyers waiting to take the case for injuries from a pharmaceutical drug trial. That said, it is not without constraints and ethical practices that pharmaceutical companies pursue these drug trials in countries in Africa. The International human subject testing guidelines require all the precautions be taken that are normally taken in any country, including the United States and the United Kingdom.

In *The Constant Gardner* (2005), a United Kingdom company named the Three Bees Pharmaceutical Company, perhaps a thinly veiled reference to 3M Companies, comes to northern Kenya to distribute AIDS drugs. They are also testing for MDR-TB, multi-drug resistant tuberculosis, and then treating those who are diagnosed with the disease with an experimental drug, Dypraxa, manufactured by KDH Pharmaceuticals.

Tessa Quayle (Rachel Weisz), the wife of Dr. Justin Quayle (Ralph Fiennes) is a political activist who is hoping to expose the corporate and political corruption she suspects when Mwanza Kibulu, an African woman dies after taking the drug. Mwanza was an acquaintance of the Quayle family, and Tessa knew her well enough to know that she should not have suddenly died. She suspects the pharmaceutical company is covering up deaths from their drug trials of Dypraxa and begins to investigate the company with a doctor, Arnold Blohm ( ), without the knowledge of her husband, who would disapprove of her investigation.

Tessa's desire to help those in poverty-stricken Kenya was evidenced when she saw a child and tried to save him, and over her protests that the child needed help, Justin told her, "There are millions of people who need help."

Tessa is found murdered in northern Kenya early in the film, which sets Justin Quayle on a course of unrelenting investigation to find the reason for his wife's death. Because she is traveling with the local physician, there are rumors that she has been unfaithful to Justin. It turns out that the doctor is gay and based on that he concludes these were only rumors.

Even when Justin is told to go home after the death of his wife and forget about it, he says he has no home, and Tessa was his home portending the ultimate conclusion of the film.

With everything at stake, Justin Quayle relentlessly pursues Three Bees Pharmaceuticals to find that they are the instigators of the death of his wife, but not only that, they are also engaged in political corruption with the British government who allowed the drug trials of Dypraxa despite the deaths of the patients. Justin returns to the United Kingdom to meet with his friend, Arthur "Ham" Hammond, and discovers Tessa had sent a report through their friend in Africa, Sandy Woodrow, to Sir Bernard Pellegrin of the British

High Commission for investigation of Three Bees Pharmaceuticals. In the report, Tessa had alleged the motive for Three Bees Pharmaceuticals was to avoid reformulating the drug at great cost, and to cover up the deaths during the drug trials in Kenya, ultimately with the goal of getting the drug approved. The report was quietly covered up. It was thereafter, that Tessa was also silenced in a brutal murder while traveling with a physician who was also suspicious of the Three Bees Pharmaceuticals motives.

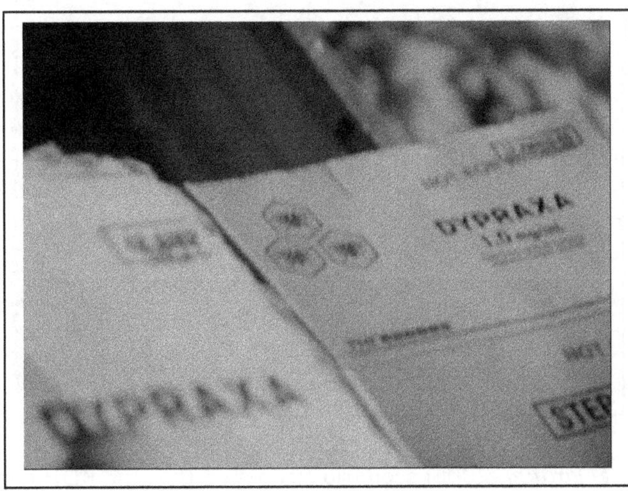

A closer examination of the methods used in the film by the Three Bees Pharmaceuticals to coerce individuals to take the drug, Dypraxa is shockingly unethical. In order to get the drug that they need for AIDS, they are forced to take Dypraxa in order to receive it. They are given an impossible choice of slow and certain death from AIDS or the risk of an unknown drug Dypraxa which they can see is killing other people. This is contrary to the Nuremberg Code which is an internationally recognized norm in international law, which prohibits nations from experimenting on humans without their consent.

In the United States, a regulation for informed consent for such research called "the common rule"[45] is required as part of every human subject research protocol. The National Institutes of Health (NIH) of the Department of Health and Human Services (DHHS) administers this code. Further, as part of the approval process a committee of institutional representatives for every university and company which receives federal funding, are required to have an Institutional Review Board (IRB) to approve the language of the informed consent disclosure to those who are subjected to the testing.

Human drug trials such as the Dypraxa drug trial would require the informed consent, and also notification to the IRB and cessation of the trial if deaths were occurring associated with the drug. The card that was signed by each of the recipients of the drug had a block to check with the initials "IC" for informed consent, indicating that they had been informed of the risks in accordance with their approved research protocol. Clearly, that informed consent was not being given to any of them, which means a knowing

[45] 45 U.S.C. §46 (2013).

understanding of the risks and benefits of the treatment. If they refused to initial the card and take Dypraxa, they were refused the AIDS drug, Navorpine.

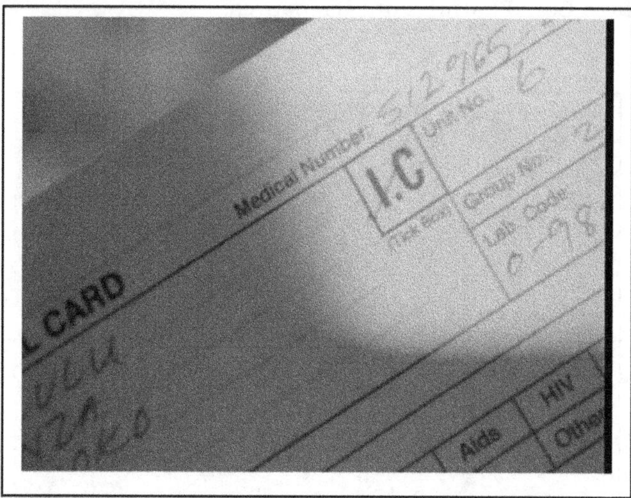

The Constant Gardner (2005) scenario suggested that the KDH company would submit the drug trial data that had been sanitized by Three Bees to omit the deaths from the drug, for approval of its treatment of MDR-TB. The United Kingdom is bound by international law, as well as international human subject testing guidelines. The United Kingdom also has a similar human subject testing regulation.

The film captured the element of "the innocent" well, featuring the poverty-stricken Kenyans, desperate for a treatment for AIDS, willing to accept a drug that they knew had a high likelihood of death. The villain, the corruption of the collusion of both the government and industry, driven by greed provided a plausible motive for the plot.

Le Carre's entry in the biohorror/biothriller subgenre received four nominations for Academy Awards, including best screenplay adaptation from a book. Rachel Weisz won an Academy Award for Best Performance by an Actress in a Supporting Role.

The Hades Factor (2006)

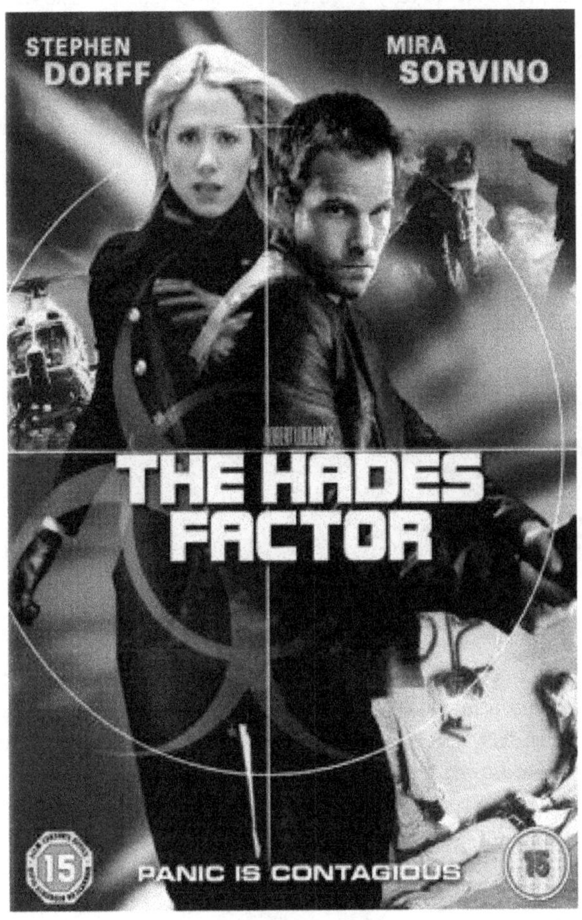

RATING

Chechnyan terrorist

We will turn America against itself. Let them feel the sting of their operation.

--*The Hades Factor* (2006)

The Hades Factor (2006) is one of the Covert One series made for television pilot and series based on the Robert Ludlum books and co-written by Gayle Lynds.. The tagline, "Panic is Contagious" is as good as any tagline for a bioterrorism movie. Two out of three words are at the core of the entire subgenre.

The movie opens with a father of a young family mowing with his daughter when his hands show subdermal hemorrhages, his nose starts to bleed and then he throws up blood and is dead in the next few seconds. The same thing happens to a waitress, and a prisoner in what appears to be a Guantanamo Bay while the Muslim call to prayer plays in the background.

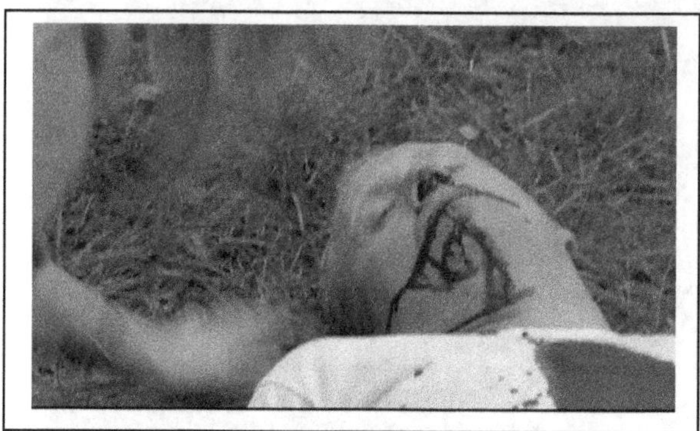

The next scene is a world health conference where the American panelist Dr. John Smith (Stephen Dorff) is questioned about what the U.S. is doing to prepare for a bioterrorism attack. He quips that "we are still looking for weapons of mass destruction" which gets a long (too long) laugh from the audience. Like much of the drama, it just lasts too long.

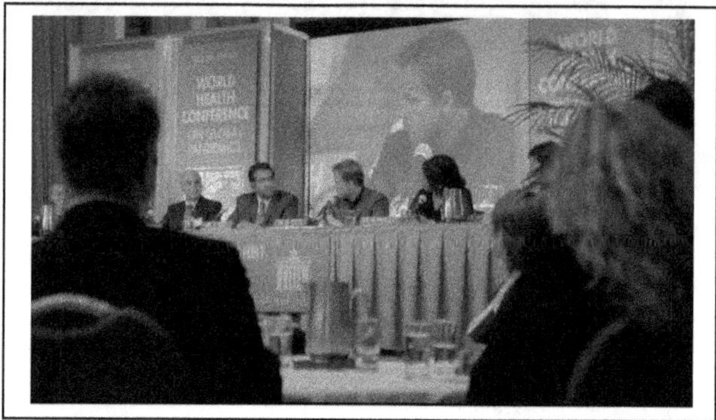

The most important lines from the conference scene are the ones about the readiness of the United States. The questioner asks Dr. J. Smith (Stephen Dorff)

Conference questioner

How is the United States preparing

for the possibility of
a bioterrorism attack?

Dr. Smith

If you are asking me if
such an attack can
be prevented --- probably not.

A transaction to get the "virus" involves Rachel Russell (Mira Sovino) and some thugs on one side and some Muslim terrorists on the other. Between them she escapes with the virus, but not before torching the car with the two men who kidnapped her, in it.

This was in the first 15 minutes of the film, which sets up the plot for the next 2.5 hours.

Fred Klein (Danny Huston) and Palmer Addison (Blair Underwood) the operatives of Covert One, are uncertain about Rachel's allegiances at this point and believe she has taken the vial with the bioweapon for personal gain. At least that is the impression the viewer gets. They order her to be "erased", and she spends a good part of the movie avoiding being "erased" by the Covert One "clean up crew."

The bioweapon, the viewer learns, is an ebola-variant. It acts quickly, with the victim showing symptoms within the first 48 hours, which include hemorrhagic rashes on the hands and face, headaches and bleeding from the orifices.

Anyone having contact with someone with the infection is subject to quarantine. This is consistent with Constitutional due process which includes a standard for quarantine, then some hearing would be required to quarantine each individual.

The President's powers present at least two legal issues in this film. Here is a screenshot of the President (Angelica Huston).

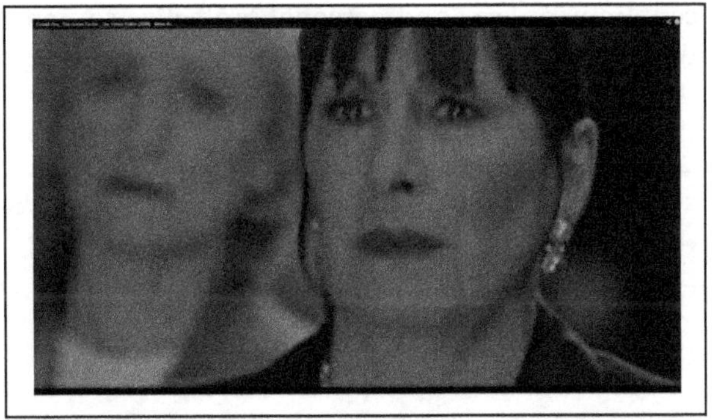

As for the Covert One agency, it reports directly to the President of the United States and officially does not exist. First, it is highly unlikely that the President would want to be that close to an operation that was being kept secret from the "Gang of Eight" in Congress, since that would violate the intelligence statute which requires the President to inform Congress on convert operations. The President has the Director of National Intelligence (ODNI) to coordinate covert operations and if he cannot trust his own appointee to the ODNI, then the President is already in jeopardy. The idea of a secret agency that reports only to the President is strictly fantasy without a lot of logic.

The two lead characters, Smith and his fiancé, work at USAMRIID, the U.S. Army research laboratory for biodefense and countermeasures. The viewer learns that Simitar is program to test bioweapons on U.S. troops run by a rogue CIA agent. Troops who served in Afghanistan were intentionally exposed to the bioweapon --- and here begins the unraveling on the U.S. Simitar program. This is the scene in the biosafety laboratory at USAMRIID where the team discovers the deaths of the three soldiers who served in Afghanistan were killed by the Hades virus.

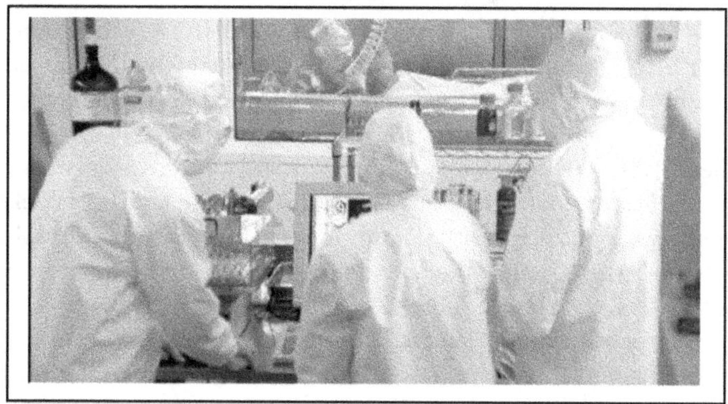

The team is working at biosafety two conditions given there is no evidence that they are in a negative pressure room. A BSL-3 laboratory would be pulling air from the room and the researchers would be wearing individual respirators. With a virus that is unknown and highly lethal, they should have been working at BSL-4 which would require negative pressure and air hoses in complete containment biosuits. As the scene progresses in these three screenshots, the containment level and personal protective equipment becomes greater. Here the containment for the autopsies increases to complete eye and skin protection.

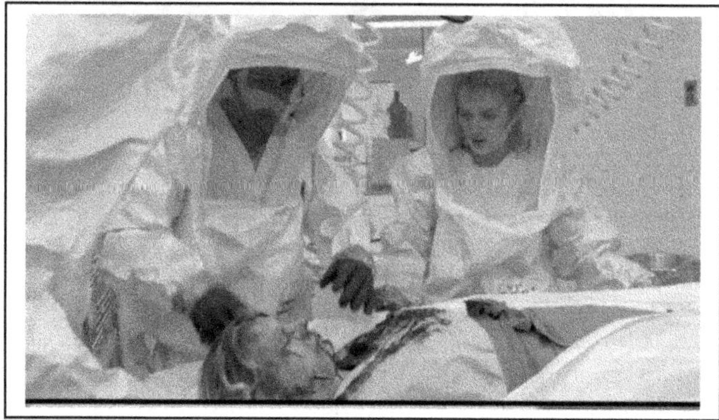

In this next screenshot where Dr. John Smith is interviewing one of the surviving soldiers who is ill, they are using containment with duct tape around their wrists and headgear.

Testing any kind of experimental drug on soldiers requires at a minimum, informed consent, and the soldiers understanding the effects of the treatment. "White coats" are human laboratory technicians who have agreed to be experimental subjects for vaccines and other countermeasures, when a human test is essential. These "White Coats" are some of the most sophisticated human subjects who are well aware of the risks involved.

However, in The Hades Factor, the use of soldiers for experimental bioweapons would be similar to the experimentation on soldiers for the effects of radiation or the experimentation on government personnel with LSD in the 1960s. Both of these experiments were eventually exposed, and restitution was made to the families of the victims of these misdirected experiments. The experimentation on soldiers in this scenario would suffer the same consequences, and hopefully restitution. This kind of experimentation is a violation of the Nuremberg Code, to which the United States and all countries have agreed to be bound. This requires informed consent for any experiment on a human subject, which means knowing consent.

A French scientist who worked in Afghanistan for WHO knew about the Hades virus and that it is an "extremely rare" variant of ebola virus. Rachel reaches him while on the run and being chased by an assassin and he helps her to identify what she has in the vial.

A word about covert operations: no covert operation can exist without the approval of the President of the United States. The President is required by law to inform the Senate Committee (Gang of Eight).[46] In this movie, the President has authorized Covert One as well as Simitar. In her meeting with the Director of National Intelligence, Frank, she says she will deny any knowledge and deny authorizing any of it if they do not find the missing virus.

Meanwhile, a terrorist group from Berlin, has been infected with the Hades virus, the way that the virus will enter the United States.

---

[46] 50 USC § 413b (2013).

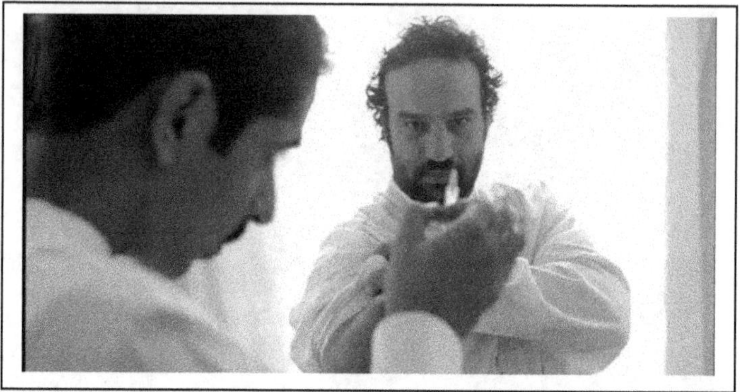

Once in the United States, despite being pulled aside at immigration, the infected suicide bioweapon terrorist enters the country and proceeds to his meeting point to give his blood to the terrorist cell in the United States. They take him to their makeshift biosafety laboratory where they draw his blood.

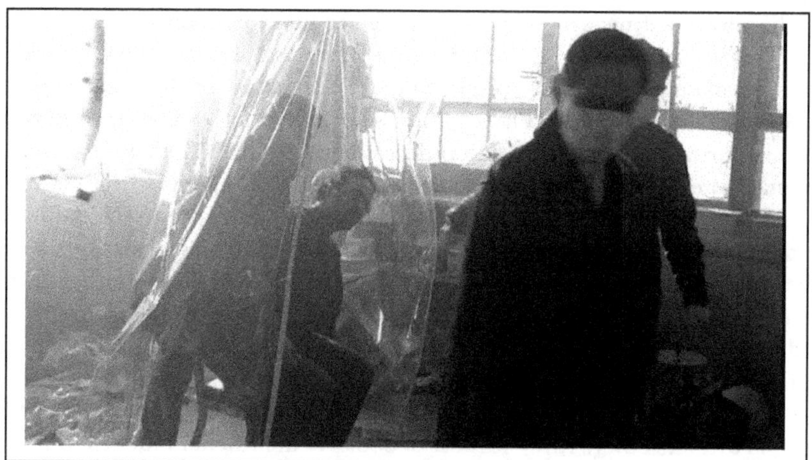

The terrorists plan to use an aerosolization activation device to release the virus into the ventilation system of the Washington Dulles Airport.

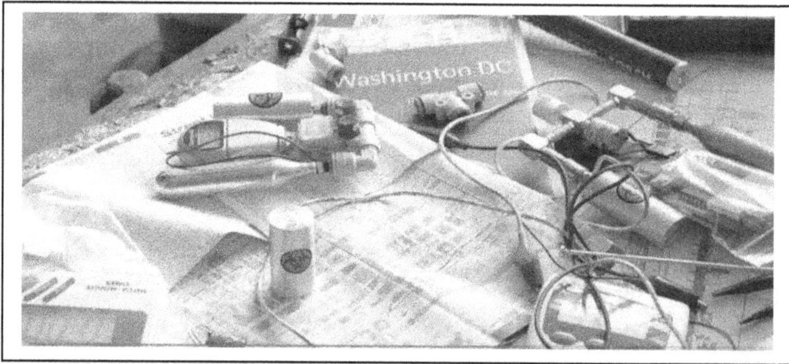

The terrorist dropped off at the Dulles International Airport in Washington, D.C. sees friends, children and people he realizes he will kill with the virus in the ventilation system. As he prepares to remove the cover from the ventilation system, he was apprehended by airport police. Three other terrorists have been dispersed to plant aerosolization bombs with the Hades virus.

The company, Maisser Pharmaceuticals eventually contacts the CDC and tells them that they have a vaccine for the Hades virus. The concern that it is not ready for human use is considered, but the President of Maisser, says that he "will let the government make that call."

Eventually, Rachel and ___ break into the computer website of Maisser Pharmaceutical to see the vaccine and compare it to antibodies in the soldiers and find it is a match. Maisser had used the soldier's immune systems to react to the virus and took their antibodies to develop the vaccine.

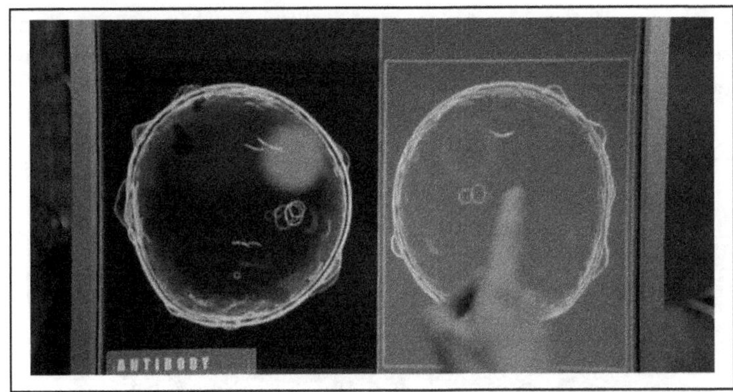

While the military may use a drug that is provisionally approved --- an IND (Investigational New Drug) if the President waives the FDA final approval step and waives informed consent requirements. However, civilians have no such exception and any civilian use would require full FDA approval before use, even in an emergency. However, 21 CFR 312.34 is a regulatory exception to full FDA approval for a new drug that is intended to treat a serious or immediately life threatening disease.

If Maisser Pharmaceuticals manufacturers the vaccine, they would need indemnification and probably for fairness to the public, a compensation act, all of which would need to be approved by Congress. Also, if the vaccine is patented, the U.S. could take the patent rights for responding to the public health emergency, or they could negotiate favorable terms for purchasing the vaccine.

The terrorists are successful with one detonation in the Hubert Humphrey building and the next screenshot is a low light view of the President and the Cabinet watching the news cast of the chaos of the attack.

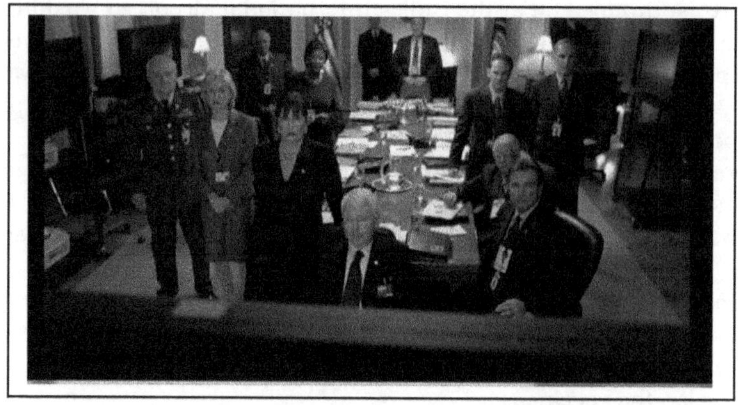

Nothing expresses the result of bioterrorism like a cemetery scene, and that is exactly what we see in the last scene as Dr. John Smith leaves the cemetery where Sophie, his finace is buried.

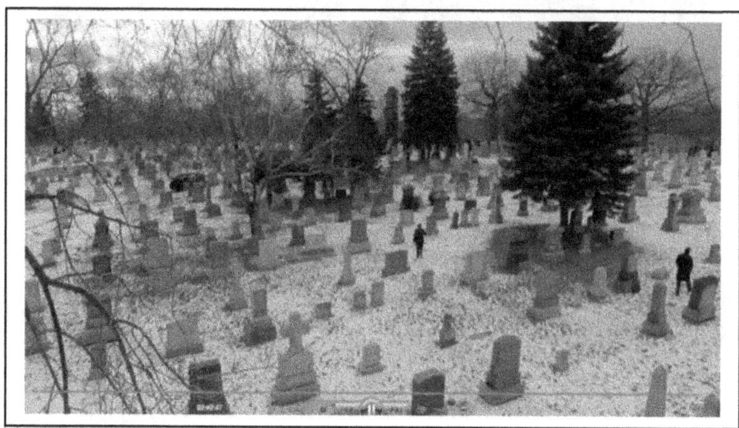

The Hades Factor (2005) was the first movie to use the suicide bomber model for bioterrorism and presents a possibility which is undetectable. The immigration of the suicide bioterrorist demonstrated how even if the person is on a watch list for Customs and Border Patrol, they are not being monitored for illness. The movie's virus, the ebola variant was not an unreasonable scenario as a realistic bioweapon. However, the technique of infected the soldiers at a much earlier time with a long period of latency is another method that was not portrayed in any other movie at this point.

The movie's villain was the drug company in collusion with a rogue CIA operative, making greed the motivation. The innocent victims were the targets of the terrorists weapons and the American people. The President's remarks sum up the message in the movie, when she is informed that the Hades virus was inside the terrorist's aerosolization device: "How do I tell the American people that their government made the virus?"

Fatal Contact: Bird Flu in America (2006)

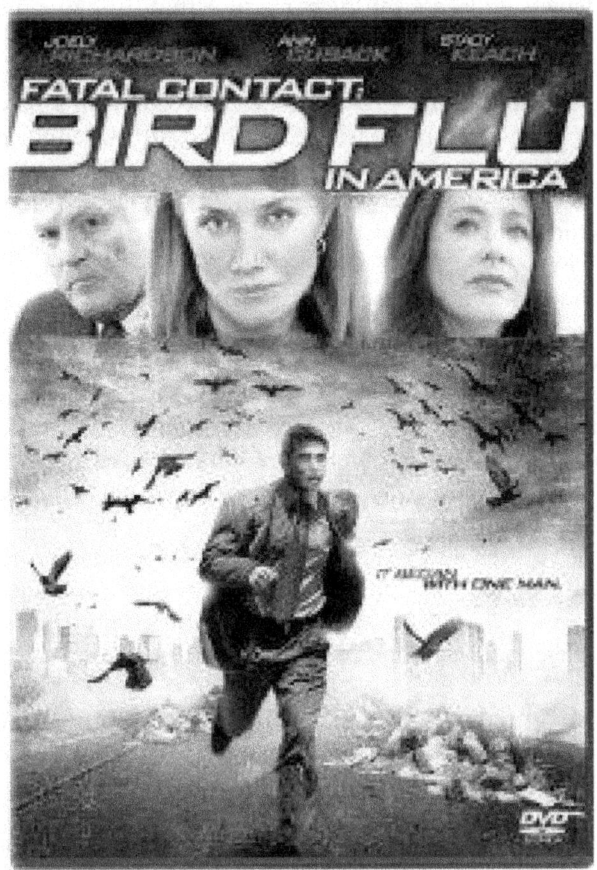

RATING

Stacy Keach

I want to re-iterate. There is absolutely no need for panic.

****

Gov Mike Newsome

What's the use of having a plan if nobody wants to *follow it.*

---*Fatal Contact: Bird Flu in America* (2006)

Fatal Contact: Bird Flu in America (2006) is a made-for-television movie which was developed and released during the height of federal planning for a bird flu pandemic. It is the only movie that depicts a disaster at the same time that the same disaster is looming, making this a unique brand of terror for this movie.

At the time, I was living on Pennsylvania Avenue in Washington, D.C. watching this movie, while working on planning for federal agencies to cope with a potential bird flu outbreak. I was Chief Counsel of the Research and Innovative Technology Administration, of the U.S. Department of Transportation, and we were leading the Department of Transportation's effort for the continuity of government should bird flu become a pandemic reality. Every federal department and agency was developing a plan when the made-for-television movie was aired. The CDC (U.S. Centers for Diseases Control and Prevention) was so concerned about the panic and the unrealistic symptoms portrayed in the movie, that in cooperation with the producers they included an announcement at the end of the movie directing viewers to the CDC website where they could obtain accurate information about the bird flu. (The CDC website discussion is in Appendix 1). But the reality is that we had considered many of the things that were depicted in the movie. We anticipated that fully 30% of the workforce in the transportation sector --- bus drivers, pilots, attendants, mechanics --- would be either sick or absent from work to avoid coming in contact with the sick.

The viewing public was well aware of calling for federal assistance in a disaster with the experiences in Louisiana, Mississippi and Texas after Hurricane Katrina in 2005, just a year before this movie was released. This collective experience may have made asking for federal resources for police assistance in time of a public health emergency as depicted in this movie, more realistic.

From the opening credits, it is clear that a worldwide pandemic is in the making. Scenes of world maps with counters and dots suggest an ominous scenario.

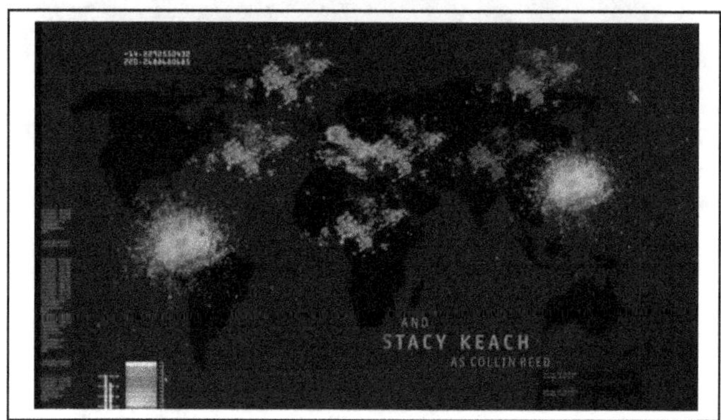

The perspective of the epidemiologist is very evident in the camera shots of the movie. After the American businessman is infected in a China manufacturing facility, the opportunities for transmission serve as close-ups. In the first screenshot there are two transmissions and the frames on the screen multiply to depict the exponential increase in exposures to the virus from the first index case, Mr. Connelly.

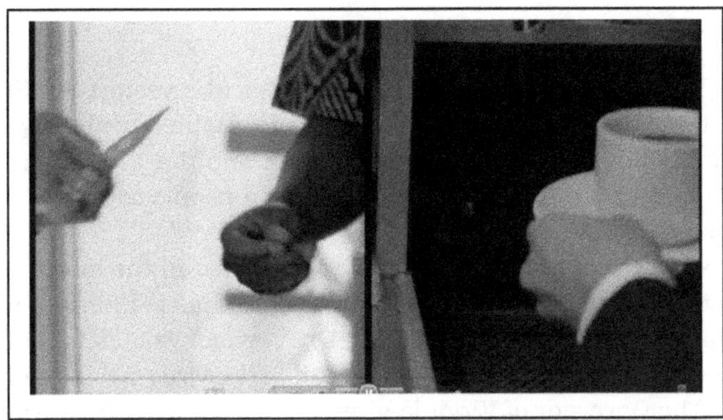

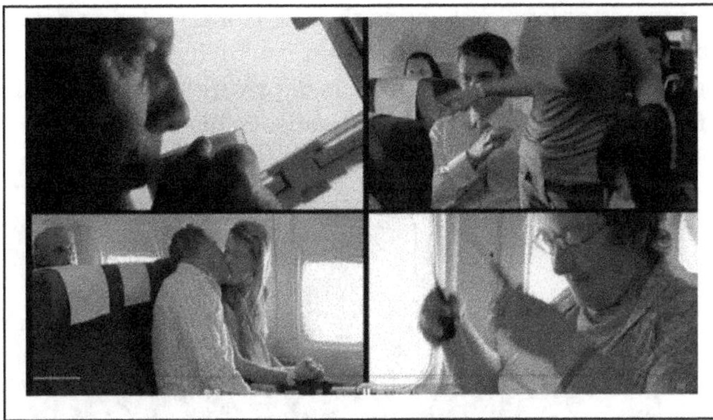

The movie begins with an American returning from a business trip to China after inspecting a facility. While there, he comes in contact with a man infected with H5N1, the bird flu strain, and brings the disease to America. He becomes the "patient zero", or index case. The graphics in the movie effectively show the bird flu virus spreading through coughing, touching, ingesting and inhaling. The realism with which the movie depicts the spread of the disease plays on the terror of the possible. The first death, is Mr. Connelly, and it is dramatic. This screenshot shows the closeup of his bleeding which preceded his collapse in the store. This is the most unrealistic part of the public health aspects of the movie, which are otherwise very accurate. The dramatic death and collapse was a concern that CDC had with this movie, considering the panic that might come from these depictions of these violent and sudden deaths.

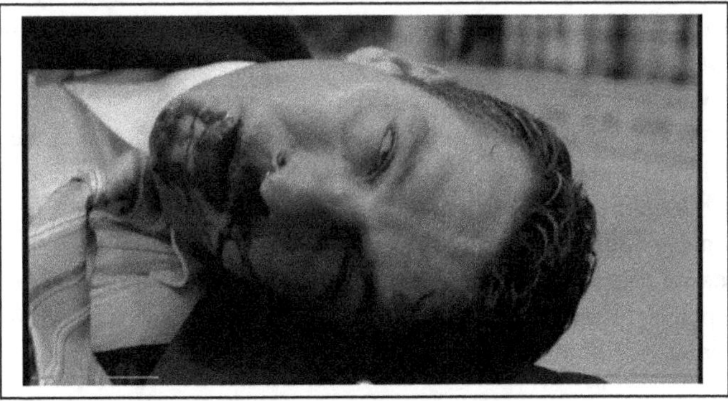

Dr. Iris Varnack from the CDC, Epidemiological Investigation Service, is called to investigate and then present to the briefing Governors who have been called for a special briefing. At this briefing, Dr. Iris Varnack informs them that the H5N1 has now become transmissible to humans, and more than 350 million people could die. That is is worse than the 1918 Spanish flu because it is more deadly.

A number of containment measures are depicted in the movie. The Governor of Virginia has instituted neighborhood quarantines. He has set himself up in a fortress with glass between him and the rest of the world. Dr. Varnack comes to talk to him about stopping his quarantine of neighborhoods, because the virus has already spread and so it will do no good. The Governor of Virginia gives her a talk about how Americans are different and will not wait around for their fate. The Governor said, " What we do in this country is to use every weapon in our arsenal." He adds that he is interested in providing the citizens of Virginia with "continuity of leadership" and that is why he is secured in this biosafety containment space. She tries to tell him he is depriving them of humanity the only thing that will get us through this pandemic. He dismisses her and continues with his plan.

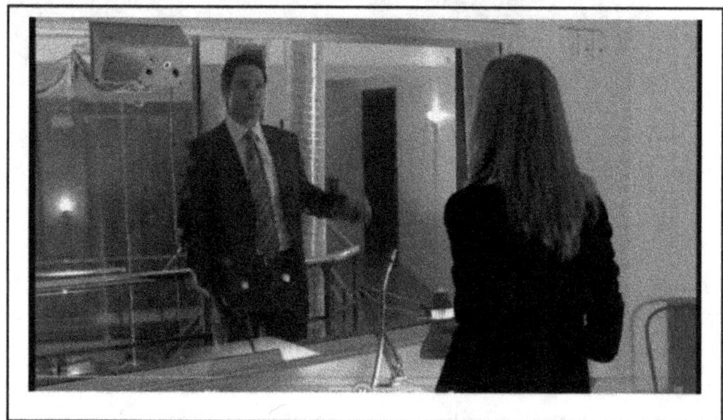

Another measure is in Moscow and they have prohibited public gatherings over the protests of citizens.

Another news cast announces that insurance companies are filing for bankruptcy because they cannot pay all the life insurance policies due to the high number of deaths from the Bird Flu.

Another state has requested their portion of the drug stockpile, a function of public health planning and they are told they cannot get it. The reason is that California and New York both have priority because of the high number of cases. "What's the point of having a plan if you don't follow it?" is the dialogue that follows this news.

Fatal Contact: Bird Flu in America (2006) is the best in the subgenre for depicting Constitutional federalism issues. In addition, the movie tackles legal issues that would be raised in this scenario unlike most of the other movies which either ignore the legal issues, are ignorant of the legal issues, or hope to use the absence of law as part of the terror and fear. The movie takes on quarantine legal issues for individuals, area quarantines and due process; intellectual property and patent ownership of drugs; international intellectual property law issues; whether health care workers can be ordered to go to work in a public health disaster; whether the National Guard can be used for civilian law enforcement; whether vaccines can be selectively distributed to the public without equal protection or other infringements on rights.

Of the movies depicting quarantine, this movie is the most thorough in its treatment of the problems that arise in the administration of a government quarantine.

In Virginia, where patient zero originates, the Governor of Virginia must make a decision about whether to quarantine. Rather than quarantine individuals, he attempts to quarantine large areas.

There is a large difference in constitutional due process for these two legal actions. In fact, many question the constitutionality of an area quarantine at all. Why? To ensure that our liberty interest is protected and only burdened in the narrowest way to serve the government purpose of protecting the public's health, each person is given a due process opportunity to understand why they are being quarantined or isolated and here the evidence for it. Then the individual has an opportunity to challenge the quarantine or to re-assess the isolation after a reasonable amount of time required to await the individual no longer being infectious. This is Constitutional due process. However, an area quarantine would not recognize individual reasons for exclusions from the quarantine, meaning that many people would be swept into the quarantine based on an area, not on specific facts to that individual's risk to society should they not be quarantined. Due process is compromised for the individual and such actions should be limited in time and scope to make them as narrow as possible.

The Governor defends his quarantine with his actions to deliver food and supplies to the neighborhoods. This scene depicts the families standing in line at distribution points and they are told there is enough for three days in the boxes they are distributing. Distributing food is a humanitarian action but does not address the due process and freedom of travel issues that are at stake in the area quarantine that the Governor has ordered.

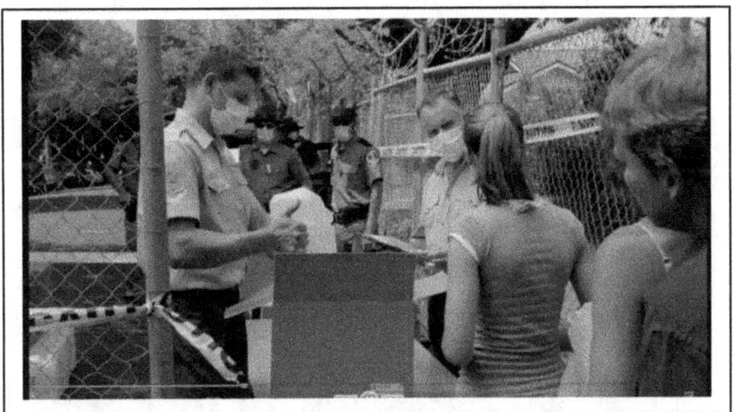

Also in this distribution scene, the government representatives are asked for more rubber gloves and masks and they are told that all these things are made in China and there is nothing coming out of there right now. This suggests that trade embargos are preventing China from trading with the world. The International Health Regulations (IHR, 2005) were intended to prevent such economic injury when it is not a reasonable public health measure to take in response to the threat. There is nothing about H5N1 that would suggest not shipping goods would be protective of public health and would be an action that would not be approved under these binding regulations.

The Emergency Rooms are experiencing panic and the worried well, who crowd emergency rooms in times of public health disasters. Here is a screenshot of an ER in New York City.

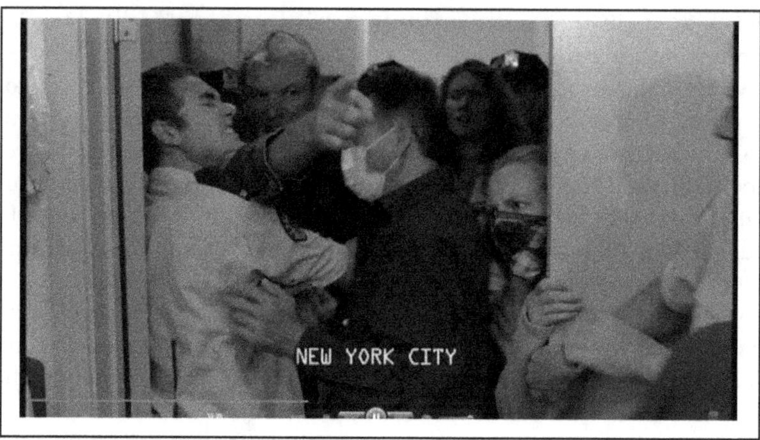

The Model Public Health Act, drafted by Lawrence Gostin in cooperation with the Association of Governors in 2001, provided for an area quarantine which as controversial among those whose who would find the balance against the burden on due process and liberty to be too great to be constitutional.

The next screenshot depicts the rising body count, and the Governor must conclude that the area quarantine is not working. The Governor is told that if they lift one quarantine they will need to lift all of them, or they will be seen as prejudiced.

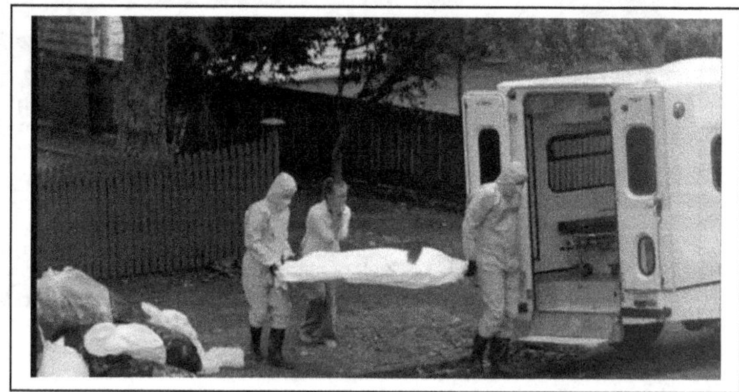

The first case to establish this principle on similar facts was *Jew Ho v. Williamson*[47] which found unconstitutional the quarantine drawn around Chinatown for reasons other than compelling public health.

Physicians and nurses began to not come to work for fear of being exposed to the deadly flu. The nurse, (Justina Muchiado), who works in a New York City hospital, struggles with the decision each day as to whether to go to work, feeling pressure from her boyfriend, who is a member of the National Guard, not to go to work. This temporary hospital is a scene which shows the desperation to provide care for the growing numbers of victims of the pandemic.

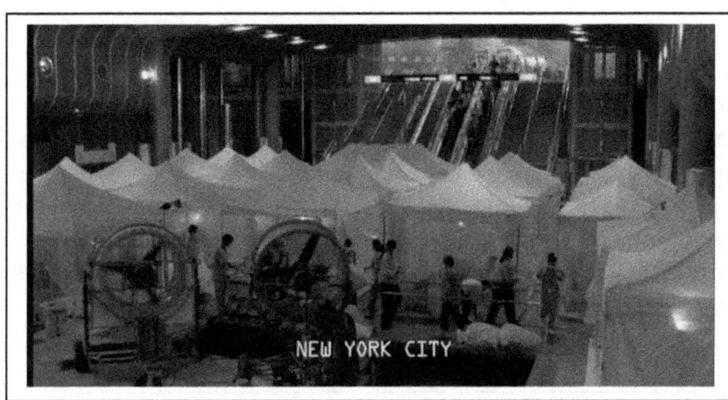

The nurse's boyfriend, a member of the National Guard is ordered to keep law and order on the streets as the pandemic escalates. This is the controversial issue of the military interface with civilians. The National Guard is better suited to provide law enforcement but they are still trained primarily for military activities, not civilian activities. The activation of the National Guard under Title 10 which gives the Governor the power to order the National Guard leaves the government power in the state government. However Title 58 gives the power to the President of the United States to order the National Guard to enforcement the law, shifting the power from the state government to the federal government. This is an extreme act and requires this only be done at the request of the Governor of the state, unless the government has completely collapsed.

Grocery stores are empty and this next screenshot shows the panic and desperation of people who have waited to get into the grocery store for so few goods on the shelf. A fight occurs over the scarce commodities depicting the rising desperation and panic as the pandemic escalates.

---

47 103 F. 10 (1900).

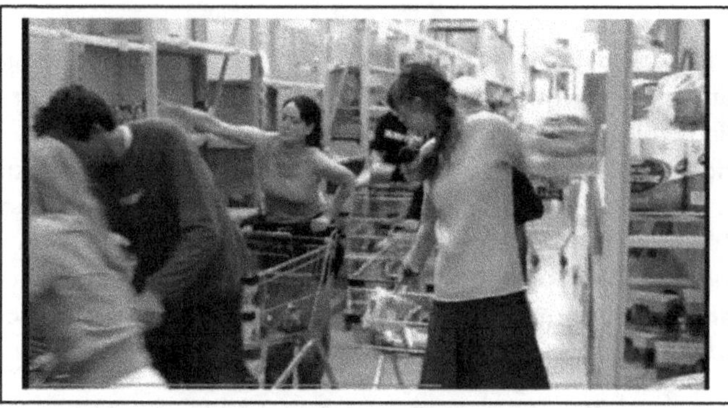

In another scene, the Governor of Virginia's son who is a diabetic runs out of insulin and goes into diabetic shock. He tries to revive his son with CPR, and an ambulance is not available for another 30 minutes. He does not want his son to go to a hospital, because of the exposure, but it is unlikely that he will survive if he does not get to a source of insulin.

Governor Newsome walks over to view the huge field of body bags and this dump truck dumping another load of bodies. He has just seen his own son die of diabetic shock due to a shortage of insulin, something that could be easily prevented in a normal environment. After viewing these bodies in this dark scene, he concludes that the area quarantines are not working and he ends these quarantines in Virginia.

The revelation that a vaccine had been developed by France was in keeping with France's long history in advances in vaccine development. But when France refused to supply the vaccine to other countries, including the United States, the U.S. used the authority to disregard their intellectual property rights in their patent in the United States, which would have allowed the U.S. to manufacture the vaccine with no income to the French pharmaceutical company. This was enough of a threat to cause the French company to provide the vaccine to the U.S.

There is not enough vaccine to be given to everyone in the United States and a determination for how to distribute the vaccine must be made.

Can vaccines be selectively distributed to the public without equal protection or other infringements on rights? There is precedent for this question in the United States from the flu season of 2003. There was a rapid escalation of seasonal influenza and the United

States was faced with a shortage of vaccine due to a tainted lot that had been produced for the U.S. in France. The United States was faced with long lines of elderly people, many of which fainted while standing in line.

In this movie, they are getting only 200,000 doses and everyone needs two doses to be effectively immunized.

The patient zero's wife, Denise Connelly (Ann Cosack) is prompted to follow a neighbor's dog since it is unusal for the dog to be out. She discovers her neighbor, Ms. Jasper is starving to death. She brings her home and starts to rescue other people in the neighborhood who are starving and her daughter is helping the children reconnect with society. The feeling that the pandemic has peaked and things are going back to normal is depicted in these scenes in the last third of the movie.

Dr. Vancek sees Collin Reed dying in the hospital with H5N1 and she runs from the room. In a break with a movie that has been concerned about accuracy, Dr. Vancek runs to the bathroom and puts her gloved hands on her face after exposure to sick patients. That would be an action that a trained epidemiologist would never do, having developed these habits over years of training.

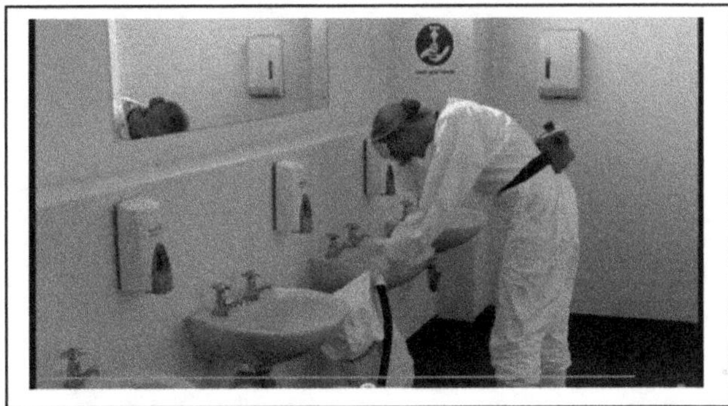

With five minutes left in the movie at week 17, 23 million deaths, the CDC is tracking a mutation in Angola in West Africa.

Bacterium (2006)

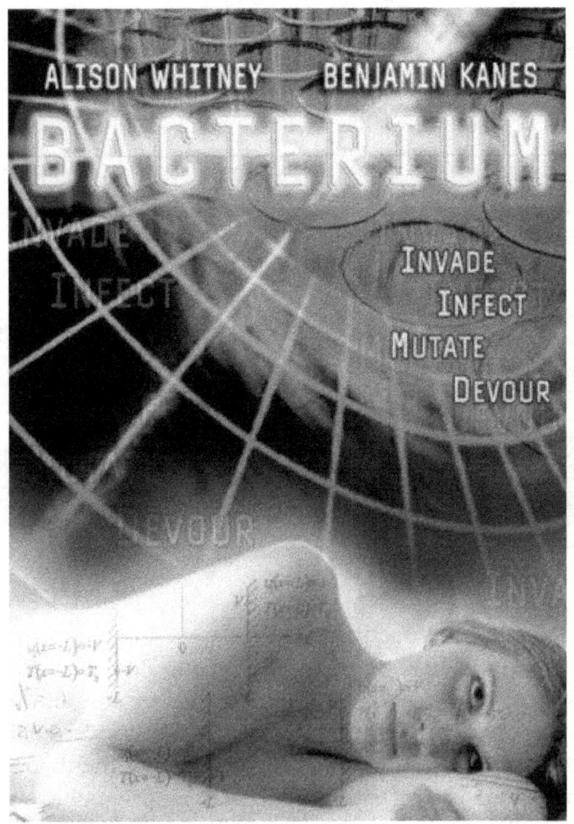

RATING

Dr. Philip Boskovic

Only two of you left. Who is going to be the next one to give his life for science, huh? Sorry little fella it can't be helped. It is a couple of lab rats verses 5 billion human beings. Sometimes it doesn't seem like a fair trade. Oh well, I might not be far behind you. In you go. . . .

---*Bacterium (2006)*

Bacterium (2006) opens with a helicopter chasing a car with a driver whose face is disfigured we come to learn is a bacteria. Two biosuited people in a helicopter jump out to recover what he has in the front seat in his car which has crashed into a tree. One of the biosuited men in the helicopter searches for the "sample" and finds it. The other man asks if he touched the sample. He then torches him and says, "you shouldn't have touched the sample.

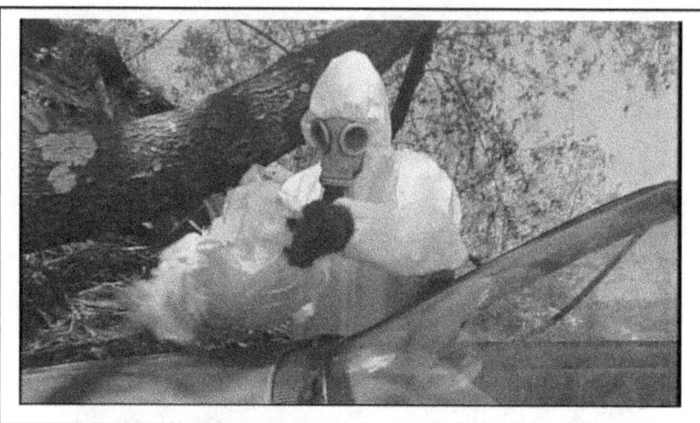

The next scene is a group of teenagers who are having a paintball fight in the forest and stumble upon a cabin. Inside they confront Dr. Philip Boskovic, Chuck McMahon, a mad scientist who is experimenting with something obviously contaminating, because he makes the young woman disrobe and enter the shower. The viewer becomes sympathetic with him when he is so kind to his laboratory rats as he experiments on them. However, in the next screenshot, Dr. Boskovic wipes his face with his glove as he is removing his personal protective gear (PPE) which would make any biosafety officer cringe. The purpose of the biosuit is to avoid contact with its surface which has been exposed to air and other potential contamination in a laboratory. Proper biosafety protocol would require he shower off, just like he had the teen remove her clothes and shower to decontaminate -- presumptively.

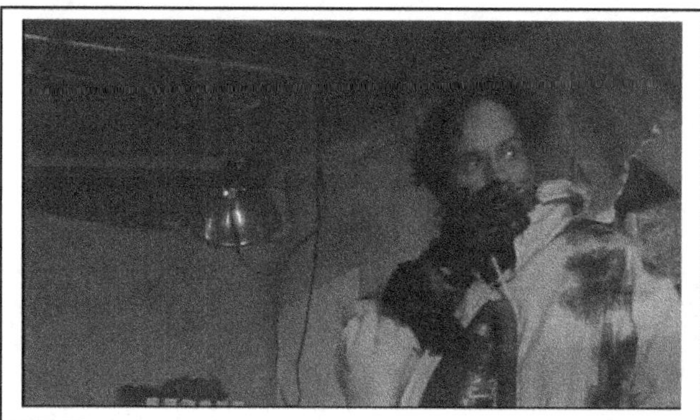

He explains to the group that he is a government scientist who was charged with creating a biological weapon for military use that could multiply in a target area and then die out when the project is over. He started to mutate unpredictably and now it can destroy the planet if it gets out of control.

Dr. Boskovic told the teens that he was hiding in the old house to find a cure before it is too late.

Major Larson, Jessica Day, comes to the old house to take control of this rogue bioweapon scientist.

Dr. Boskovic has violated the law by leaving his laboratory with the bioweapon which we will assume is on the "select agent list", a list of bacteria, viruses, fungi and prions, etc. that are required to be registered and kept in specific biocontainment levels and laboratories. There are no criminal penalties with the "select agent regulations" but there are criminal penalties for violating the Biological Weapons statute.

Dr. Boskovic has nothing to worry about because he is consumed by the bacteria while trapped in the laboratory.

The military have surrounded the house, and Major Larson, a military commander appears on the scene to take control of the operation. She determines that they made a mistake by letting people in, and shooting one of the teens as they tried to escape was also a bad decision. The teens retreat inside and spend the rest of the movie trying to escape.

Another government scientist, who comes into the room with Dr. Boskovic is also consumed by the bacteria. The doctor outside Dr. Chandler, called upon to treat the teen who was shot by the military snipers. It reproduces by fission. She communicates with the headquarters staff and they say that "in 18 hours there will be over 250,000 of those things." The response from his co-workers? "That's a lot of blobs!"

The next screenshot is the only movie that depicts a biosafety suit failure and they do so with great effect. Dr. Chandler's partner is consumed by the bacteria which invade his biosafety suit.

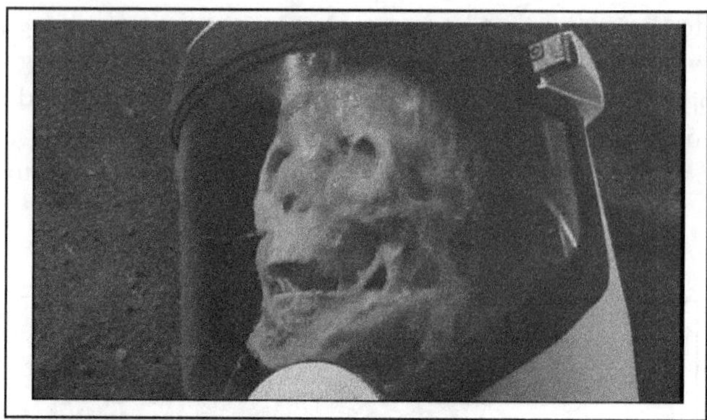

Dr. Chandler is communicating with the military headquarters about the bacteria and the status of its growth. At one point, this exchange takes place at the headquarters.

Techno-Geek 1
In just 48 hours they will
cover the surface of the earth.

Techno-Geek 2

Does that include the ocean?

Techno-Geek 1
Yes.

The next screenshot shows the "emergency operations center" for the military who are deciding how to address this bioweapon that has escaped and mutated. When discussing the policy options for eradicating the bacteria they have this conversation:

Techno-Geek 3
Using a nuclear weapon to
Control a biological weapon
that has gone out of control?

Techno-Geek 4
If we don't make a
decision in 48 hours,
life on this planet is finished.

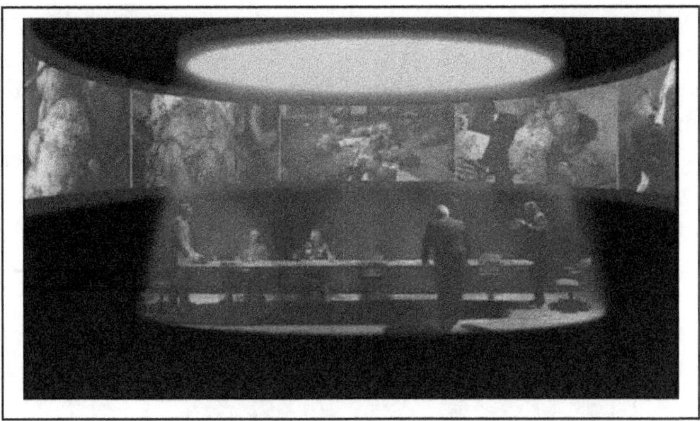

The scientist in the headquarters discussion in the military situation room explains the physics and they have no idea what he explained to them. They have a discussion privately to decide whether to use the "bomb" and finally flip a coin. This is probably the funniest scene in the entire movie, and may have more truth than any policymaker would ever want to admit.

Predictably, the bacteria blob is out of control and growing exponentially. It has fallen off of the ceiling when Dr. Chandler and the teens confront it as they try to escape from the old house.

The tagline for the movie is: *Invade. Iinfect. Mutate. Devour.* Soon, the viewer will understand the tagline because Dr. Boskovic is exposed to his own bioweapon which escapes from its laboratory containment unit which appears to be a tabletop bioreactor, which would be used to multiply the bacteria.

Dr. Chandler is eventually consumed by the bacteria but the teens escape from the old house and conveniently a motor cycle gang is driving by and can provide transport for the teens out of the forest.

The military team decides they have to use the "atomic bomb" and send the helicopter pilots.

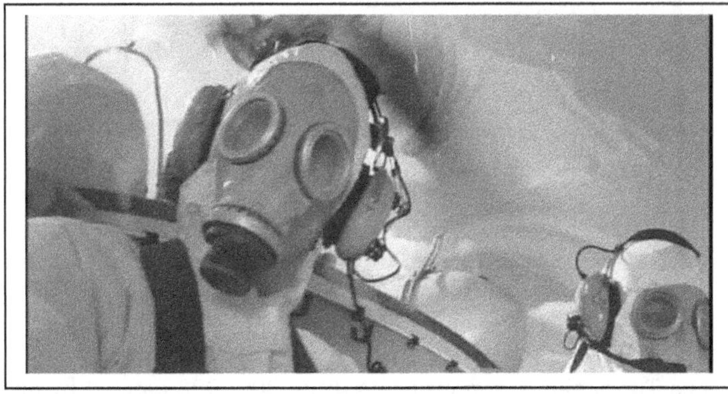

The blob uses its tendrils to capture the helicopter and then rolls over the bomb just in time for it to explode.

Back in the military control room, they find they may have miscalculated the range of the bomb and end up being blasted by the bomb.

News reports compare it to the incident in Russia almost a century ago, which was determined to be a black hole explosion. The newscaster interviewed a scientist who dispelled any notion that this was an atomic bomb.

A newscaster calls this the worse natural disaster in 70 million years on earth and compares it to the Tunguska region of Siberia where a similar incident occurred over a century ago. This is followed by headlines in the "New York Daily Post" that the incident is being investigated.

Early during the policy discussion, the Techno-Geeks suggested that an explosion in the Tunguska region was explained away as a natural disaster suggesting that an atomic bomb might also be explained away as a similar disaster.

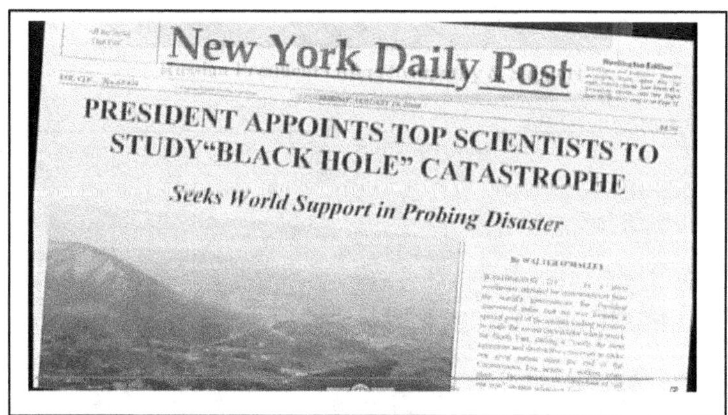

New York Daily Post

PRESIDENT APPOINTS TOP SCIENTISTS TO STUDY "BLACK HOLE" CATASTROPHE

Seeks World Support in Probing Disaster

There was a Tunguska region event on June 30, 1908 caused by an asteroid hitting the earth. It is recorded as the biggest natural disaster to hit earth in recorded history. The movie makes an interesting use of this extreme natural disaster to use it as a "cover" for the atomic bomb – never mind that such a coverup could not have occurred in 1908, since the atomic bomb had not yet been invented. Nonetheless, it was a useful tool to coverup the destruction of the bioweapon and everyone associated with it – except the teens.

The teens are in the last scene watching the news reports of the event, eating popcorn and reclining on the couch. This is an apropos conclusion to a movie which did not take itself too seriously but had a wickedly talented crew with silly string for the special effects.

The science was depicted as difficult to understand with policy makers who made decisions without fully understanding it. This is one of the most intriguing issues presenting in the movie, and should not be overlooked. However, the implications of bombing within the United States and killing civilians as well as military personnel cannot be taken lightly. The effect of the movie was to raise a number of interesting science and law questions despite the premise of a bacteria that would eat the earth.

I Am Legend (2007)

RATING

Anna

In 2009, a deadly virus burned through our civilization, pushing humankind to the edge of extinction. Dr. Robert Neville dedicated his life to the discovery of a cure and the restoration of humanity. On September 9th, 2012, at approximately 8:49 P.M., he discovered that cure. And at 8:52, he gave his life to defend it. We are his legacy. This is his legend. Light up the darkness.

---*I Am Legend* (2007)

I Am Legend (2007) is the third movie based on the novel by Richard Matheson. The first is *The Last Man on Earth* (1964); then *The Omega Man* (1971). *The Stand* (1994) by Stephen King was loosely based on the book, but did not have a plot that centered on the cure or the contagion. Then *I Am Legend* (2007) revived the plot, again.

The movie opens with a television interview of a Dr. Alice Krippin, Emma Thompson, who describes the alteration of the measles virus to produce a cure for cancer. She declares cancer to be cured. The next screenshot is of the city of New York with a legend on the screen which reads, "Three Years Later". It is 2009 and the City is in shambles, the pandemic virus has the moniker of its creator, the Krippin Virus (KV). There is no discernible human life in the day except for one man, Dr. Robert Neville, Will Smith.

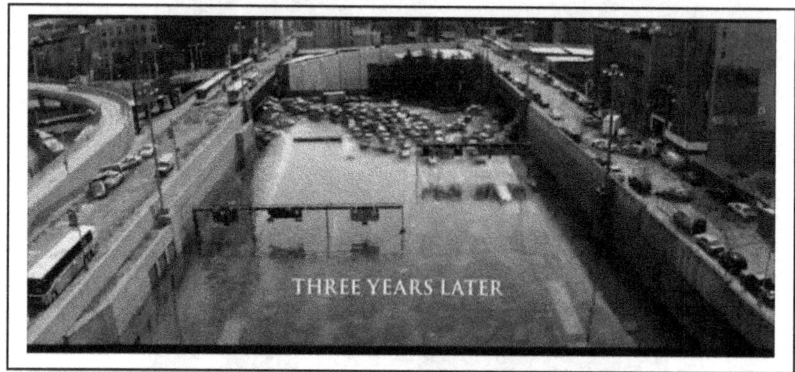

Lt. Col. Neville is a military research scientist who is determined to find the cure for this contagious disease that is bringing humans to the brink of extinction. In the next screenshot he is about to begin "human trials" on a young woman. She appears not to be cured and he is disappointed, again. He keeps her alive and sedated while he continues his search for a cure.

Interjected during the chronological order of the movie were frequent flashbacks that told the backstory about his family who were no longer with him. His last moments with his wife, Zoe, Sallie Richardson, and his daughter, Marley (Willow Smith, his daughter in real life) are spent as he hurries to the edge of New York where a helicopter is waiting to carry them away from the City.

This screenshot shows the chaos in a traffic jam at what is now a quarantine checkpoint.

Dr. Neville is stopped in the traffic jam and he and his family get out of the car and walk to the quarantine checkpoint. Each person's eyes are scanned with a device that indicates whether they are infected or not. Dr. Neville and his daughter are cleared, but he notices his wife is detained and taken into custody as "infected." He asserts his rank as Lt. Col. and orders them to stand down and re-scan her. After some resistance, they rescan her and find she is clear and she is free to go. The next screenshot shows the eyescanner device.

The human experimentation with the vaccine trials would normally require an Institutional Review Board (IRB) to review the experiment to ensure that the experiment's risk did not outweigh its benefits and whether the human subjects were treated humanely. In this movie, there is no IRB because there are no other humans that he knows. Dr. Neville is free to experiment with abandon, with no regulatory constraints and no ethical considerations.

Interestingly, the humans that appear to be creatures or zombies are still humans and despite their transitions to monsters with aggressive behaviors, they still must be treated as humans. Experimenting on them with the likely possibility of killing them would not be approved by an IRB. However, the viewers as well as Dr. Neville have made the determination that the risk of their death outweighs the possibility of saving humanity with this cure, even if it is not likely to succeed. Who is to say the zombies' lives are worth so little? Do they not deserve to have their lives protected? Zombies and mutated humans tend to lose human empathy the further away from normal humans that they become.

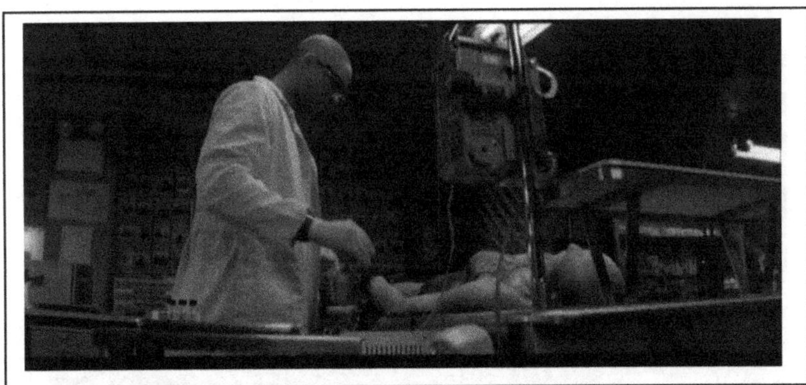

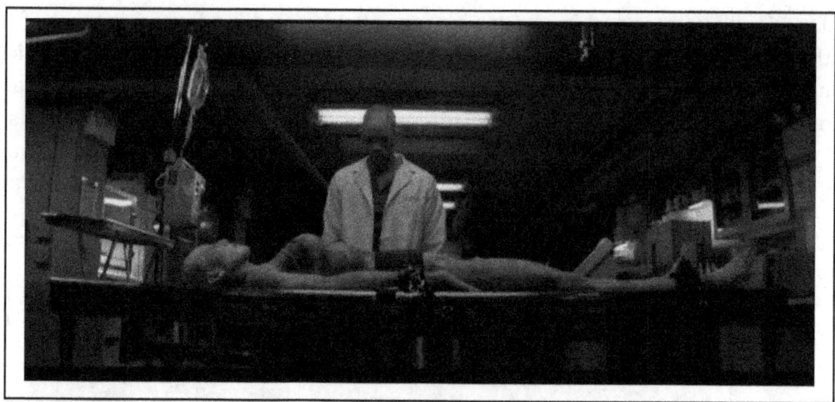

Dr. Neville shows compassion for his rat test subjects, and cares for them. He expresses sadness when he has to destroy them. The experimentation on animals also requires a review board to give an approval for the experiment, the pain to the animals and whether the experiment is being done in the most humane manner. Regulations also require that laboratory animals that must be euthanized, be out of the sight of the other animals, since seeing one of their same species being killed creates a high level of stress in the other animals.

Dr. Neville's daughter Marley, portends the references to Bob Marley throughout the movie. He compares Bob Marley's philosophy to that of a virologist when he describes him as saying, "He [Bob Marley] believed that you could cure racism and hate... literally cure it, by injecting music and love into people's lives." He also listens to Bob Marley's "Everything is Going to Be Alright," as the ironic background music to his vicious flashbacks and feelings of impending doom. Interestingly, before Bob Marley worte the song, Charleton Heston used that line as dialogue several times in *The Omega Man (*1971), another film interpretation of Richard Matheson's book, *I Am Legend* on which both of these movies are based.

Lt. Col. Robert Neville sees the end coming and passes a vial of blood with immunity to the disease to Anna, Alice Braga, and asks her to take it with her when she goes to Vermont, where she hears there are still people alive. Dr. Neville uses a hand grenade to end his life and prevent the zombies from having their final victory. Anna and her son escape to Vermont and pass along the "cure" to what appears to be a provisional government and society. The next screenshot is the arrival of Anna and her son at the gates of Bethel, Vermont, where the survivors were colonizing.

The last lines of the movie are a voice over from Anna, telling about Dr. Neville's cure and his legendary status. We want to believe that the serum will be the cure for the virus.

The causes of the pandemic in each of the three movies depicting *I Am Legend,* the novel, are different for each of the movies and they reflect the concerns of society and culture at the time. In *The Last Man on Earth* (1964) the cause was a surprise that a "germ" traveled from Europe around the world killing everyone; in In *The Omega Man* (1971) during the Cold War, the cause was a bioweapon bomb that was deployed against the United States and they failed to intercept it. In *I Am Legend* (2007) the cause is genetic engineering of viruses with good intentions but which goes badly wrong when it mutates.

28 Weeks Later (2007)

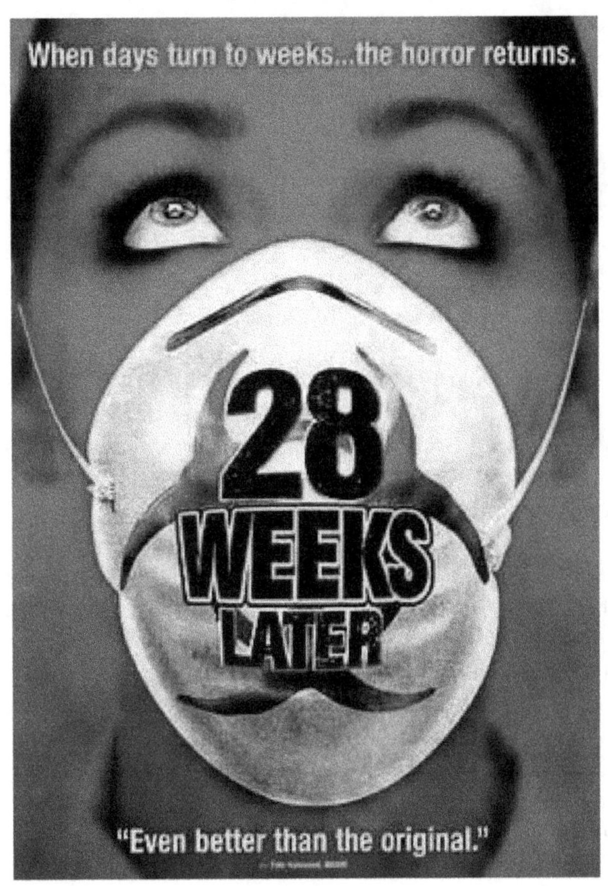

RATING

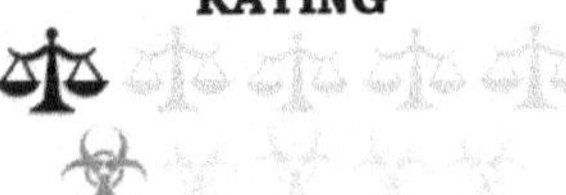

Gen. Stone

Abandon selective targeting. Shoot everything. Targets are now free. We've lost control.

--- 28 Weeks Later

28 Weeks Later (2007) is the sequel to *28 Days Later* (2002) which follows the devastation of the Rage virus in London with a repopulation phase.

The opening of the movie begins with some human survivors in a house in Britain just before an attack of the infected. One man gets away but his wife is left behind. Then, the following legends appear, one after the other, with a background of ominous, repeating, monotonous music:

15 days later, Mainland Britain is quarantined

28 days later, mainland Britain has been destroyed by the Rage Virus

5 weeks later: the infected have died of starvation

11 weeks later: an American-led NATO force enters London

18 weeks later: mainland Britain is declared free of infection

28 weeks later reconstruction begins

The disease, the Rage virus, has not mutated since the first movie five years ago, *28 Days Later* (2002). The infected are still immediately turned into raging killing machines within 60 seconds of exposure to saliva. All of the infected are believed to have died of starvation but here is close containment for the repopulating individuals.

The repopulation of Britain is a hopeful opening after the legend gives us the expectation that Britain can return to normal, but the viewers are probably skeptical that the Rage virus is gone, and they would be right.

Re-immigrating, a scanner is used to examine them for signs of the Rage virus. This screenshot is a look at the young boy's eyes which are different colors – one brown and one blue.

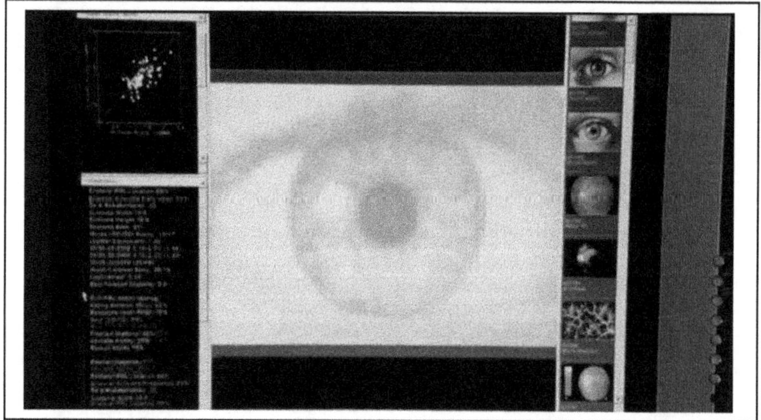

When the boy and his sister are cleared to enter Britain they find their Dad, Don, played by Robert Carlyle, has survived but their Mom, Alice, played by Catherine McCormack, was attacked by the infected. Soon thereafter in an escape from the compound, the two children search out their old home for a photo of their Mom, and instead find her there. She is normal but she has been bitten and has some signs of infection but not the rage symptoms.

When the children are found they retrieve the mother and bring her back for examination. The physician determines that she has immunity to the Rage virus because although she has been bitten, she does not have the symptoms of the disease other than one bloody eye. The physician also suggests that she is probably a carrier can can give the disease to someone else.

The fact that the physician works with the infected mother without any biosafety personal protective equipment is the real rage in this movie. It is outrageous that of all the knowledge about this rage virus that they are taking zero precautions when they encounter someone who has obviously been exposed to the infected.

An equally outrageous decision was to allow her normal husband to see her strapped to a bed and allow him to kiss her, infecting him, and then he tries to kill her. He escapes and then once again, the Rage virus sweeps through Britain in no time.

Outrageous.

Our due process requirements for detaining people who are well, but are carriers would require a hearing to determine if there was good reason to hold the Mother against her will. Was she a serious enough threat to the public health to warrant the burden on her individual freedom? Was there a narrower way of protecting the public's health? For example, if the Mother had been ordered to stay away from all well humans, and she agreed, we would have a social contract with her to uphold her agreement in the interest of society. If she breached that agreement, the consequences would be deadly to the entire population. The gravity of the consequences may very likely be enough to outweigh the Mom's individual freedoms and this is a very high standard. The case of Mary Mallon at the turn of the century involved the detention of a cook who was spreading typhoid fever to families for whom she cooked. She was ordered not to be a cook on more than one occasion and each time she violated her social contract and infected more people. She could not believe that she was a carrier since she did not have any symptoms of typhoid fever. A similar analogy could be made to the Mother.

Trying to excape from the infected is the continuing theme, when the two children , a physician and one man from the military compound find themselves together.

This is the bloodiest movie by far. The helicopter slices off heads and body parts of the infected running through a field, and blood spews everywhere with each attack.

The physician believes that the son may have inherited the immunity from his mother, but it is uncertain. All traits are not inherited, and whatever the genetic anomaly the mother had to create immunity may not be present in her son. The fact that they both have the unusual feature of different colored irises -- one blue and one brown --- is an indication that he may have inherited her immunity.

By the end of the movie, the theory is tested when the son is attacked by his father and his daughter has to shoot her father to keep him from attacking her. They soon learn that the son does indeed have his mother's immunity but that also means he is a carrier. His sister protects him as they are rescued by a military helicopter as the only two survivors left in their group.

A legend appears on the next screen:

Then, a visual of the infected running toward the Eiffel Tower leaves us with the thought that the Rage virus has reached Paris, France. Interestingly, they skipped across the countryside and targeted the capital --- but then, Paris is a nice location to film a sequel.

The legal issues in this movie are broad sweeping and uncertainty about order is what contributes to the creation of the horror. The opening movie quotation for this chapter reflects the breakdown of order and the lack of the Rule of Law --- "Shoot everything. . . . We've lost control." This movie is frightening, too, not only because the Rule of Law gone, but because the usual last resort is martial law and it has utterly failed to bring order to this chaos of blood and death.

Pandemic (2007)

RATING

Dr. Kayla Martin

A pandemic is like a forest fire, we have to get a ring around it to slow it down . . . Federal regulations give CDC --- that would be me --- broad powers to contain a virus that is in danger of spreading across stateliness. I am ordering you to quarantine Los Angeles!

---Pandemic (2007)

Pandemic (2007), is one of the movies falling squarely into the realism category. It is an unusually long 170 minutes so the development of the disaster response is more detailed than many 90 minute movies. This made-for-television movie is a very real scenario of a deadly respiratory illness in a young man traveling from Australia to Los Angeles International Airport (LAX). This movie is an excellent depiction of the conflicts between state and federal governments, city and federal governments and city and state governments. The science is very realistic. The plot follows the normal course of a pandemic.

This movie does a very good job of exploring relationships between friends, lovers and families during a pandemic. The producer had the luxury of time – a movie that is 2 hours and 45 minutes long --- but the time was used effectively to portray the issues that may arise, and this made for television movie is the best of the movies in depicting Constitutional federalism issues between local, state and federal government.

The protagonist is a public health physician from CDC, Dr. Kayla Martin, Tiffani Thiessen.

The passengers on the flight from Australia are quarantined at LAX and each of them present an interesting conflict. One is a federal prison being escorted by an FBI agent; another is a real estate agent who is so desperate to make his business deal that he breaks from the group and escapes unnoticed; another is a rebellious passenger who questions whether his Constitutional rights are being violated and wants to escape; another is a model-turned-photographer.

This next screenshot shows the CDC entering the aircraft to examine the passenger who has died of an acute respiratory illness while in flight from Australia to LAX.

First, the FBI, Troy Whitlock, played by Vincent Spano, demands the FBI's priorities be served by releasing a federal prisoner on board, and she rebukes him and says he will have to wait like everyone else.

The Federalism Debate

This next scene is a good example of a Constitutional federalism conflict when jurisdictions overlap. In this dialogue, there is an overlap of federal and local government responsibility which causes friction between them when the city was not notified of the federal action at the local level, which is the best step to take, if shared jurisdiction is reasonable. In this movie, the local, state and federal government work most effectively by sharing emergency response operations.

Mayor's assistant
Whose Dr. Martin?

Dr. Martin, CDC
I am.

Mayor's assistant
This airport is city property.

Dr. Martin, CDC
Understood, however, technically it is CDC . . .

Mayor
Don't give me technicalities, you opened the
city's health emergency response
center without even consulting my staff

Dr. Martin, CDC
Actually, I have the emergency authority here.

Mayor Delasandro
You have the authority for nothing unless I say it first.

Dr. Martin, CDC
I just want to be prepared for the worst.

Mayor Delasandro
I appreciate your concern.
Next time you want anything from
this city go through my
office first, understood?

This controversy between the city and federal government is very realistic because the relationship is unclear where governmental authorities have jurisdiction when areas of shared federalism are involved, like public health that involves federal issues.

In this case, the Mayor was right. Dr. Martin from the CDC had no authority to take control of local public health assets or activities without the express request from the state or city. Dr. Martin's actions were a violation of the separation of powers and the constitutional concept of federalism, where the federal government does not have authority in areas where states have authority without specific legislative actions.

International Health Regulations trigger notification

The Australian public health officials discovered a dead body in a surfing hut and found the flight itinerary from the American, Ames Smith, who was visiting and who died on the flight. Australia is bound by the International Health Regulations and when this movie was made in 2007, the IHR had gone into effect June 7, 2007. This unknown lethal disease and the known fact that an American passenger was exposed on the way back on a flight to the U.S. is required to notify the World Health Organization which would also notify the U.S. In the movie, Australian authorities contacted the CDC which is not the protocol in the IHR, but it is reasonable and not illegal.

In an interesting scene, the Mayor Delasandro, Eric Roberts, of Los Angeles was visiting with a school and chatting with the students when his assistant came and whispered something in his ear, and he excused himself. This was clearly a reference to the notification to Pres. George W. Bush when he was informed that the World Trade Center had been hit by terrorists.

This screenshot is a birdseye view of the CDC personnel removing the body from the flight.

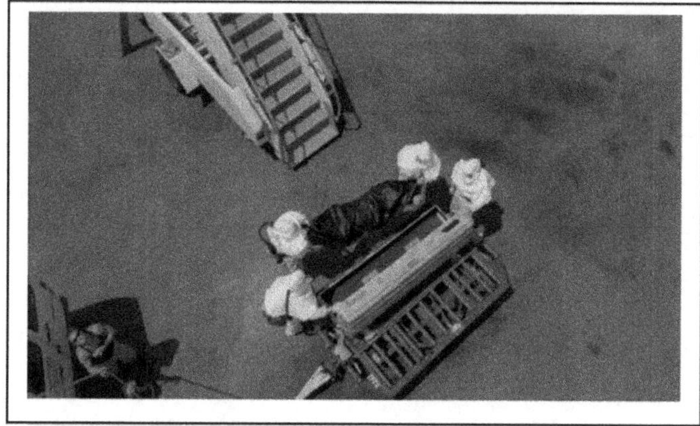

Right to detain passengers and to quarantine consistent with individual rights under the U.S. Constitution, Bill of Rights

The businessman who was determined to make his meeting escaped from the quarantine and the music and slow motion that depicts his spread of the infection is very accurate. The passenger who is rebellious says to the businessman, "Where in the Constitutional does it say they can treat us like this?" Immediately afterward, the businessman makes his escape.

The sequence of flashbacks to the origin of the infection are very effective when the real estate agent coughs as he speaks to the taxi station personnel. The taxi driver handles money that he gives to a nun, potentially passing along the infection. The next day, the same taxi driver hands money to a co-taxi driver who needs change, again, potentially passing the infection. The co-taxi driver picks up Dr. Martin's niece after a skating practice and coughs in the taxi as he drives her to her destination.

Next scene the Governor of California, Lillian Schafer, Faye Dunaway, is involved and having a discussion with her staff about how this might be used politically by her political rival, the Mayor.

Back at the airport the CDC is confronted with the mother who wants to see her son, and she takes her to a window where the CDC opens a steel coffin in a body bag. CDC accommodates the parents.

The CDC has set up a triage operation in the emergency response center, and different wings for those exposed and those under surveillance. Three basic areas: area 1 people who haven't been exposed; area 2 are for people who have been exposed but have no symptoms; area 3 are for people who have been exposed and have symptoms.

CDC is informed that they have a passenger missing from the manifest of Flight 182.

Unfolding the Science of the Riptide Virus

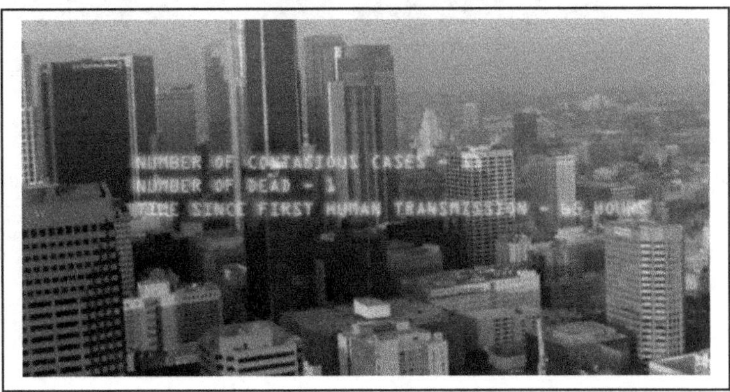

CDC gave a press conference on Day 2, and he is lecturing the media about their reporting methods and how they want to cause panic with their reporting. The Governor and the Mayor both get involved with the CDC press conference. The news conference triggers grocery store purchases that are greater than normal.

When they finally get a characterization of the virus, they find that it is an antigen shift that is typical of a pandemic virus. It is now called the "Riptide virus", named after its origin from the surfer who returned from Australia carrying it on flight 182. The next screenshot is a depiction for the viewer while Dr. Martin explained the action of the virus to government officials.

One of the most surprising misrepresentations of the movie which was otherwise very accurate and realistic was the level of personal protective equipment (PPE) worn by Dr. Martin and her colleague as they researched a cure for the virus. In this screenshot the viewer sees Dr. Martin and her colleague with masks that are not sufficient to guard against viruses and labcoats with exposed skin and goggles that are not completely protecting their eyes from splashes. With a virus this lethal with no cure, Biological Safety Level 4 (BSL-4) conditions would be mandatory. This would involve a room with air that had to be filtered and biosuits with contained air supplies, including a washdown and disinfection of their suits before they left the laboratory. This contrasts ironically with the full PAPR suits which are contained air supplies and complete body protection when they are visiting patients.

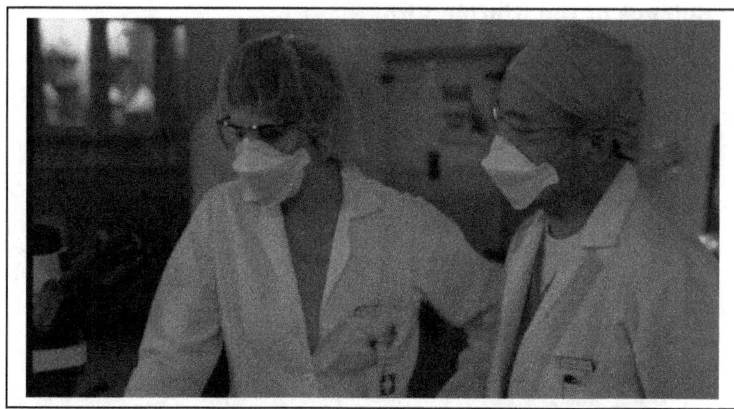

The Ethics of Human Subject Experimentation and Informed Consent

One of the ethical questions in the movie is the choice by CDC to administer only one of two possible treatments for patients. The CDC lead, says it is the only way they can determine which one works. This amounts to a human subject experiment, and is illegal as well an unethical without informed consent and informing the patient about the experiment and allow them to make their own choice.

The federal prisoner is forcing the CDC lead to tell him what kind of drug he is giving to the patients and it is simply "Tamiflu". The criminals then proceed to rob the pharmacies of Tamiflu.

When Dr. Martin found that her niece was one of the patients with symptoms, she clearly received special treatment with specific personnel assigned to her.

Mayor Delasandro is reassuring people that it is safe to stay in Los Angeles, yet the graphic displays the spread of the virus and the projection of tens of thousands of deaths.

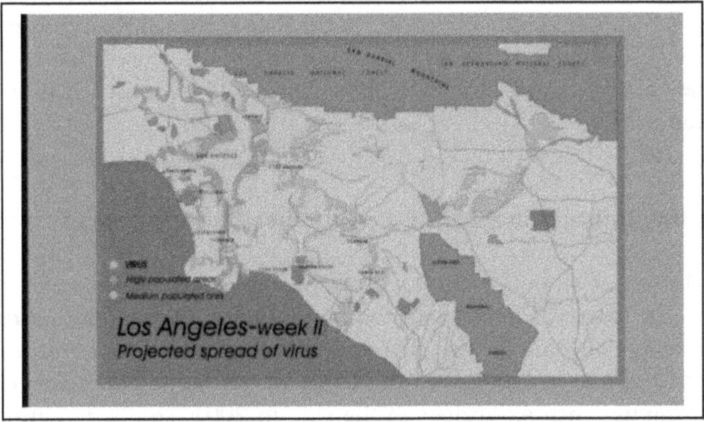

Dr. Martin asks the Mayor to quarantine Los Angeles. The amount of time that has passed since the first infection suggests that a quarantine is probably an exercise in futility. With the publicity and attention to the Riptide virus, many people will have already fled Los Angeles, potentially taking the virus with them. The Governor and the Mayor disagree on the decision to implement a citywide quarantine.

Who has a right to the human remains of those who died of the Riptide virus?

The CDC eventually needs room for bodies and they utilize the ice rink in Los Angeles. The reference is made that they did the same thing in 1918 with the Spanish Flu. The federal government taking of private property for a public use, while legal, also requires just compensation under the Fifth Amendment of the U.S. Constitution. The owner of the ice rink who says, "I never thought it [the ice rink] would be used like this," would be given a just amount of money to compensation for his losses during the use of the ice rink for this purpose.

As the body count begins to increase exponentially, the city begins to worry that they will run out of space for the bodies. They have already taken over the ice rink for storage of bodies, which is a scene in the next screenshot.

The right of families to the remains of their loved ones is not explored in this movie, but it is one of the most controversial processes that I encountered in federal, state and local bioterrorism table top exercises to plan for a public health emergency. These decisions are emotionally charged and are issues of the greatest importance to families. The risk of releasing remains which may still be infective to the living is a concern that public health agencies must weigh. However, if the bodies are recorded and stored in a cold place until such time that they are not longer infective, then they could be returned to the families for burial or cremation.

Who provides public information during a public health emergency?

Meanwhile, the news that Tami-flu is completely ineffective was announced in a press conference. Dr. Martin followed with the announcement that another drug looks promising and is being delivered for use. There is still a great deal of uncertainty, and the only public health information is coming from CDC, which is one of the successful processes in the movie. During the anthrax attacks in the U.S. in 2001, conflicting information came from local, state and federal public health agencies, confusing the public. President Bush issued an Executive Order making the CDC the point for announcements in the event of an outbreak of a disease.

Will the federal government assist with drugs and antibiotics?

In another subplot, the federal criminal has hijacked the truck carrying the Cotoxil, the drug developed to treat the virus. Public health emergencies planning would almost certainly involve the use of armed guards for transport of such emergency treatments in time of a public health emergency.

The Mayor expresses disappointment with his cell phone conversation with the President of the United States regarding the drug stockpiles and reports that the President says he will try to get "15% of the cotoxil stored in Tennessee" for Los Angeles. The reality that they cannot rely on the federal government for help begins to become a reality for the city.

The reality is that the Department of Health and Human Services which began with the National Strategic Stockpile for drugs and countermeasures has continually cautioned cities that they cannot rely on the federal government for their emergency needs, but should provide for their own emergency stockpiles. Part of the reason for this is that multiple cities could be involved in a disaster at the same time, making supplies inadequate.

Challenging the Quarantine of Los Angeles

The rebellious passenger has organized his friends to challenge the quarantine as a violation of their Constitutional rights. Here we see the meeting to plan to breaking of the quarantine of Los Angeles. The rebellious passenger believes it is all a government conspiracy and there really is no virus.

In the next screenshot, the friends drive three pickup trucks through the barricade and the National Guard do not stop them after they have been warned. This breach of the quarantine is reported to the Governor.

This triggers the Governor's office to declare martial law in the city and to issue new orders to use force to stop anyone who breaks the law, including breaking quarantine.

The discussion about whether the Governor or the Mayor would issue a quarantine resulted in a compromise where the Governor would make an announcement from the Mayor's office --- a good depiction of a political decisionmaking process. This announcement was made by Governor Schaeffer:

Governor Schaeffer

There is no justice without security, although we believe in the rule of law, the law is not effective if it is only words.

I have issued an Executive Order imposing martial law. From dawn to dusk curfew will be enforced and I have ordered the national guard to preserve the quarantine. Order and safety will prevail.

In the next scene, the National Guard are at the quarantine check point and have received their new orders to stop anyone who tries to break quarantine.

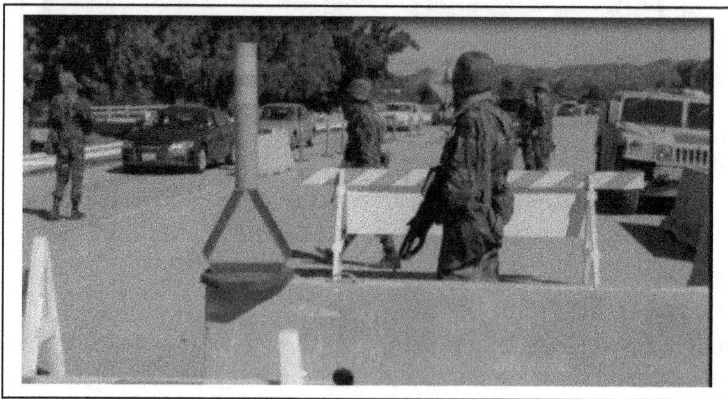

The subplots cross when the federal criminal, Vicante, has his henchman meet his lawyer for exchange of some documents, and in an encounter which turns deadly the henchman drives away and kidnaps a young hitchhiker to drive the car for him, since he has been shot and is unable to drive. He forces the young man to drive through the barrier and the National Guard following their new orders shoot the young man as he makes a run from the car. This is a scenario that challenges the wisdom of using lethal force on those who break the quarantine, because such force ignores due process and can result in the deaths of innocent people.

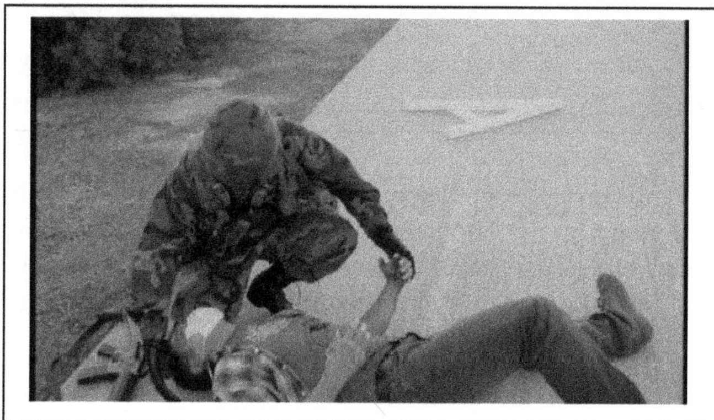

Crimes committed during the Emergency

The suggestion is made in the movie that those who committed crimes during the public health emergency may have not done so during the course of normal life in Los Angeles. Another subplot was used to development this idea when the FBI agent's son became so worried that his Mom was sick that he took the gun his father left with them and robbed a man at an ATM machine. He uses the money to buy some black market Cotoxil for his mother. At the end of the movie, his mother recovered from what was pneumonia, not the Riptide virus, and his father resolved the situation by meeting with the victim of the robbery. The idea that many of these incidents had occurred during the emergency period was an important part of the legal discourse that was so well addressed throughout this movie.

The Cure

Dr. Martin and the FBI agent both do investigations to find out how the federal prisoner, Vacinte, survived and did not contract the Riptide virus. He explained that he was in prison in Australia and was a test patient for a flu vaccine. Dr. Martin decided to use the antibodies in his blood as a quick way to save her niece. This is clearly human experimentation but the fact that it was her niece suggested that her aunt was authorized to be her guardian and informed consent was not necessary for a minor child although, even a minor child is expected to be informed at the level that they can understand. Since her niece was not capable of understanding at this point, Dr. Martin may have been justified in her actions.

The cure was to use blood donations from those who had been treated for tuberculosis, and take those antibodies and use them for the vaccine--- an interesting and creative turn in the story to put an end to a disease epidemic.

Flight of the Living Dead (2007)

RATING

Frank
What is it going to take to
Convince you that I'm innocent?

Truman
An act of God.

---*Flight of the Living Dead (2007)*

Flight of the Living Dead (2007) subtitled "Outbreak on a Plane" fulfills some of the unfullfilled hopes from other movies of this subgenre. No other movie addresses the very interesting legal issue of taking a bioweapon in the cargo section of a plane that is in an infected human. All the rules are broken on this flight in this made for television movie. The opening dialogue between the pilot and the co-pilot set the background for the movie's conflict.

Capt. Banyan
So what the deal with the special cargo?

Co-Pilot Randy
Some last minute special cargo shipment.

Capt. Banyan
It says there is an armed
guard in the cargo hold.

Co-Pilot Randy
What are we carrying?

Capt. Banyan
I am not sure I want to know.

Capt. Banyan
If there are any abnormalities
involving the cargo area we are to contact. . .

Co-Pilot Randy
Abnormalites?

. . . Dr. Bennet and Dr. Sebasitan. These
are the passengers who secured
the cargo. They are in First Class.

Capt. Banyan
I am glad this is my last flight.

In the next scene, the military commanders are discussing whether to tell the President of the United States that the Dr. Bennett has escaped with the engineered biological weapon that he has been developing. They explain that Dr. Bennett found a malaria strain in Vietnam that is 100% fatal and kills immediately. It then regenerates that organism for a few seconds or longer.

Soon into the action, turbulence causes the cryogenic tank in which Dr. Kelly, played by Laura Cayouette, is stored, to topple over and open. The armed guard then has to cope with his leg being amputated from below the knee due to the falling tank.

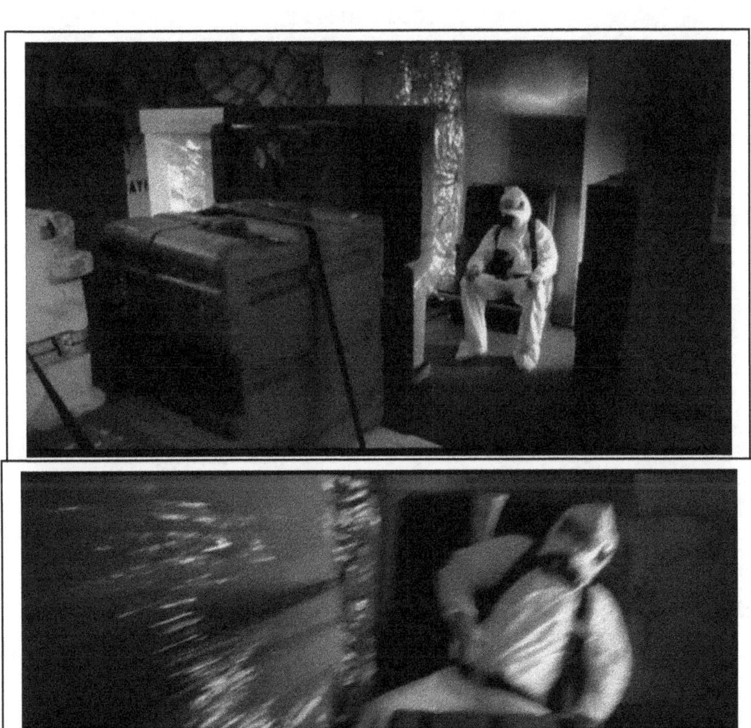

A discussion between the military and the CIA lets the audience know what they can expect to see on the aircraft with the biological weapon infecting the passengers, and the nature of the infection and why it was developed. This dialogue also poses some of the most important legal issues in the movie – whether a civilian aircraft can be shot down under these circumstances.

Dr. Conroy

The overall feeling among the scientists working on this is that we are working with a serum transfer virus. This virus is without a known curevaccine or cure. But this
This type of virus transfers onl through body fluid them most effectively from blood froman infected victim enters a cut or saliva

Col. Wolff

The MedCon scientists believe they can make this work despite the side effects from being being brought back from the dead. In fact they looked upon the side effects as a benefit.
Let me paraphrase these notes we found in Dr. Bennett's desk:

They wanted this virus as a bioweapon to keep soldiers fighting after they were mortally wounded. To release a captive enemy infected with the virus and let him infect others, until they all kill each other.

I am going to recommend to you ---and to the President--- that we destroy Flight 239 before it can reach a populated area.

CIA Director

Let me get this straight. You want our forces to follow a shoot to kill order regarding a civilian aircraft?

Col. Wolff

We have received no communication from the aircraft. We must assume the cargo has been breached and the virus has spread among the passenger compartment. The only way we have to contain this is to vaporize every living thing on that aircraft---before the virus can reach a major population center.

CIA Director

Do you concur?

Dr. Conroy

I am afraid I do.

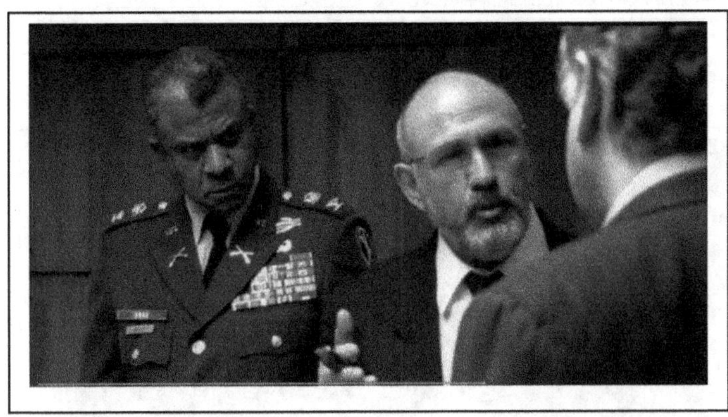

The three individuals making the decision to shoot down a civilian aircraft are military and CIA leadership. The President ultimately makes the decision with the telephone call made by the CIA Director. However, the 2004 reorganization of the intelligence agencies of the United States,[48]would have required the Director of National Intelligence, not the CIA Director, to have participated in this decision.

Can a civilian aircraft be shot from the air? The simple answer is, yes. During the events of 9-11, the United States was being attacked by terrorists who had hijacked civilian aircraft and used them as weapons to crash into buildings. To counter this attack, the strategic air command had orders to shoot down aircraft that did not land when the FAA ordered them to do so, which would have included commercial aircraft. The President has the power to act to protect the security of American citizens and to minimize the lives lost, in this case. Article II of the U.S. Constitution gives the President these executive powers in an emergency.

---

[48] Intelligence Reform and Terrorism Prevention Act of 2004 (IRTPA) 50 USC §§ 401 (2013).

Perhaps these before and after screenshots of Dr. Kelly might be convincing as to the public health threat. This is before she is "re-animated" by the virus.

This is after she is "re-animated" by the virus.

Another question, is whether this virus development by MedCon is a violation of the Biological Weapons Convention. Returning to the premise of the movie, that MedCon was developing a biological weapon for the Army to use on enemy prisoners who would be returned with the virus to the enemy, and then infect and attack each other. Under the Biological Weapons Convention, a biological weapon is defined in Article I and subsequent Conferences of the Parties in interpreting Article I have only broadened the scope. Here is the definition:

ARTICLE I

Each State Party to this Convention undertakes never in any circumstance to develop, produce, stockpile or otherwise acquire or retain:

Microbial or other biological agents, or toxins whatever their origin or method of production, of types and in quantities that have no justification for prophylactic, protective or other peaceful purposes;

Weapons, equipment or means of delivery designed to use such agents or toxins for hostile purposes or in armed conflict.

The development of a virus to infect the enemy would meet the definition of a "biological agent" . . . "for hostile purposes." Therefore the United States would be in violation of the treaty, and would be subject to global community approbation if this program was revealed.

If there is a virus being shipped in cargo, what is required for the virus to be legally transported? Dr. Bennett and his colleagues were anything but secret about the fact that they were transporting cargo that was in a cryogenic container and required an armed guard. The shipment of viruses and bacteria are regulated by IATA, the International Air Transport Association, in consultation with ICAO, the International Civil Aviation Organization. The regulations are called "Dangerous Goods Regulations." Interestingly, these are created by a commercial association but are recognized and binding. These are not governmental regulations, but airlines will not accept cargo without compliance, thus making compliance for those who make use of airlines for transporting dangerous goods, essential if they wish to continue using air transport.

Section 9.5.1.3 addresses the "in-flight emergency" when there is dangerous cargo on board. It reads, in full, as follows: *If an in-flight emergency occurs, the pilot-in-command must, as soon as the situation permits, inform the appropriate air traffic services unit, for the information of airport authorities, of any dangerous goods carried as cargo on board na aircraft. Whenever possible, this information should include the proper shipping name and/or UN/ID number, the class/division and Class 1, the compatibility group, any identified subsidiary risk(s), the quantity and the location on board the aircraft or, a telephone number where a copy of the information to the pilot-in-command can be obtained. When it is not considered possible to include all the information, those parts thought most relevant in the circumstances or a summary of the quantities nad class or division of dangerous goods in each cargo compartment should be given.*

Once the communication system was disabled, there was no chance of this communication. However, if it had become possible the pilot-in-command would have probably used Section 9.6.2 *Undeclared or Mis-Declared Dangerous Goods which requires that "An operator must report any occasion when undeclared or mis-declared goods are discovered in cargo. Such a report must be made to the appropriate authorities of the State of the operator and the State in which this occurred. . .s*

The Flight of the Living Dead (2007) was not a movie that took itself too seriously, and has a special focus on producing zombie interactions, but despite the ridiculousness of the viral effects, the legal aspects of this movie turn out to be significant ones.

Bats: A Human Harvest (2007)

RATING

Nature Made Them Predators.
Science Made Them Killers.
A Madman Made Them An Army.

-- *Bats: A Human Harvest(2007)*
(tagline)

Bats: A Human Harvest (2008) may be a surprising entry to the biohorror/biothriller subgenre, but it has some elements that make it qualify. The bats are biological weapons, biologically engineered to attack on command from various bat-like sounds from loudspeakers. But is this kind of weapon prohibited by international law? The definition of a biological weapon in the Biological Weapons Convention probably does not prohibit such biological weapons. So what crime has been committed here?

The story begins with some Russian Spetsnaz officers patrolling the edge of the forest, only to be attacked by the bats and dismembered. This is followed by several orienting shots, one with a C.I.A. briefing in Belgrade. Here Russo (David Chokachi) is introduced to his leader, Katya (Pollyanna McIntosh) with whom he has an immediate conflict because she is Russian. The next orienting scene is a fleet of Delta force helicopters going to North Ossetia, disputed territory from the U.S.S.R. dissolution. Their mission is to find "WMD" in the Chechen Forest. Here, they say, the "locals believe there is a beast easily awoken."

After discovering the remains of the patrols who were patrolling in an earlier scene and dismembered the bats, they are cautious of the threat. They also find radar devices mounted on the trees, as seen in this screenshot. Eventually the Delta team discovers that these speakers give signals to the bats to attack.

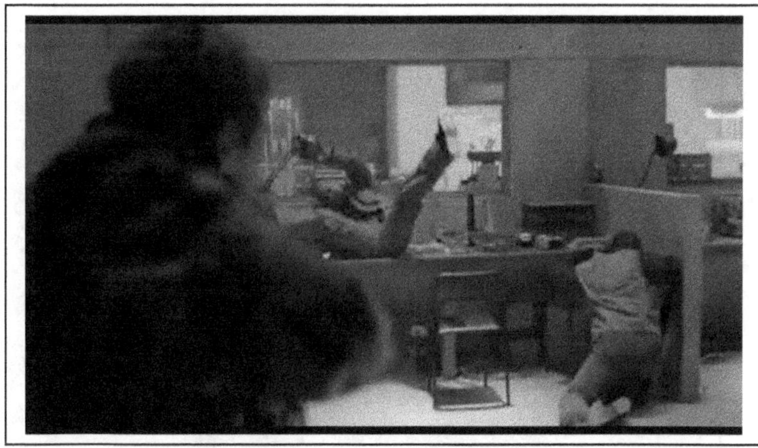

The laboratory was located and invaded by the Delta force and they captured Dr. Benton Walsh (Tomas Arana), the scientist and creator of the bats and told him that he was "now the property of the United States." Since no humans are property in the United States, it could only be an attempt at cleverness by his captor.

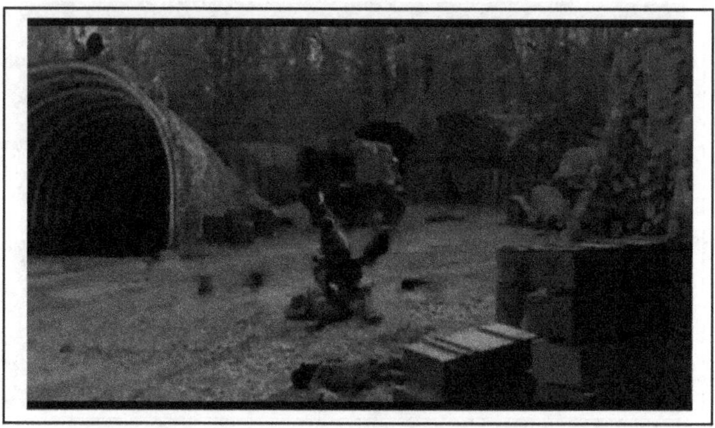

A bat attack on Katyna (Pollyanna McIntosh) and O'Neal (Melissa DeSousa) is being watched on a video screen by her Delta force team members who are powerless to stop it. They try to "shut down the sequence" which is the description of an apparent experiment that is being done by Dr. Walsh with the bats. He warns them not to interrupt the sequence, but they do so anyway to save their team members.

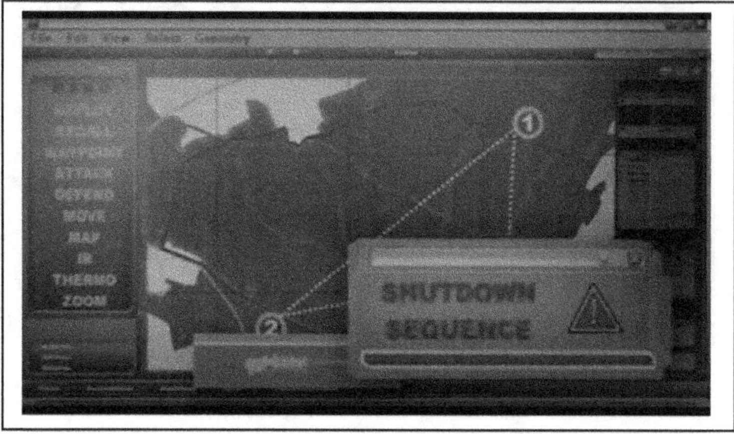

The attack does not stop and another of the Delta team is killed (ONeal). Eventually almost every one of the Delta team was dismembered by the bats.

Dr. Walsh, the creator of the bats, reveals that he has the bat DNA in his blood which makes them unable or unwilling to attack him. Later, when Russo shoots Dr. Walsh and causes an explosion, he is covered in Dr. Walsh's blood, giving him a temporary immunity to the bats. A downpour starts, threatening to wash off the blood that is giving him the immunity but just in the last moment, he is able to get the bats into the laboratory and implode the building with the bats.

Then, he is captured by Russian soldiers who suspect they may be Americans helping the Chechens. But Katya saves Russo by infiltrating them as a Russian guard and escorting Russo to an American helicopter painted like a Russian one. Appearing under a "false flag" is strictly again the Geneva Convention in a conflict, but then foreign espionage is illegal under domestic law in Russia, too. No international law prohibits nations from spying on each other, however.

So does the Biological Weapons Convention (BWC) prohibit animals from being transformed into biological weapons? Article I of the BWC provides the only definition of a biological weapon in the treaty:

> ARTICLE I
>
> Each State Party to this Convention undertakes never in any circumstance to develop, produce, stockpile or otherwise acquire or retain:
>
> Microbial or other biological agents, or toxins whatever their origin or method of production, of types and in quantities that have no justification for prophylactic, protective or other peaceful purposes;
>
> Weapons, equipment or means of delivery designed to use such agents or toxins for hostile purposes or in armed conflict.

But international treaties are typically clarified and interpreted by subsequent meetings of the parties to the treaty. Every five years, the parties meet for a review conference to do such needed clarifications for the BWC.

The documents from the Sixth Review Conference (2006) and Seventh Review Conference (2011) of the BWC do not define the term "bioweapon" or explain what "or other biological agents" might mean; however, there is evidence that the intended meaning of this and related terms is restricted to microorganisms. The use of the term "bacteriological (biological) weapons and toxins" is used in the title of both final reports and in all major sections of these documents (including the sections pursuant to the Articles of the BWC.[49] Given the apparent synonymity of the words "bacteriological" and "biological" in this descriptor, it would seem that the BWC views "or other biological agents" as bacteriological weapons. Interestingly, the use of the word "bacteriological," and "microbial," conveys an image of a small organism being used as a weapon. From this, it is unlikely that anything larger than a bacteriological or microbial agent would be prohibited by the BWC.

This movie takes place in Chechnya, not in U.S. jurisdiction. But the U.S. federal law defining biological weapons in Title 18, Chapter 10 of the United States Code, passed as the Biological Weapons Act of 1989 was intended to implement the BWC but the statute expands on the Treaty definition.

The provisions of Title 18, Chapter 10 of the United States Code provide a substantially clearer definition of the term "bioweapon." Title 18, Section 175(a) provides for criminal penalties to "whoever knowingly develops, produces, stockpiles, transfers, acquires, retains, or possesses any biological agent, toxin, or delivery system for use as a weapon . . . ." 18 U.S.C. § 175(a) (2002). Additionally, in Title 18, Section 175(c), the term "for use as a weapon" is further narrowed to encompass certain uses ". . . for other than prophylactic, protective, bona fide research, or other peaceful purposes." 18 U.S.C. § 175(c) (2002). Although this section does not provide a definition of the term "biological agent," such a definition is given in Title 18, Section 178. According to Title 18, Section 178:

> *As used in this chapter—(1) the term "biological agent" means any microorganism (including, but not limited to, bacteria, viruses, fungi, rickettsiae or protozoa), or infectious substance, or any naturally occurring, bioengineered or synthesized component of any such microorganism or infectious substance, capable of causing—(A) death, disease, or other biological malfunction in a human, an animal, a plant, or another living organism; (B) deterioration of food, water, equipment, supplies, or material of any kind; or (C) deleterious alteration of the environment. . .*

So, the definition of a bioweapon is specifically limited to microbial-size biological agents, and so would exclude invasive or non-indigenous plant or animal species (such as feral Burmese pythons), or in this case, engineered bats as weapons.

So using a bat to kill people would likely be criminalized by the same state and local statutes that make an owner liable for the actions of their dog if they attack and kill someone, particularly if they have intent to use their dog to kill someone. Local criminal laws will come with substantially reduced penalties than crimes for weapons of mass destruction.

In the last scene, after Katnya has saved Russo from the Russians after he was captured, they are sitting together in a hospital room, Katnya the only one not in a hospital bed, and Downey (Martin Papazian) asks, "did we complete our mission?" Katnya responds with these memorable lines;

> Doctor's dead. You're not. Mission accomplished.
>
> ---Katya (Pollyanna McIntosh)

[49] *See* Sixth Review Conference of the States Parties to the Biological Weapons Convention, Geneva, Switz., Nov. 20-Dec. 8, 2006, *Final Document*, U.N. Doc. BWC/CONF.VI/6 (2006); Seventh Review Conference of the States Parties to the Biological Weapons Convention, Geneva, Switz., Dec. 5-22, 2011, *Final Document of the Seventh Review Conference*, U.N. Doc. BWC/CONF.VII/7 (Jan. 13, 2012).

Quarantine (2008)

RATING

Angela Vidal
[*after witnessing Bernard being killed by a government sniper*]
Scott... They're not gonna let us out of here alive, are they?

Scott Percival
No... I don't think so.

---*Quarantine* (2008)

Quarantine (2008) begins innocently enough as a night reporter gives us her behind the scenes takes of her broadcast which is spending some time at the local fire fighter station, in a kind of realty show format, making regular eye-contact with the camera. She begins with interviews with the Fire Chief, has fun sliding down the fire station pole, chats with the fire fighters in their dining hall, and meets the Dalmatian mascot for the fire station. The Fire Chief introduces the reporter to the fire fighters she will be "shadowing."

The fateful fire alarm comes eleven minutes into the movie, and rapidly the funny scenes turn into scenes so horrific they stand in stark contrast to the earlier light-heartened realty show banter.

The scene where the night begins to unravel is where the firefighters enter the apartment of the old lady who has been screaming and then has gone silent. Neighbors mutter about the horrific screams they heard as they watch the firefighters ascend the steps in the apartment. As they enter a prophetic dog leaves the small dark room of the apartment as they approach the old lady who is clearly suffering from a horrific disease that has caused her bluish skin and bleeding from her mouth. When the television camera lights pop on, the horrified old lady turns into a monster and provoked by the noise and lights she attacks a firefighter and bites a large hole in his neck.

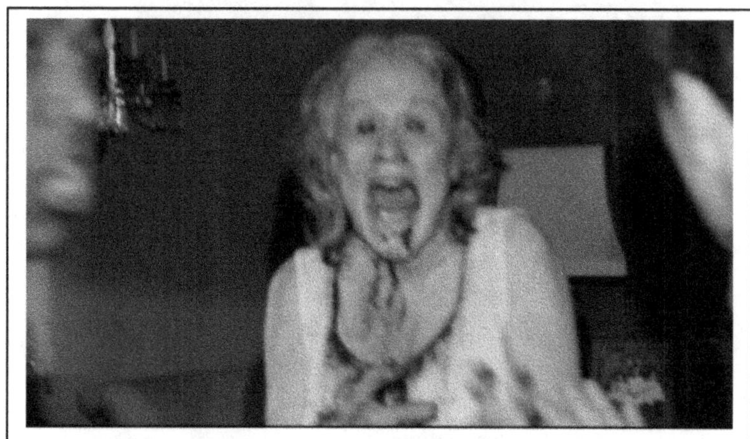

As they carry the wounded firefighter toward the door, they realize the door has been locked. They radio, "office down," but to no avail. A police officer outside is directing people to obey on a loudspeaker.

The police officer has a gun and eventually has to shoot Miss Espinoza the old lady when she is about to attack them. The firefighter puts his hand on the gun as if to subdue the office, while the officer looks for reassurance from the fire fighter that he shot the old lady in self-defense. A tazor or tranquilizer gun would have been more appropriate force, but they are unaware that even those means would have been unable to subdue the infected old lady. This is a Los Angeles firefighter and police officer, clearly anticipating litigation.

The firefighters try to evacuate the apartment building and struggle with language barriers and confusion. One woman is foaming at the mouth and gasping for air, which become recognizable symptoms of this disease.

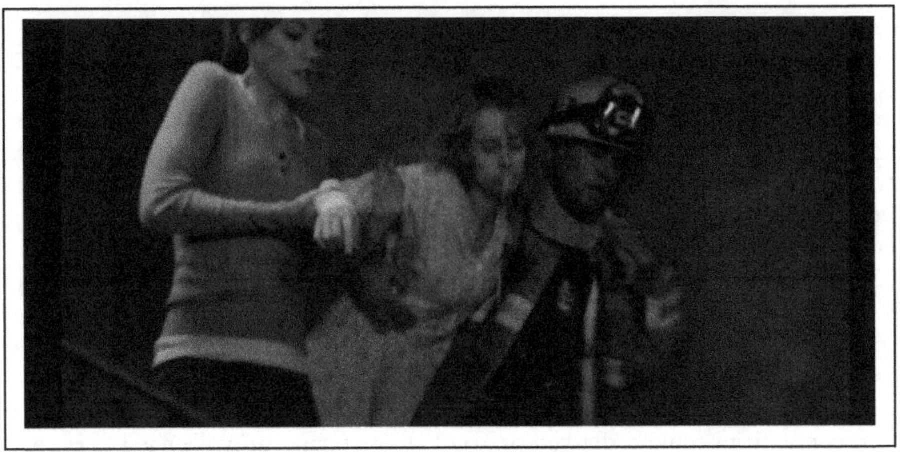

The loudspeaker announces that the building has been "sealed" and "thank you for your cooperation." No one seems to be panicking. They conclude there is a biological, chemical or nuclear threat.

The apartment owner shows the reporter and firefighter a room with a window which could be an escape. As they reach the window, two military troops appear with rifles and full personal protective equipment including a respirator. The screenshot shows both rifles are pointed at the inhabitants through the glass window. They immediately begin to seal up the window over the screams and pleas of the reporter. It has been said that if we do not learn history, we are doomed to repeat it; but in the case we might say, if we do not learn history, we are doomed to be surprised by it when it happens again. This is no exception. In the years of the plague, or Black Death, of the 1350s period of Europe, Italy addressed the problem of plague sickness by sending a government crew to seal up the windows and doors of the cottages and buildings where the sick person lived, along with any of their family who happened to be inside, presuming they were already on the way to dying themselves. They knew nothing about the germ theory but they had a sense of how contagion worked. Although draconian and a violation of human rights law, today, it worked to slow down the plague deaths in Italy. Today, this government strategy would not only violate the international human rights treaty, but also the Constitutional Eight Amendment for cruel and unusual punishment, Constitutional Fifth and Fourteenth Amendment procedural due process before being sealed in a tomb. Destroying the apartment owners building would likely not be a violation of a Fifth Amendment taking, however, because the threat of the disease spreading to the public makes it a public nuisance and those properties can be destroyed without just compensation.

But this is just the beginning of the inhabitants problems. They firefighters and police officer set up a makeshift hospital for the wounded who have been bitten by the infected. A veterinarian is attending the wounded. Which raises another interesting question about whether a veterinarian can provide medical care for humans in a public health emergency? Veterinarians are licensed to practice on animals, but in an emergency a government official could order veterinarians to be temporarily licensed to render medical treatment, give vaccinations, but this would be a extreme measure which might ultimately leave the state or federal government open to compensating anyone injured as a result of this treatment.

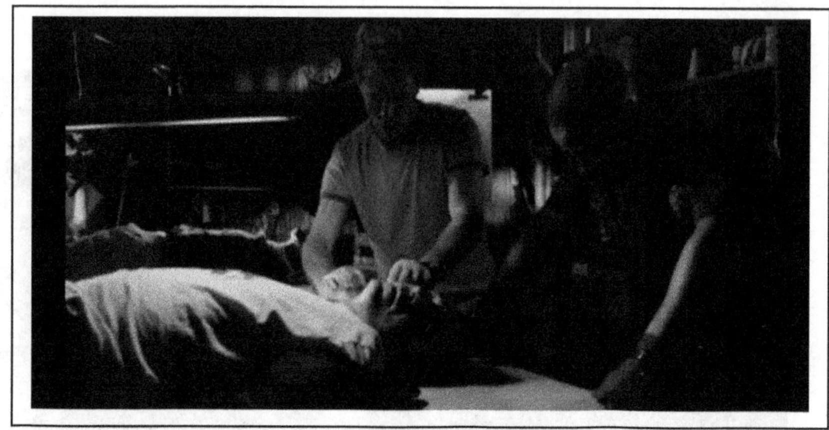

It is the veterinarian who makes the diagnosis, 42 minutes into the 89 minute movie -- it is a rabies like disease. He describes the symptoms of rabies and points out that the disease spreads through blood or saliva that enters another body, but normally it takes years to show symptoms. However, in this case, it is only minutes.

The next scene the inhabitants begin to panic. Dogs in the building begin to show symptoms and attack. One tenant turns on the television, with rabbit ear antennae and static to pick up the live station with breaking news that "CDC Surrounds Building" and for the first time, the tenants know that it is CDC that has ordered the quarantine.

Using the military to enforce a quarantine is extraordinary, and even if the military were ordered by the President (not CDC) to enforce the quarantine, the rules of engagement would have to be limited. For example, even in the Yellow Fever outbreak in New Orleans in the early 1900s, instructions to public health officials in enforcing public health orders required them to refrain from "brute force."[50]

Next, the CDC has the power shut down in the building, leaving the inhabitants vulnerable to attacks from the infected humans and animals. Almost immediately, an infected woman attacks the cameraman who kills her with his camera, and the next screenshot shows the effective view of the cameraman as he looks at the dead woman through his blood-spattered lens.

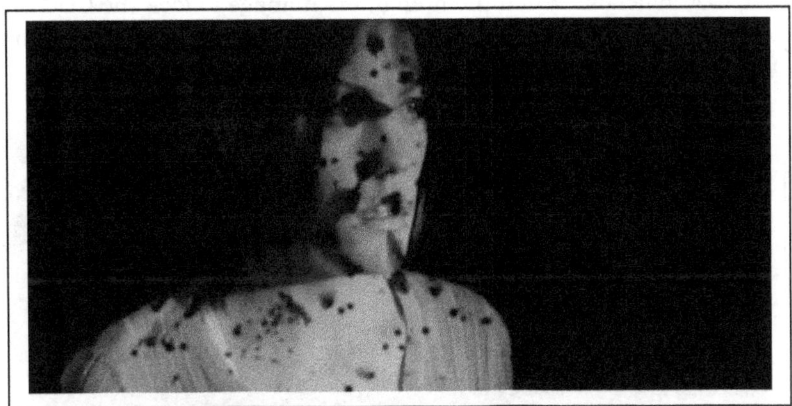

The next move is the loudspeaker announcement that CDC will be coming in to take blood samples. The veterinarian points out that that doesn't work with rabies, that you have to get brain tissue. He is berated by the inhabitants just to "shut up."

---

[50] Alfred J. Sciarrino, The Grapes of Wrath & The Speckled Monster (Epidemics, Biological Terrorism and the Early Legal History of Two Major Defenses – Quarantine and Vaccination), 7 Mich. St. Univ. J. Med. & L. 117, 167 (2003).

One of my favorite scenes in this movie is the entry into the apartment building in this shadowy scene, with who is reported to be the CDC official carrying a large rifle and wearing a respirator. The sounds are like an underwater breathing sound from the perspective of the "outsider." When CDC officials enter wearing full personal protective suits with respirators and no one else is wearing protection, there is an immediate realization that you are in danger.

Two CDC officials go to the makeshift hospital and the reporter and her cameraman spy through a wall and note that they are using a drill into the sick man's brain. "The veterinarian was right," the cameraman remarked. Then the sick man goes into a rage and attacks one of the CDC officials. When the firefighters manage to lock the CDC official in the room and the other one safely out of the room, in a moment of irony, the CDC official mutters, "it isn't right!" referring to locking his bitten friend in the room to die.

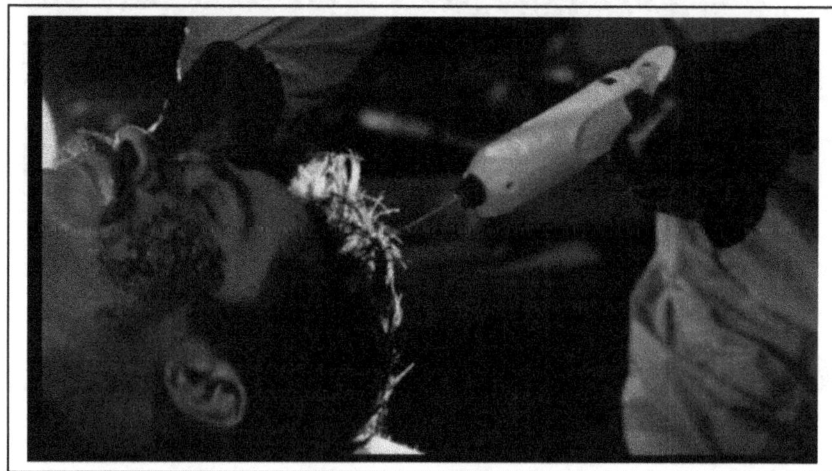

But the big question in this movie is whether it is ever constitutionally permissible to use lethal force to enforce a quarantine? In the next scene, snipers positioned on the adjacent rooftop shoot through the window when a grieving husband tries to escape through the window on an upper floor.

The rules of engagement for the military should be clear about this decision long before they are presented with the escaping man. To use deadly force against a person in the United States who is escaping a CDC ordered civilian quarantine would be weighed against the threat to public health. Even if the escaping individual was a lethal threat to public health, using lethal force is more than necessary if a tranquilizer gun or something more humane could be used to detain his entry into the public where the disease would then become a threat. There has never been a quarantine order that authorized the use of deadly force in the U.S. (However, there are some facilities that once were locations of biological weapons which were guarded with the threat of lethal force if anyone tried to enter them. Signs were posted to that effect.)

In 2008, when this movie was made, the International Health Regulations (IHR) had been effective since 2007. These regulations bind members of the World Health Organization (WHO). These regulations require reporting any event which meets the criteria for a Public Health Emergency of International Concern (PHEIC). The *Decision Instrument for Assessment and Notification* of the IHR asks a series of questions to make that determination. Is it a listed disease? Is it a disease that is a threat to the International community? Or, is this a "unexpected" or "unusual" for this area or time of year? If the answer is yes, and in this case, the virus was determined to be unlike any they had seen according to the CDC official who talked to the inhabitants. The next questions ask if the disease would have a serious public health impact, and whether it has occurred in a highly populated area? The apartment building is located in the densely populated area of downtown Los Angeles. Further, if there is a chance for international spread, in the final series of questions, then the designated official for the United States must make a decision within 24 hours of notice of the disease to the World Health Organization that this is a PHEIC. Some may argue that the quarantine and sealed building with the inhabitants inside eliminates the risk of international spread, but we know from seeing the infected rat inside the building that efforts to contain this zoonotic disease is doomed.

A split second before the apartment building owner is attacked through the door by an infected human, he tells the group that there are some keys in his office that will allow them to escape. Three people eventually survive for the last twenty minutes – the firefighter, the cameraman and the reporter. After fighting their way to his office, finding a ring of about a hundred keys they get to the secret room in the basement. They find it is full of rat cages. That is not all they found.

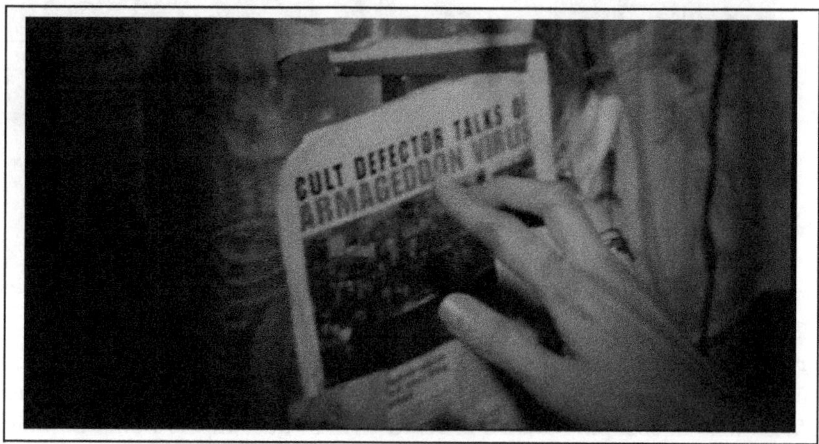

The yellowing newspaper articles pinned to a bulletin board, suggest that the apartment owner was engaged in a mad scientist experiment in his basement with rats on a biological weapon. One article headline reads, "Life on Remote South Pacific Island Wiped Out. Scientists Baffled." Another, "Cult defector talks of Argeggadon Virus," and "Doomsday Cult Suspected in Weapons Lab Break In."

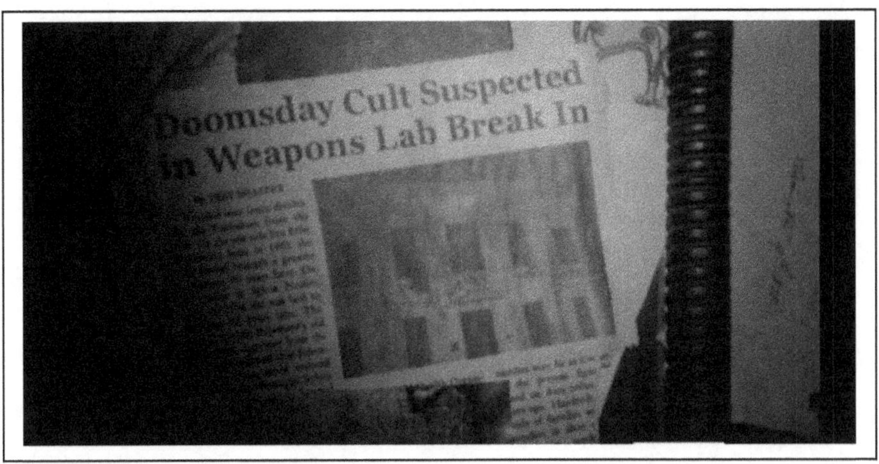

The article is quite authentic looking, but upon closer examination, the text appears to be an article about Zimbabwe and women's mortality rates. Nonetheless, the headlines which move quickly, coupled with the frantic and panicked breathing of the reporter signals the tension that is building in the basement with the rat cages.

They enter another door which seems to be his autopsy room for his rats. The reporter is riffling through papers in a laboratory with a deadly virus, which is further showing of her commitment as a reporter. With ten minutes left, the cameraman says he is going to use his "night vision" on the camera. In the meantime, a couple of humans break into the laboratory and throw things around. There is no happy ending for the reporting team, and unfortunately. But what will happen to their capturing of the events on the news camera?

Pandemic (2009)

RATING

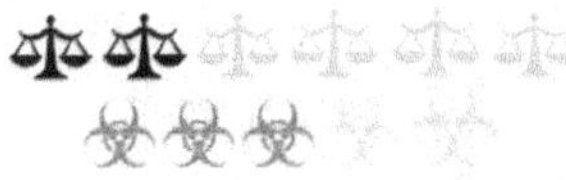

Dr. Sydney Stevens
I have an idea. Let's call the CDC.

----*Pandemic* (2009)

Pandemic (2009) opens with a cowboy riding his horse back to the barn, and shortly thereafter he dies a terrible death, blackening blood vessels creeping over his face. The scenes alternate between the dying man and the explosion of blood vessels inside his body, giving a graphic depiction of an attack from the inside that kills in minutes.

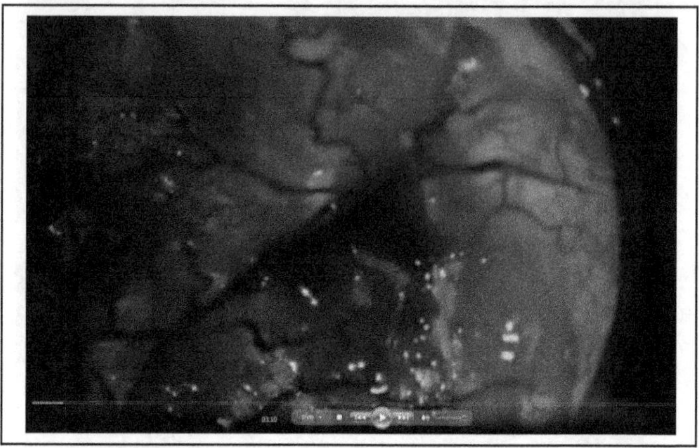

The hero, veterinarian, Dr. Sydney Stevens, played by Alesha Rucci, is called by a local eccentric, Spenser, whose horse has collapsed. She examines the horse, shown in the screenshot, and concludes it "looks viral." Spenser mutters about keeping his barn locked so "they" can't get in, and the impression is that he may be a bit paranoid. The scene progresses through an argument between Spenser and the veterinarian about whether he should shoot his horse and put it out of its misery. The shotgun sound ends the scene.

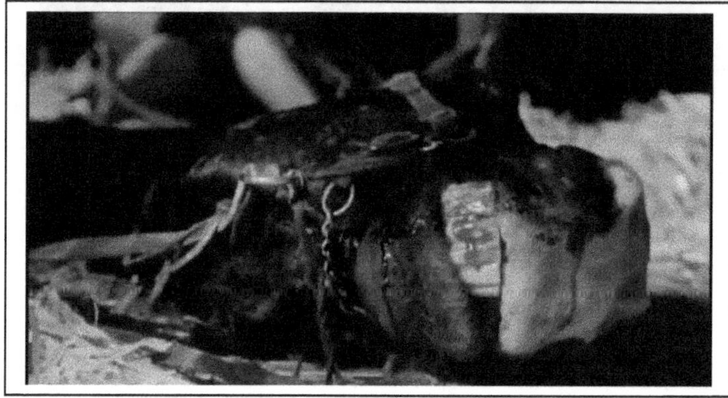

Dr. Stevens returns to her home to research the virus when she hears a report from the Diablo County, New Mexico coroner announcing the death of a rancher. Dr. Stevens departs for the coroner's office and demands to see the body. The coroner Dr. Greene complies despite the heroine's unnecessarily abrupt demand. The lowlight filming is carried through except for the occasional scene outside in the bright New Mexico sunlight. Here is the coroner's office which should normally be well lit.

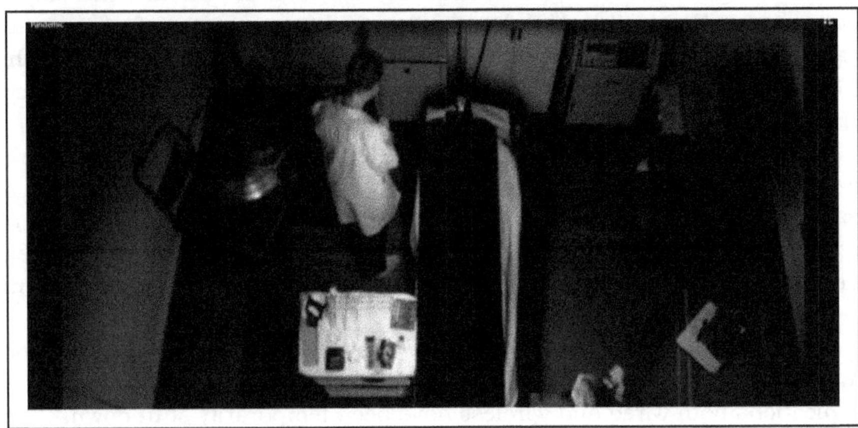

They begin to discuss the diagnosis and first say it is *Ebola*, but there is no bleeding from the orifices, the most obvious symptom of *Ebola*. Then they say it looks like West Nile Virus (WNV), but there are no symptoms with WNV that match the blackened face of the dead rancher. Then the veterinarian says, "I have an idea. Let's call the CDC." Any contagious disease that is unknown is required by federal law to be reported to CDC, immediately, and physicians have a particular duty to do so. Dr. Green, the coroner, played by Kristi Green, seemed to be surprised by this suggestion.

The film loses a good bit of the tension built up around the deadliness of the disease when Dr. Stevens enters the coroners examining room where the bodies, admittedly infectious, are exposed to the air and she dons a minimal surgical paper mask not even up to the simple N-95 surgical mask. If this disease is as deadly as depicted, they would be expected to work at BSL-4 conditions or the closest duplication in field conditions if such a laboratory was not available.

Interestingly, Dr. Stevens suggests to the coroner they call the CDC but since she is a veterinarian in New Mexico, her first call would more likely be to her contacts in the New Mexico Livestock Board or the U.S. Department of Agriculture, Veterinary Services.

Dr. Green and Dr. Stevens with the office clerk, observed the approach of a military caravan during the night. General Matthews introduces himself and has a quick chat with the doctors, telling them that they will "quarantine the area." He asks for their cooperation.

According to General Matthews, the CDC alerted the military who are quarantining the area. Dr. Green questioned why the CDC would want to quarantine without a diagnosis? The authority for the quarantine is "guaranteed by the U.S. Code of Justice Quarantine and Containment Act." The quarantine was ordered by an Executive Order issued by General Matthews. There are a number of major errors with this scenario. First, the CDC cannot give authority to the military to enact a civilian quarantine. Only the President can order the U.S. Army under the *Posse Comitatus Act* to enforce martial law on a civilian community, and this would be only in extraordinary circumstances where there is no functional local or state government. The *Posse Comitatus* Act was enacted after the U.S. Civil War in response to the disastrous martial control of the South during Reconstruction. The sentiment of Congress was that the military should never be ordered to have martial control of civilians without extraordinary circumstances. Second, the implementation of a quarantine would have to be ordered by the state public health agency, because public health law is an area of state sovereignty. Even if they had deemed the need for a quarantine was a matter of national security, thereby inviting federal jurisdiction, the U.S. CDC would be the agency to advise on the quarantine and the U.S. Department of Health and Human Services would be the department to order the federal quarantine.

Later a local citizen, Clay, questions the quarantine and raises "New Orleans", "Three-Mile Island" as examples of how the federal government handles things. Interestingly, Hurricane Katrina was the biggest natural disaster in the history of the United States, while nothing happened except a scare at "Three-Mile Island" when a near melt-down was prevented but disclosed at Three Mile Island, a nuclear power facility in Pennsylvania in 1979.

A quarantine is only the first step, and when no one can get a call out of the town, Dr. Stevens heads off to find out why. At the checkpoint, she is told that "all communications both wired and wireless have been temporarily shut down." She is told that they have to shut down communication because he wants to prevent "widespread panic." He tells her that her work is done. Her response? "This is bullshit!" Then walks calmly from the military tent and mutters, "Asshole!" followed by accelerating away in her red pickup truck.

A vocal, "we have come this far," plays over scenes of Dr. Stevens driving through her town and seeing military confrontations with citizens and just a military presence with no real action or turning point events. As she is arriving back to her home, she suspects an intruder and takes out her cattle prod to investigate while calling out, "hello," which may be a bit unrealistic. She spies someone running from her back door but enters still leading with the cattle prod. The tension is broken when she electrocutes Spenser with her cattle prod. Again, it is unrealistic that a friend would hide in her house without saying something. He tells her they are after him because of all the "things he saw." He then explains to her – "it's the water." He explains it is a delivery device for the virus. His logic revolves around their geographic location near the continental divide (which is the place where all the rivers flow the other direction into the nearest body of water). The logic is never really explained. But his claim that their isolation makes them a good testing ground is the only logic he offers for his claims of their experimentation on the community but no explanation why they would be experimenting on the community. Dr. Stevens is understandably in disbelief.

Dr. Stevens

They're not just going to kill
innocent Americans.

Spenser

Well innocent is debatable. But ---
Need I remind you of the history of
this part of the country? This state
has been relentlessly scorched by
nuclear testing. . .

Dr. Stevens

That was decades ago. . .

Spenser
If I am so wrong, so fucked in the head, why did they cut off all communications?

Dr. Stevens
Because of people like you.

A group of citizens confront the military guards at the checkpoint, in the screenshot below, and they are turned away when they demand to see the General who has ordered the quarantine. This confirms the lack of even minimal due process to allow individuals to have a hearing with a stated reason for why they are being detained and a chance for them to respond.
The guard fires a shot into the air and that is enough to discourage the local citizens and they get back in their trucks, not without first shouting, "This is bullshit!" A favorite line in the movie.

Spenser
They're not testing preparedness, they are testing a weapon.

Dr. Sidney Stevens
What?

Spenser
A biological weapon. A perfect one. Look how fast this virus is moving.

Dr. Sidney Stevens
The U.S. government is not going to test weapons on its own people.

Spenser

Really, well you better believe it
baby because the Army is taking over.

Spenser is a local eccentric who believes the Army is testing a weapon on them, but the veterinarian, Dr. Stevens is not ready to believe him. As they are pursued by the military while driving around at night, she begins to become suspicious that he may be right.

The last third of the movie involves Spenser and Dr. Stevens making a break for the county border to tell the world. But it is not until they are on the run that Spenser gets the epiphany that this is a biological weapons experiment.

They apprehend the two fleeing hero and heroine and they divide them and convince Dr. Stevens that Spenser is a dissonant, anti-American associating with the Cubans embarking on a revolution building weapons. Then General Matthews discloses that he is actually his son. Dr. Stevens does not seem to be very affected by this revelation.

The question of a vaccine is raised, and the General tells Dr. Stevens that they experimented on Brian, the coroner's clerk, with the vaccine. Previous scenes showed that Brian took the vaccine believing with no idea that this was an experiment. Dr. Stevens took some time to realize that Brian was probably not a volunteer.

Surprisingly, they let her return to her home, with no sign of Spenser, and she slept on her couch until the sun arose and then made her escape. She takes a trail through the desert with music that was eerily reminiscent of *28 Days Later* (2003). Crossing over the county line, she appears to be succumbing to the deadly virus.

This movie plot exploits the fear of government, lack of due process and government experimenting on its own citizens with biological weapons. The characters fit the unfolding of such a plot: Spenser, the eccentric, paranoid character turns out to be right and not just paranoid. Dr. Stevens, the heroine, is the voice of reason but is ultimately forced to conclude that her government is the enemy and the villain in this story pushing her to the extremes of life and death choices.

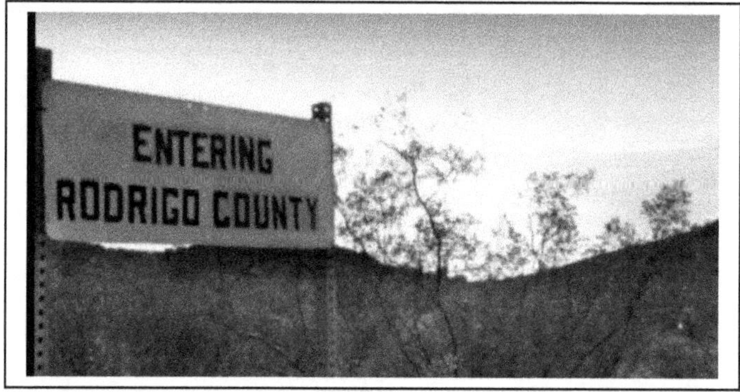

In her final dying scene, Dr. Stevens reflects back on her encounter with General Matthews and the glass of water she gave her to drink in their meeting.

The real payoff in the movie comes as General Matthews is seen stoically sitting in a comfortable chair and watching the newscaster who reports first that Dr. Stevens died in an unfortunate accident when her truck veered off the road. But in the next story on international news, he reports that a mysterious illness has struck Afghanistan, and strangely enough it has infected and killed an "Al Qaeda leader of a splinter group" in Pakistan, killing him. Thus, the message is clearly that we are defeating the enemy but at what cost?

But the writers are not through with the lessons, yet. A dog has wandered out to the highway from the infected county and a boy asks his dad if they can take him back to Los Angeles with them, which he affirms. The familiar exploding of blood vessels confirms the infected dog will open up the floodgates of death and destruction, the true costs of our government's wins in the war on terror, is clearly the message.

Pandemic (Japan) (2009)

RATING

Japan Council Member

Tamiflu is our only hope.

--Pandemic (2009) (Japan)

Pandemic (2009) a Japanese movie, has the distinction of being the most expensive movie ever made in Japan at the time it was made. It runs a long 138 minutes and the only English subtitles are available with this hard-to-find foreign film. The cast leads with popular stars in Japan. Tsumabuki Satoshi plays Dr. Tsuyoshi Matsuoka, the ER physician and Dan Rei, plays the World Health Organization medical officer, Eiko.

The movie begins with a scene in North Phillipines in an avian flu outbreak. Biosuited personnel are in the village. A man is leaving the village for a wedding in town, taking a chicken as a gift, touching off the spread of the epidemic.

A year or so later, in Japan, avian flu is suspected in a few patients who are ill. The god shots of the poultry farm that reported the outbreak showed massive destruction of poultry. One memorable visual is all of the workers bowing in prayer together in a perfect line. Throughout this movie, the uniformity of lines of people whether in ques, chairs in a room or cleaning up poultry, was remarkable.

Dr. Tuyoshi Matsuka, the protagonist, misdiagnoses a patient with ordinary flu, only to have him decline rapidly with a deadly flu-like illness. His girlfriend, also sick, accuses Dr. Matsuka of being a murderer. While he did misdiagnosis the patient it was the first patient to present in the hospital with the bird flu and the flu-like illness did not show on the "flu kit."

The scene switches to government processes. The Japan Councilmembers recall the outbreak in the Phillipines and the 32 deaths from birdflu the previous year. They predict it could affect 2.5 million. They begin to raise quarantine as a solution and there is disagreement about quarantine. Some argue they want to avoid frightening people. Discussion of whether a vaccine could be used, but experts respond that it takes six months to develop a vaccine. One of the councilmembers concludes, "Tamiflu is our only hope."

There is a scene which focuses on the family of the chicken farmer, as he witnesses a stone being thrown through his glass window of his home. He receives a threatening phone call thereafter, blaming him for the outbreak. "You and your damn chickens!" the caller says and the farmer apologies.

The chicken farmer is on his way to be questioned by Japanese authorities. His daughter, Akane, goes to school and her friends shun her saying she will make them sick. They have drawn a huge sick chicken on the black board. She defends herself by telling them they have not proven it is the chickens which caused this illness.

The two stars are former lovers who confront each other in a chance meeting at the hospital Eiko is the medical officer sent from the World Health Organization and she has been sent here to investigate the outbreak. They have not seen each other since medical school. Apparently, Tsuyoshi was unaware that Eiko had gone to work at her dream job at the World Health Organization.

Eiko tells Tsuyoshi that the hospital will be taken over by the health ministry. She convenes a meeting of the hospital staff and asserts that she will be in charge. She fields questions about whether this is H5N1 and what will happen. She has no answers but gives them some order of the process. First to find the first contact with the patients who presented with the illness. She looks around the room and Tsuyoshi raises his hand. It is her ex-lover who was the first contact in the dramatic end of this scene.

Eiko tries to question the female partner in the couple who first presented with the the illness. The husband has died, but Eiko is relentless in her questioning.

A various points in the movie, Eiko and Tsuyoshi catch up on the lost years between them since they left medical school. She tells him that she got her dream job because she left him and Japan and went to England. He tells her he would rather have empathy than to be like her.

The hospital staff grow to dislike Eiko and her imposing control. Dramatic orchestra music plays as she writes her instructions (in Japanese) on the white board.
"Bloody WHO" someone mutters and walks out. She is assigned a "keeper" but asks instead to have Dr. Matsouka as her liaison.

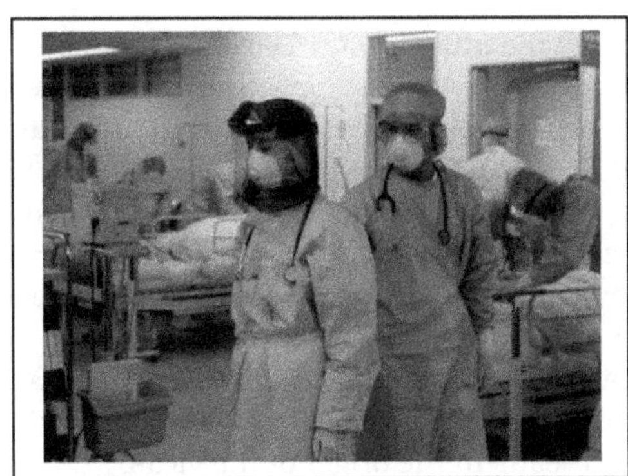

Next, they have to witness the painful death of the physician, Dr. Ando, who was sprayed by the blood of the first death (when he inexplicably removed his goggles). His wife and daughter look on, with details the movie never overlooks to drain more sympathy from the audience. The slow zipping of the body bag at an altar with candles and the widow and daughter in surgical scrubs and masks further the tension with the death.

Tsuyoshi is feeling very guilty about misdiagnosing the first patient who was negative for influenza. But the test kits are not showing this new influenza. Of all the movies, the expression of guilt and personal acceptance of blame is never more evident than in this movie which in part, must be attributed to Japanese culture. In fact, the name of the disease takes on the name, "Blame."

People are amassed at a makeshift hospital under tents outside the hospital because the hospital is quarantined. The hospital conditions and the crowds are very authentic. Extremely ill people are waiting outside among well patients. One of the women runs away when she is asked to assist and the other female doctor mutters, "bitch."

The text shows the body count periodically throughout the movie. At this point, the body count is 832 by day two.

Eiko and Tsuyoshi go to inspect the chicken farm and they are required to have their temperature taken before entering the farm. This is a widespread mechanism of monitoring for illness in Asia. During the SARS outbreak, heat detection monitors were set up on the Guangdong airport and in Hong Kong for monitoring travelers. The false positives were high, according to reports, but the method is still used. In the U.S. and in Europe this would be considered an unacceptable invasion of privacy.

The chicken farmer is very apologetic, and bows in apology to the inspectors.

Then the inspectors and others spot an intruder. The dialogue that follows raises the possibility of bioterrorism:

Government inspector 1
There have been rumors that this might be bioterror.

Government inspector 2
Terror? I never thought of that.

The military pursue the intruder but Tsuyoshi finds him first. The intruder is an unknown scientist who is trying to get a sample and analyze the virus. He gives Tsuyoshi his card. Later in the movie, Tsuyoshi decides to give the scientist samples of the virus, and meets him in a secluded forest. While you might expect this to be a set up for an ultimate betrayal by the scientist, the scientist actually succeeds in isolating the virus and identifying it. However, the point seems to be that when the announcement is made the scientist is not given credit to his dismay, and the cultural disapproval of those who work along, not with the group seems to be the lesson here.

Eiko communicated with WHO via video on her laptop and English is spoken in these exchanges. This contacts prove to be troublesome and WHO is uncooperative and refuses to follow up on her leads to the origin of the virus.

Panic increases in Japan and scenes of Tokyo look like a war zone. Buses are overturned and cars and stores are looted. The hospitals are overrun.

Eiko gives an impassioned plea to the staff of the hospital to asks them to stay and not go home with a deep bow as she waits for a dramatic pause for the volunteers. The volunteers raise their hand and they give a count of 23 doctors and 54 nurses volunteer to stay and live in the hospital. She bows, the doctors and nurses bow. Deal struck.

The Japanese are barred from other nations and the Japan government orders "all regions quarantined in 72 hours." The staff grumbles that the public will be unhappy. They have military check points and stop any mass gatherings.

Another text on the screen announces there are 1,989 dead.

Meanwhile, the drama with the chicken farmer, his daughter and her boyfriend continues. The daughter calls her boyfriend and asks him to meet her at the abandoned amusement park. He refuses because he is already packing to leave with his family which is trying to get out of Tokoyo. They are eventually turned back by the military which is enforcing the quarantine. Interestingly, this is the only quarantine enforced by the military in any movie that portrays the military as unarmed. The boyfriend's family breaks the quarantine in their car and the military troops just scramble – but there are no weapons and not even an attempt to stop them. There is not even a question of lethal force.

To make matters worse for the daughter she finds her father has hanged himself blaming himself and his chickens for the disaster. Just at the moment the doctor pronounces the chicken farmer dead, a scientist announces that the lab has determined it is not bird flu further adding to the misery felt by the daughter. She calls them all murders.

The intial patient who survives finally gives Eikos enough information about where she got the virus. Her father was a physician from Minas Island off the coast of Japan, and he was sick.

The stress level at the hospital spirals out of control when one of the doctors becomes violent and shoves Eiko and another doctor, but then breaks down into tears and wants to go home.

News reports in English show the headlines:
"Satanic virus attacks Japan".

The virus is named "Blame" for divine punishment and the discussion is about why Japan is being punished. Predictions now put infections at 80 percent of the population. More news: "Transit is shut down and the social fabric begins to unravel." They announce laws that make it is a crime to conceal the sick. Looting and theft abound. The military (still unarmed) take people from hiding who are sick. Food distributions are made every two weeks. In this scene Eiko and Tsuyoshi are walking through the city as they observe the military taking some sick people out of hiding.

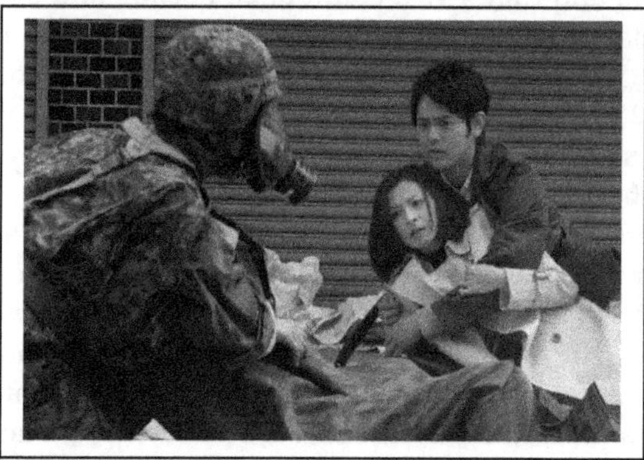

The hospital begins to run out of supplies and they are forced to take them from the patients with the least chance of survival. The staff and Tusyoshi watch Eiko remove the respirator from a small boy in favor of a more promising patient in terms of survival. As she walks around removing the respirators from less promising patients, there is silence, then heart monitors begin to buzz the flatline sound. Body bags come out and the staff is further demoralized. Many of them walk out in frustration. The count --twelve patients died and the rest were stable in the process leaving a grim, quiet over the emergency room.

Once outside, Eiko breaks down into tears when she is with Tsuyoshi.

Further trouble for the investigation of the disease occurs when the scientist who first diagnosed the disease as bird flu, Dr. Nishi, and caused the chicken farmer to commit suicide walked out. Tsuyoshi convinced him to stay, telling him that he too felt guilty of misdiagnosing the first patient but now he only wants to keep people from dying.

So Dr. Nishi the scientist and Tsuyoshi team up to investigate the origin of the disease on Minas Island. They find many dead people and in the clinic, the scene is as close to zombies as this movie gets to anything other than pure realism. But even the zombies are very real. They are told that it was a witch from the forest that gave a man the disease that started the tragedy.

A huge wave of bats fly out of one of the huts when Tsuyoshi opens the door. Again realism instead of zombies works well. They find dead bodies with a symptoms of the disease. They find dying patients in the clinic and they move like zombies with a realism that makes them pathetic as sad music is heard in the scene. Yet they are still able to come after Tsuyoshi, pull off his mask and grab his leg.

The theme of the virus and human interaction is carried into this scene where Dr. Nishi says he is sharing his body with a virus, a cancer, and has accepted the coexistence. Tsuyoshi knows he will die and bows deeply to him as he walks away. Dr. Nishi decides to stay on the island and treat the sick.

It is Dr. Nishi who eventually traces the "Witch" in the forest to a cave of bats as the reservoir for the deadly virus.

On the 50th day 2.5 million are infected and 900,000 are dead.

Scenes of body bags line the open spaces and the downtown is a warzone.

Eiko seems defeated when she tells the staff that they can only treat the symptoms right now, but not to give up hope. Then she announces she has been transferred to Nagano by WHO. There is an exchange of bows and clapping. As she leaves in the taxi she discovers that she has the disease as she coughs up blood.

The chicken farmers daughter, Akane becomes sick just when her boyfriend finds her in the amusement park in the snow and he is apologizing for abandoning her when his family tried to leave Tokyo. Apologizing for mistakes is a theme throughout the movie.

Every relationship in the movie is destroyed by the virus. For example, a nurse's little girl is outside the hospital with her father in the snow. The little girl holds her phone waiting for her Mom to return her text. But her Mom dies while they are waiting outside but Tsuyoshi sees the text and responds on behalf of the mother, ". . . Mommy loves you."

After watching more than fifty of these movies from the biohorro subgenre, it was surprising to me that this one was so extraordinarily sad. It is one of the most moving and tragic of all of the movies.

Then another text on the screen: 10 million infected, 3 million dead.

Eiko reaches Tsuyoshi via video on his laptop in the ER and tells him that she is sick but she is going to try a new remedy. She remembers a remedy used in Zaire in the ebola outbreak, where they transfused patents with blood from blood of survivors of ebola. About 5 out of 8 survived. The European doctors were against it, but the Zaire doctors were in favor of trying it.

Tsuyoshi is about to lose Akane, the chicken farmer's daughter in the ER so he tries that approach on her. He uses the blood of the woman who survived who was the first to come into the hospital. The transfusion is working on Akane in Tokoyo but Eiko in Nagano seems to be having trouble.

Tsuyoshi jumps in his car and drives toward Nagano, but his car runs out of gas. He gets out of his car and finishes the trip at a run. When he gets there they take him to Eiko and he speaks to her. He begins to take off his facemask (reminiscent of the scene in Outbreak (1995) with the two doctors, Dustin Hoffman and Renee Russo) but she stops him. Then her heart monitor flatlines and blood runs out of her eyes in a dramatic death scene. Tusyohi runs out of the hospital and begins to scream.

He remembers something Eiko said to him in medical school, "Even if the world ends tomorrow, plant an apple tree today." This seems to sustain him.

The movie ends with a vaccine that begins to bring "Blame" under control after 1.12 million are dead. Akane, the chicken farmer's daughter survives and she is happily riding a bicycle with her boyfriend.

Tsuyoshi goes to a small town where they don't have a doctor to set up a practice. In the last scene, he is happily treating an old farmer.

This movie at 138 minutes had time to explore several complex relationships and to develop the plot more extensively than the shorter 89 minute movie.

Carriers (2009)

RATING

Doctor

Sometimes choosing life is just choosing a more painful form of death.

---*Carriers* (2009)

Carriers (2009) begins with a foursome, two girls two boys, on a road trip to the beach with two surfboards on the top of the car. They laugh and it appears to be a carefree trip but we soon learn it is anything but that. They laugh about driving a stolen Mercedes. Then on the road encounter a man outside his SUV which is blocking the roadway. They see his daughter is infected and speed away while the man clubs the driver's window with a wrench, breaking it.

The driver, Brian Green, is in charge and has set the rules stated by his brother, Danny, in a voice over:

Danny Green
(voice over)

The rules are simple. At least that's how my brother sees it. One, avoid the infected at all costs. Their breath is highly contagious. Two, disinfect anything they've touched in the last 24 hours. Three, the sick are already dead, they can't be saved. You break the rules, you die. You follow them, you live. Maybe.

Soon, they find the Mercedes has lost all of its oil due to damage sustained in driving around the SUV. (A Mercedes has a solid under cover that protects it from damage, but apparently this one was missing.) They realize they will need the SUV, so they drive back to confront the man and make an agreement to travel together ---his car and their gas.

This screenshot shows the masks that the foursome put on to approach the man. The masks are N-95s which is a basic mask for dust, but not protective against viruses, although it is better than nothing, but not by much. The problem with N-95s is that the wearer can have a false confidence that they are protected and be less careful with exposures. After the initial meeting with the man and his infected daughter, astonishingly they took the masks off and traveled in the car with them without masks. They used a plastic screen to separate the father and his daughter in the back, but that would not have been effective in a closed car for long periods of exposure. World Health Organization (WHO) guidelines suggest that a person with tuberculosis should not travel on a commercial flight for any duration of more than 8 hours, or they will endanger the other passengers. That is a rough guideline for other infectious diseases. As they discuss traveling together, they learn that the father was heading for Farmington, New Mexico to a hospital where he heard that the Centers for Diseases Control (CDC) had developed a cure for the virus. The foursome chided him for his naivette, but agreed to go.

When they stop at night, the couples pair off, and Brian's girlfriend, Bobbi, says the memorable line, "I think we should see other people." In the middle of a pandemic with no one else in sight, it was a bit of irony but not meant to be humorous.

In the next scene they see an Asian man hanging from a tower with a sign, "Chinks brought it."

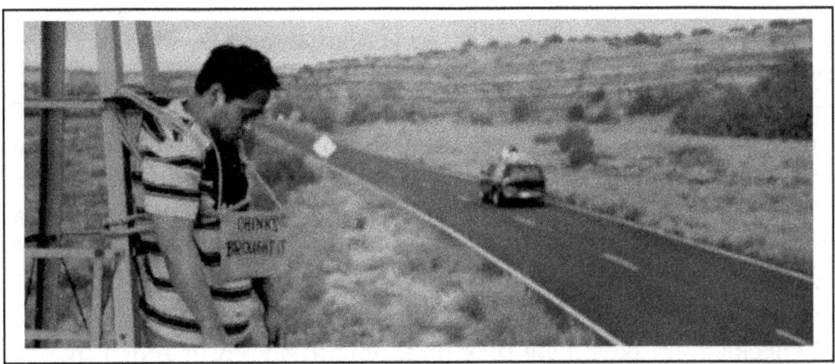

This is reminiscent of the blame placed on Chinatown in San Francisco during the 1901 outbreak of plague. The consequences of quarantining the entire Chinatown led to the court striking down such prejudice on the basis of Constitutional equal protection in *Jew Ho v. Williamson.*

They found the hospital empty in Farmington, but explored all the abandoned corridors. They found a doctor in the hospital and he told them the "cure" lasted only for three days. In the meantime, he was developing a potassium drink that would kill the children so they wouldn't have to die a painful death. The father got the gun from Brian and threatened the doctor not to euthanize the children. When the doctor told him, "sometimes chosing life is just chosing a more painful way of death," he seemed to understand and backed away from the doctor who was pulling the curtains in the makeshift tent, seen in this screenshot.

The scene with the makeshift temporary tents was frightening because in reality, hospitals currently have only one or two such beds for patients with respiratory distress. In a flu-like outbreak everyone would need one, which would lead to the makeshift oxygen tents as seen in this scene.

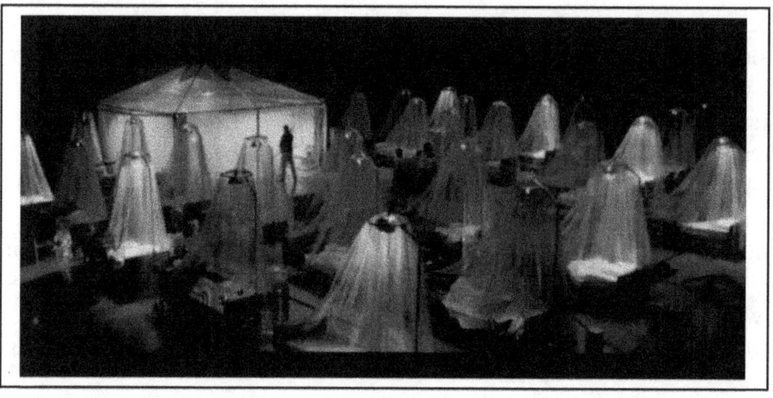

As the father's daughter worsens, she is unable to walk, so he takes her out of the car to an outhouse, and Brian convinces them to leave them having brought them to where they agreed to bring them. Brian has to make the hard decision to leave them – Brian's brother, Danny, reluctant to make the hard decisions. They continue to drive and stop at an abandoned Homewood hotel for the night. Brian narrowly misses jumping into the swimming pool with a floating bloody body. They decide to play golf and enjoy a moment of wild abandon driving a golf cart all over the course. Then they delight in swinging golf balls through the hotel glass doors and windows.

Back in the hotel, Kate, Danny's girlfriend, is disturbed that she can't reach her parents and checks every payphone they find, only to be reprimanded by her friend, Bobby, that all the phones are dead and all of their parents are dead.

Then, while Brian is still out on the golf course long after dark hitting golf balls, a biosuited man comes to investigate inside the hotel where Danny and the girls are located. Brian comes back and attacks one of them in the parking lot, in the screenshot below.

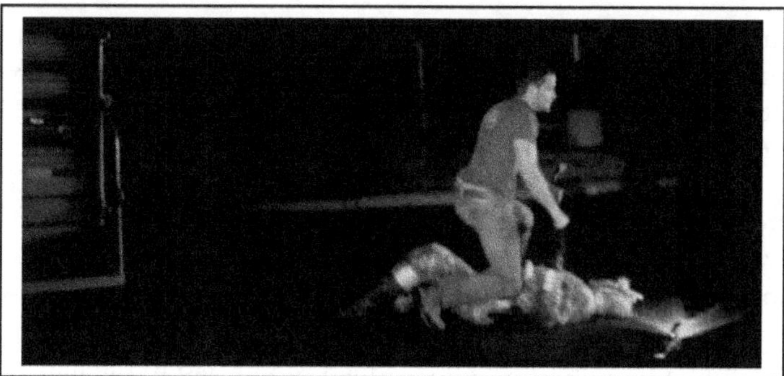

Two of the three men decide to take the girls but want to see if they are "clean" first so they make them strip. The have an internal conflict among the biosuited men but the two men prevail and demand the girls strip. The boys, Brian and Danny, see to their dismay that Bobbi, Brian's girlfriend is infected and has the symptomatic rash all over her body. The three remaining symptom-free travelers all have to face the fact that they have to abandon Bobbi so the three of them can survive. Before Brian leaves his girlfriend beside the road, he tells her where to go to find shelter and to get a blanket before she gets too weak. He is angry with her for breaking the rules – getting close to the infected little girl that they picked up when they had to travel in the SUV.

They begin to run out of gas because the men at the hotel stole their cans of gasoline and they become more aggressive.

Danny, the moral compass of the group, lies to some women in a car they have struck on the road in order to stop them. Danny notices that the women have a Christian fish symbol, so he tries to play on their sympathy by telling tell them his wife is pregnant and they are looking for a place for her to have a baby and appeals to them as Christians. Then things turn lethal. Brian ends up shooting the two women out of desperation. The brothers get into a fight over Brian's shooting of the woman and Danny's "self-righteousness." Brian is distraught over losing his girlfriend, Kate, and having to do all the dirty work for the group. To make matters worse, Brian was shot in the leg during the shootout with the women.

They come upon an abandoned house with the windows boarded and Danny decided to stop to get some materials to bandage his wound. Brian was wounded so Danny had to get into the house and find the supplies. Danny found a shotgun in the house. He came upon a German Shepherd eating the remains of his owner who had died of the virus. The dog attacked Danny and he was forced to shoot the dog, splattering blood everywhere. He scooped up the bottles of drugs he found in the house and left.

When Danny got back to the car, he had his brother take off his pants to dress his wound and saw that Brian, had become infected. He had a rash on his leg – the symptom of the pandemic virus, with 14 minutes left in the 84 minute movie.

At the end of the day, Danny talked to his dying brother as they sat around the fire, and told him a secret. The secret was his haunted memory of burying people with the virus who are still moving and still alive. Danny and his girlfriend tried to leave Brian at the fire, but he kept the keys so they wouldn't leave him. He stumbled over to the car and tried to get in but his brother, Danny wouldn't let him in. His girlfriend, Kate, tried to get Danny to shoot his brother and gave him the gun. Brian told Danny to shoot him or take him with him. Now that Brian was sick with the virus, he said he didn't care about the "rules" anymore. He laughed and told Danny that he had taught him everything he knows. Those would be his last words. Danny was forced to shoot his brother, despite his brother's pleas.

Danny and his girlfriend, Kate, eventually make it to the shore in Corpus Christi from their origin in Farmington, New Mexico. Danny sees visions of his past with his brother playing on that very beach. The movie ends with a sense of hopeless apocalyptic despair of loneliness.

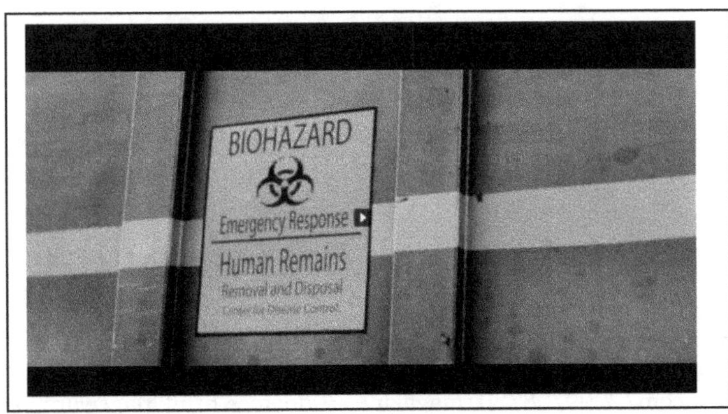

One of the unique questions raised in this movie is whether a physician can euthanize his or her patients when there is a greater chance of dying a painful death than finding a cure to survive.

This question arose in a disaster at Memorial Medical Center in Uptown New Orleans in the disaster of Hurricane Katrina, which had similar tensions and pressures as would a pandemic. The physicians and nurses at this hospital worked tirelessly according to reports to get patients out, but they had to make choices. At one point they decided that patients with DNR orders (Do not resuscitate) would not want to take the place of someone else who could be evacuated first. Eventually, it became clear that they were helpless to save 7 people on respirators that shut off when the last generator stopped. One nurse used a hand pump for an hour on the roof on a man, until she was told there was no more oxygen and she had to stop and see the man through to his death. It was this context of desperation that Dr. Pou and neck surgeon made the decision to euthanize patients who could not get out. The discovery of 52 bodies in the hospital in the aftermath triggered suspicions since this death count was higher than anywhere else in the city. Dr. Pou was arrested for second degree murder of four patients, but a grand jury refused to indict her. She appealed on national television that her job was to help patients "through their pain." In the four years since her indictment, Dr. Pou has helped write and pass three statutes in Louisiana to protection healthcare professionals from criminal and civil liability for taking similar actions in situations like hurricanes, terrorist attacks or pandemics.[51]

Perhaps the doctor in the movie made in 2009 had taken some cues from the Hurricane Katrina 2005 disaster. Liability was the least of his worries.

---

[51] Sheri Fink,"The Deadly Choices at Memorial," *The New York Times* (Aug. 25, 2009) at http://www.nytimes.com/2009/08/30/magazine/30doctors.html?pagewanted=all&_r=0.

Black Death (2010) Germany

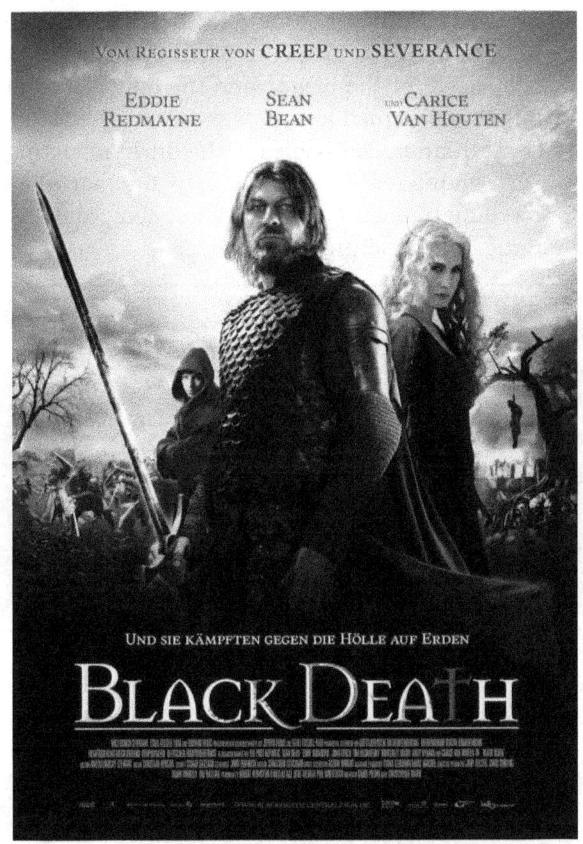

RATING

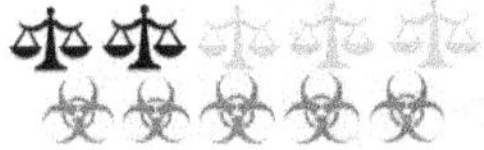

Priest
Even if you survive, the world out there will change you.

Young Monk
Perhaps that is what I want.

---**Black Death** (2010)

Black Death (2010), Germany, is a very authentic historical narrative of the black plague period that lasted from 1346-1350 A.D. The opening voice over tells the viewers that the priests told the people that the plague was from God, punishing them for their sins. But people were quick to find other scapegoats including the Jews and women. Women, as it turned out, were witches who brought the plague to particular villages or people. This movie focuses on women as the scapegoat for the plague and the ugly consequences of the lack of the rule of law in a pandemic that spanned almost five years.

From the scenes of death and dead bodies in the dark, misty night, the morning opens in the monastery with a young monk, Osmund. His first act when he awakes is to check under his arms for swelling buboes – one of the first symptoms of the plague. Finding none, he makes the sign of the cross and prays.

He heads off to join his brothers at an early mass where they are mourning the loss of one of their brothers.

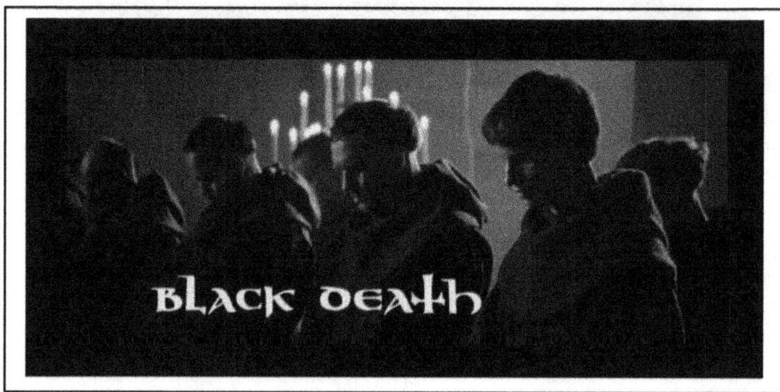

Ulrich, Sean Bean, is the Bishop's envoy who has arrived at the monastery to announce his need for a guide to find the reputed village that has not been visited by the plague. The village lies in the Great Marsh and despite the obvious fact that it is isolated, Ulrich insisted that it had not been hit by the plague because it was inhabited by a necromancer. The young monk has prayed for guidance to serve outside the walls of the monastery. He says he was raised near the Great Marsh and knows the area better than anyone. The Priest tells the young monk that the Bishop's envoy is more dangerous "than the pestilence itself."

Along their journey the men speculate about the plague, and Osmund listens. It is the folklore that grew up around the plague. "It came from France where all bad comes from," they explained. The men told the story of the slaughter of the French in the day of a great battle between England and France (the Hundred Years' War). King Edward ordered all the Frenchmen to be kept alive so that they could be killed by dismemberment and tortured. They believed that it was that day that they began being punished by God and the plague was sent as punishment for that day.

They see some approaching people and it is a parade of flagellants (not to be confused with "flagellates" named for a similar reason, for the microbiology readers of this book). The flagellants are men of the church and their followers who beat themselves with straps, walking village to village, to assuage an angry god thought to have brought the plague as punishment. This ritual grew from impatience with the Church for having no affect on the continuing plague and death. The Church began to see the flagellants as an affront to Church control of the people and their trust in the Church, as a result many were killed.

Through their journey they encounter a band of thieves that result in at least one death. They continue on until they reach the Great Marsh and the men announce that the "cage" or punishment device will never make it through the marsh. The Bishop's envoy shouts that they will leave it and bring the heretic to it -- when they find him.

They reach the village and are greeted by Hob, the male leader of the village. But behind the man is the real power – a woman, Averill, who gives the viewer every indication she is the necromancer the Church is looking for. The men are allowed to stay when they tell Hob that they are there for refuge, only.

The woman with long blond hair braided wearing a simple light blue linen dress saw that the young monk was wounded (he had been wounded in the robbery) and offered to dress his wound. She told him that she was widowed. When she dressed his wound the pain went away immediately. The young monk asked her why her husband had died. She replied, “He was killed by men like you – men of God.”

After being drugged at dinner, the men were all captured by Hob and the villagers and tied up in a water trough causing them to shiver incessantly.

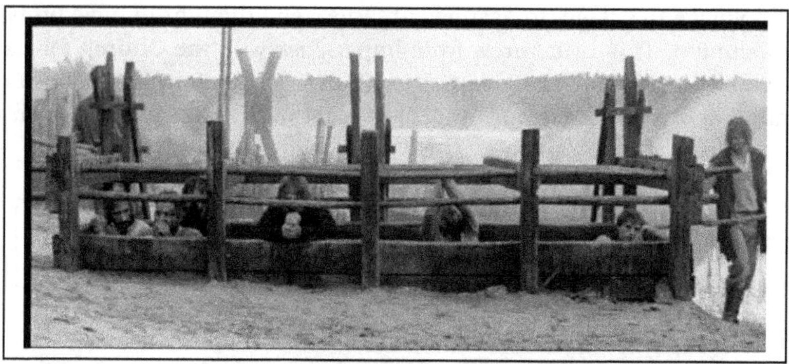

While the men were drinking at dinner, Averill took the young monk to the marsh and in the mist, he saw her raise his dead girlfriend from the dirt and he believed, re-animate her to life.

The villagers had been convinced that their village was spared by spilling the blood of Christians. So they took one of the men as the first sacrifice and then another. They gave them a chance to recant their belief in God, and one did. They led him to the edge of the village and hanged him.

Then it is the young Monk’s faith that is tested. Averill offers Osmund the woman who is his girlfriend who she found in the forest. She tells him she is waiting for him in the house nearby. He walks away to the house where he finds her hysterical and insane. But he had to renounce his faith to be with her. Once he found her he stabbed her to end her necromantic existence. Only later did he learn that she had never been dead and the witch, Averill, had drugged her into her insane behavior. The young monk had to confront the fact that not only had he renounced God and the Church but he had murdered the woman that he loved.

The young monk was correct that this journey would change him, challenging him to deny the Church and God to whom he had dedicated his life. The plague had driven people to kill each other in the name of God. Averill reminded them of the Commandment, “Thou shalt not kill,” in an irony that ran through the movie.

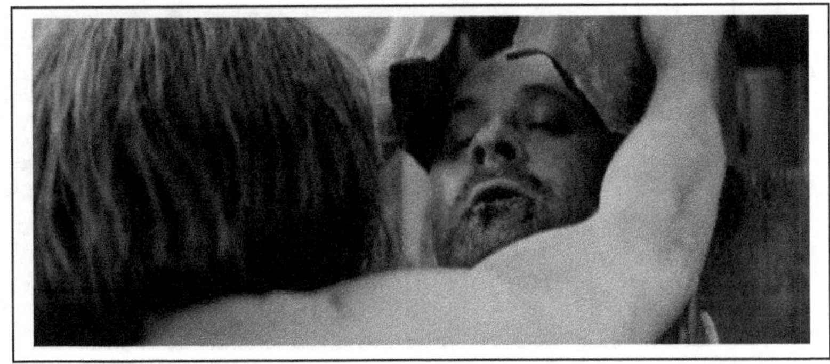

In his final moments in the torture device, when the last man freed himself from his capture and caught Hob by surprise. Hob continued to renounce God to his final breath. When he was asked why he followed "her", he replied simply, "she was beautiful and she was real."

Having his necromancer caught in the torture cage, the one man on the journey who was left returned back to the monastery to deliver Osmund back to his Priest. The young monk, Osmund, returned to the monastery but he became cold, and hate grew until he took up the sword to get revenge on Averill, the witch. He traveled to her village and captured her and tried to force her to confess. He tortured her as he had seen her torture his friends.

He continued to burn women everywhere, and when he looked at them, he saw only Averill. The plague had changed him, indeed. In the last scene, he is looking through the fire, having burned the women, and his eyes are distant and cold and souless.

The theme of change in the world during the plague years was certainly true. However, change of a magnitude never before seen was about to take place at the end of the pandemic. The elimination of one-third of the world's population lead to the greatest redistribution of wealth in the history of the world. The system of land tenure and fiefdoms, the foundation of property law, was forever changed because there were often no lords left to serve. The peasants and fiefs began working for themselves and would never return to this kind of captivity again. Peasant uprisings and unrest would prevent the ruling class, even after recovery, from ever enslaving such a large part of society.

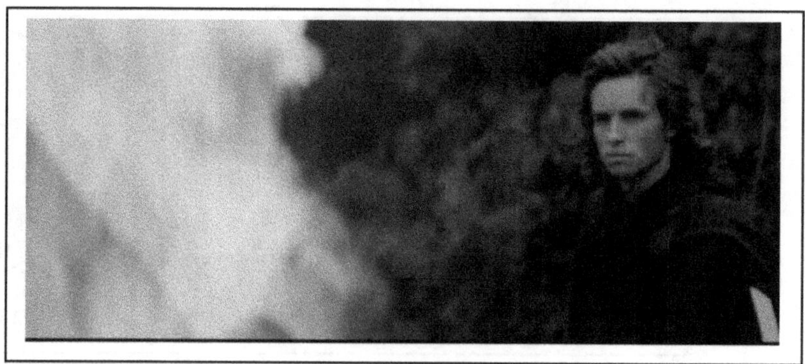

The Church lost favor after the plague in part because many people saw it as failing to stop the black death. In part, because of a number of scandals that followed the Church. Some saw the Church as the last bit of security in a world filled with chaos and uncertainty. The plague hit monasteries and churches as well as everyone else, and the Church was threatened by the flagellants so well depicted in this movie. The Church was threatened by the idea that witches might be seen as more powerful than the Church in warding off the plague. All of these threats had to be eliminated --- in the name of God.

The monk, Osmund, was one of the social and moral casualties of the black plague, depicted with amazing cinematography and writing in the way only Europeans, who live with the memory of the black plague in their villages, could do.

Contagion (2011)

RATING

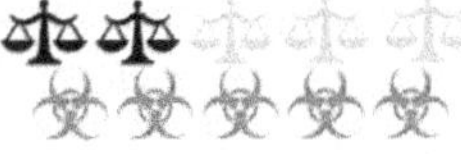

[During the autopsy of Elizabeth Enhoff, the index case, the two coroners see something unusual in their view of her brain.]

Coroner 1
I want you to back away from the table.

Coroner 2
Should I call someone?

Coroner 1
Call everyone.

---*Contagion* (2011)

Contagion (2011) takes the subgenre to its purest level of fright and thrill by taking the minimalist gesture, touch, handshake and bat dropping to the level of true horror. It is the realism wherein lies the horror. Instead of zombies leaping off the screen, the simple cough sends chills down the spine of the viewer. The last breath of a victim escalates the tension to ever increasing heights.

In the opening, Matt Damon, the husband of Elizabeth Enhoff, played by Gwyneth Paltrow, sees his wife and son die in the first few minutes of the movie. His wife who travels the globe carrying out the capitalist investment strategy of her company AIMM, a thinly veiled reference to a real corporation in Minnesota, has returned home sick from her travel to Macau and Hong Kong.

It is not her death so much as her autopsy which triggers notification to the CDC of the seriousness of her deteriorated condition.

The movie appears to have employed no legal specialists in this field, or they would have immediately engaged the "focal point" of the United States which has an obligation to notify the World Health Organization. The United States has only 24 hours within the time of determining that the disease is a Public Health Emergency of International Concern, or a "PHEIC" as those in the field would know it. This is all required, indeed binding law, under the International Health Regulations which the United States signed and ratified and agreed to be bound by in 2005, effective 2007. This movie was made in 2011.

The International Health Regulations or "IHR" another acronym signifying that you are in the "know" ask several questions to determine if you have a "PHEIC." The first question which would apply to this outbreak is defined in the regulation to include "Any event of potential international public health including those of unknown causes . . . " which would prompt the next question --- "Is the public health impact of the event serious?" If you didn't answer, "yes" to this question, you haven't been paying attention to the movie! By all accounts we have a serious public health impact and stand on the precipice of a pandemic even at this early point in the movie. The answer of "yes" prompts you to answer the next question: "Is the event unusual or unexpected?" The answer in this movie would certainly be another "yes!" Matt Damon was certainly not expecting his wife to convulse and die and his son to follow within hours of exposure. Having answered "yes" to these regulatory questions, a determination would be that this is a Public Health Emergency of International Concern and the event would be reported within 24 hours to the World Health Organization. But the failure to recognize this international agreement portends just the beginning of ignoring the "rule of law" in this story.

International Health Regulations, Annex II

FIGURE

Decision instrument for the assessment and notification of events that may constitute a public health emergency of international concern

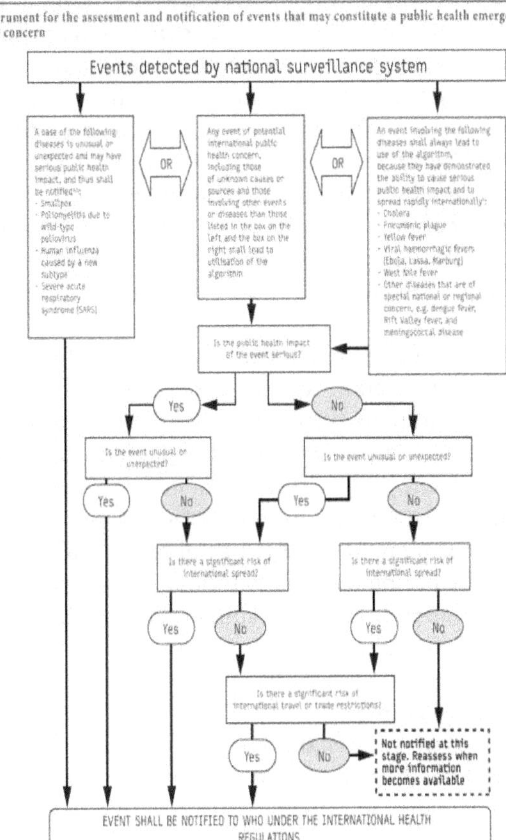

a. As per WHO case definitions

b. The disease list shall be used only for the purposes of these Regulations

Genre/Subgenre

The genre is identified as drama, thriller and so we have a biothriller, biodrama. It shatters the heroes and villains that we have come to expect early in the subgenre by making the villains hard to determine, and the heroes complex and seriously flawed characters.

The Biological Agent

The most creative part of this movie was probably the choice of a real biological agent that turned into a pandemic based completely on plausible reality. To the Director's credit, he utilized some top research scientists in biodefense as consultants. Ian Rivkin, research scientist from Columbia University and co-researcher with me on a major National Institutes of Health biodefense research grant, was one of the experts used. In the scene where Ian Sussman, hero for his work in developing the humanity-saving vaccine (probably no coincidence that his first name is also "Ian"), the real-life scientist, Ian Rivkin has a cameo appearance in the on-looking crowd watching him receive his award.

From the first mention of diagnosing the disease, the physician walked through the logical steps of making a diagnosis. First, the emergency medicine physician who was there for Beth's emergency visit which ended in her death, said he didn't know what killed her. He guessed encephalitis or meningitis, first, both having symptoms not unlike those shown by Beth. Then he guessed maybe West Nile Virus, another disease that affects the central nervous system and would cause seizures. He added that the autopsy probably would not tell them anything, but they would probably ask his permission to do one.

The diagnosis of the disease takes days as the death toll continued to rise. The Department of Homeland Security staff asked whether it could be a weaponized bird flu. The CDC responded , "No one has to weaponize it. The birds are taking care of that." But it is determined not to be a bird flu. The virus is compared to all known viruses and they find there are none that match with this one, finally concluding it is a newly emerging, and horrific disease.
This is a realistic depiction of the steps to determine what it is. Beth is the index case.

The disease is finally described in the last three minutes of the movie by showing the probably way that it evolved and emerged. The company that Beth worked for, AIMM is clearing rain forest in Hong Kong to build a new facility, causing the bats to flee to shelter, having had their habitat destroyed. The bats take shelter in a barn housing pigs, and as the bat droppings are picked up by the pig and ingested, the viruses of both the bat and the pig meet. When the chef in Hong Kong is interrupted from his preparation of the pig for the restaurant, he simply wipes his hands on his apron and goes out to meet Beth, shaking her hand in another one of those understated horrifying moments when the deadly virus is passed to Beth as the first human infection.

Individual rights issues and Quarantine?

In only one instance do we see isolation where Matt Damon is held for observation right after the autopsy determines his wife has a deadly infectious unidentifiable disease. It appears that Matt Damon is staying voluntarily but the public health authority in the city could have quickly issued an administrative quarantine to hold him there until they had determined his release would not be a threat to public health. Reasonable? The U.S. Constitution and state constitutions provide for this kind of state power to protect the public health. However, a balancing test determines for how long and under what conditions is it reasonable to deprive Matt Damon of his freedom. In keeping with the theme of no rule of law in this movie, no use of quarantine, quarantine orders or public health authorities are mentioned.

The use of "social distancing" an authentic measure used by public health authorities as a method of reducing the spread of an infectious disease. Social distancing is avoiding contact with crowds or other people to avoid contracting the virus. This was seemingly accomplished voluntarily by the 300 million people in the United States, again, without the suggestion of the rule of law playing any part in maintaining order and civility.

Eventually, Chicago is put under a city perimeter quarantine, and the National Guard, presumptively under the command of the Governor, here, are enforcing the quarantine. The scene depicts cars stopped in a line up over a bridge, but it is very unlikely that any car would be allowed to stop, because cars that run out of fuel, become problems for those enforcing control of the quarantine perimeter. No one tries to break the quarantine and no one is angry. No suggestion that anyone is acting other than as a model citizen.

Crime and the Model Citizens

Then civility and order eventually do break down and succumb to looting and vandalizing. Calls to 9-1-1 go unanswered as Matt Damon found out well into the pandemic when he called to report a burglary in his neighbor's house. Looting in time of a disaster typically carries a higher criminal penalty in state law. Any hoarding of scarce supplies in times of disaster is a federal crime, and the hoarding of drugs or vaccine could have been a crime. The movie does not suggest that anything other than looting is a problem. Nor does it depict the price gouging that is typically during shortages due to disasters or emergencies, which is also a crime that is punishing by criminal penalties under state law. In declared emergencies, any retailer who increases the price of goods more than 10% over its normal retail price, is violating the price gouging statutes. None of this was depicted or occurred in this movie, and most people seemed to behave as model citizens. This may have been the most unrealistic part of the otherwise realistic movie.

Human Remains Regulation

Then there is the issue of the body bags running out and the matter-of-fact conversation between the workers disposing of the bodies in long trenches. This is a scene that is always part of the end of a tabletop exercise conducted by the FBI, local and state governments. The white powder sprinkled over the bodies is likely the depiction of lime, which would accelerate the decomposition of the bodies. The only part the movie omitted was the option to use refrigerated trucks as a temporary morgue.

But human remains are controlled by state law, and in one scene Matt Damon is having trouble with the cemetery and funeral service who have refused to accept his wife's remains. It is highly unlikely that Matt Damon would have been given custody of her remains until CDC had ensured that the body was not infectious and without a diagnosis and characterization of the disease, they were certainly unable to give those assurances. The reality of this scene was likely that CDC would have either placed the remains in a freezer until and when they could determine whether the remains were infectious or they would have destroyed the remains by cremation. State law requires as a general matter than relatives have a right to take custody of human remains of their family, but where public health concerns outweigh the individual right to possession of these human remains even for a short time, the public health purpose will outweigh any right that Matt Damon has to Beth's remains.

A Constitutional Federalism Moment

A subtle yet very important constitutional issue was raised by Dr. Cheever in his television interview with Dr Gupta. When Dr. Cheever was asked how many people had died, he said "we don't know." He then went on to explain quite truthfully and realistically why CDC or any other federal agency will have difficulty determining how many people have died in a pandemic. There are "fifty different states and fifty different protocols," he explains. But how does this keep CDC from knowing the number of deaths? Because the reporting of deaths and disease statistics other than for a very few half-dozen specific diseases is not information the federal government is entitled to from a sovereign state. That's right. State governments are sovereign governments and do not have to disclose information about the public health of the people who live in the state, including the number of deaths from this outbreak. Even though a national surveillance system for disease would ensure that we learned at the earliest possible time that we had a pandemic, the fifty different states and fifty different protocols put up a barrier at each border to this kind of federal information collection. It is a barrier to having a true national system of defense against bioterrorism and emerging infectious diseases and neither the U.S. Department of Homeland Security or the Dept of Health and Human Services of CDC has changed that in any way since 9-11 or the anthrax attacks. It is a politically charged issue which has so far eluded repair or shifting to accommodate today's realities.

Plot device for horror and thrill

"We don't even know what to tell you to be afraid of." This is what Dr. Mears, played by Kate Winslett tells her waiting local public health colleagues in Minnesota upon her arrival to brief them about the disease. Add to this uncertainty, the "R-naught" number to which she refers in her briefing --- another teaching moment for the film. R0 is the rate at which the infection is spread by the carriers and the rate of infection based on their average contact. Dr. Mears gives us something to compare this horrific disease to: Flu, she says, is usually one person, polio before the vaccine was between four and six. This disease, however, she adds with the ominous dread we are expecting, could have an R-naught number much greater than these.

The uncertainty and the unknowing about this new disease reaches back to the days of the spring of 2003 and the outbreak of SARS, an emerging infectious disease which rapidly spread around the world and triggered a pandemic killing hundreds of people before it could even be characterized.

The birds, Mother Nature, both uncontrollable forces that were credited with the deadly disease added to the uncertainty and unpredictability of a fate that seemed unstoppable and incurable.

The Unethical Heros

Dr. Hextall, one of two research scientists working tirelessly to develop a vaccine is clearly a hero, but she steals the honor when she valiantly, but unethically, injects herself with the vaccine that seems to be effective against the virus in the monkey with the vaccine number 57. Once protected with her vaccine, she immediately challenges her vaccine by visiting her father and removing her protective equipment to the horror of her father. But she explains to him her actions, attributing her decision to the story her father told her of the Nobel prize winning Barry Marshall who intentionally infected himself with H. pylori to demonstrate that the bacterium caused stomach ulcers. Explaining why you are a hero may have gone far beyond acceptable dramatic arts boundaries and into the realm of term paper standards, but this movie never missed a "teaching moment."

Dr. Cheever, CDC physician is the unethical hero taking chances that are unethical that the story tells us are altruistic, unselfish and yes, heroic.
His first misstep is leaking in advance news of a citywide quarantine in Chicago to his finacee who lives there and tells her to flee immediately and come to Washington. Though sworn to secrecy, she tells her best friend. This communiqué ends up quoted and attributed to Cheever by his fiancées best friend in Chicago. This results in a censure Cheever's agency and a promise of a federal investigation. But into what, it is not clear, other than an ethical violation.

A civil servant would normally be guarded about further temptations to engage in unethical conduct, but not our Dr. Cheever. No sooner than he has been assured that his federal hearing and investigation has been scheduled, does he proceed to pretend to have been vaccinated by using the identifying band. But the story doesn't let us get angry with him for potentially making himself susceptible to an infection because he uses the vaccine that was specifically intended for his use, on his building custodian's son at his home. Altruism but unethical. Then he goes home and gives his fiancée a vaccine which she would only be entitled to if she was his wife and would otherwise have had to wait seven months for it. Noble and caring. But all unethical.

This is the message that physicians and healthcare workers do not need laws or regulations or even ethical guidelines, but instead will deem themselves the arbiters of good and they alone will make the right decision outside of the constraints of some predetermined guidelines. These predetermined guidelines called ethics, regulations and laws are strictly followed under the principle we call "The Rule of Law, not the Rule of Man." This depiction of the Rule of Law being subjugated for the greater good by those god-like individuals who will make all the decisions for us when they deem it is the right thing to do, is the "Rule of Man."

But the story carries us into a lull of blissful gratefulness for their altruism and risks to their own lives to save others, and we ignore the fact that the Rule of Law has been made a step child to the wisdom of the White Coats.

The Villains

The Department of Homeland Security representative, Haggerty asks if they might be looking at a weaponized bird flu and Dr. Cheever lectures, "They don't need to. The birds are doing it for us."

We have become accustomed to the journalist being the hero breaking open the government conspiracy, but in Contagion, make no mistake, the blogger who wants to be called a journalist, is the closest thing to a human villain the movie has to offer. Dr. Sussman's contempt for Allen is clear when he slings an insult at him that "Blogging is graffiti with punctuation."

Ending

The filming location for the movie was in Germany. Urban settings, airports and government buildings are all completely not recognizable Washington or Atlanta institutions, but most viewers were probably not looking for a familiar landmark CDC building or the Washington FBI building.

The ending was a return to normal, with everyone appearing to be going about their daily routine. But amidst what appeared normal was the abnormal---t one of the last scenes was of the armory-like building marked "MEV-1 vaccination center" guarded by uniformed military personnel each holding an AK-47, with the blogger photographing the scene. Although the blogger "made bail" he would still have his evidence heard by a grand jury which would decide whether to indict him or not. Then the case would proceed to scheduling and to trial. His ominous presence suggested that justice was never done for the people who died as a result of his blogging, and it also continued with the theme of the lack of the Rule of Law.

Quarantine 2: Terminal (2011)

RATING

Jenny
What is the truth, Henry, huh?

Henry
Earth could use a good plague.

---*Quarantine 2: Terminal* (2011)

Quarantine 2: Terminal (2011) is the sequel to *Quarantine* (2008). Whereas, Quarantine 2 used the realty show-type plot with a television crew on a regular night of finding a story at a firestation that turns into a biological disaster, *Quarantine 2: Terminal* (2011) is a continuation of that disaster. This sequel shows what happens when the virus from *Quarantine* (2004) predictably escapes into Los Angeles from the quarantined apartment building.

The movie opens with the flight crew boarding their flight for Nashville from Los Angeles.

The first clue that something bad is going to happen came about three minutes into the movie. The pilot who looked ill, said that he was sick and he caught it from his dog. All the dogs in the neighborhood have it. If you remember the rabies-like virus from *Quarantine* (2008) and the infected dogs, this will be an immediate sign that this flight is in trouble.

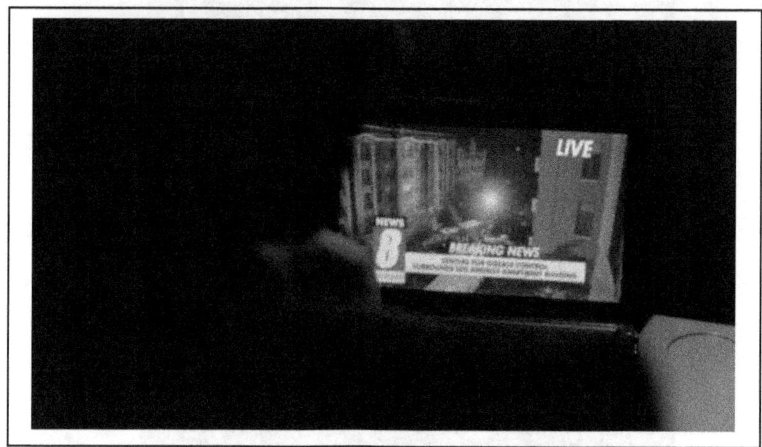

As the passengers are boarding, Jenny tells a passenger that they cannot take their "hamsters" on board, and that they have to be in the cargo section of the plane. He was trying to put his pet carrier with the rats in the overhead compartment, rather than under his seat, where legitimate onboard pets travel. Another passenger is traveling with her cat in the seat next to her (rather than under the seat in front of her, as required.) The stewardess tells her she has to put her cat back in the bag.

After takeoff, one of the passengers is watching the news on his laptop and sees a disaster happening in an apartment building. Then a large man of about 300 pounds in the back, Ralph, who was bitten by a rat that was in a carryon on the plane, throws up on the stewardess, Paula. He then goes into a rage and demands to get off of the plane. Chaos breaks out on the flight only 15 minutes into the movie.

The pilots call ground control and announce they have a "code red." Passengers and crew all manage to subdue the 300 pound passenger and tie him up, face down on the floor.

The pilot is going to attempt to land the plane but there is turbulence and they instruct the passengers on assuming the crash position. Note, that the flight only just took off for a flight to Nashville from Los Angeles, about a 3.5 hour flight, so they will have a full fuel tank, making it potentially dangerous to land. But this issue is not even raised.

In the meantime, the stewardess, Paula, struggles to comply with FAA seatbelt rules when she tries to seat the 300-pound man from the floor into his seat and fasten his seatbelt, but the stewardess has trouble fastening his seatbelt because he is too large for the seatbelt. Just as she is in his face, the man becomes conscious and bites the stewardess's face and blood is everywhere. Some of the passengers manage to get the large man into a bathroom and lock the door. All this occurs, while the flight is landing, so turbulence becomes a minor issue when the passenger attacks Paula, the stewardess.

Once on the ground, the pilots are unable to get clearance for a gate. One man who is the only ground crew agent present, Ed, wants to allow the passengers to deplane, but the gate door into the terminal is locked and no one will open it. The ground crew guy takes them through the back "staging area" to get them to the terminal but then finds the door is locked --- that has never been locked before.

Here is a dark scene in the "staging area" of the terminal where most of the movie will be filmed. The dark lighting and the use of flashlights keeps the mood dark.

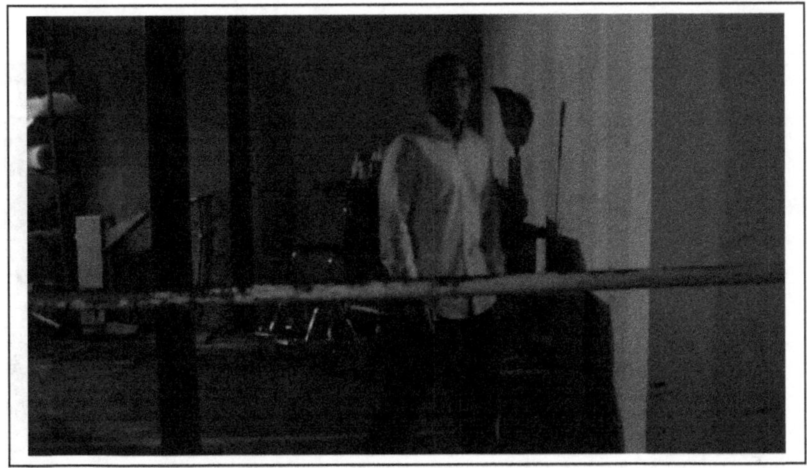

Discovering the locked door, the passengers then realize they are in "lock down" and think it is terrorism. They begin to argue among themselves about this but are interrupted by sirens outside. Their fears are confirmed that they are being held inside.

So far, the passengers are still within FAA federal jurisdiction because they have not yet entered the terminal. That means they have not yet entered state jurisdiction where local public health officials and law enforcement would have jurisdiction. But if terrorism is suspected, the President's directives give the FBI the lead on any suspected case of bioterrorism. This would invoke federal authority as well, but FAA would no longer be the lead federal agency in this matter. Once in the terminal they would be subject to state jurisdiction and public health law which might include isolation or quarantine as the name of the movie suggests. But that does not look likely at this point in the movie.

With the electronic communication explosion from 2004 when the first movie was made to 2011, the year of the sequel, cellphone calls to the outside are now important to the reality of the quarantine.

Some 15 minutes after the stewardess is bitten and bleeding, they are still discussing emergency measures to stop her blood loss. However, with the loss of 3 pints of blood, a human has already reached a dangerous 30 percent loss of blood and is in danger of passing out and dying. This does not look like the kind of slow bleed that would take 15 minutes to reach a critical level. She would likely already be unconscious and minutes away from death. Do you think she will become infected with the virus and turn aggressive?

Helicopter sounds and shadows of helmeted-military troops hovering outside their windows in the dark set the stage for this quarantine inside the bowels of the terminal.

Some of the passengers go back to the plane to see if they can find the pilot as their leader. They also check on the bathroom which became a confinement space for Ralph, the 300-pound passenger who had the disease and bit the stewardess's face. They open the door and discover he has escaped. (If you have been in the four square feet of an aircraft bathroom, you may question how a 300-pound man was lithe enough to escape it, but that is another matter.) The passengers began to look for him and cut into the floor of the plane to go into the cargo area of the plane. (It is not clear why they have to find Ralph.) This scene perspective up into the cabin from the bowels of the plane created the suspense of the crew before entering what was certainly omniscient of bad things to come.

And it was. Rats that were infected were aggressive and attacking. The woman with the cat had been infected by her cat and the stewardess finds her whimpering in the dark. Perhaps not coincidentally she attacks and grabs around the door with "claws" in a cat-like manner, as they try to subdue her.

At 41 minutes into the movie, they finally cut the cellphone communications to the passengers in the terminal.

The stewardess who is left, declares that she will be in charge until they are released. The dialogue goes as follows:

Jenny, the stewardess
We have to make sure no one else gets infected.

Passenger
Oh that's fuckin' brilliant.

They have a discussion about the quarantined building in L.A. and they make the connection to the rabies-like virus. Another woman complains their behavior is "inhumane". (Not sure what is inhumane.)

The aggressive rat attacks the man with dementia and they corner the rat and the ground crew guy, Ed, picks it up in his hand so everyone can see it. Someone declares it's an albino and therefore a laboratory rat. The 12 year old boy, George, accuses the teacher of bringing the lab rats on board. The teacher defends himself and says they were hamsters and a gift from parents who had just returned from Ecuador where they got them. (There's a red flag.) But the teacher's story is not believable, and George doesn't believe him. Even his friend questions his story and he tries to explain:

Henry, the teacher
You can't bring rats on in your carry on --- I never would have made it through security.

Girl
I am just accusing you instead of…

So is it true that you cannot bring rats onto the plane? Well Jenny told the passenger that they could be kept in the cargo section. But can he bring them onto the plane in the passenger section? The answer to both questions is, yes. There is an additional fee and health certificate requirements. Even a goldfish can be brought on as a pet, for an additional fee. However, it is not clear how more than 2.5 ounces of liquid, i.e. Water, for the fish will clear through TSA screening.

However, if the rats are laboratory rats that have or are likely to have an infectious disease, there is a different process for shipment. Because of research needs, there are methods devised for shipping these kinds of materials safely. The airline has no way of knowing this without the transporter disclosing the nature of the rats that are being shipped. No reputable animal supplier would violate these airline regulations or CDC and DOT regulations.

First of all, rats that were brought into the United States by parents traveling back from Ecuador is a violation of the import permit program, unless they received an import permit from the Centers for Diseases Control for rats which are "vectors, including animals/animal products . . . that are known to transfer or are capable of transferring an infectious biological agent to a human."[52] Rats are one of the scourges of humankind, having brought the plague through their fleas as one example of the kind of animal that CDC would want to regulate. Here is page 1 of a 2-page form that the parents would have had to complete, at the time of the writing of this book.[53]

U.S. DEPARTMENT OF HEALTH & HUMAN SERVICES
Public Health Service

APPLICATION FOR PERMIT TO IMPORT BIOLOGICAL AGENTS OR VECTORS OF HUMAN DISEASE INTO THE UNITED STATES

FORM APPROVED
OMB NO. 0920-0199
EXP DATE 01/31/2014

Application Number:

Permit # Issued

(For Program use ONLY)

Guidance for completing this form is available at www.cdc.gov/od/eaipp/ImportApplicationForms.htm. This form may be submitted by mail, fax, or email attachment to the Centers for Disease Control and Prevention, Import Permit Program. Mailing Address: 1600 Clifton Road NE, Mailstop A-46, Atlanta, GA 30333. Fax: 404-718-2093. E-mail: ImportPermit@cdc.gov. Telephone: 404-718-2077.

Please submit completed form only once by either email, fax, or mail

SECTION A, Person Requesting Permit in US (Permittee)

1. Permittee's Last Name	2. First Name	3. MI	4. Permittee's Organization
5. Physical Address *(NOT a post office box)*	6. City	7. State	8. Zip Code
9. Telephone	10. Fax	11. Email	
12. Will the permittee be the courier of the imported biological agent? ☐ Yes ☐ No	13. Will other members of the organization listed above, in Section A Block 4, be authorized to use the approved permit? ☐ No ☐ Yes *if Yes* ⇨	14. Check here ☐ if you have included a Continuation Form to list others authorized to use this permit	

SECTION B, Sender of Imported Biological Agent(s)

1. Sender's Last Name (☐ Check if same as Sec A)	2. First Name	3. MI	4. Sender's Organization	
5. Physical Address Outside of the US *(NOT a post office box)*	6. City	7. State/Prov.	8. Country	9. Postal Code
10. Telephone	11. Fax	12. Email	13. Check here ☐ if you have included a Continuation Form to list multiple senders	

SECTION C, Shipment Information

1. Method(s) of Shipment	2. Number of Shipments	3. Shipment Temperature(s)	4. Anticipated U.S. Port(s) of Entry
☐ Commercial Carrier *(e.g., FedEx)* ☐ Hand-carried by *(provide name of person)*:__________	☐ Single Shipment ☐ Multiple Shipments i. Estimated # of shipments:____	☐ Ambient ☐ Frozen/Refrigerated	

SECTION D, Final Destination of Imported Biological Agent

1. Is final destination of biological agent(s) different from address in Section A? ☐ No (skip to Section E) ☐ Yes ⇨	2. Last Name of Recipient at Destination	3. First Name	4. MI	
5. Destination Organization	6. Final Destination Address *(NOT a post office box)*	7. City	8. State	9. Zip Code
10. Telephone	11. Fax	12. Email	13. Check here ☐ if you have included a Continuation Form to list multiple final destinations	

CDC Form 0.753, Revised January 2011 Page 1

Second, for Henry to take these rats onto a plane as laboratory animals if the parents brought the rats into the country with the appropriate form, block 5, would note whether Henry could further transfer the rats within the U.S. and how that is to be done.

However, we learn that the back story about the parents bringing in the rats was a lie, and that Henry infected these rats in the apartment building basement in furtherance of his terroristic agenda. However, if Henry were to comply with the law while he is transferring his rats on this commercial flight he would have to have completed a transfer form from a registered laboratory. His laboratory was in the basement of the apartment and not registered from every indication.

[52] CDC, "Import Permit Program," Office of Public Health Preparedness and emergency Response, Division of Select Agents and Toxins, guidance brochure.

[53] http://www.cdc.gov/od/eaipp/forms/Permit_to_Import_Biological_Agent_or_Vector.pdf .

Henry would also have to comply with IATA regulations which are not government regulations, but the International Air Transport Association regulations which require compliance, require special packaging, special labeling and special certifications, including a phone number to reach someone in case of an emergency. As you can see from this movie, an infected rat that escapes can present an emergency.

IATA regulations stipulate in general, that:

> *9.1.5.2 A live animal which has been intentionally infected and is known or suspected to contain an infectious substance must not be transported by air unless the infectious substance contained cannot be consigned by any other means. Infected animals may only be transported under terms and conditions approved by the appropriate national authority.*

7.3.15 specifies the type of label that would be on the container. It would look like this but have specific contact information on it. Failure to complete this label correctly can itself be a felony. However, this is not one of Henry's concerns.

The Department of Transportation also regulates the transfer of infected live animals that are NOT livestock or fall into the regulated animals of the USDA. In this case, these are laboratory rats that are infected with a disease that infects humans, dogs and cats, but no livestock infections have been indicated for this virus, at least so far. Here is the section and the division responsible at the U.S. Department of Transportation:

> ***Transportation of Live Animals Containing or Contaminated with an Infectious Substance. 49 CFR 173.196(c).*** *An animal containing or contaminated with an infectious substance must be transported under terms and conditions approved by PHMSA's Associate Administrator for Hazardous Materials Safety.*

(PHMSA is the pipeline safety administration and they are the designated agency to implement this regulation, believe it or not.)

Now, let's turn to CDC's role in this incident:

Ed, the ground crew guy, gets a call on his radio that "CDC is coming." To their astonishment, CDC arrives with AK-47s and demands that everyone put their hands up and obey them. They tell the passengers to cooperate and "we will get you out of here as quickly as possible."

The CDC personnel vaccinates the man with dementia with something that sounds like a staple-gun. The CDC says to everyone, "if you want to be released, take the protocol." There are objections to putting things in their bodies without knowing what it is. The CDC officer says, "it will all be explained later."

This is exactly contrary to the requirement to have the informed consent of an individual before administering an experimental drug or "protocol" whatever you want to call it. Informed consent is a knowing or understanding of what is being given to them and the likelihood of what will happen when they take it. Then man with dementia stood up out of his wheelchair and took a large bite out of the CDC personnel's neck from behind. Panic ensues and the CDC personnel try to escape but the door has been locked behind them. They shoot the door with their AK-47s until it opens and they run out but sniper fire shoots them and a couple of the passengers who ran out behind them.

So far, the story has been completely from the perspective of the passengers and crew, except for the rare communication on the cell phone or the laptop with news about the L.A. apartment quarantine in the first scenes of the movie. Now, one of the CDC personnel has been trapped inside and the outside perspective is now revealed.

The CDC personnel tells the passengers and crew that the Biological and Domestic Terrorism (BDT) response team was called. LA is under quarantine. Our units just arrived. We found the lab in the apartment ---some kind of doomsday cult. (This is the plot of *Quarantine* (2004).) We ran a clinical trial and found a survivor. Whatever they were given it was making it worse, much worse.

Rats are the carriers.

CDC officer

If what I see spreads into the general population we have no way to cure it.

Passenger

So we are the lab rats now?

One of the passengers recognizes that the injection that the CDC official calls the "protocol" which "will be explained to you later," is an experimental drug being used on the people who are infected inside. They can't determine who is infected and who isn't but they are using it anyway. Soon, it becomes clear that it is not working at all.

The Federal Drug Administration (FDA) regulates the use of drugs and vaccines and requires three levels of testing. First, animals are tested for toxicity, then a small group of humans are tested for safety of the vaccine, then another group of humans are tested for efficacy of the vaccine. However, in the case of diseases for which there are no cures, humans cannot be used in the third stage because they would have to be given the disease to challenge the vaccine, and if it didn't work, there would be no cure for the human experimental subject. So the action taken by CDC is entirely illegal. However, that said, the President is the only one that can waive the IND status (investigational new drug) for humans before it is fully tested. The President did this for the anthrax vaccine for the military when it was determined that a military threat existed. This lasted only as long as it appeared a military threat of an anthrax attack against them was a high probability event. In this case, the IND status could have been waived for use on the people inside, but informed consent regulations would still apply, and "we will explain to you later" would not comply!

George, the 12-year-old, finds some medicinal effects in Henry's briefcase and asks Henry if this is the antidote. Henry is bitten and demands that George give it to him and he shoots Ed when Ed tries to intervene. As Henry is giving himself the eye-drops which is the antidote, George asks him the following about the antidote:

George, the 12-year-old
How did you get that on the plane?

Henry, the teacher
The same way I got the rats on ---friends.
Friends of the cause.

Henry explains his motivation by telling George not to believe in that "big government" line. That government calls them terrorists or domestic terrorists, but they are going to save the world. Henry believes there are too many people and they are ruining the planet. He says we need a good plague to wipe out a lot of people to save some of the people. Too bad, Henry, the teacher hasn't kept up with the population estimates that shows the earth is not headed toward overpopulation as we once believed in the 1970s due to a drastic reduction in per capita childbirth rates than was projected. In fact, the population of the world is projected to decline in our lifetimes.[54]

Henry injects his brain, to prevent the virus from damaging his brain, as he explains, by going through his eye with a very long needle to the amazement of the passengers who looked on. This is his "antidote." Then Henry and George disappear.

---

[54] Jeff Wise, "About that Overpopulations Problem," Slate, Future America, Jan 9, 2013 at http://www.slate.com/articles/technology/future_tense/2013/01/world_population_may_actually_start_declining_not_exploding.html.

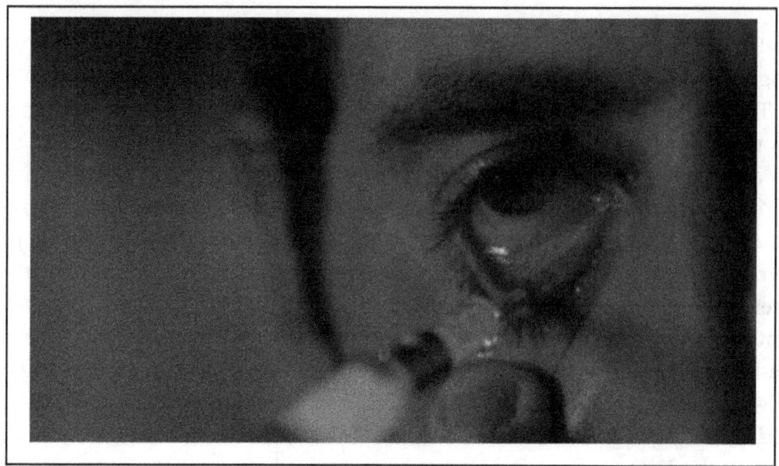

Jenny begins to look for George, the 12-year-old. She finds George sitting in the dark with Jenny's new-found night-vision goggles and he pleads with her not to come down. He says Henry's cure didn't work. George finds the gun and shoots Henry as he is attacking her. The movie is interjected with footage from the night-vision goggles worn by Jenny as seen in this scene:

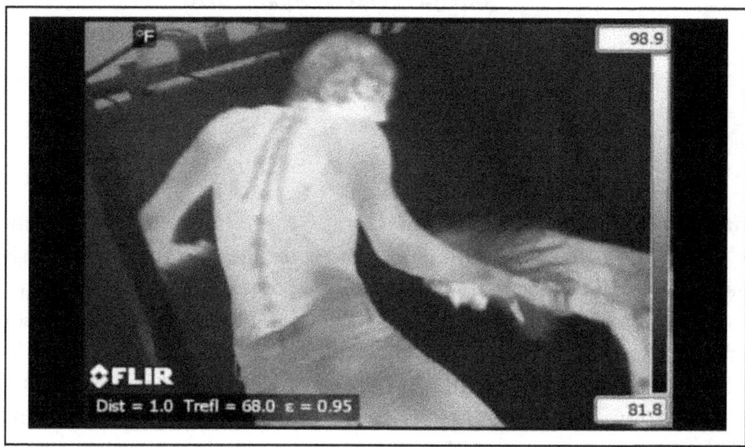

Jenny is able to finish off Henry with a crowbar, but not before he has bitten her. George also shoots Henry with Henry's gun that was left on the floor. George doesn't want to leave without Jenny but she pleads with him to leave as we see her rapidly evolve into rabid dog behavior on all fours. Then George sees a bomb hit part of the terminal. In the final scene, George has escaped from the perimeter of the airport through the unfinished corridor that they had followed. He throws down the night-vision goggles he had taken and the audience has a rare moment of relief that maybe George is safe.

But then, we have what is almost guaranteed to be the segue to the next sequel, a cat shaking foam off of its mouth, seen through the night-vision goggles that George dropped on the ground as he emerged from the tunnel outside the perimeter of the airport terminal.

Season of the Witch (2011)

RATING

Priest
We're going to need more holy water.

----*Season of the Witch* (2011)

In *Season of the Witch* (2011), a U.S. interpretation of the return of the crusaders in the period of the black plague, one of the most disastrous events of human history, killing one-third of the civilized world's population.

The opening scene peaks into the life of a medieval priest having a "trial" for three women accused of witchcraft. This screenshot shows the tremendous cinematography of the drama of hanging three convicted witches and then drowning them in the river below the bridge. The priest insists on pulling them back up but his men abandon him. He is left to do it himself and in a scene which suggests the priest was correct in determining that one of the women was a witch, one of the women comes up and lethally attacks the priest.

Nicolas Cage plays a Templar knight, Behman, and is introduced in this dramatic scene of the march of the crusaders in 1332 A.D. The Templar Knights are captured in the village after they desert their cadre out of a fit of moral predisposition to give up killing women and children.

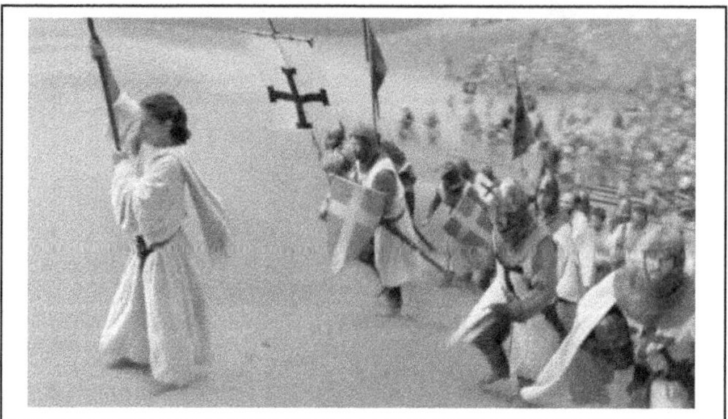

Nicolas Cage and his companion crusader, Felsen (Ron Perlman), leave the group with disgust with the killing of women and children. As they travel on their own they come to the first house after a day's walk, only to discover dead bodies in their beds. This scene of death portends the plague that they will confront as they continue on their journey.

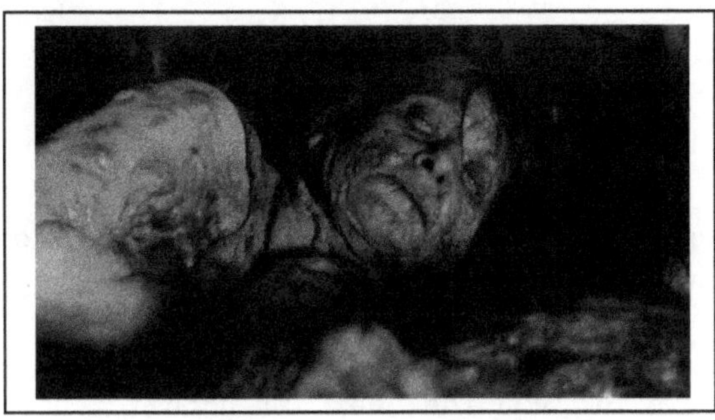

Entering a village, the pair are quickly exposed as deserters from the crusades and arrested. They are questioned by the priest, Debelzaq (Stephen Campbell Moore) who takes them to their dying priest. In one of the most incredible scenes, the doctors attending to the dying priest all turn to look at the knights revealing the coarse reality of the leather beaks that were worn by doctors to treat plague patients.

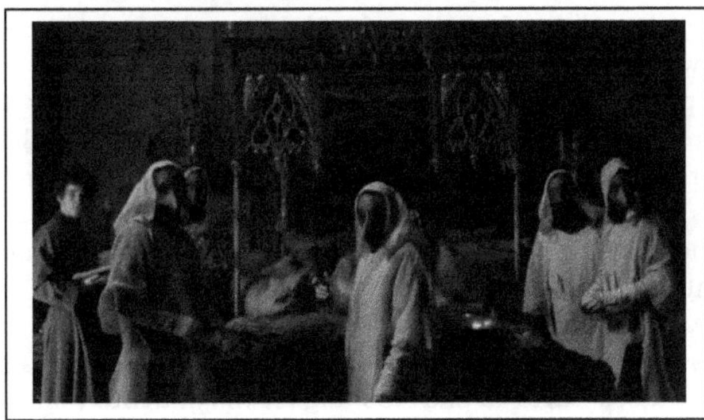

The cause of the plague is blamed on the "black witch" by the dying priest. The knights question the connection, saying "no one saw the girl pass by my village, yet the plague came." This did not deter the priest. The priest continues:

Old priest
At the Abby of Severak there is an ancient
book of rituals that will destroy
the witches powers and end the plague.

Knight
What has this to do with us?

Old priest
Our ranks have been decimated.
You must deliver her to the Abbey of Severak.. . .

Old priest
Do you serve God and the church?

Knight
I serve the church no more.

The subtle message of how men can be deceived by women is only thinly veiled by the reference to her as a witch, as started in the following dialogue:

Priest
Did you feel her strength?

Knight
I have seen women destroy men
without lifting a finger.

The mission to deliver the black witch to the Abby of Severak carries the plot. The conflict between the witch and the character of each of the knights and men on the journey is challenged. Many who are mean to her are cruelly killed.

Nicolas Cage promises the girl (Claire Foy) that she will get a fair trial.

But what is a fair trial for a witch in 1332? The plan for her trial is to go to the Abby of Severak and read the passage in the book there which will determine her guilt or innocence. That does not comport with due process or a fair trial in the sense of modern due process, hence the horror of being tried by the laws of man rather than the rule of law.

The first night, the witch steals the key and escapes leading to a night chase through a cavern.

After Edgar is accidentally killed by the witch, the priest explains that the witch caused his death and caused Edgar to start looking for his daughter, Milo. The priest tells Nicolas Cage that the witch overheard them talking about Edgar's daughter, Milo, and said, "It was the witch which killed Edgar. . . . She sees the weakness that lies in our hearts and what she sees there she will use against us."

Everyone who tried to harm the witch came to some sudden and dreadful death on the journey to determine her guilt or innocence. Even Nicolas Cage was finally convinced after the wolf pack attacked their guide who had just threated to kill the witch.

The wagon finally reached Severak, the destination which held the last copy of the book with the words that could be repeated to end the witch's powers. Once they reached the village they discovered the plague had killed all of the monks and priests in the entire village. The priest was distraught.

The one monk barely alive pointed to the book --- the book with the ritual.

Nicolas Cage asked the priest if he could perform the ritual and the next challenge on their journey began.

As the girl begins to tell them things she had no way of knowing, they began to realize she was not just a witch, she was Satan himself.

The priest, Debezaq, began the ritual and the girl confessed she had deceived everyone. At one point, the priest declared, "this is no witch" and he turned the pages in the book to a new ritual. When he began to read those words, the witch went into a frenzy.

The funniest line in the movie was delivered by the priest after the witch was stopped when he doused her with holy water, and she flew away. In the next beat there was a moment of calm and the priest said, "We're going to need more holy water."

As they explored the Abby they found monks who had tied themselves to their desks before they died miserable deaths. They realized that the creature was not a witch but if they believed she was a witch then they would bring her to the place where the last book existed that contained the ritual that would eliminate the evil, satan.

The ritual was read in latin first by the priest and then by the alter boy who had come along to become a knight.

The movie ends with a discussion of what caused the black plague and how many thought it was just a pestilence that came and went, but they knew it was truly evil. The pestilence left and life returned to normal and these two people who left the Abby, the altar boy and the girl, once possessed, were the only two who knew ---

"The darkness that almost was. . . "

When a plague or pandemic occurs that is truly out of the ordinary many turn to their faith for protection or to their belief in the supernatural as a cause. It is no surprise that diseases were called curses in the Bible.

In a time with no knowledge of germs, bacteria or viruses, turning to religion and the forces against good were obvious tools to cope with the unknown and unpredictable future for humanity. The end of the crusades with the priests still leading society, provided the context for dealing with witches and those that would cause the plague. The horror of this period has never disappeared from our collective memories and the recreation of this horrific historical reality will remain forever a subject for the biohorror subgenre.

The Gerber Syndrome (2011)

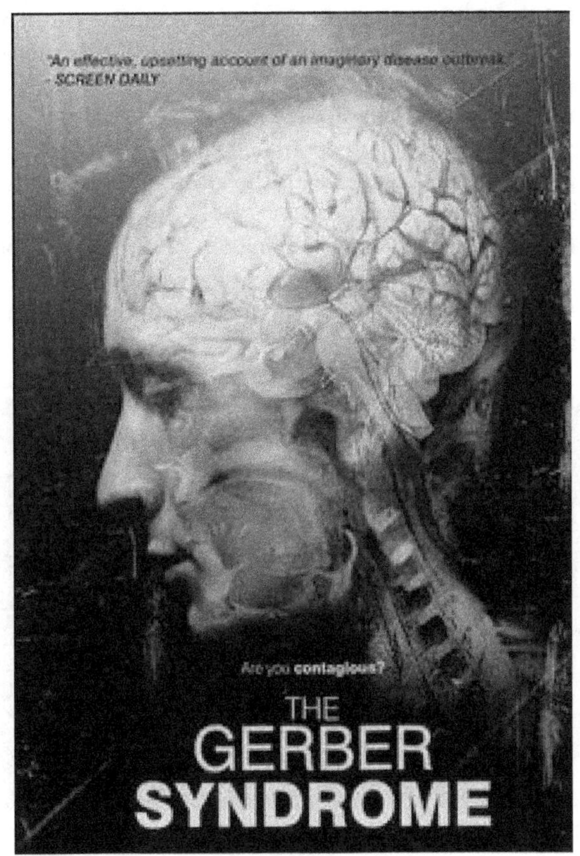

RATING

TopoTino, the Mouse

And today, I want to talk to you about Gerber's Syndrome!

---*Gerber's Syndrome* (2011)

The Gerber Syndrome (2011), Italy, is filmed n the documentary style much like *Quarantine* (2004), where the public security personnel are followed by the media reporter to see the plot develop and the character arc progress. In this movie, three people are followed in their role and response to Gerber's Syndrome. The realism of this movie may lead you to believe there is really such a disease as Gerber Syndrome! (Some chatter on the internet actually investigated whether it was a real disease in Italy.)

Luigi, a Central Security officer is responsible for patrolling the streets and responding to calls to pick up peope infected with the virus. Dr. Ricardi diagnoses and attends to the people with the virus.

The end stages of the virus which affects one out of a thousand people, results in irrational aggression.

The movie leads with convincing statistics about viruses and that 2 million people get sick in Italy each year.

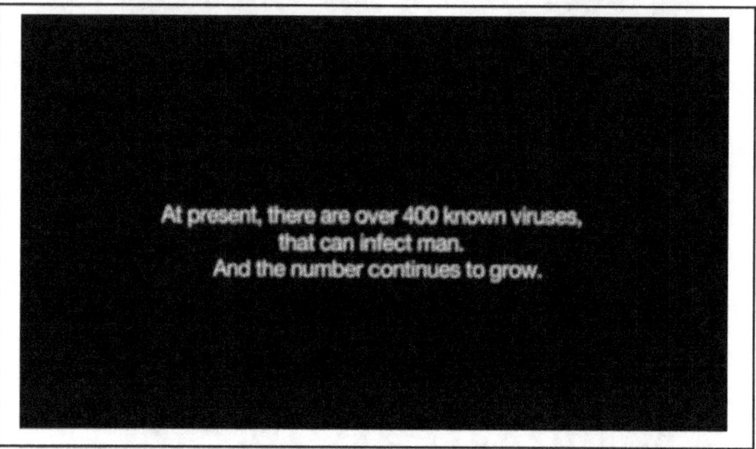

In this television-documentary type format, the first interview is with a doctor and he explains his background and then talks about Gerber's Syndrome, which interestingly has been isolated as he shows in this screenshot:

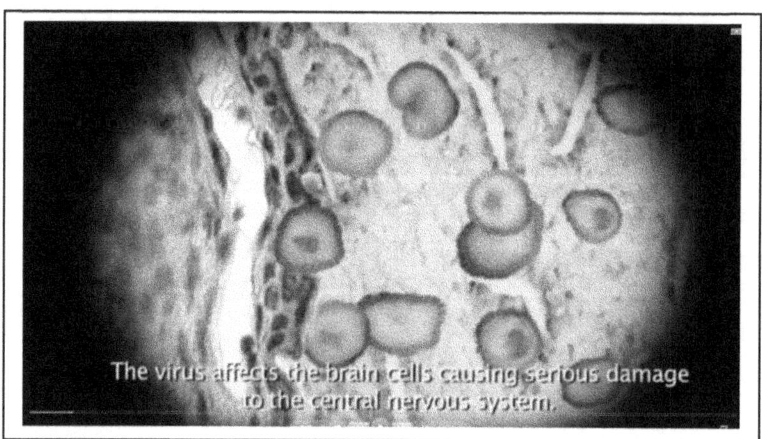

The subtile and frightening mood of the movie is one that is calm and accepting of an epidemic that is 99% fatal. The doctor describes the symptoms which slowly end in death. He adds that he is obligated to report anyone with the disease to the CS board. He says the CS board was formed very quickly after the discovery of Gerber's Syndrome.

Next we see the children's playful television show with TopoTino the Mouse talking about Gerber's Syndrome and the requirement to report it. Making the acceptance of death an inevitable consequence of citizenship, almost.

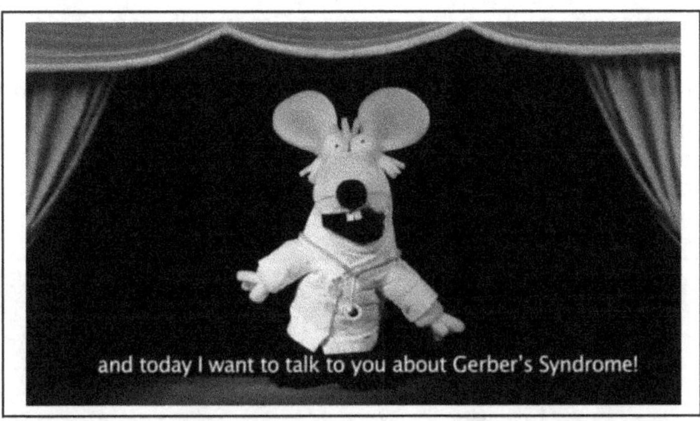

TopoTino has a very misleading message asking children to have their parents call this number if they have any of the symptoms. But when they call, the children are taken away. The doctor admits that the people who see the television ad and report are making an "unwitting report."

Dr. Ricardi is followed by the camera when he makes a call to the house of a friend whose daughter has a fever and was attacked and bitten by a homeless man no her way home from the university where she is taking classes. One of the interviewers stays at the home with Melissa and interviews her. They ask her if she is frightened and she says not anymore because Luigi reassured her.

The next scene interviews Luigi, a 23-year old emergency response officer. They also interview a prostitute and ask her what she has seen. She replies in Russian and tells them to look in the market area. Then he goes to check areas that he is assigned to patrol. The interviewer asks what he thinks about Gerber's Syndrome and he says he feels it has gotten out of hand. Then he tells him the people with the syndrome are not even like humans "They are the lowest form of life." This is an indication of how they are able to capture these people like animals and bring them into quarantine a violation of the International Human Rights Treaty with regard to the humane treatment of the sick. However, under the circumstances, with government having limited funds and the need to prevent further infections, there is a good argument to take these people off the street. However, state law in the United States generally agree with arguments from the ACLU that homeless people suffering from schizophrenia should not be forced to accept treatment and they should be allowed to decide whether they want to take the drugs that would change their behavior and make them function in society. Ironically, about 40 percent of people with schizophrenia have lost the ability to make self-assessments because of damage to that part of their brain, thus making it impossible for them to conclude that they need treatment. An analogy could be made to the neurologically damaged victims of Gerber's Syndrome in this movie.

Meanwhile back at Melissa's house, Dr. Ricardi talks to the parents and informs them she tested positive for Gerber's Syndrome and that there is no treatment. He tells them they are lucky they called him because if they had called CS, they would take her and put her in quarantine and then central security and she would never come out. Dr. Ricardi then talks to the camera outside without the parents and shares that there is an experimental treatment, not approved for use in Italy that has some small chance of survival but also has serious side-effects. He has contacts in Geneva where he is going to check about this treatment.

They interview a priest about Gerber's Syndrome and he says it is spread through venereal disease. However, they distribute advice about how to avoid it by avoiding crowds. The interviewer asked him if Mass wasn't a crowd? The priest replied that repenting and praying at mass was the best way to avoid contagion.

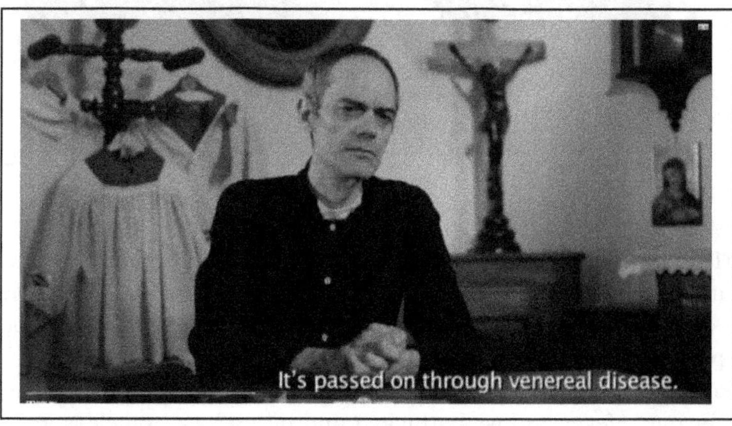

Meanwhile, back with Luigi he enters the house he is inspecting and finds an infected man who is in the aggressive phase, and has to bring him in for quarantine. The interviewer asks him if he was frightened, and he said yes, but he was used to it --- another sad commentary on the acceptance of this plague. One has to wonder at this point if the Italians accepted the plague which ravaged Italy in the 1340s with the same coolness? They were the ones, afterall, who devised the method of bricking up the home of anyone with the plague – while they were inside. That definitely kept them from infecting anyone else.

When Luigi approaches Central Security headquarters, he is warned by his radio dispatch officer that there is a demonstration at the entrance. The demonstrators beat on his van and tell him to "free them!" They are wearing gas masks, carrying sticks and signs but otherwise do not seem very violent.

Flashes of Melissa's agonizing degradation are used to remind us of the human process of dying with Gerber's Syndrome. Eventually, they accept an experimental drug with horrendous side effects from Geneva.Outside, the protesters are interviewed and the responses are varied. One woman from Sweden is waiting outside to get word about her husband who was taken. One protestor's mother was taken inside about amonth ago. One protester said his cousin was taken and he had no symptoms at all. None of them were able to get any information or to learn about what has happened to their loved one. They all say that the same thing is happened in their countries.

The cameras enter the Central Security quarantine area and they see inside padded rooms in a dazed state, many of them oozing vomit and foam.

The government officials are interviewed about Gerber's Syndrome and they simply say they are following protocols the same as the rest of Europe.

Street gangs have formed to protect their neighborhoods from the plague-infected, and they are angry that the CS is not doing enough to protect them.

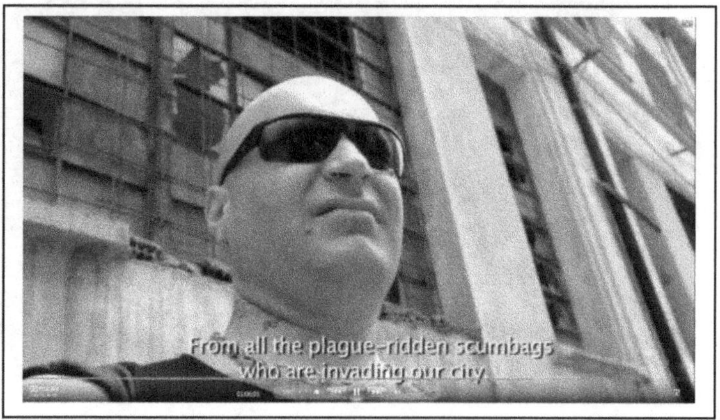

When asked how they take care of these people, there are flashes to fields with gasoline being poured on the sick and lighting them on fire – reminiscent of destroying plague-ridden corpses.

The clubs in Italy have been reopened and everyone has their temperature checked at the door. If they have a temperature, they are turned away. Then Luigi and his crew attend to the people outside the clubs.

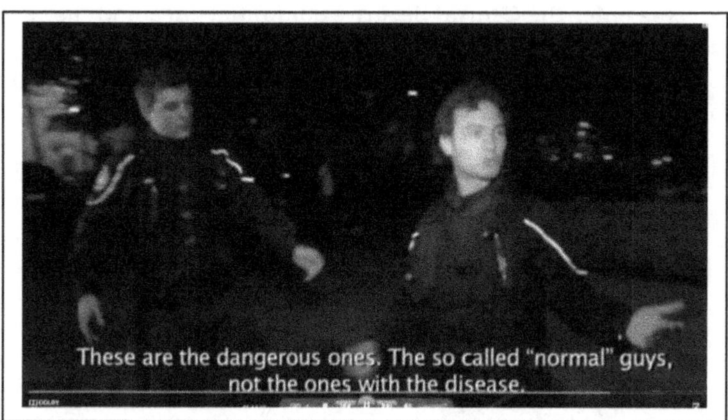

Melissa survived the disease and the cure but she had permanent brain damage and was speechless and sat in a wheelchair.

Luigi was killed on one of his calls by a gang when one of them shot him. His epitaph was on the final screens.

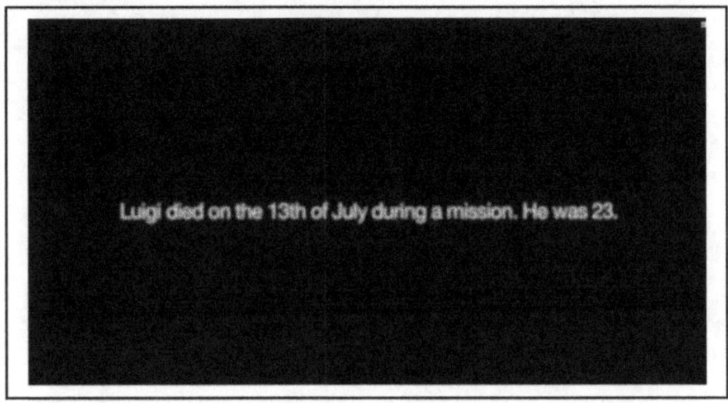

In the last scene Dr. Ricardi is interviewed about Melissa's outcome, and they note he has an open wound on his finger --- the last dialogue of the movie:

Interviewer

Dr. Ricardi, what happened to your hand?

Azaan (2011)

RATING

The Doctor

Think of the beauty of the thought of 8 billion suicide bombers . . . it will turn every Indian into a suicide bomber . . I have made this into an age of proxy wars.

---*Azaan* (2011)

Azaan (2011) opens with an Indian politician, Indian Home Minister Manohar Kamat, played by Sachin Khedekar, talking about their soft power over China's economic power. When he raises his hand to the crowd his sleeve pulls back and exposes sores on his arm. His eyes begin to bleed. At the same time, individuals who are visibly dizzy and sick are put on the street and moments later they explode.

The next scene is a meeting with Interpol and they discuss Mossad, CIA. In a video communication they discuss the virus as a very rare, variant of ebola.

A terrorist has opened a shop of biological viruses. They claim he has one for Arabs and one for Jews. Then their computer system crashes and a little man appears on the screen, laughing, then the computer system returns to normal. They complain the terrorist cut through their "level 3" security with no problem.

The Interpol official asked the Indian officials about Operation White Tiger and who is Asaan Khan? They began discussing their operations in Paris, London, and Waziristan.

The backstory shows his training beginning with three days of torture and then he is sent on his way to meet the Doctor.

The man called "Doctor" is the one who has created the virus attack. The Indian secret service agency, RAW, officials use Azaan to track down the "Doctor". The next screenshot is a bioterrorism operation underway.

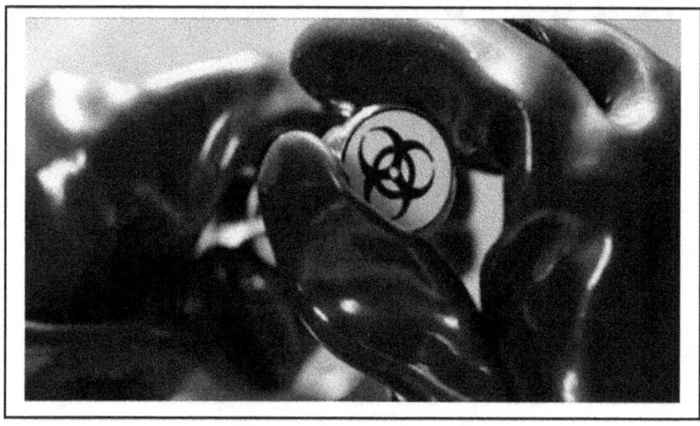

After several contacts he reaches a building where scenes in a laboratory show what appears to be a bioweapons operation finishing with a deposit of a glass vial into a metal container with a biohazard symbol on it.

Meanwhile the investigators identify the agent as an engineered strain of ebola. The investigator said "it has been tampered with." They identified the mastermind, Dr. Mahfouz as the suspect because he has worked on a cure for ebola. In the next screenshot they find a summary of their criminal, Dr. Mahfouz.

Further investigation and discussion is that he is behind "America's biological weapon" and Israel's biological weapons program, saying that they are the most advanced biological weapons program in the world.

If their claims were true that the U.S. and Israel have biological weapons programs, then the U.S. would be in violation of the U.N. Biological Weapons and Toxins Convention (BWC) signed by the U.S. on April 10, 1972. India signed the BWC, January 15, 1973. Israel has never signed the UN Biological Weapons Convention and so, ironically, if their claims were true, then Israel would not be violating the BWC by engaging in a biological weapons program.

Indian companies have sold dual-use biological equipment to the former Saddam Hussein regime in violation of their own export regulations. These companies were sanctioned by the United States for their role in contributing to WMD programs in Iraq.

This movie follows the Mumbai attacks in December 2010, when the public's awareness of terrorists is very high. The RAW Director, Ms. Choudry, tells her colleagues that there is one man who can do the job, and that is Azaan Khan, played by Sachin Joshi. Azaan is the Indian equivalent of a mix of James Bond and Jason Bourne, and for unknown (commercial) reasons, he is killed off at the end of the movie, foreclosing any hope of a sequel.

The mastermind criminal, the Doctor, played by Sajid Hasaan through some deception meets our hero, Azaan in an art gallery in London where he takes him to the laboratory where the bioweapons are being made. Here we have an omniscient view of an injection in a terrorist who is going to become a suicide bioterror bomber. As the Doctor explains, they can make a billion people in India into suicide bioterror bombers by injecting suicide bombers with the ebola variant, and strapping explosives on them to disperse the disease? Given the difficulty for a fragile virus like ebola to survive an explosion, this seems to be an additional element that is not needed to spread the infection when walking around sick is enough. However, in one scene, they stage an explosion and the vial of ebola stays intact, but that is equally unclear as to how that would disseminate the virus. As one reviewer put it, "The story by itself is something we have seen in non-Indian cinema earlier. But not too much has been done in the area of bio-terrorism and more importantly the psyche of terrorists hasn't been talked about a lot in our cinema."[55] Despite some of the gaps in the plot, it is a thriller and poses an interesting socio-economic motive.

---

[55] See Azaan review, http://wogma.com/movie/azaan-review/#sthash.jTqmnFmn.dpuf (7-22-2013).

In the next screenshot there is a closeup of one of the terrorists injecting himself with another terrorist looking on.

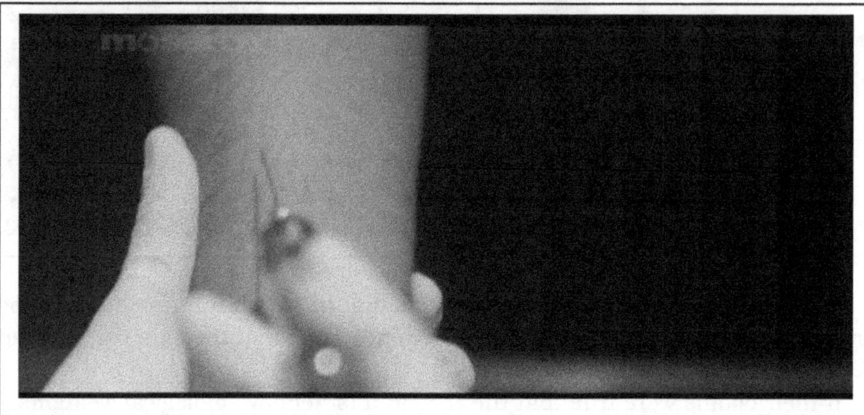

Nicely labeled bioweapon canisters add to the suggestion that the United States and Israel have sophisticated bioweapons operations.

The mission of Azaan was to find Dr. Mahfrouz because they believed he had a cure for the bioweapon, although he was involved in making it? In the next screenshot, the researcher is testing the effectiveness of the Mahfrouz "cure" against the ebola variant. A closeup of his computer monitor shows the result of the test, which is that the cure is not effective against the ebola bioweapon.

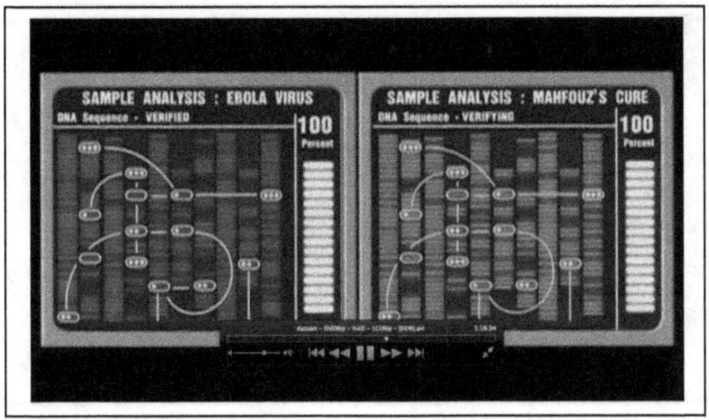

The movie had about 30 minutes of swirling scarves and close-ups of faces looking adoringly at each other --- or something. This made up the romantic element of this movie, where Azaan was deeply made human by his encounter with a beautiful Moroccan woman, Afreen, played by Candice Boucher, who was a sand artist, believing that she knew something deep about his past and connected with her from seeing her performance of sand artistry.

Right before Dr. Mahfrouz died, he told Azaan to go to Morrocco and find this sand painter because she had the cure. Her daughter, Zara, has the antibodies against the virus. This encounter with the sand artist resonated with Azaan as he saw her telling his own life story. Azaan had learned that his brother was suspected of being one of the terrorists, but had been killed. She told him that he was the good brother. He asked her how her story ended, and she told him to come back to her performance tomorrow to see how the story ends. The story ends by saying that everyone has control over their destiny. Little did she realize that she had just lost control over hers. She is eventually gunned down by the forces that are out to stop Azaan.

Azaan valiantly seeks out the Dr. Mahrfouz but Dr. Mahrfouz is used as a suicide bioweapon bomber himself when he is injected with the disease and then rolled in a wheel chair into the city square with explosives strapped underneath his blankets. Azaan tries to disarm the bomb, but cannot and the Doctor is detonated.

Then Azaan's mission changes and he decides he must stop the terrorists his own way, and he goes after them and destroys many of them in high action, thrilling gun fights and car scenes. However, in the end, he is able to save Zara, the sand painter's daughter, by throwing her off a cliff with a parachute. He stays to battle the black-shirted SWAT teams that are intentionally made to look like a foreign spy mission that is conspiring with the local terrorists to destroy India.

The RAW headquarters and Ms. Choudry look on as the city becomes more chaotic with the disease and the overflow in the hospitals. The scenes in the last ten minutes are the most that the viewer will see of the attack but the scenes are dramatic.

In this screenshot, the crowds are watching a large screen television in the city square.

The next screenshot is a patient being wheeled through a hospital corridor.

In a very effective directing moment, a patient's view of the biosuited personnel above him, looking down at him is the only point where the biosafety protection used with infected patients is shown.

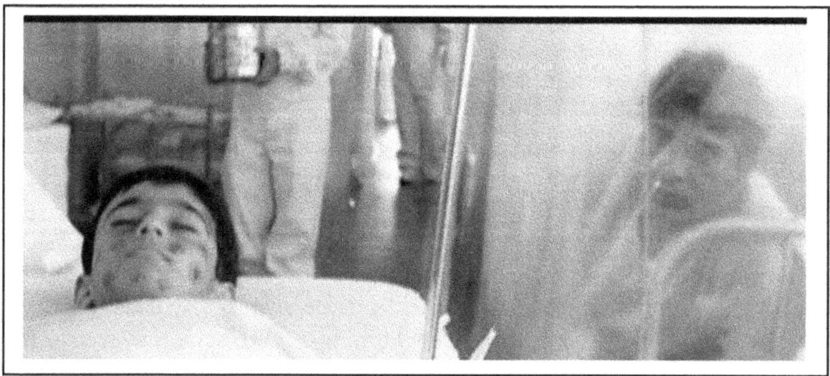

Had the star of the movie, Sachiin J Joshi, been one of the Bollywood regulars, the reviews would have been kinder; however, watching the movie from outside the Bollywood culture, he appeared to be as good as any other Bollywood actor I have seen. The use of the biohorror, biothriller subgenre as a premise for a Bollywood movie is probably good evidence that it is a subgenre that has broad appeal far beyond the U.S. movie industry.

Patient Zero (2012)

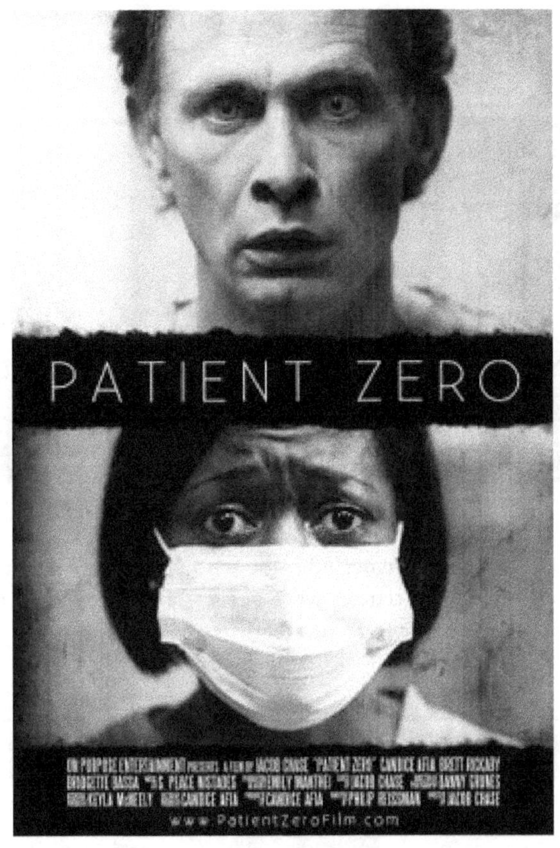

RATING

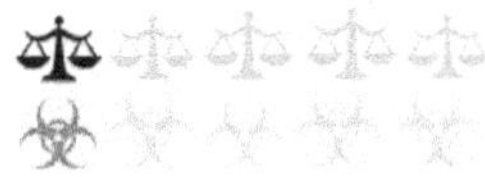

Dr. Jonathan Wright
Honey, do you really believe all we do here is conduct agricultural research?

Dr. Jenna Barnes
Well, that s what you told me in the interview

Dr. Jonathan Wright
Well, then I am sorry.

----*Patient Zero* (2011)

Patient Zero (2012) also named *Biohazard: Patient Zero* (2012) opens with a scene with a newly engaged couple in bed together in the morning before going to work where he is her boss. The names are introduced with their two company identification badges hanging from the rearview mirror.

The Sheriff takes a call at a farmer's house who says there was shooting on his property last night and a lot of black trucks were seen. Then they have a chat about all the bad things going on at the company where he used to work which must be Gem Laboratories.

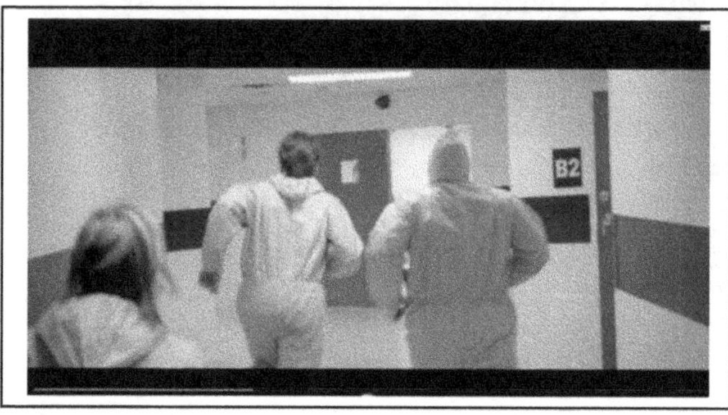

The contamination alarm went off and everyone ran for the door. Normal response strategies involve those involved take care of the response. The boss, John, looked at his computer and said there is a little problem with the "red lab."

The Sheriff's daughter works for Gem Lab and called her father to alert him something serious had happened. He heads in that direction.

John and his finance go to investigate what was happening and they had to hack to death a couple of scientists-turned-aggressive-monsters, almost immediately. This screenshot shows the hacking of the first scientists. But we soon learn that the Department of Defense will be killing everyone in the building.

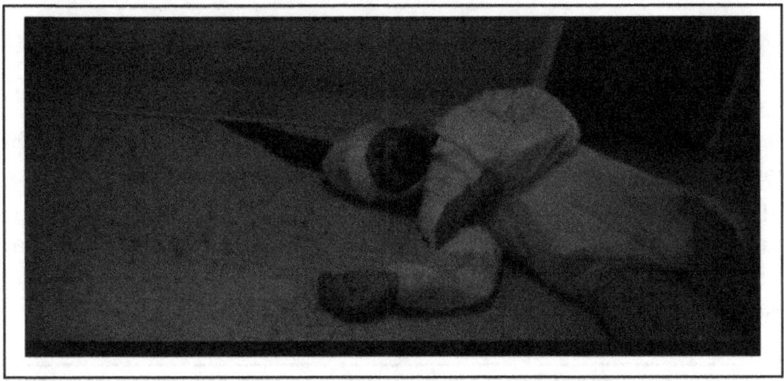

The other scientists locked into the laboratory, plead with the receptionist to let them out. This part of the plot is very similar to *Warning Sign* (1985) in a release in a government bioweapons laboratory. Jenna's good friend is the scientist pleading to get out behind the door in this screenshot.

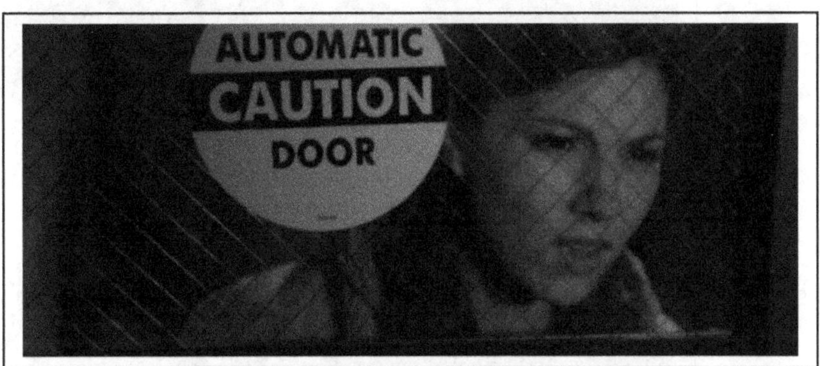

John tells his fiancé that he inherited this project when he became the boss, and had to continue with the development of bioweapons contract with the Department of Defense. John's fiancé, Dr. Jenna Barnes, is surprised by his revelations about what is being done there at Gem Laboratories:

Dr. Jonathan Wright
Honey, do you really believe all we do here is conduct agricultural research?

Dr. Jenna Barnes
Well, that s what you told me in the interview

Dr. Jonathan Wright
Well, then I am sorry.

He explains to her that the bioweapon is a combination of smallpox and viremic encephalitis.

He calls it "H4IV2".

They continue to hide in the air ventilation system and hope that the virus does not become airborne. But one has to wonder how so many scientists in one space became infected in such a short time if the virus was not already airborne?

In the meantime, the pair of scientists, Dr. Wright and Dr. Barnes are having to avoid being shot by the DOD killing force as well as avoid being attacked by one of the zombie–like scientists.

The two made their way to the exit fan and stopped it manually. But just before she exited up the vent, John gave her an engagement ring and told her he loved her.

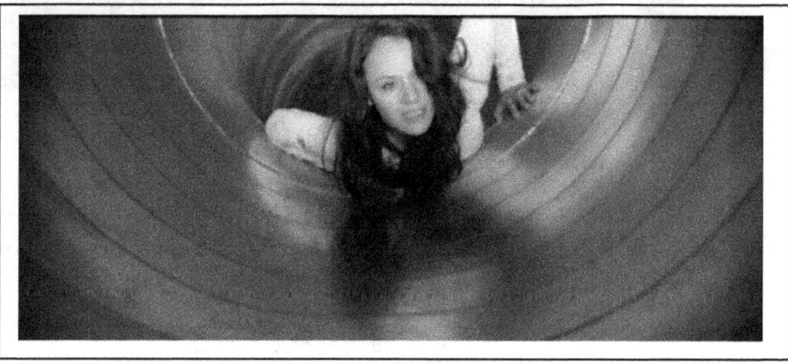

Although the DOD killer team suffered 100 percent casualties, the DOD control room operators were able to continue with the next phase by blowing in poisonous gas. One has to wonder why they didn't use that technique in the first phase, rather than risking military casualties.

Unfortunately, John was one of the last casualties, gassed in the vent, just behind Jenna who managed to get out, but without John.

Meanwhile, the DOD team leader gives a press interview and talks about how they have everything under control although they did suffer a few casualties. (From the counts in the movie, there were 53 scientists in the building in addition to the Sheriff and the receptionist as well as the lost military team members.)

One has to question why a Department of Defense representative, the Major, would do a television interview in a small town that never knew that DOD was involved in Gem Laboratories? Further, the sub-headlines read, "rumors persist about biological weapons testing," which would tend to be substantiated by the spokesperson being from the Department of Defense. His interview in front of Gem Laboratories in the next screen shot is also dubbed as a "World News Alert."

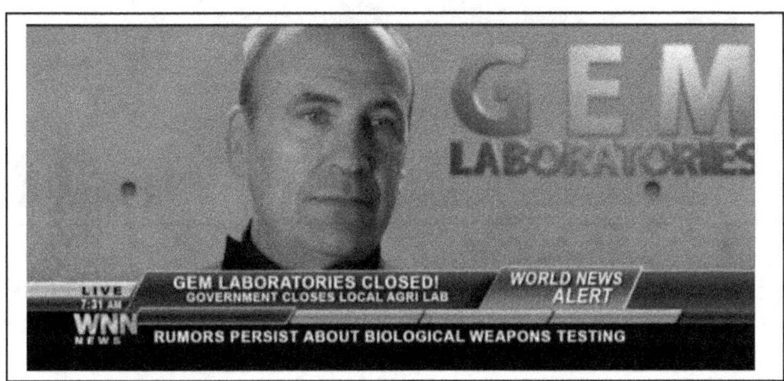

Given that the world will be notified, the United States can expect to get some inquiries about the rumored violation of the U.N. Biological and Toxins Weapons Convention that we signed in 1972 and it went into effect in 1975. At that time we confirmed that we had ended all of our bioweapons programs and destroyed all stockpiles. If the United Nations decided to investigate this disaster at Gem Laboratories, they would convene a vote and decide the terms under the UN 1540 mechanism which allows for an inspection with a special team. Having ratified the BWC, the nation thereby gives its consent to allow this kind of inspection when there is a suspicion that warrants a United Nations action and vote.

Would the scientists inside (if any had survived) been liable for their activities on a government contract? The answer is probably yes, because courts have found that there is no "government contract" defense. For example, if a company follows a receipt for government paint, and the materials cause toxicity and organ damage to the users of the product, the company is still liable, even though it used the exact formula provided by the federal government. So Gem Laboratories may be facing a number of wrongful death lawsuits for employees killed in this incident. In a secret killing operation, like this depicted, the DOD may simply deny they did any of the killing and it was just a casualty of the "accident."

This short, 70 minute movie, was the first movie that portrayed the United States as making bioweapons since *The Hades Factor* (2006) and before that, then *Day of the Dead: Contagium* (2004), *Venomous* (2001); *Outbreak* (1995); *Warning Sign* (1985) and the first, *The Satan Bug* (1965).

One final word about the title of the movie, *Patient Zero* or *Biohazard: Patient Zero*, is a term that denotes the first person in an epidemic to start the contagion or the first person to have the disease if it is a zoonotic disease that is jumping from animal to human.

Although this was the name of the movie, there was nothing that used this concept in the plot, other than this screen of a label on a body bag from the trailer.

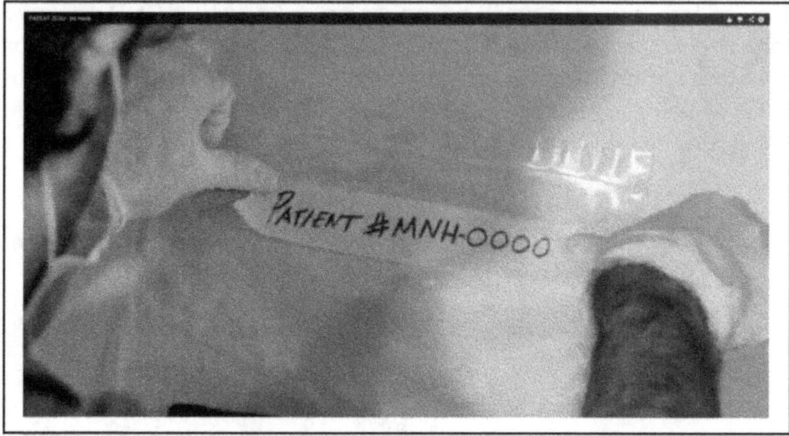

Another important issue raised in the movie is the ethics of the scientists in developing a bioweapon. In the scene where Dr. Wright reveals to his fiancé, Dr. Barnes that they are developing a bioweapon at Gem Laboratories, he told her that he never wanted to tell her because he knew how she "felt about those things." He assumed the contract with DOD when he was promoted into his position and it was at that point he would have had to withdraw from the promotion. Given the secret nature of the program and his knowledge of the depiction of the violation of international law by the United States, he may have had very little choice.

John also told his finace that they were not experimenting, only developing, but this appears to be another coverup. When John was in the laboratory before lunch, he launched the virus into a host, thus suggesting they were engaged in an experimental infection with the virus.

World War Z (2013)

RATING

Constance Lane

Daddy, what is martial law?

----*World War Z (2013)*

World War Z (2013) depicts a global pandemic which resorts to zombies as the end result of the disease. The plot centers on finding a way to save the world which is to find a cure or a defense against the attacking zombies. As expected in the universal rules of zombies, the bite of the zombie will turn the person into a zombie.

As the last movie to be analyzed in this book, it is significant that it seals the importance of this subgenre with the bidding war that took place between the Brad Pitt production company and the Leonardo DeCaprio production company:

> *Pitt's production company, Plan B, pursued the rights aggressively, winning them for $1 million over competing bidder Leonardo DiCaprio. But though Pitt was initially attracted to "World War Z" for its provocative hypothesizing of various nations' handling of a worldwide epidemic, the need for a more linear narrative soon took precedence.*[56]

According to reports, the fact that Pitt's attraction to the movie was because of the movie's core conflict of how nations deal with a pandemic makes clear that it is this subgenre that is key to the producer's interest.

But getting to the plot and the characters, this movie was remarkable in that it was not a movie that I anticipated including in this book because it was a zombie movie. Certainly the trailers showing incredible CGI dynamics of zombies scaling walls that were at least a half a mile tall, suggested that zombies would drive the story. Yet, the plot did center on the pandemic and finding a cure, which made it fit squarely in the subgenre of biohorror, biothriller movies.

[Publicity image released by Paramount Pictures shows a scene from "World War Z." (AP Photo/Paramount Pictures)]

One characters in the movie signaled a reversal of a trend that had been evident since the first epidemiologist hit the silver screen, and that is ever one of them have been females, up until World War Z. As I watched Andrew Fassbach, played by Moritz Bleibtreu

---

[56] Jake Coyle, "Israel in 'World War Z': Curious Wall Draws Speculation As to Movie's Message," http://www.huffingtonpost.com/2013/06/26/israel-world-war-z-wall_n_3502076.html?utm_hp_ref=world&ir=World (June 25, 2013).

in the theater, as the "last best hope" as he was described, I wondered why they had cast a male for the part of the epidemiologist who would save mankind when every other previous movie had cleverly cast a woman even when the original script or book called for a male? (See Chapter on Heros). But it was made painfully clear when the writers killed off their epidemiologist in the first minutes of the movie when he apparently slipped and his gun went off, killing him in a tragically stupid accident. So much for male epidemiologists in the subgenre, and it was only one bit of information that our hero, Brad Pitt, would need to find the cause of the great plague.

The heros in this movie appear to be the United Nations and the World Health Organization who are benevolently continuing to show up for work at the only WHO laboratory that can reasonably be expected to work on a cure for the plague. Astonishingly it is only staffed by three researchers, but we soon find out it is because the other half of the laboratory was compromised when one of the doctors infected himself with the zombie plague and then immediately infected the rest of the researchers. Only a stack of folding chairs against some double doors, separate the living from the "undead" in the laboratory.

One of the best moment so of the visuals of the film was the news cast filming of the U.S. Constitution being carried out of the U.S. Archives in Washington, D.C., presumptively to an underground hiding place. Since society had collapsed as far as we could tell in the movie except for international intergovernment rule by the United Nations, the U.S. Constitution had become largely irrelevant for this film.

"Life as we know it will come to an end in 90 days." The commanding officer tells the troops as we see a visual of the U.S. Constitution being carried out of the U.S. Archives to who-knows-where?

The suggestion that martial law is the government is met with complete indifference by the Brad Pitt family, the Gerry Lane family. The youngest daughter asks what is "marital law" which she hears on a news cast, to which she gets no answer. Perhaps the parents don't know what it is, otherwise they would certainly have responded with more than indifference.

In this movie, martial law would be reasonable where there is no longer local, state or federal governments to keep order, but there is very little of military governance in the United States. Martial law is very evident when Gerry Lane goes to Israel on one of his bootstrapped missions. There, general chaos is the order of the day, and martial law seems to have little relevance. Rather the people are motivated and driven by religious needs, not martial law, and perhaps this is why Israel is a good demonstration of the lack of real power that martial law can have on a society when religion and the end of life as you know it is very real.

The Cure

At this point, it is significant to talk about the "cure" or defense against the zombies. The identification of the disease, the identification of the perpetrator whether it was Mother Nature or a terrorist was never explored in any way, leaving this film as one of the very few in this subgenre to ignore the villain behind the disaster.

The "cure" as it turns out based on the clues that Gerry Lane gathered as he watched the zombies ignore people who were in chemotherapy (Who knows how that was organized in a society without civil law enforcement?) or other people on the verge of death. To that end, Gerry Lane decides to risk his life to reach the part of the WHO Laboratory with the zombie doctors, to find an incurable disease and hope that someone can give him the cure. He has the chance to test his theory when he ends up in the laboratory with only the deadly disease vials and zombies waiting outside the glass doors.

At this point, if there is anything positive to say about resorting to zombies as the result of the plague which is about as serious a literary crime as resulting to the *deus ex machine* device to get the writer out of any conflict – these zombies were greatly done. They were convincing and scary and the makeup and acting were phenomenal as far as zombies go.

But back to the cure. Gerry Lane doesn't have a clue which virus to infect himself with and randomly selects one from the drawer. He finds a hypodermic needle conveniently in a nearby drawer and injects himself after holding up a crayoned sign to tell his family that he loves them. Then he walks through the zombies, untouched, after they recognize that he is not healthy since he has injected himself with the disease.

The reality is that for any disease in the incurable drawer, it would take hours at the minimum for the body to manifest some response that might be detectable to a disease. The movie gave us a few minutes.

Miraculously, he is quickly injected with the antidote to whatever random virus he picked and one has to wonder how they knew which virus he injected himself with, but it doesn't pay to think too much about the logic in this movie. It lacks a lot of it.

Acknowledgements

Law students in my courses over the years at Texas Tech University School of Law---Law and Bioterrorism and Global Biosecurity Law---have been helpful to me as I conceptualized the idea for this book. I also benefited from their research, writing, presentation and discussion of many of these movies. These students are: Kelsey Brock, Austin Carrizales, Alexandria Dover, James Austin Franklin, Nadia Haghighatian, John Hardy, Peyton Kampas, Bradley Lewis, Kiara Martinez, Elena McCoy, Audrey Rugg, Jessica Schneider, Son Trinh, Adam Varvel and Lara Wynn (2013 course); Juliet Azarani, Heather Carson, Eloy J. Hita, Marta Hoes, Marissa Marino Lydon, Benjamin Robertson, Yolanda Catalina Rodriguez, Brandon Schwarzentraub, Declan Sullivan (visiting from Australia's Melbourne Law School), Brian Thornton, Colin Wooldridge (2012 course); Zack Allen, Kyle Baum, Jared Burr, Lisa Danley, Chad Davis, Marissa Dunagan, Floyd Taylor, James Garrett, Courtney Graft, Evan Jackson, Katie Maxwell, Kenneth Morris, Lorenzo Sierra, Jordan Surratt, Bryan Tate and Karla Valles-Gonzalez (2011 course); Allen Ayers, Bradley Anderle, Arthur Chaslot, Michael Choate, Andrew Hefferly, Jeansonne, Laci Lawrence, Kelly A. Morrison, Jeff Mustin,, Palisano, Colby Rideout, Shelton (2010 course); William Black, Katie DuBois, Russell Frost, Brandon Gaines, Matthew Keslin, Brad Kvinta, Julia Thomas, Natalie Vanhouten (2008 course); Jaume Canaves, Lindsay Epley, Christopher Gardner, Lani Hoffman, Ashley Hutchison Knight, Michel Manuel, David Morehan, Whitney Boatright, Sara Thornton and Lindsey Wachsmann (2007 course). Thanks also to Joel Aldrich, Ph.D. and Cory Davenport, PhD., Center Fellows who contributed their comments and thoughts during the course of this project.

Thanks is also due to my law librarian, Eugenia Newton, who took time to search out exactly what I needed for this project, with professionalism and speed.

Michele Thaetig, my able assistant, was invaluable at every step of this project.

I would especially like to thank my non-fiction writing workshop colleagues, Jerry Staley, Chloe Honum, Andrew Berthrong and Jason Farrell led by Dennis Covington, professor and National Book Award finalist, Texas Tech University, who read and commented on my first chapter. Their comments were insightful and had a lot to do with the shaping of this book.

I would like to acknowledge the fair use of the movie posters and movie packaging covers to ensure that the movie has been accurately identified. Many of the movies in this subgenre re-use titles, and the identification of the movies with their poster is helpful in properly attributing and distinguishing the work.

The diagram of the map of the movement of the plague in the chapter on plague is from Wikipedia.

I thank Dennis E. Hackin who was always willing to read another draft and to make comments and suggestions. His depth of knowledge of film history and structure was invaluable in informing my work in the development and writing of this book. No one knows more about movies. He's the movie expert's expert.

Thanks also to my parents who influenced my love of the horror and thriller genre with the consistent viewing of every single episode of the television works of Alfred Hitchcock and Rod Serling's "Twilight Zone" as well as introducing me to the classic biological horror film, *The Fly* (1958) and others.

Finally, I would like to thank Summer S. Sutton and Remington J. Sutton who spent a lot of time with me watching almost all of these movies plus a lot more that did not make the cut for this book. They, too, had a lot to do with the shaping of this book and in many ways.

Annex 1

February 1, 2007 CDC Update

1. **How much truth is the May 9th ABC television network made-for-TV movie titled "Fatal Contact: Bird Flu in America" which follows an outbreak of the H5N1 avian flu virus from its origins in a Hong Kong market through its mutation into a pandemic virus that becomes easily transmittable from human to human and spreads rapidly around the world?**

   The ABC Movie "Fatal Contact: Bird Flu in America" is a movie, not a documentary. It is a work of fiction designed to entertain and not a factual accounting of a real world event. Please remember that there is no influenza pandemic in the world at this time. It is important to also remember that H5N1 avian influenza is almost exclusively a disease of birds. The H5N1 virus has not yet appeared in the U.S. Should the H5N1 virus appear in the U.S., it does not mean the start of a pandemic.
2. **Is a pandemic imminent? Will the bird flu cause the next influenza pandemic?**

   Many scientists believe it is a matter of time until the next influenza pandemic occurs. However, the timing and severity of the next pandemic cannot be predicted. Influenza pandemics occurred three times in the past century — in 1918-19, 1957-58, and 1968-69. Avian influenza (bird flu) is a disease of wild and farm birds caused by influenza viruses. Bird flu viruses do not usually infect humans, but since 1997, there have been a number of confirmed cases of human infection from bird flu viruses. Most of these resulted from direct or close contact with infected birds. The spread of bird flu viruses from an infected person to another person has been reported very rarely and has not been reported to continue beyond one person. A worldwide pandemic could occur if a bird flu virus were to change so that it could easily be passed from person to person.
3. **Is it safe to eat poultry?**
   Yes, it is safe to eat properly cooked poultry. Cooking destroys germs, including the bird flu virus. The US bans imports of poultry and poultry products from countries where bird flu has been found.
4. **Is influenza A (H5N1) virus the only avian influenza virus of concern regarding a pandemic?**

   Although H5N1 probably poses the greatest current pandemic threat, other avian influenza A subtypes also have infected people in recent years. For example, in 1999, H9N2 infections were identified in Hong Kong; in 2002; and 2003, H7N7 infections occurred in the Netherlands and H7N3 infections occurred in Canada. These viruses also have the potential to give rise to the next pandemic.
5. **Why won't the annual flu vaccine protect people against pandemic influenza?**

   Influenza vaccines are designed to protect against a specific virus, so a pandemic vaccine cannot be produced until a new pandemic influenza virus emerges and is identified. Even after a pandemic influenza virus has been identified, it could take at least six months to develop, test and produce vaccine.
6. **How much time does it take to develop and produce an influenza vaccine?**

   The influenza vaccine production process is long and complicated. Traditional influenza vaccine production for the U.S. relies on long-standing technology based on chicken eggs. This production technology is labor-intensive and takes nine months from start to finish.

The flu vaccine production process is further complicated by the fact that influenza virus strains continually evolve. Thus, seasonal flu vaccines must be modified each year to match the strains of the virus that are known to be in circulation among humans around the world. As a result of this constant viral evolution, seasonal influenza vaccines cannot be stockpiled year to year. The appearance of an influenza pandemic virus would likely be unaffected by currently available flu vaccines. Researchers are making and testing possible H5N1 vaccines now. Large amounts of vaccine cannot be made before knowing exactly which virus will cause the pandemic. It could then take up to six months before a vaccine is available and in only limited amounts at first. Research is underway to make vaccines more quickly.

7. **How will vaccine be distributed if a pandemic breaks out? Who will decide who gets vaccination first and who will have priority?**

   Most likely, the federal government will work with manufacturers, distributors and states and the states will develop distribution plans at the local level. States are developing and improving plans to distribute a vaccine rapidly. These plans build on experience gained from other emergencies. The greatest risk of hospitalization and death—as seen during the last two pandemics in 1957 and 1968 pandemics and during annual influenza—will be in infants, the elderly, and those with underlying health conditions. These individuals, along with health care providers, who are critical to maintaining a health care system in a pandemic, would likely be the first individuals to receive the first supplies of vaccine. However, in the 1918 pandemic, most deaths occurred in young adults, highlighting the need to remain flexible on determining priorities for vaccination groups based on the epidemiology of an emerging pandemic.

   As part of planning efforts, two Federal advisory committees—the Advisory Committee on Immunization Practices and the National Vaccine Advisory Committee—have made recommendations for prioritizing critical populations that might receive the first supplies of vaccine. These recommendations can be found in the Health & Human Services Pandemic Plan, which is available at http://www.pandemicflu.gov.

8. **Is a shortage of Tamiflu (or other anti-virals) anticipated? If so, what is the government doing to prevent such a shortage?**

   HHS is stockpiling enough anti-virals to treat 25% of the U.S. population should a pandemic occur in the U.S. This figure is based on historical data from past pandemics indicating that roughly 25% of the population would get sick in a pandemic and would benefit from antiviral treatment if started early in the course of illness. To date, the U.S. government has purchased 26 million antiviral treatment courses and expects to have on hand a total of 81 million treatment courses by the end of 2008.

9. **What strategies will help protect Americans?**
   In the event of a pandemic, certain public health measures may be important to help contain or limit the spread of infection as effectively as possible. This could include:
   a. Isolating sick people in hospitals, homes, or other facilities,
   b. Identifying and quarantining exposed people,
   c. Closing schools and workplaces as needed,
   d. Canceling public events, and
   e. Restricting travel.
   In addition, people should protect themselves by:
   f. Getting seasonal flu shots,
   g. Washing hands frequently with soap and water,

   h. Staying away from people who are sick, and
   i. Staying home if sick.

10. **Will wearing a surgical mask protect people from the flu?**
    Surgical masks are recommended for health care workers who are subjected to repeated exposure to multiple patients. For health care workers performing certain medical procedures on infected patients, respirators are recommended. Surgical masks are also recommended for patients who are infected to help reduce the potential for spread of virus when these people cough or sneeze.
11. **In addition to coughing and sneezing, can one acquire the virus by handshakes, kissing, sharing drinks, etc.?**
    Influenza virus is primarily spread by airborne droplets that reach the eyes, nose or mouth but can also spread by touching contaminated surfaces and then touching one's face. This highlights the importance of learning and practicing good personal hygiene, including:
    a. Wash hands frequently with soap and water.
    b. Cover your mouth and nose with a tissue when you cough or sneeze.
    c. Put used tissues in a wastebasket.
    d. Cough or sneeze into your upper sleeve if you don't have a tissue.
    e. Clean your hands after coughing or sneezing. Use soap and water or an alcohol-based hand cleaner.
    f. Stay at home if you are sick.
12. **Could terrorists spread the avian influenza viruses to create a worldwide pandemic?**

    Experts believe it highly unlikely that a pandemic influenza virus could be created by terrorists. Developing a pandemic influenza virus would require extraordinary scientific skill as well as sophisticated scientific equipment and other resources.
13. **How would pandemic flu affect communities and businesses?**

    If an influenza pandemic occurs, many people could become sick at the same time and would be unable to work. Many would stay at home to care for ill family members. Schools and businesses might close to try to prevent disease spread. Large group gatherings might be canceled and public transportation might be scarce. These are examples of challenges that local communities, schools, civic organizations, and businesses will have to work together on to plan for a pandemic response.

February 1, 2007 Update From CDC
Found at http://www.dpi.state.nd.us/pandemic.shtm .

The

End

www.ingramcontent.com/pod-product-compliance
Lightning Source LLC
LaVergne TN
LVHW061249060426
835507LV00017B/1982
9780991420711